FLIGHT AND CONCEALMENT

FLIGHT AND CONCEALMENT

Surviving the Holocaust Underground in Munich and Beyond

SUSANNA SCHRAFSTETTER

TRANSLATED BY

ALLISON BROWN

INDIANA UNIVERSITY PRESS

This book is a publication of

Indiana University Press
Office of Scholarly Publishing
Herman B Wells Library 350
1320 East 10th Street
Bloomington, Indiana 47405 USA

iupress.org

The translation of this work was funded by Geisteswissenschaften International—Translation Funding for Work in the Humanities and Social Sciences from Germany, a joint initiative of the Fritz Thyssen Foundation, the German Federal Foreign Office, the collecting society VG WORT, and the Börsenverein des Deutschen Buchhandels (German Publishers & Booksellers Association).

The translation was also funded by the REACH Grant Program of the Office of the Vice President for Research at the University of Vermont.

Manufactured in the United States of America

First printing 2022

Cataloging information is available from the Library of Congress.

ISBN 978-0-253-06402-8 (hardback)
ISBN 978-0-253-06403-5 (paperback)
ISBN 978-0-253-06404-2 (ebook)

CONTENTS

PREFACE AND ACKNOWLEDGMENTS

This book is the revised and updated English version of my book *Flucht und Versteck. Untergetauchte Juden in München—Verfolgungserfahrung und Nachkriegsalltag*, which was published by the Wallstein Verlag in Göttingen, Germany, in 2015. The English version has been made possible by a grant from Geisteswissenschaften International—Translation Funding for Work in the Humanities and Social Sciences from Germany and by a REACH grant from the office of the vice president for research at the University of Vermont. Over the years, the Miller Center for Holocaust Studies at the University of Vermont has also provided financial support and a congenial intellectual climate. I would like to thank these institutions for their generous funding. The original German manuscript has been altered in many places. The introduction has been substantially changed to make it accessible to an international audience. In addition, the text has been revised to reflect a broader perspective on the situation of German Jews in hiding in Munich and elsewhere in Germany. With that goal in mind, some sections of the German version have been removed, while some new information has been added. A significant number of relevant publications has appeared since the German edition was published, and in many places, the text has been revised and updated to reflect the latest state of the historiography.

There are numerous individuals to whom I owe thanks for making the original German book and the English translation possible. At Indiana University Press, in Bloomington, Indiana, Dee Mortensen brought this project on its way, while Gary Dunham, Ashante Thomas, Anna Francis, and Darja Malcolm-Clarke oversaw the process of publication. I'm grateful to Jamie Armstrong for the meticulous copyediting. In Berlin, Allison Brown translated the book in the midst of the COVID-19 pandemic. She is a great translator and editor, who had an incredible amount of patience with me. In Munich, Germany, Eva Schrafstetter scanned literature and documents that I could not access because of the COVID-19 pandemic. In Burlington, Timber Wright took great care in designing several maps that indicate most of the places mentioned in the book, while Liam Hilferty got the bibliography into printable shape. Alan Steinweis remained by my side, kept calm, and kept telling me that, one day, I would be able to fly back home to Germany again. He was right, and I brought the project to fruition in Munich in early 2022.

The original German book was the result of a research project that grew over time. I owe a great debt to many people who helped me turn a small case study into a book. The Lehrstuhl für Zeitgeschichte (Chair for Contemporary History) at the Ludwig-Maximilians-University in Munich and a number of individuals who are connected to it played a key role in making the original publication of the book possible. My greatest thanks go to the chairholder, Margit Szöllösi-Janze, for funding the publication of the German edition. Margit Szöllösi-Janze, Hans Günter Hockerts, Christiane Kuller, and Winfried Süß, who have been directing a research project on the Munich city administration under National Socialism, supported my work through to its completion. Their profound knowledge and constructive criticism of the manuscript have been invaluable. All four of them, each in their own way, have shaped my development as a historian and a scholar.

From the start, I have profited immensely from Maximilian Strnad's knowledge and friendship, and I'm very grateful for his ideas and recommendations as well as his enthusiasm about this project. In addition to the individuals already mentioned, Annette Eberle, Anna Hájková, Beate Kosmala, Eva Schrafstetter, and Jürgen Zarusky read the manuscript in whole or in part, providing numerous valuable suggestions. For insights, ideas, constructive criticism, and encouragement, I am indebted to Natalia Aleksiun, Frank Bajohr, Michael Brenner, Marion Detjen, Atina Grossmann, Angela Herrmann, Dominique Hipp, Anna Holian, Marion Kaplan, Rudi Armin Kitzmann, Katja Klee, Philipp Lenhard, Antonia Leugers, Andrea Löw, Ilse Macek, Heinrich Mayer, Beate Meyer, Armand Presser, Ellen Presser, Edith Raim, Rebecca Raue, Mark Roseman, Daniela Schmidl, Barbara Schieb, Claudia Schoppmann, Katharina Seehuber, Dana Smith, Manfred Struck, Dietmar Süß, Adi Trumpf, Martina Voigt, Maria von der Heydt, Gerhard Weinberg, and Angela Zieglgänsberger. At the Wallstein Verlag in Göttingen, Germany, Hajo Gevers and Stephanie Mürbe oversaw the publication of the German manuscript with great care.

Hugo Holzmann, Charlotte Knobloch, Bernhard K., Richard Marx, Herta Pila, and Klaus Vrieslander graciously shared their memories with me. I'm deeply grateful for their willingness to talk to me.

Sadly, three individuals who were instrumental in the genesis of this project are no longer alive to see the English edition. Bernhard K. told me his story of hiding and rescue in 2012, when I had just started my research. After that conversation, I knew that this would become a bigger project than I had originally planned. Brigitte Schmidt generously shared her unique expertise, her dry wit, and good food. When I knocked on the door of her office for the first time, I did not know that this archivist at the Munich City Archive possessed an encyclopedic knowledge of the Munich Jewish community past and present. I also did not know that this was the beginning of a wonderful friendship that was ended much too early by her untimely death. Jürgen Zarusky, at the Institute for Contemporary History in Munich, gave me the original idea for the project. For more than twenty years, Jürgen was a colleague, mentor, friend, and source of inspiration and advice to me.

Archivists in many archives and libraries assisted me with my research. I am especially indebted to Robert Bierschneider (Munich State Archive) and Sigmund Bornstein (Bavarian State Compensation Office), who went the extra mile and allowed me to benefit from their profound knowledge. Andreas Heusler (Munich City Archive) provided generous help in the beginning phase of this project. I wrote large sections of the original text and made many of the revisions in the reading room of the Institute for Contemporary History, where the librarians were immensely helpful ordering books and documents.

My colleagues and friends in Vermont—Jonathan Huener, Frank Nicosia, Adriana Borra, Antonello Borra, Marc Heinzer, Michael Johnson, Marilyn Lucas, Judith Müller, Annegret Schmitt-Johnson, Sandra Sonntag and Meša Tuco—contributed in many different ways to the completion of this book as well as to the earlier German edition. I benefited immensely from their knowledge and insights and from their continued intellectual and emotional support during a difficult year of COVID-19, when we were all grounded in Vermont. The congenial and friendly atmosphere in the Department of History at the University of Vermont has made my work very enjoyable overall. I would like to thank the chairperson, Paul Deslandes, and all of my colleagues in the department for their support and for their constant efforts to maintain a spirit of solidarity and empathy in the department. It is not to be taken for granted.

Fritz Schrafstetter and Rosalie Steinweis have followed this book project (and others) with keen interest and encouraging comments. Sadly, Fritz

Schrafstetter did not live to see the English edition. Eva Schrafstetter has always been there for me and provided so much support. Alan Steinweis knows all the ups and downs of this project. Not only did he read both the German and the English versions of the manuscript and make extensive comments, but he also had to live with the author. This has been no small feat—even before COVID-19. For all of these reasons—and many more—this book is, with my deepest gratitude, for him.

Munich, Germany, April 2022

ABBREVIATIONS

AA Arolsen Archives
AG Amtsgericht (local court)
AIM Archiv der Inneren Mission, München (Archive of the Inner Mission, Munich)
AWL Archive of the Wiener Library, London
BArchB Bundesarchiv Berlin (German Federal Archive, Berlin)
BayHStA Bayerisches Hauptstaatsarchiv (Bavarian Main State Archive)
BBC British Broadcasting Company
BDC Berlin Document Center
BEG Bundesentschädigungsgesetz (1956) (Federal Compensation Law)
BErgG Bundesergänzungsgesetz zur Entschädigung für Opfer Nationalsozialistischer Verfolgung (1953) (Federal Supplementary Law of Compensation for Victims of National Socialist Persecution)
BLEA Bayerisches Landesentschädigungsamt (Bavarian State Compensation Office)
BMW Bayerische Motorenwerke (Bavarian Motor Works)
BVP Bayerische Volkspartei (Bavarian People's Party)
CCL Allied Control Council Law
CJH Center for Jewish History

CSU Christlich-Soziale Union (Christian-Social Union)
DAF Deutsche Arbeitsfront (German Labor Front)
DDR Deutsche Demokratische Republik (German Democratic Republic, East Germany)
DiCV Archiv des Caritasverbands der Erzdiözese München und Freising e.V. (Archive of the Caritas Association of the Archdiocese of Munich and Freising)
DP displaced person
EG Entschädigungsgesetz (compensation law)
e. V. Eingetragener Verein (registered association)
FDP Freie Demokratische Partei (Free Democratic Party)
Gestapo Geheime Staatspolizei (Secret State Police)
HJ Hitlerjugend (Hitler Youth)
HSSPF Höhere SS- und Polizeiführer (Higher SS and Police Leaders)
ID identification card
IfZ Institut für Zeitgeschichte (Leibniz Institute for Contemporary History)
IKG Israelitische Kultusgemeinde (Jewish Community of Munich)
ITS International Tracing Service, Arolsen
JDC/Joint American Jewish Joint Distribution Committee
KPD Kommunistische Partei Deutschlands (German Communist Party)
KZ Konzentrationslager (concentration camp)
LAN Landeskirchliches Archiv der Evangelisch-Lutherischen Kirche in Bayern, Nürnberg (Archive of the Lutheran State Church of Bavaria, Nuremberg)
LEA Landesentschädigungsamt (State Compensation Office)
LBI Leo Baeck Institute
Mem. Memoiren (memoirs)
NL Nachlass (personal papers)
NSDAP Nationalsozialistische Deutsche Arbeiterpartei (National Socialist German Workers' Party, Nazi Party)
NSFK Nationalsozialistisches Fliegerkorps (National Socialist Flying Corps)

NSKK Nationalsozialistisches Kraftfahrerkorps (National Socialist Motor Vehicle Corps)
NSV Nationalsozialistische Volkswohlfahrt (National Socialist People's Welfare)
OdF Opfer des Faschismus (Victim of Fascism)
OT Organization Todt
PK Parteikorrespondenz (party correspondence)
Pol. Dir. Polizeidirektion (police directorate)
RM reichsmark
RSHA Reichssicherheitshauptamt (Reich Security Main Office)
RSI Repubblica Sociale Italiana (Italian Social Republic)
SA Sturmabteilung (Storm Troopers of the Nazi Party)
SD Sicherheitsdienst (Security Service of the SS)
SPD Sozialdemokratische Partei Deutschlands (Social Democratic Party of Germany)
SS Schutzstaffel (Protection Squadron, Nazi party paramilitary organization)
Spk Spruchkammer (denazification tribunal)
Stanw Staatsanwaltschaft (public prosecutor's office)
StadtAM Stadtarchiv München (Munich City Archive)
StAM Staatsarchiv München (State Archive, Munich)
UNRRA United Nations Relief and Rehabilitation Administration
USEG Law for Compensation for National Socialist Injustice in the US Zone (1949)
USHMM United States Holocaust Memorial Museum
VVN Vereinigung der Verfolgten des Naziregimes (Association of Persecutees of the Nazi Regime)
WB Wiedergutmachungsbehörden (restitution offices)
YV Yad Vashem
ZAL Zwangsarbeitslager (forced labor camp)
ZfA Zentrum für Antisemitismusforschung (Center for Research on Antisemitism)

MAPS

Germany, 1939.

German Occupation of Europe in 1942.

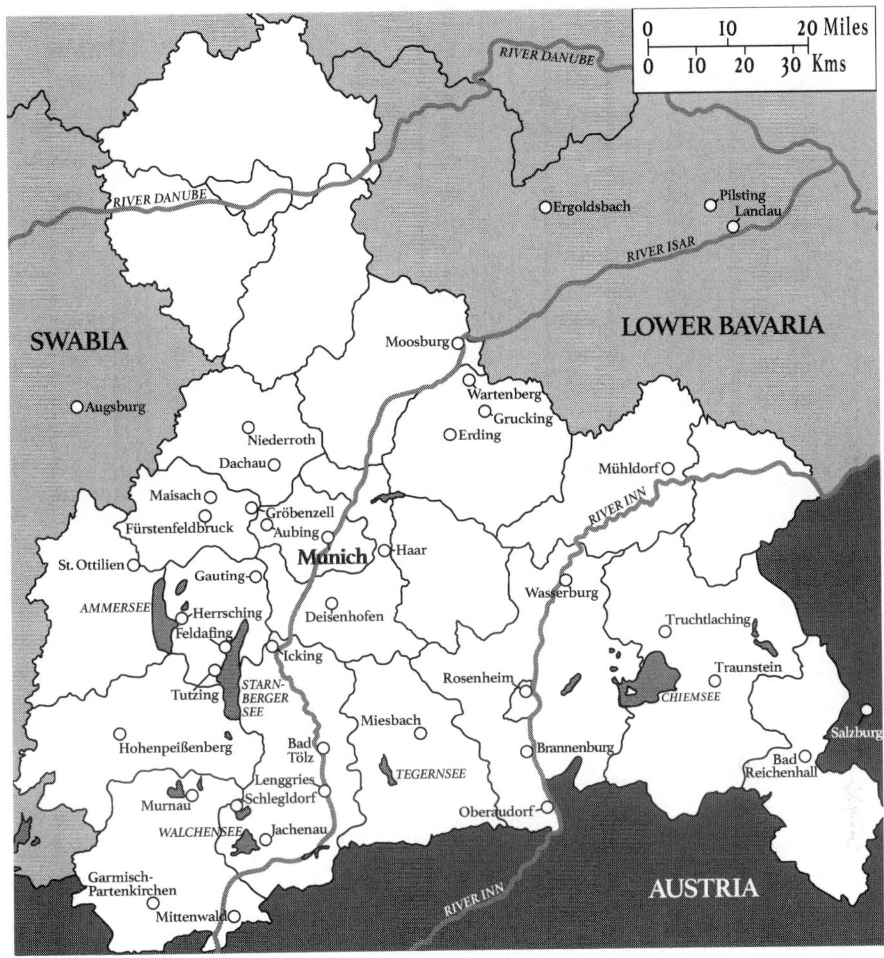

Upper Bavaria.

FLIGHT AND CONCEALMENT

INTRODUCTION

ON JULY 10, 1942, SOPHIE Mayer, a German Jewish doctor from Munich, learned that her deportation was imminent. In a couple of days, she was to be included on a transport to a Jewish ghetto in German-occupied Poland. With the help of an old acquaintance, she fled from Munich to Lenggries, a small town in the foothills of the Bavarian Alps. She remained in Lenggries until the war ended in 1945. For almost three years, she was hidden in the attic of the home of a local family she had not previously known.[1] Sophie Mayer was one of an estimated ten thousand to twelve thousand Jews in Nazi Germany who went underground, defying deportation orders that would have ultimately led to their deaths.[2] With the help of relatives, friends, neighbors, and strangers, these Jewish fugitives attempted to survive the Holocaust by living in "illegality."[3] Without a home, without food ration cards, and under constant fear of denunciation and arrest, they were dependent on their helpers, some of whom were altruistic, and some of whom were selfish profiteers. Only a few thousand of these Jews survived until the end of the war.[4]

Sophie Mayer's case was unusual in a number of ways. First of all, she survived. The majority of the Jewish fugitives were eventually caught, deported, and murdered. Most Jews who went into hiding did not remain in one place for the entirety of their time in hiding, as Mayer did. Instead, they changed their quarters frequently out of fear of being discovered or denounced. Typically, a large number of helpers, rather than just one family, facilitated their survival. Food and clothing had to be arranged, new hiding places found, and, if possible, forged identity papers procured. In some cases, up to fifty helpers were involved in saving a single individual.[5]

The largest number of fugitive German Jews lived in Berlin, not Bavaria. In 1941, when the deportations began, about 40 percent of all Jews still in Germany lived in Berlin.[6] Roughly five thousand to seven thousand Jews, that is, about 50 percent of all Jewish fugitives in Germany, went into hiding in the capital city. An estimated 1,500 to 2,000 of them were able to hold out until liberation.[7] In Berlin, the Jews who lived in hiding sardonically referred to themselves as "U-boats" (submarines), as they had "submerged" below the surface. Most of them did not, however, live in constant hiding as Sophie Mayer did, but rather they resubmerged and resurfaced frequently; many of them even lived quite visibly within German society.[8] Those who were able to obtain false identity papers were able to move about more freely in public if the false papers were good forgeries, but they also had to convincingly live as their assumed identity. On the streets, they risked ID checks and raids or being recognized by old acquaintances or Jewish "snatchers" (*Greifer*), collaborators who were used by the Gestapo to track down fugitive Jews.[9] In war-torn Berlin, thousands of Jews submerged in the anonymity of the big city. Many knew of each other, and sometimes they even met. These Berlin U-boats and their helpers have become a focus of postwar memory, commemoration, and scholarly research on hiding and rescue of Jews in Nazi Germany.

By contrast, far less is known about the situation of Jewish U-boats in other German cities and regions. It can be assumed that hardly more than two hundred hidden Jews survived in most of those cities. Petra Bonavita estimates that roughly 225 Jews lived "illegally" in Greater Frankfurt.[10] Beate Meyer has stated that an early postwar figure of only fifty people having survived in hiding in Hamburg "needs to be corrected upwards somewhat, but not terribly much."[11] This book is the first comprehensive study of Jews who went underground to avoid deportation in Munich or elsewhere in southern Bavaria. My research findings allow me to conclude that a total of roughly 110 to 120 Jews went into hiding in the Greater Munich area.[12] In some cases, there are only vague indications or anecdotal knowledge without any names. Especially with respect to failed escape attempts that ended in deportation or murder, we must assume that a certain number never became known because those who attempted to escape were not necessarily arrested in Munich.

In comparison with Berlin, the number of Jewish U-boats in other regions was small. Moreover, the conditions for escaping deportation and living in illegality were different in different parts of the country. The focus on Berlin has, therefore, led to an incomplete and somewhat distorted picture of Jewish flight and rescue in Germany. The conditions for hiding in Munich differed from those in Berlin. For example, Sophie Mayer went underground much earlier than most Jews in Berlin; she did not live under the constant threat of Allied air raids; she could not shop on the illegal underground market; and she could not leave her hiding place, as everyone in the village would have recognized her as a stranger.

This book tells many stories of Munich U-boats and their helpers that have not been previously known. It focuses on several questions: When and under what circumstances did Jews from Munich make the decision to go into hiding, and who helped them? How and where did they survive or perish? From a comparative perspective, it examines how the conditions in Munich differed from the situations in Berlin, Vienna, Frankfurt, and other cities and regions of the German Reich. What common ground and what differences can be recognized? The comparative approach paints a more precise picture of regional differences and peculiarities in the history of the deportation of German Jewry. Escape and hiding were often dynamic processes in the course of which hundreds, or even thousands, of miles were covered.[13] Many Jewish U-boats from Berlin or other parts of Germany ended up in Upper Bavaria, while many from Munich and environs went to Berlin or elsewhere in Germany. And some of them managed to escape abroad. Looking at Jewish fugitives who left Munich and Bavaria and at those who arrived there from other places, this book illustrates the transregional and transnational dimensions of flight, hiding, and rescue. Throughout German-occupied Europe, Jews on the run from persecution and deportation crossed multiple borders in the hope of reaching safety.

This book does not end with 1945. It documents the process of reemerging from hiding and traces the postwar fates of many former U-boats. What did their postwar lives look like? The postwar phase involves questions of the relationship between survivors and helpers after the persecution, struggles for financial compensation, punishment of the perpetrators, and recognition of the assistance provided by helpers. It also addresses how German cities dealt with expressions of solidarity with Jews during the Nazi period and how hiding and solidarity with Jews have been remembered in Germany.

Following Saul Friedländer's integrative history *Nazi Germany and the Jews*, the persecution measures, the experiences of the Jews, and the behavior of the non-Jewish population are analyzed here from multiple perspectives.[14] In contrast to Friedländer, however, the focus of this book is not on the political measures,[15] but instead on the victims' perspective, though not limited to it. In a complex web of relationships involving Jews in hiding, helpers, helpers' helpers, people who silently knew of the actions, sympathizers, financial profiteers, denouncers, and perpetrators, far-reaching conclusions can be drawn about the social history of the persecution, which was a process determined not only by state and police actions but also by the actions of ordinary people responding to everyday conditions in Nazi Germany. Since my analysis continues beyond 1945, it can also show how the experience of persecution was dealt with in postwar society among perpetrators, victims, and the entire spectrum of additional social actors ("bystanders," as Raul Hilberg referred to them).[16] This study can thus be viewed as a contribution to the social history of German Jewry during the Holocaust, to the postwar history of the survivors, and to how persecution and its victims were addressed and remembered after 1945.

The Nuremberg Race Laws of the Nazi regime distinguished among different degrees of Jewishness based on ancestry rather than by religion or identity. Thus, the people in hiding belonged to different categories of people who were targeted in different ways and at different times. The race laws differentiated between "full Jews" and certain categories of people of "mixed blood," or *Mischlinge*.[17] The laws prohibited marriages between Jews and non-Jewish Germans. Existing marriages were not terminated, but mixed-marriage couples had to live as social outcasts under precarious economic conditions and they faced harassment by the authorities. Germans who were classified as *Mischlinge* were generally not deported, but some of them went into hiding because they feared they might ultimately be included in the deportations. *Geltungsjuden*, those of mixed descent who were legally treated as Jews, were often, but not always, deported later than full Jews.[18] Jews in mixed marriages were targeted for deportation if they lost the protection of a non-Jewish spouse through death or divorce. In the final stages of the war, all Jews still in mixed marriages were scheduled for deportation. How did these classifications impact an individual's perception of the persecution and the decision to go into hiding? What did they mean for mixed-religion families? We must also ask to what extent assistance for Jews in hiding was offered by people in mixed marriages or "half Jews." Many people who suffered persecution were not Jews in a religious sense but were the children of Jewish converts to Christianity, had been baptized as Christians, or had left the official Jewish community. According to the Nuremberg Race Laws, they were nevertheless considered Jews and were persecuted as such. One must thus ask who the helpers actually helped or wanted to help: a Jew or a Christian coreligionist? Regrettably, it is impossible to avoid using Nazi terminology in this context because that is the only way to understand the specific living conditions and maneuvering room under which individuals attempted to flee and live in hiding or to help others.

The sources for this book have very varied provenance. Works on the history of Munich and on the Jewish Community of Munich during the Nazi period were key in identifying individual stories for the present study.[19] The Munich

City Archive's database of the Biographical Memorial Book of the Jews of Munich, 1933–1945 (*Biographisches Gedenkbuch der Münchner Juden*) and the database of Jews known to have gone into hiding located at the German Resistance Memorial Center in Berlin provided valuable information about individual cases across Germany.[20] Memoirs, diaries, and eyewitness accounts by Jews—whether they were published or not—also constitute an essential foundation for this book. Some authors describe their own survival underground, while others refer either in detail or in passing to the rescue attempts of friends and acquaintances. Personal testimonies from the postwar period offer insight into decisions and strategies for action among the Jews and their helpers, as well as into how they coped with the persecution emotionally. Of course, as with all primary sources, it is necessary to read these documents critically and to compare them with other contemporaneous materials. Unfortunately, only isolated diaries of Munich Jews who went into hiding are extant, to some degree due to the fear of their being discovered.[21] The most comprehensive and well-known such diary is that of Else Behrend-Rosenfeld, who worked as the director of the Jewish predeportation internment camp in Berg am Laim (on the outskirts of the city of Munich) and went underground in 1942.[22]

The point of departure for my research were lists of names—more or less incomplete—of perpetrators, helpers, survivors, and victims.[23] The lists contained intriguing clues. For example, a list of the members of the Jewish Community of Munich included numerous handwritten notes scribbled next to individuals' names. The notes usually related to matters of health, marital status, and changes of address, but next to a few names stood the simple comment "missing."[24] In many cases, persecution narratives could be researched in historical records, such as the restitution and compensation files of persecutees, the records of postwar trials against perpetrators, and the denazification files of the helpers for whom Jews had provided affidavits. Some former U-boats testified in denazification proceedings or postwar trials against the perpetrators. In their petitions for restitution and compensation, Jews had to document their whereabouts during the war years. In doing so, some revealed—frequently more in passing than deliberately—extraordinary stories of flight, persecution, denunciation, and betrayal, but also of support and a readiness to help. Others offered only short, general descriptions of their survival, thereby obscuring the precise circumstances of their life in hiding.[25]

Some survivors wanted to thank their helpers after the war. Their first opportunity to do so came when the helpers had to go through denazification proceedings. Some Jews, however, also made an effort to have their helpers honored by seeking to have them included among the Righteous Among the

Nations at Yad Vashem—the World Holocaust Remembrance Center in Israel. Since 1963, when the program started, almost twenty-eight thousand Righteous have been honored, among them 641 Germans.[26] Hence, the holdings of the Righteous Among the Nations collection in Yad Vashem have also provided valuable information about individual stories of rescue. To be recognized as one of the Righteous, a helper had to have "risked his or her life, freedom, and safety in order to rescue one or several Jews from the threat of death or deportation" without demanding anything in return.[27] In other words, helpers had to have been motivated by altruism.

Obviously, the motives of the helpers varied greatly. Some did not (or not exclusively) act out of altruism. Some provided help on the basis of family ties or friendships or even on a spontaneous impulse. Political convictions sometimes played a role, but there were also financial and sexual interests, prospects of inexpensive labor, or even hopes for a religious conversion of the person(s) to be rescued.[28] Assistance was often conditional or connected to expectations of rewards or return services. Altruistic motives could change over time and were frequently mixed with other feelings or financial motives. For example, largely unselfish helpers could sometimes not avoid demanding financial assistance to afford to help out in the first place.[29] The personal relationships between helpers and those in hiding were often complicated. A previous relationship could have played a role, as could hardship on both sides, emotional dependencies, and the psychological stress resulting from the extreme situation. In addition, many survivors remained silent after the war concerning the darker sides of these relationships. Who really wanted to talk or write about sexual or financial exploitation, beatings, humiliation, or (emotional) extortion? For all these reasons, a strict distinction between "righteous" and "other" helpers can be problematic. Many helpers certainly satisfied the criteria to be acknowledged in Yad Vashem as Righteous Among the Nations, but many cases of assistance unfolded in a gray area of implicit and explicit expectations or relationships that were not entirely voluntary.

MEMORY, LITERATURE, AND TERMINOLOGY

In postwar West German society, which collectively viewed itself as the victim of a criminal regime that had made it impossible for individuals to resist in any way, most people did not want to hear about the civil courage of the few Germans who showed solidarity with those facing persecution and supported them in their struggle to survive. The survivors themselves, who attempted to (re)build their livelihood in postwar Germany, rarely spoke about their experiences. For a long time, very few people posed questions about (the lack of) assistance for Jews during the Holocaust. Memoirs and efforts to honor the helpers remained isolated cases.[30] This began to change in the early 1960s, when some Germans were recognized as Righteous Among the Nations and a select few even received Germany's highest honor, the Federal Cross of Merit (*Bundesverdienstkreuz*).[31] They were presented as proof that not all Germans had been collectively guilty and that there had been courageous individuals who served as "counterimages" to Nazi perpetrators such as Adolf Eichmann, who was standing trial at the time.[32] Over time, younger generations of Germans increasingly developed positive associations with "good Germans" who had helped Jews, and more than a few believed that their grandparents were among those who had helped.[33] Yet overall, public interest in the issue remained limited.

Things changed dramatically in 1993 when Hollywood took up the fate of Oskar Schindler and the film *Schindler's List*, based on the book by Thomas Keneally, was shown in German cinemas. Schindler had rescued roughly 1,200 Jews in occupied Poland and Czechoslovakia. Within two months, 3.4 million Germans had seen the movie,[34] and the subject of rescue became a topic of broad public interest for the first time.[35] When in the early 1990s, after the Cold War had ended, memories of the Holocaust were revived and there was increased research on the subject in Germany, Britain, the United States, and Israel, *Schindler's List* reached audiences of millions in many countries. Since then, not only have numerous stories of rescues become the subjects of successful films,[36] but the memoirs of prominent figures in Germany who had survived in hiding, such as television host Hans Rosenthal, also received broader attention.[37] Many new memoirs have appeared since 2000.[38] Interest has been particularly strong in Berlin, where most of the rescues took place and where survivors such as Inge Deutschkron were actively engaged in the public commemoration of helpers.[39] In 2008, the Silent Heroes Memorial Center opened its doors in the heart of Berlin. The phrase "silent heroes" refers to the fact that most of the helpers had remained silent about what they had done during the war. The Memorial Center informs visitors about "the persecution and plight of Jews facing imminent deportation," "how some of them decided to resist the threat to their lives by going underground," and "the actions and motivations of the men and women who helped them."[40]

Scholarly research has also shown an interest in survivors and their helpers. In the mid-1990s, Wolfgang Benz, the then director of the Center for Research on Antisemitism (ZfA) in Berlin, launched a historical research project on the rescue of Jews in Nazi Germany. Under the title "Solidarity and Assistance for

Jews during the Nazi Period," multiple volumes eventually appeared, covering not only assistance to Jews in Nazi Germany but in all the countries of German-occupied Europe.[41] These volumes and other works produced by Benz's project document cases of rescue by individuals and networks of helpers, in addition to the treatment of survivors and helpers in the postwar period.[42] As part of the project, the Center for Research on Antisemitism also set up a database containing all known cases of rescue in Germany.[43]

Subsequently, scholars in Germany and elsewhere published a number of studies about Jews in hiding, most of which focus on individual cases of rescue and on the situation of Jewish U-boats in Berlin.[44] In the most recent works, a focus on the motives and networks of helpers is apparent.[45] Overall, these publications are part of a broader, growing scholarly interest in the history of flight, hiding, and rescue of Jews across German-occupied Europe.[46] Many focus on specific cities, regions, or countries, while comparative and transnational aspects of the subject still require further examination.

In German historiography, especially in some of the works that appeared in the early 2000s, helping Jews escape from the deportations has been termed *Rettungswiderstand*, that is, rescue as a form of resistance against National Socialism.[47] The term was coined by the Holocaust survivor and historian Arno Lustiger, whose efforts established the rescue of Jews as a category of resistance against the Nazi regime.[48] Previously, the scholarly literature on resistance in Nazi Germany had not dealt with such rescue efforts, addressing instead anti-Nazi activities in social groups such as the military officer corps, the working class, and youth.[49] Much of Lustiger's efforts were motivated by his rejection of Raul Hilberg's claim that the European Jews had done little to resist their own destruction.[50] Lustiger saw the refusal to let oneself be deported as part of the extensive and multifaceted resistance that Jews across Europe carried out against Nazism. Others also recognized efforts to escape deportation as acts of noncompliance and, as such, a form of resistance.[51] Lustiger had another motive: he wanted to honor all those individuals who had helped Jews escape deportation. To him, these individuals were the "heroes of *Rettungswiderstand*."[52]

The term *Rettungswiderstand*, rescue as resistance, has become established in the German discourse about Jews escaping deportation, but it is not unproblematic. The focus on rescue comes with a clear emphasis on "rescuers" or "silent heroes,"[53] implying a certain passivity on the part of those rescued[54] and, more importantly, reducing complex social encounters and interactions to a simplistic relationship between rescuer and rescued. Not everyone who helped became a rescuer, much less a hero.[55] There were differences between those who housed a fugitive Jew for weeks or months, those who regularly donated ration cards to feed a Jew in hiding, and those who occasionally served as messengers.[56] Also, if we examine all the individuals who came into contact with U-boats, we find courageous, selfless rescuers, pragmatic helpers, selfish helpers, and those who saw the plight of others as an opportunity for self-enrichment. Of course, even individuals with selfish reasons could provide effective help.

There was also a market for escape assistance, involving lodgings, food ration cards, clothing, ID documents, weapons, and human smugglers. Not everyone who offered their services was an honest trader. The spectrum of demands ranged from moderate sums of money for caring for someone in hiding to exorbitant sums that were extorted from the U-boats, for which they received little or nothing in return. Berliners called this practice *Judenfledderei*, or "Jew fleecing," which was evidently so widespread that it was worthy of its own very telling neologism.[57] The verb *fleddern*, "plundering," is generally used in German in connection with corpses, that is, the plundering of corpses or grave robbing. So here people spoke of plundering those doomed to die, which might allow conclusions about the knowledge of many Germans about the fate awaiting the Jews. Jewish flight and concealment was, therefore, a social process within the framework of the history of deportations, involving much more than so-called rescuers and the rescued. It also involved traders, profiteers, extortionists, casual thieves, denouncers, silent confidants, indirect helpers (such as those who passed on news and messages, donors of money or food ration coupons, and employers), and non-Jewish relatives. On top of that were all those who did not know whether the people they were hosting, sheltering, or employing were Jews. Once we expand our perspective in this way, it becomes obvious that many more people than is generally presumed determined the fate of the U-boats in some way. The subject is much broader than the story of resistance and thus must be considered part of the social history of the deportations.

Most studies of survival in hiding end in 1945 or a short time thereafter. The state of research on survivors of the Holocaust is relatively good with respect to the displaced persons (DPs) and the DP camps, but far less is known about German Jews outside the DP camps and their contacts with the German population. Atina Grossmann's study, *Jews, Germans, and Allies*, is pioneering in this regard, also shedding light on the "resurfacing" of the U-boats, their specific problems among survivors, and their perspective on postwar Berlin society.[58] There have also been some publications about the recognition of the helpers and the commemoration of their aid to Jews in Nazi Germany.[59] Surviving U-boats have rarely been perceived as a distinct group. Particularly with respect to compensation for victims, they were legally in a worse position than survivors of the death camps, as having lived in hiding was initially not recognized as a form of imprisonment. The historiography of compensation and restitution shows a transition in recent years from a focus on state measures to "compensation in practice," in which the individual experience of the victims is placed at the center of the story.[60] In this regard, the present study can also be viewed as a contribution to the history of compensation.

Stories of living illegally are also stories of the emotional and psychological stress of hiding, painful postwar reunions, and struggles for recognition as victims of persecution. As Alexandra Garbarini has shown in her study of the diaries of Jewish victims, the diarists wanted later generations to learn something about what Jews who lived at that time had been feeling.[61] Although the present study does not pursue an approach based on the history of the emotions, it does aim, as far as the sources permit, to highlight the emotions experienced by persons who lived in illegality. This pertains also to the postwar period, especially regarding the experiences of former U-boats in their dealings with the bureaucracy of compensation and in their participation in trials against former perpetrators.

STRUCTURE OF THE STUDY

The following analysis is divided into two parts and a total of twelve chapters, in which the first part covers the period of Nazism and the second part, the postwar period. The first two chapters are dedicated to the predeportation history of Jewish persecution in Nazi Germany and the unfolding of the deportations starting in 1941. The book begins with an outline of the persecution of the Jews in Germany up to 1939 as illustrated by the demise of the organized Jewish community in Munich. A particular focus is placed on the assistance offered Jews during the pogrom of November 9, 1938. After the pogrom, Jewish men who had gone on the run to avoid arrest needed food and shelter. Did non-Jewish friends and neighbors help them? This also raises the question as to whether, in the years from 1941 to 1945, Jews could rely on people who had helped them in 1938. The pogrom was not the prelude to the Holocaust, but it was when mass flight and going underground began.

The focus of the second chapter is the deportation of German Jewry. Here, escapes are placed within the context of the initial deportations and the subsequent deportation waves. Regional differences are especially significant here. In contrast to Berlin, the vast majority of Jews in Munich had already been deported in 1941–42, when knowledge of the murder of European Jewry was still rather vague or barely existent. While there were still more than 3,400 Jews living in Munich in early 1941, by December 1942, the number had dropped to only 645.[62]

The chronology of the deportations forms the context for the next three chapters on the various phases of escape. Chapters 3 to 5 distinguish three phases of escapes: early escapes from October 1941 to August 1942, escapes in the course of the final mass deportations in early 1943, and the relatively large wave of escapes in February 1945, when Jews in mixed marriages were deported. By presenting multiple individual stories, it is possible not only to describe the different waves, but also to analyze the social background, motives, strategies for action, and personal circumstances of U-boats and their helpers. A comparison of German cities reveals substantial regional differences. Whereas most of the Berlin Jews went underground within the scope of the so-called Factory Operation in February 1943, that is, during the final major wave of deportations, a very different picture is evident for Munich and Frankfurt.

Chapters 6 through 8 focus on particular themes deserving special attention. These include failed escape attempts, Christian help organizations, hidden children, and the regional, national, and international geography of the routes along which Jews sought to escape. Chapter 6, which analyzes failed escape attempts, describes not only a wide spectrum of dangers threatening Jews in hiding, but also the risks and consequences for their helpers. A major risk both groups had to face was denunciation. How often and why were Jews and their helpers denounced? The seventh chapter focuses on hidden children, most of whom were sheltered away from their hometowns in completely new social environments, and on transregional Christian networks and aid provided by church representatives. Just as important as the chronology of submerging is the topography of flight and concealment. Chapter 8 describes Jews who sometimes covered thousands of miles while on the run and living in hiding. Escape routes throughout all of Germany are presented, as are examples of escapes to other countries. This chapter closes the first part of the book with an analysis of flight and hiding as dynamic processes.

Beginning with chapter 9, the second part of the study illustrates the fate of survivors and helpers in the postwar period, with a focus on the U-boats' process of resurfacing and on the key dilemma for many survivors of whether to emigrate or remain in Germany. Did the U-boats' experience with "other Germans," that is, German helpers, play a role in their decision? One of the most famous surviving U-boats was the postwar television game show host Hans Rosenthal. He said that the support and solidarity he had received during his time in hiding made it possible for him to continue living in Germany "without hatred."[63] Chapter 9 also discusses the possible long-term consequences of the emotional and physical stress of life in hiding.

In denazification proceedings and postwar trials, survivors who remained in Germany sometimes reencountered not only their former helpers, but also those who had persecuted, extorted, threatened, and denounced them. These "second encounters" are analyzed in all their different facets in chapter 10. How could the surviving U-boats contribute to the trials against the perpetrators? How was support for Jews assessed by the denazification tribunals? How important, and credible, were statements made by Jews to postwar tribunals testifying to the support and good treatment they had received from their helpers? How were denouncers and so-called Jew fleecers treated in criminal proceedings? A comparative analysis of denazification judgments against people who denounced Jews and those against Munich Gestapo agents adds to our understanding of the history of denazification.

The last two chapters revolve around how postwar society treated the surviving U-boats and their helpers. Chapter 11 analyzes compensation for the former U-boats based on a series of individual cases. It focuses on the legal discrimination the U-boats faced as compared with survivors of concentration and death camps, as well as on their perceptions of the compensation process more generally. The twelfth chapter is about the evolving and regionally very different forms of remembrance of the surviving U-boats and their helpers. Were the helpers publicly recognized? How was the persecution perceived? With respect to Munich, it can be shown that the city leadership in the postwar period created a mythology of Munich as a city of numerous helpers of Jews, a claim that was intended to reinforce positive memories of emigrants toward their former hometown and to contribute to the moral rehabilitation of an economically expanding region. Even though the memory of surviving U-boats and their helpers is much more visible in remembrance of the Holocaust in Munich today than it was thirty years ago, it is apparent that Berlin is largely recognized as the main site of remembrance for this aspect of the Holocaust. Finally, the key findings of the study are summarized and placed into the broader context of the history of the deportation of German Jewry.

ONE

UNDER NAZI RULE

Jews in Munich, 1933–1941

IN 1933, THERE WERE ROUGHLY ten thousand to eleven thousand Jews living in all of Upper Bavaria and only a few hundred in Lower Bavaria. Whereas in Munich alone there were nine thousand to ten thousand Jews, constituting the seventh-largest Jewish community in Germany, the rural regions of Upper and Lower Bavaria were home to very few Jews.[1] Conditions also varied considerably between northern and southern Bavaria. Far more Jews lived in Franconia (in the north) than in Upper and Lower Bavaria (in the south and east). It is not possible based on this data to generate precise numbers for those facing persecution, as the statistics only apply to people who were members of officially recognized Jewish communities and do not include Jews who had converted or had canceled their memberships in the official communities. Such individuals, however, were equally affected by Nazi persecution. As Nazi measures of persecution impacted all Jews in Germany in similar ways, the situation of Jews in Munich can serve to illustrate the disenfranchisement and exclusion experienced throughout Germany. There were nevertheless always regional and local differences in how the persecution was carried out; these will be discussed at the end of the chapter.

The Jewish Community of Munich (IKG) had grown steadily in the nineteenth century, experiencing its heyday in the two decades prior to the First World War.[2] Germany's defeat in 1918 was followed by the revolution, Kurt Eisner's government, and, after Eisner was murdered in February 1919, the phase of the Soviet Republic. Prominent Munich Jews publicly distanced themselves from socialist revolutionaries such as Eugen Leviné, Gustav Landauer, and Max Levien. They feared having Jewry associated with socialist revolution.[3] Many people in Munich saw the Jews as being primarily responsible for revolution, the Soviet Republic, and civil war–like circumstances. It was irrelevant that many socialist revolutionaries had long since abandoned their Jewish roots and that the Jews of Munich largely supported bourgeois parties and viewed Eisner's government as a catastrophe.[4] It was also deliberately overlooked that Jews fought in the notorious Free Corps units, which were responsible for brutally quashing the Soviet Republic.[5]

As a result of the political radicalization, the city changed in the early 1920s. People who lived through the time described how the climate of "live and let live" transformed under the growing presence of *völkisch* (ethnic-nationalist) groups.[6] Long before the Nazis came to power, Munich's Jews had already begun to suffer from an emerging ostracism and antisemitic graffiti, flyers, and even acts of violence. During the Beer Hall Putsch in November 1923, these excesses reached an initial peak.[7] A particular stronghold of antisemitism was Munich's Ludwig Maximilian University, where antisemitic machinations and discriminatory personnel policies prompted Nobel Prize laureate Richard Willstätter to give up his professorial chair as early as 1924.[8] Although the volatile atmosphere abated somewhat in the following years, discriminatory everyday experiences remained part and parcel of Jewish life, as did antisemitic rabble-rousing.[9] For example, the Jewish community had to defend itself several times against press campaigns on the subject of "ritual murder."[10] The Jewish Community of Munich responded to this development by turning inward. For many members, Jewish tradition and customs took on greater meaning.[11]

EXCLUSION, PLUNDERING, EMIGRATION, 1933–1938

When the Nazis took power in 1933, the systematic exclusion of the Jews from social, cultural, and economic life began in Munich as everywhere else.[12] This was followed by the economic plundering, ghettoization, and, ultimately, the physical extermination of the Jews. The economic exclusion started in March 1933 when Mayor Karl Fiehler issued a directive to no longer award municipal contracts to Jewish companies.[13] The announced boycott of Jewish businesses that was to take place on April 1, on the other hand, turned out to be a failure in Munich, since long lines had formed in front of the Jewish stores in the preceding days, clearly demonstrating that the Munich populace in no way wanted to refrain from shopping in these stores.[14] This behavior cannot be interpreted as far-reaching solidarity, however, but might instead have arisen from an unwillingness to change old habits or do without certain goods.[15]

The exclusion from professional life took various forms. In 1934 and 1935, there were repeated attacks on Jewish-owned shops. Customers were prevented from entering, "*Jude*" ("Jew") or "*Saujude*" ("Jew-swine") was painted on the facades, and windows were smashed.[16] Civil servants were removed from their positions in compliance with the Law for the Restoration of the Professional Civil Service, which was enacted only a couple of months after the Nazis came to power. Jewish lawyers were shunned, and, pursuant to the Fifth Decree to the Reich Citizenship Law of September 1938, they lost their license to practice. Munich lawyer Dr. Benno Schülein had run a flourishing law practice with six staff members. In 1935, he had to lay off five of them because his income had dropped so dramatically that he could no longer pay their salaries. In 1938, his admission to the bar was revoked.[17] The physician Magdalena Schwarz was refused approval by a health insurance fund in 1933 and could only treat patients with private health insurance. In 1938, her license to practice medicine—like that of all Jewish doctors—was rescinded.[18] From then on, Jewish doctors could treat only Jewish patients and had to refer to themselves as "treaters of the sick" rather than as physicians. Physicians and lawyers are only two examples of a systematic and all-encompassing elimination of Jews from the economic life of the city. As Peter Hanke put it, "after Jews in Munich had been removed from practically all positions in the civil service and the municipal administration, the number of dismissals in the private sector also increased continually, which meant that the number of those who had to seek assistance from Jewish aid organizations in Munich also rose steadily."[19]

The economic impoverishment inevitably led to social and cultural exclusion as well. This was carried out through a plethora of regulations that banned Jews from participating in public life. For example, Jews could no longer attend concerts or theater or visit public libraries, nor could they enter cinemas or public swimming pools. The list of prohibitions continued to grow, gradually covering all public spaces, even public transportation. After 1933, only 1.5 percent of all secondary school students could be Jewish, and many Jewish high school students thus had to leave school. For those who could continue, the time they spent in school often came with daily humiliation from the other students and even the teachers. As of November 1938, Jewish children were permitted to attend only Jewish schools.[20]

Due to the persecution, 646 Munich Jews had already left the city in 1933. An additional 369 departed in 1934, and in the following year the figure was 379. After the Nuremberg Race Laws took effect, the number of emigrants in 1936 climbed back up to 581.[21] Many who wanted to leave Germany as quickly as possible sold their possessions under great pressure. Numerous Munich residents participated in the Aryanization of Jewish property in hopes of finding a good deal. Jews often felt compelled to sell their property below market value, and the tax offices made sure that only an increasingly small part of their assets could be transferred abroad.[22] In response to any indication that Jews were planning to emigrate, tax offices could demand "securities."[23] When actually leaving the country, they had to pay the Reich Flight Tax and foreign exchange duties. To transfer capital abroad, Jews had to acquire foreign exchange currency via a frozen account, into which a disagio payment had to be paid. This was increased from 20 percent in 1934 to 81 percent in 1936 and to 95 percent in 1939.[24] Consequently, anyone who decided to emigrate could only take a small fraction of their assets with them. This process was accompanied by harassment and arbitrary actions by the authorities. Richard Willstätter recounted the tribulations: "I would have to emigrate, and seek a refuge for the balance of my life. . . . And now, for many months to come (an aspect for which I was not prepared at all), began the daily running around to the many agencies involved, the standing in line at municipal and state cashiers' offices, the customs search department, the foreign exchange department and the foreign exchange control department, the almost daily hours-long waiting in corridors, the humiliations by overbearing minor officials."[25]

For the Jews remaining in Munich, the tax law meant an abundance of discriminatory measures. As of 1934, according to the Tax Adjustment Act, "the tax laws shall be interpreted in the spirit of the National Socialist ideology."[26] That opened the floodgates to arbitrary fiscal practices. Consequently, the tax offices could strike tax allowances and deductions for Jewish taxpayers at their discretion.[27] The case of the industrialist Max Bachmann is a good example of how someone's livelihood could be destroyed through the interplay of individual financial interests, Nazi Party agitation, and arbitrary bureaucratic actions.[28] Bachmann operated a millinery factory from his building at Rosenstrasse 11. A dance café, Tanzcafé Lieselott, occupied a space rented from Bachmann on the ground floor. Not only had the proprietor of the café accumulated a significant sum of rent arrears, but he also maintained good connections to the party leadership. On June 24, 1933, an article appeared in the Nazi paper *Der Stürmer* accusing Bachmann of charging exorbitant rents and closing with the sentence: "The Jew Bachmann should be sentenced to penal servitude."[29] As a result, Bachmann had to stand trial. Although he was "amnestied," as the charges were obviously untenable, he was harassed constantly by the authorities in the years that followed. Not only the party members from the Tanzcafé Lieselott but other tenants as well did not hesitate to take advantage of Bachmann's plight. They now felt encouraged simply to pay reduced rent. "The building thus ceased to be profitable, while on the other hand the tax burdens continued to their full extent in this peculiar rule of law,"[30] a resigned Bachmann wrote. The tax offices demanded taxes for income that Bachmann had long since stopped receiving. Ironically, it was not until Bachmann's building was Aryanized that these actions came to an end, since unauthorized rent reductions were not enforceable if the owner was not Jewish.

THE POGROM OF NOVEMBER 9, 1938

In Munich, Hitler and Goebbels had decided on short notice to stage the *Kristallnacht*, a pogrom throughout the German Reich, on the evening of November 9 as an ostensible "eruption of the German people's anger" at the assassination of German diplomat Ernst vom Rath by a Jewish teenager in Paris. SA hordes, the Nazi paramilitary stormtroopers, raged through Munich, as in other cities as well.[31] The main Munich synagogue on Herzog Max Strasse had already been torn down in June 1938 on orders from Hitler. The destruction of the other two synagogues followed on the night of November 9. A driving force was a particular unit, the Stosstrupp (Shock Troop) Adolf Hitler, which had played a key role in the attempted putsch in 1923 and was therefore given a position of honor at the annual celebrations on November 8–9.[32] Rabbi Ernst Ehrentreu was almost burned alive by SA men as he tried to rescue the Torah scrolls from the burning synagogue on Herzog Rudolf Strasse.[33] The Jewish businessman Joachim Both was murdered on the night of November 9 as he and his wife were returning home late in the evening. The defenseless man was shot in his apartment. Leaders of the Hitler Youth had moved through the city, extorting "monetary donations" from businesspeople and chasing Jews out of their apartments.[34] Over the next few days, roughly one thousand Jews were arrested and put in the Dachau concentration camp, at least twenty-six of whom did not survive the incarceration.[35] Eighteen suicides were officially registered, but as Andreas Heusler emphasizes, "the actual number of suicides was presumably much higher."[36]

How did Munich residents conduct themselves during the pogrom? Is it possible to draw conclusions based on their behavior on those days in November 1938 as to whether, or to what extent, the population would respond to the deportations three years later? In particular, one must ask if people were willing to help Jewish men who tried to avoid arrest following the pogrom. Among the many onlookers who witnessed the destruction of synagogues and Jewish stores, more than just a few were part of a grateful audience to the orgy of destruction;[37] this was the case in Munich as well as other German cities. One man who was walking past the burning synagogue on Kanalstrasse stopped and watched the fire and the idle firefighters, when a woman next to him said,

"It would be nice if there were a few charred bodies in there."[38] There were also some Munich residents who did not hesitate to participate in the looting during the pogrom.[39]

At the same time, Munich Jews recounted in postwar testimony the help they received from neighbors and friends in those days. The family of Dr. Else Behrend-Rosenfeld, who on orders of the local Nazi leadership had to abandon her residence in Icking (a small town south of Munich) on November 10, described how, after arriving in Munich, she wandered through the streets in search of a place to stay: "We kept running into people gathered in front of Jewish stores who wanted to look at the destruction, or in front of those that had been skipped over, whose windows were now being shattered. The crowd was calm; even their expressions rarely revealed what they were thinking. Here and there you could hear some gloating, but occasionally also words of disgust."[40]

Behrend-Rosenfeld and her family were not able to find shelter with Jewish acquaintances, as they had originally planned, since they would have risked being caught in one of the numerous raids in which the Jewish men were arrested and put in concentration camps. Throughout the country, thirty-one thousand Jewish men were arrested and brought to Sachsenhausen, Buchenwald, and Dachau; from Munich alone, roughly one thousand men were brought to Dachau.[41] A good number of men attempted to evade these arrests. Else Behrend-Rosenfeld turned to her non-Jewish dressmaker and asked the woman if her husband and son could stay with her for a while. Her request was granted.[42]

Julius Spanier, a physician, had been warned of the arrests by telephone, so he and his wife rode aimlessly around the city on the streetcar. The couple was finally taken in by non-Jewish patients of Dr. Spanier.[43] They then fled to the Jewish hospital in order not to endanger their helpers. Even at the hospital, SA squads looked for Jewish men to arrest and send to Dachau.[44] The Hirsch family had also been informed, and they fled to Lina Hirsch's Christian parents.[45] Ernst Daffinger, managing director of the Schauspielhaus theater, hid his neighbor, the doctor Raphael Levi, together with Levi's two children and the Jewish household staff, at his home for several days.[46] The Jewish lawyer Siegfried (Fritz) Neuland had also been warned, and he found refuge with friends, thus avoiding arrest.[47] In addition to these specifically named cases, a number of other men managed to flee;[48] however, most people were caught totally unawares by this wave of arrests. In addition, presumably very few men were willing to leave their wives and children alone in the destroyed apartments.

The situation of the Jews in Munich was also exacerbated by a shopping ban for Jews that lasted several days. Behrend-Rosenfeld reported that there was nevertheless a significant willingness to help in this situation: "The neighbors and friends, in many cases also the shop owners who had Jewish families as customers, hurried to bring everything they needed—often to an excess—into the apartments. These were not isolated cases, but the rule! At that time Helene often joked that it was such a stroke of luck that we four were also being fed, or else she wouldn't have known what to do with all the blessings that people were bringing her."[49]

These impressions, regarding both food provisions and spontaneous offers of lodgings, were also confirmed by other Munich Jews.[50] Still, it would be wrong to conclude widespread displays of solidarity based on these statements. Many Munich residents might have felt ashamed and secretly given neighbors some food, but there was no general public outrage.

Those who wanted to flee or provide assistance had to fear being denounced to the Gestapo. This happened not only to people in Munich who placed food at the doorstep of their Jewish neighbors following the pogrom,[51] but also to people who spoke candidly about the persecution. A police lieutenant was denounced for allegedly saying, "It is a scandal that the synagogues are being set on fire; it is also what is most sacred to them."[52] A former employee in the household of Moritz Klar, a Jewish doctor, was denounced by a neighbor when she declared that, contrary to official claims, her former employer had not simply died in Dachau, but had been murdered, and that, moreover, a ring and a fountain pen had been stolen from the deceased.[53] Emma Wallach was denounced by the sister-in-law of an SA man. On the night of the pogrom, she had been told by the stormtrooper that she and her child would have to vacate her apartment by November 12 at the latest. The next day, she ran into the SA man's sister-in-law in a store and said to her: "I just wish that you and your brother-in-law and his wife and child would all have to leave Germany without a cent."[54] For this, Wallach was sentenced to two months in prison.

CONCLUSION OF ARYANIZATION AND THE EXPULSION OF THE JEWS FROM THEIR RESIDENCES, 1938–1939

The year 1938 also marked the transition from "wild" (i.e., unregulated) Aryanization to state-regulated, mandatory Aryanization.[55] An ordinance of April 1938 compelled Jews to declare all bank accounts and possessions. The sale of Jewish businesses had to be officially authorized. After the pogrom, an ordinance of the Regional Tax Office prohibited Jews from withdrawing more than 100 marks from their accounts without special authorization from the tax office. Many Jewish businesses were closed permanently on November 10. Only a few days later, the Ordinance on Jewish Reparations went into force, according to which German Jews owed one billion reichsmarks as a collective "punitive tax" for the assassination of Ernst vom Rath. There was a flood of ordinances assuring that all Jewish stores would be Aryanized or liquidated. The final point in this development came in December 1939, when Jews were generally banned from running businesses.[56]

Stores operated by non-Jewish Munich residents who were in mixed marriages with Jews were also threatened with closure. In these cases, the trade licensing office cited "Jewish influence" over the businesses. These businesses were registered as Jewish enterprises and therefore also threatened with closure in late 1938.[57] In some cases, couples tried to transfer businesses from the Jewish spouse to the non-Jewish spouse to evade the discrimination.[58] The municipal trade licensing office acknowledged the non-Jewish status of Ellen Kuhn's art dealership even though Kuhn was married to the Jewish lawyer, Dr. Fritz Kuhn. When in 1939 Ellen Kuhn was denounced as "married to a Jew" by an artist who owed her money, she started to experience problems with the authorities.[59] As a result of the denunciation, the Gestapo intervened, and Kuhn had to give up her business. Her argument that her husband worked twelve hours a day as a forced laborer and therefore had no influence at all on the art dealership had been accepted by the trade licensing office, but not by the Gau leadership. She, nevertheless, did not divorce Fritz Kuhn.[60]

As of November 1938, the Asset Realization Munich Company (*Vermögensverwertung München GmbH*), a private company, operated to acquire property and real estate that was still in Jewish hands. This company had been founded by Gauleiter Adolf Wagner to assure that party offices would obtain access to Jewish real estate assets. It bought lucrative real estate for far below value and then resold it at market value. The lawyers Andreas Kügle and Kurt Wolf functioned as receivers for Asset Realization Munich, pressuring the Jewish owners to transfer the rights of disposal for their property to them.[61] The two lawyers showed up in the Dachau concentration camp and forced the incarcerated Jews to sign pre-prepared powers of attorney for the Aryanization and liquidation of their businesses.[62] Dr. Benno Schülein later described how a week after his arrest, he was brought to the camp administration building. Kügle and a notary public were already seated there and demanded that he sign a notarized power of attorney. Although Kügle and Schülein had known each other previously as colleagues, Kügle refused to greet Schülein. Instead, Schülein was simply told to list his real estate property and sign the powers of attorney.[63] "The price for the regained freedom," as Andreas Heusler and Tobias Weger have written, "could have meant renouncing one's entire assets."[64]

In Munich as elsewhere, Aryanization was marked by individual greed. Neighbors sensed an opportunity to acquire property, senior managers suddenly saw themselves as business proprietors, competition was eliminated effortlessly, and the property of friends and acquaintances was willingly taken "for safekeeping." Interactions with the apparatus of persecution were marked by corruption and greed. The staffs of the Gestapo and of Asset Realization Munich (later known as the Aryanization Office), in particular, were mindful about securing the best items of Jewish-owned property for themselves. Hedwig Geng of Munich recounted the following episode:

> A relative of mine had a house in Munich and also owned a country house at a lake in Upper Bavaria. The agents from the Jewish Property Department wanted to buy it for themselves personally. My relative was a courageous woman. She responded that she was not selling it voluntarily. One of the agents who definitely wanted it for himself arranged a meeting with her on a Sunday morning at her country house. She asked me to accompany her, since she wanted to have a witness to the meeting. I was the witness. The agent offered her authentic rugs and other easily transportable goods for the house, ones my cousin could take with her if she emigrated. She refused, as she later told me, and didn't let herself get caught up in their illicit deals. At that time you had to learn complicated thinking. It was prohibited to take these things with you and they would have simply confiscated the shipping container and punished the woman beyond measure.[65]

Expensive cars were also very sought-after. In 1939 a Jewish man was forced to sell his car to a Gestapo agent for fifteen percent of its actual value.[66]

From 1939 onward, Munich Jews were evicted from their houses and apartments and forced to move into overcrowded *Judenhäuser* ("Jew houses"). Munich, along with Berlin, took on a leading role in the Aryanization of housing. This was due, first of all, to the already existing shortage of apartments. Secondly, there were plans to transform the urban landscape of Munich, as in Berlin as well. This required the large-scale demolition of housing, and substitute housing was needed for the tenants in the teardowns.[67] Already in early 1939, the leases for apartments of Jewish tenants that became available could not be rented out again, but instead had to be given to non-Jewish "demolition tenants." In late April 1939, the Law on Tenancy Agreements with Jews ensured that Jews could live with or rent from only other Jews. Jews were compelled to take Jewish tenants or boarders into their apartments. This legislation led to the ghettoization of the Jewish population in these so-called Jew houses, such as at Thierschstrasse 7, Frundsbergstrasse 8, and Herzogstrasse 65.[68] Munich residents participated in the eviction and Aryanization through targeted denunciation of Jewish tenants and landlords or through extortion attempts.[69] There are records, for example, of a building caretaker in Munich who reported the owner of the building to the police to place her under pressure. The caretaker wanted to purchase her weekend house in the Upper Bavarian town of Grainau for a low price, but ultimately had to settle for the household effects.[70]

The driving force in this process was the Munich Aryanization Office; in April 1939 it replaced Asset Realization Munich, which had been created by Gauleiter Adolf Wagner. The Aryanization Office was formally a state fiduciary agency that was affiliated with a Nazi Party office. Wagner established this agency to satisfy a demand of the Reich government, according to which Aryanization was to be carried out exclusively by state authorities, with the profits accruing to Reich coffers.[71] In actuality, however, as of September 1939, both the state fiduciary agency and the party office of the Aryanization Office were run by Hans Wegner, an SA man and confidant of Wagner.[72] In this way, Gauleiter Wagner was able to assure that he would continue to have a substantial influence on Aryanization.[73] Furthermore, the Aryanization Office "developed into what for the Jews of Munich was the absolute decisive authority by which even the Munich city administration was forced into the background. This office served to register every movement within Munich's Jewish population and rigorously monitored the implementation of all relevant restricting ordinances that showered down on German Jewry since *Kristallnacht*."[74]

The Aryanization Office became the central office responsible for coordinating Jewish forced labor and carrying out the deportations. For the Jews of Munich, the address of the Aryanization Office, Widenmayerstrasse, became a shorthand reference to humiliation, plundering, and violence, and it was feared at least as much as was the Munich Gestapo.

Characteristic in this context is the following episode. Benno Neuburger was arrested in 1941 for having mailed a couple of postcards, without a return address, in which one could read expressions such as "never before was there such an idiot," "Bastard, murderer," "die a miserable death," and "beast, murderer, thug." Almost all of the postcards referred directly to Hitler, but there was also one that read "Tyrant" and, underneath that, "the underlings Mugler, Schrott."[75] Franz Mugler and Ludwig Schrott were among the most-feared officials in the Aryanization Office. The fact that they were the only people besides Hitler who were specifically named indicates that Neuburger must have had particularly bad experiences with the Aryanization Office. Benno Neuburger was transferred to Berlin, and in July 1942, he was sentenced to death by the People's Court for high treason for these postcards.[76]

PERSECUTION MEASURES AND FORCED LABOR, 1939–1941

After the so-called *Kristallnacht*, the pogrom on the night of November 9, 1938, the number of emigrations increased substantially: 2,354 Munich Jews left their hometown in 1939. Although a total of 6,661 Munich Jews left Germany between 1933 and 1942, Munich's Jewish community did not shrink noticeably until after 1938, since many Jews, especially from nearby Franconia, had moved to Munich. They went to Munich hoping that the larger Jewish community there could offer more protection and care and that life in an anonymous metropolis would be more tolerable.[77] Many of them were already impoverished when they arrived in Bavaria's state capital.

There was another wave of arrests one year after the November pogrom. Many Jewish men were arrested and imprisoned for several months in connection with Georg Elser's failed attempt to assassinate Hitler in November 1939. Dietrich Lisberger, who was jailed in Stadelheim Prison until January 1940, reported 120 arrested men, forty-five of whom were also held in Stadelheim. The men were not informed of the grounds for their arrest, but over the course of numerous interrogations, it became apparent that the arrests were related to Elser's attack on Hitler in the Bürgerbräukeller beer hall.[78] Either it had been presumed that there had been Jews behind Elser's actions or the attempted assassination had been used as a welcome pretense for arrests of Jews. Some Jewish men were also denounced because of political remarks they had made in connection with Elser's attack.[79] Franz Kohn was denounced by a remote acquaintance whom he had met on the street. She felt it was worth reporting Kohn's remark that "the attackers should be sought among NSDAP [Nazi Party] members," although she was neither politically active nor did she have any personal problems with Kohn.[80]

Starting in early 1939, the Aryanization Office instructed the employment offices to conscript unemployed non-Aryans to do forced labor. The Munich employment office set up a department "exclusively for the placement of Jews."[81] It was headed by Josef Paulus, who candidly admitted that he found Jews to be "abhorrent."[82] Even though individual staff members of the employment office helped some Jews by letting their file cards go missing, the department responsible for the Jews became an eager accomplice of the Aryanization Office.[83] Once the war started, the forced labor deployments intensified in the course of a general "war mobilization" of the labor market.[84] In Munich, as in other cities, the municipal administration assigned unemployed Jews to a variety of jobs. They were generally paid a pittance. As of May 1940, all Jews still in Germany could be conscripted to do forced labor. In Munich, some men over the age of seventy were conscripted. Thus the age limit there was higher than in other major cities.[85] Numerous Munich Jews worked in private companies deemed essential to the war effort. This included, for example, the Lohhof flax rettery, where in addition to flax, linseed oil was also produced.[86] In addition to roughly one hundred Jewish women from Munich, the workers there included French and Polish prisoners of war, Belgian women, and a smaller number of non-Jewish German employees and Polish Jewish women from the Lodz ghetto.[87] Most of the Jewish forced laborers were quartered in a barracks camp on the grounds of the rettery. Another company classified as war essential that used Jewish forced labor was the A. & R. Kammerer telephone and battery factory at Tassiloplatz in eastern Munich.

From August 1938 onward, Jews were required to use Israel or Sara as a middle name and have it recorded on their ID cards. They had to apply for one of these newly introduced ID cards that was stamped with a large J, which clearly identified them as Jewish. As of September 1941, they had to wear a yellow Jewish star plainly visible on their clothing. Numerous Munich Jews nevertheless attempted, at least for periods of time, to disguise their identities. This is indicated by the large number of prosecutions for "violation of the Jewish identification requirements" that were tried before the local courts from 1940 to 1942.[88] The cases mainly involved Jewish women in "privileged mixed marriages" who neglected to acquire identity cards with the name Sara. Mixed marriages were considered privileged if one spouse was Jewish and the children were not raised Jewish. Regarding married couples who did not have any children, the marriages were considered privileged only if the woman was of Jewish descent but the man was not.[89]

Many Jewish forced laborers at the Kammerer telephone company did not wear the yellow star during working hours, so it had to be quickly attached when there were inspections.[90] The doorman had been given instructions to warn the workers immediately.[91] Jews occasionally took off their yellow stars to use public transportation to go to work or shopping and, of course, also to avoid the constant public stigmatization. Walter Geismar and his girlfriend, Ilselotte Nussbaum, simply wanted, for a change, to feel again like normal people among normal people. On a beautiful winter Sunday, they took off their yellow stars, rode to the Isar Valley, went for a hike, and then stopped for something to eat at an inn, even though they were afraid of being recognized.[92] Anyone caught doing this in Munich had to reckon with a considerable fine, and some even received a prison sentence.[93]

Many Jews also tried to take action against their categorization within the Nazi race hierarchy. Children from unmarried couples, in particular, initiated proceedings involving proof of descent, claiming different, non-Jewish biological fathers, while others alleged that their mothers had been involved in affairs. The mothers themselves also sometimes used this argument to improve the status of their children. Klara B. petitioned an "upgrade" in 1939, claiming that her mother had not lived with her father and had had an affair with an "Aryan" man from Munich.[94] A Munich woman gave a sworn statement, according to which the father of her three children was not her deceased husband, but rather an "Aryan" with whom she had had an affair.[95] In many cases, parents working together tried to have their children classified as first-degree *Mischlinge* instead of as *Geltungsjuden*; the decisive point here was the religious affiliation of the children.[96] An "upgrade" to first-degree *Mischlinge* would have meant that the children no longer had to wear a yellow star and would receive the same food rations as those for "Aryan" Germans instead of those for Jews. First-degree *Mischlinge* were deferred from the deportations, which is why there were so many petitions in 1941 and 1942. Franz Grube petitioned in 1941 to have his three children assigned the identical status of first-degree *Mischlinge*. After this was rejected, his Jewish wife, Clementine Grube, had the children baptized.[97] These attempts were often to no avail.[98] Sometimes Gestapo officials also downgraded children arbitrarily, changing their status from *Mischlinge* to *Geltungsjuden*.[99]

DENUNCIATIONS

The subject of denunciation has not yet been systematically investigated for Munich, but there is a great deal of evidence indicating that Jews in Munich and those who helped them were denounced particularly often. This is apparent within the context of the November pogrom, Georg Elser's assassination attempt, disagreements over assets and apartments, and violations of the "Jewish identification requirements." In addition, numerous people were denounced for "defiling the race," including Magdalena Schwarz, a physician who later successfully went into hiding.[100] The doctor Lothar Gerweck and his wife Ilse were reported by a former patient of Dr. Gerweck for "suspicion of foreign currency offenses." The denouncer explained that she possessed no evidence at all of the couple's misconduct but that she had read in the newspaper that a person, presumably related to Ilse Gerweck, had been convicted of foreign currency offenses. Consequently, the denouncer said, it is probable that Ilse Gerweck and her husband were also involved in illegal dealings.[101] Josefine T., a Jewish woman, was denounced in prison by her non-Jewish cell neighbor because she allegedly had made some negative remarks about the interrogating officer.[102]

The denunciation of Jews and non-Jews who continued to maintain close contact turned out to be an effective method of eliminating professional competition.[103] Thus, a Herr Hamacher denounced the stamp trader Jakob Littner and his business partner and friend, Christine Hintermeier, to the Chamber of Industry and Commerce to sabotage the transfer of the business solely to Hintermeier, who was not Jewish.[104]

In many cases, it was about trivial matters. Strangers, neighbors, acquaintances, and even relatives denounced Jews because of carelessly made political remarks that they frequently had not even heard themselves but instead learned about through hearsay. The sentence "If today a dog were to die on the street, they would have more sympathy with it than with us Jews" became Felizi Weill's downfall.[105] Anna Burian was reported by a stranger due to a derogatory remark about the Wehrmacht.[106] The same thing happened to Eugen Oppenheimer, who was denounced by a waitress in a café because of a critical remark about Ribbentrop, this being the second time he had fallen victim to denunciation.[107] Alfred Weil had spoken disparagingly of SA-Gruppenführer Otto Gümbel, president of the Reich Railway directorate in Munich. After being denounced, he was sentenced to one and a half years in prison. Weil hanged himself in his prison cell.[108] One woman was even denounced by two neighbors because she was friendly with a Jewish woman.[109] Denouncers had a wide range of motivations for their actions. Regarding the denunciation of Jews, antisemitism or loyalty to the regime were not necessarily the (only) motives. Personal motives such as unrequited love, marriage problems, revenge, malice, economic competition, debts, and many other factors could also play a role.[110]

In this context, it is important to emphasize that the limited number of cases found in the extant court dossiers does not make it possible to draw reliable conclusions about the actual extent of denunciations.[111] Most Gestapo files were destroyed.[112] And it was not unusual for Jews to be transferred directly to concentration camps without a trial. References to denunciations can frequently be found within a different archival context, as demonstrated by the following example. A Jewish woman was reported by her former brother-in-law for disparaging the Hitler salute. She was lucky and was simply sent home after an interrogation. Mention of this was found in a compensation file from the postwar period.[113] Similarly, a denunciation charge against Gerty Spies and her daughter was mentioned within the scope of denazification proceedings.[114] Although a systematic evaluation is still needed, there are many indications that Eric Johnson's finding for the Cologne/Krefeld region—that "Jews were the most affected by civilian denunciations"[115]—also applies to Munich. In his study, Johnson shows that "during the 1930s . . . civilian denunciations initiated the same proportion of Jewish cases as they did of the cases of ordinary Germans."[116]

For Munich Jews who went into hiding, denunciations represented one of the greatest possible dangers. This subject will therefore be taken up in further detail in chapter 6. In addition, the Munich Gestapo, which had roughly three hundred employees, was far better staffed as compared with other major cities. Only the Berlin office of the Gestapo had a larger workforce.[117]

GHETTOIZATION: THE "JEWISH CAMPS"

Starting in the fall of 1940, a new regulation allowed for the liquidation of the "Jew houses," which meant that the Jews were in danger of losing even the few remaining dwellings that had been assigned to them. The displaced Jews were to be quartered in mass accommodations outside the city center. This action was intended to expedite the physical separation of Jews and non-Jews in Munich and the ghettoization of the remaining Jews.[118] In addition to the existing camps for the women working in the Lohhof flax rettery, the Gau leadership, through the Aryanization Office, had established two Jewish camps in the Munich suburbs of Berg am Laim and Milbertshofen. The Berg am Laim camp was located in an annex of the convent of the Sisters of Mercy. The social worker Dr. Else Behrend-Rosenfeld, whose husband had managed to emigrate to Britain in 1939 along with their children, served as the camp manager.

The Milbertshofen barracks camp was built in the spring of 1941 by Jewish forced laborers from around Upper Bavaria. The workers, many of whom were elderly and not accustomed to physical labor, were faced with the choice between working without pay to erect the Milbertshofen camp or being sent to Dachau.[119] The Aryanization Office oversaw the construction, which was completed early in the summer of 1941. The barracks camp had a capacity of more than one thousand people, though, like the Berg am Laim camp, which held three hundred people, it was often overcrowded.[120] Formally the barracks camp was "under Jewish self-administration," but in fact it was controlled by the Aryanization Office. The head of the Aryanization Office was de facto the head of the camp.[121]

Setting up the Milbertshofen camp did not merely serve as a way to control the local Jewish population and keep Jews segregated from non-Jews. It can also be viewed as a direct reaction to the first isolated deportations from other parts of the German Reich, such as the deportation of Jews from Baden to France

Jewish forced laborers at the construction site of the Milbertshofen camp. Munich City Archive, DE-1992-NL-MEI-1-01.

in the fall of 1940.[122] In Munich, the authorities responsible for the persecution did everything they could to create the necessary conditions for a speedy deportation of the local Jewish population. In early January 1941, Mayor Karl Fiehler submitted his plans to deport all Jews from the Upper Bavaria Gau, as had already been done for the Baden and Palatinate Gaus.[123]

In early November 1941—shortly before the Munich deportations began—the Munich registry listed 3,240 Jews still residing in the city.[124] They had long since been isolated from the rest of the population, yet at the same time they remained visible, clearly marked by their yellow stars as they marched to and from work, went shopping, performed forced labor in factories, or carried out the public works tasks to which they had been assigned, such as shoveling snow or cleaning streets. Many of them had not been able to leave the country. They were too old, too poor, or unable to find a host country and acquire a visa and valid papers in time. Others did not want to leave their homeland, hoping instead that the situation would get better, even if this appeared unrealistic after the pogrom of November 1938. There was definitely some resistance to the persecution measures. Many Jewish men had evaded the wave of arrests in November 1938, and numerous Munich Jews vented their discontent in political statements. There were very frequent violations of the identification requirements, often in connection with the use of public transportation. For the Jewish population, however, denunciation continued to represent a grave danger.

CONCLUSION: JEWISH PERSECUTION IN MUNICH AS COMPARED TO OTHER GERMAN CITIES

Nazi persecution measures in Munich did not differ fundamentally from those in other German cities. However, the way in which they were implemented on the ground shows that the "capital of the movement" played a pioneering role.[125] Other cities also distinguished themselves in various ways in their persecution of the Jews. According to Axel Drecoll, Munich and Nuremberg played leading roles in the financial plunder of the Jews. Wolf Gruner has argued that in addition to Munich and Berlin, Leipzig, Nuremberg, and Hamburg also took the lead in denying welfare benefits to Jews.[126] In both Munich and Nuremberg, the main synagogues had already been torn down before the pogrom in November 1938. Munich's zeal in implementing anti-Jewish measures had already been obvious in 1933, when local anti-Jewish regulations were enacted, including the March 1933 decree prohibiting Jews from receiving municipal contracts. Municipal welfare benefits were reduced for Jews in 1937 and, in anticipation of the measure throughout the German Reich, eliminated entirely in November 1938.[127]

The development of the Aryanization Office into a powerful authority for persecution alongside the Gestapo intensified the persecution in Munich. Control over Aryanization was placed into the hands of the Gau leadership, and the Aryanization Office expanded its own area of competence considerably. It monitored the implementation of all antisemitic measures in coordination with the Gestapo and even imposed penalties for violations.[128] The smooth cooperation between the Gau leadership, the Aryanization Office, and the Gestapo added to the persecutory pressure in Munich. The Aryanization Office made a name for itself as "clearly the most active institution."[129] In planning anti-Jewish measures, it proceeded earlier than the organs of persecution in Berlin. For example, the Aryanization Office already wanted to expel Jews from Munich in the spring of 1940 and to place them in convents in the countryside.[130] The initiatives taken by some cities, including Munich, to quarter Jews in barracks camps was rejected by the Reich Security Main Office (RSHA) even as late as March 1941.[131] The RSHA instead issued instructions to increase the capacity in the "Jew houses," as was then being done in Berlin. The Milbertshofen camp was completed in Munich notwithstanding these instructions.[132]

Not only did the "capital of the movement" outpace the planned persecution measures for the German Reich as a whole, but it was also particularly spiteful in its methods of implementation. For example, Jews received food ration coupons that could be used only in stores outside of the district where they lived.[133] In practice, this meant that Munich Jews, most of whom also had to perform forced labor and were not permitted to use street cars, could only obtain their meager food rations after completing a long trek. They were often unable to do this because of poor health or lack of time. This was the background against which the deportations of Munich's Jews began in November 1941.

TWO

THE DEPORTATIONS

EARLY IN THE MORNING OF November 20, 1941, 999 Jewish men, women, and children boarded a train in Munich-Milbertshofen bound for Kaunas/Kovno in German-occupied Lithuania. They had been brought to the Milbertshofen internment camp a few days earlier, when the security measures in the camp had been intensified, as a survivor who had been detained there reported: "Two days before the transport, the entrance to the camp, which had otherwise always been watched over by camp prisoners or workers, was guarded by the SS under the direction of an Oberscharführer. Until the transport left, there were patrols day and night inside and outside the camp enclosure."[1] Requests by various companies to defer their workers from the transport were rejected.[2] Five days after the transport departed, all of its passengers from Munich were dead. Members of the mobile killing unit Einsatzkommando 3 under Karl Jäger had murdered them in Fort IX in Kaunas on November 25.

This chapter will present the chronology of the deportation of Munich's Jews within the context of the deportations throughout the German Reich. Munich will serve as a case study for examining reactions to the deportations by the Jewish and non-Jewish populations.

THE WAVES OF DEPORTATIONS, 1941–1945

The first deportations of Jews had already taken place in 1939, from Vienna to Nisko, from Pomerania to Lublin, and from Baden to France.[3] The mass deportations of German Jews from throughout the German Reich began in October 1941. In that month alone, the deportation trains brought almost twenty thousand Jews from the major cities of Berlin, Prague, Vienna, Frankfurt, Hamburg,

The deportation of Munich Jews from the Munich-Milbertshofen train station to Kaunas on November 21, 1941. Munich City Archive, DE-1992-JUD-F-0522-7.

and Düsseldorf to the ghetto in Lodz (renamed Litzmannstadt by the Nazis).[4] More than four thousand of them died in the ghetto by the end of 1942; the others were deported to the death camps of Chelmno and Auschwitz.[5] Between November 8, 1941, and February 10, 1942, a series of frequent deportations from throughout the Reich transferred more than thirty thousand Jews to Kaunas, Minsk, and Riga in the Soviet Union.[6] Six thousand German Jews were shot shortly after arriving in either Riga or Kaunas, including those in the first transport from Munich, as well as Jews deported from Frankfurt, Berlin, Breslau (now Wrocław, Poland), and Vienna.[7] As early as September 20, 1940, 193 Jewish patients from the Eglfing-Haar sanatorium and nursing home were deported from Munich[8] and murdered, separately from the non-Jewish patients, in the Austrian "euthanasia" center at Hartheim.[9] Their relatives were told that the patients had been brought to a clinic in the General Government (the nonannexed part of German-occupied Poland) intended solely for Jews and had died there.[10]

The second mass transport from Munich took place in the course of another series of deportations from Germany in the spring and summer of 1942. At that time, there were numerous trains leaving from all over Germany, usually with approximately one thousand people each, headed for occupied Poland and the Soviet Union. On April 4, 1942, 774 Jews (about half of whom were from Munich and the other half from Swabia) were deported from Munich to the General Government.[11] The Milbertshofen camp served as an internment camp, and the trains left Munich from the nearby Milbertshofen freight station. The deportees were brought to the Piaski ghetto and from there—if they hadn't already died in the ghetto—to a death camp. There were also no survivors of this second transport.[12] Starting in June 1942, there were also deportations to Theresienstadt (Terezín) from all over the Reich. This was the destination primarily for people over sixty-five, who had largely been spared from the deportations, as well as decorated First World War veterans.[13] Between June and August 1942, twenty-five transports with fifty passengers each left Munich bound for Theresienstadt.[14] On July 13, 1942, another fifty people were deported from Munich to Auschwitz. After the first two mass deportations in November 1941 and April 1942, the trains from Munich no longer left from the Milbertshofen freight station, but from the main train station or the Hackerbrücke or Laim freight stations.[15]

On March 13, 1943, the last mass transport for the time being left Munich: 220 Jews were deported to Auschwitz, 108 of them from Munich.[16] This deportation was carried out within the scope of the Nazi leadership's decision in February 1943 to conclude the large deportations from the German Reich. A final wave of deportations in February and March targeted most of the remaining Jews, especially the Jewish forced laborers who had been exempted from earlier transports. The center of these deportations was Berlin, where in late 1942 more than fifteen thousand Jewish forced laborers were still registered.[17] Many of them were arrested and deported during the so-called Factory Operation, a large-scale raid on more than one hundred arms factories.[18] In other German cities as well, Jewish forced labor camps were being liquidated and the remaining Jews deported out of the Reich. On March 3, a train with roughly 1,500 Jews from Dresden, Erfurt, Hannover, Paderborn, and a few other cities reached Auschwitz; a day earlier, a train had arrived there that brought Jews from western and southern Germany to their deaths.[19] In Munich, within the scope of the Factory Operation, the remaining Jewish forced laborers, most of whom had worked at the Kammerer telephone and battery factory and the Luitpold works, received their notices for deportation, and the Berg am Laim camp was then closed.[20] The Milbertshofen barracks camp had already been closed in the summer of 1942 and had been used since then by BMW to house foreign forced laborers.[21] After the liquidation of the Berg am Laim camp in

March 1943, a few remaining Jews were placed in the rooms of the already disbanded Jewish Community of Munich (IKG), which now was made into a so-called Jew house in a former cigarette factory in the back building at Lindwurmstrasse 125.[22] Munich's official Jewish community had been converted in June 1942 into the Bavarian district branch of the Reich Association of Jews in Germany, which was headed by Julius Hechinger. Exactly one year later, the district branch was dissolved as well, and Theodor Koronczyk, who had succeeded Hechinger as head of the district branch in July 1942, became the Reich Association's liaison to the Aryanization Office and the Gestapo.[23] Koronczyk, who lived in a mixed marriage, fulfilled this position until the end of the war.

After this series of deportations was completed, most Jews remaining in the city were so-called *Geltungsjuden*, those "half Jews" deemed Jews according to the race laws, or spouses in mixed marriages. Jews in mixed marriages were excluded from the deportation directives of the RSHA.[24] The deportation of *Geltungsjuden* was not explicitly regulated until the edicts of May 1942 and February 1943.[25] Consequently, a few of them had already been deported on the early transports.[26] Starting in May 1942, *Geltungsjuden* living on their own were supposed to be deported to Theresienstadt. This policy was made more precise in February 1943, to the effect that all *Geltungsjuden* not living with non-Jewish family members were deported to Theresienstadt, while *Geltungsjuden* who were married to Jews continued to be scheduled for the transports to the East. *Geltungsjuden* who lived together with a non-Jewish family member were not yet slated for deportation.[27]

Between April 1943 and December 1944, numerous additional trains from throughout the Reich went to Auschwitz and Theresienstadt. During this period there were nine transports to Theresienstadt or Auschwitz from Munich, carrying a total of 79 people. These transports generally consisted of single train cars coupled to regular passenger trains or to Wehrmacht troop transport trains.[28] Those deported included the staff of the district branch of the Reich Association of Jews in Germany, *Geltungsjuden* living alone, and especially Jews who had lost the protection of living in a mixed marriage through divorce or the death of the spouse. Jews who had lost their non-Jewish spouse were supposed to be brought to Theresienstadt as of early 1944 on orders from Himmler.[29] There were regional differences in how the ordinances were implemented. The decision as to which names appeared on which deportation lists was often arbitrary or a matter of chance.[30] Consequently, some Munich Jews from divorced mixed marriages or widowed Jews had already been deported to Theresienstadt in 1943, while others did not receive their deportation notice until February 1945 (see chapter 4).

Beginning in February 1945, Jewish spouses in existing mixed marriages and *Geltungsjuden* who lived together with a non-Jewish family member (usually a parent) were also threatened with deportation to Theresienstadt. It was irrelevant whether these people lived in so-called privileged or nonprivileged mixed marriages. Throughout the Reich, there were more than thirty transports to Theresienstadt in February and March.[31] In the chaos of the final months of the war, by no means did all of these people receive notices to report for deportation, but the last two transports from Munich to Theresienstadt on February 20 and 21 did include another eighty-three people from Munich and Augsburg.[32] In all, 3,400 Jews were deported from Munich during the war.[33]

This appalling total clearly shows that the majority of people deported from Munich were sent to their deaths very early on. More than 1,700 had departed from Munich on one of the two first transports in November 1941 and April 1942. In the months from June to August 1942, another 1,245 people were deported to Theresienstadt. According to official statistics, in late 1942 there were only 645 Jews still living in Munich, the vast majority of them in mixed marriages.[34]

Being assigned to work in factories deemed vital for the war effort could offer a certain amount of protection up until the last mass deportation in March 1943. However, already in 1941 the pool of Jewish forced laborers in Munich was not large enough to constitute a critical mass for a potential workforce. Many Jewish forced laborers were not even deployed in war-essential factories in 1941–42, but instead worked at private businesses such as nurseries (Buchner), publishers and print shops (Oldenbourg), textile factories (Brettschneider millinery factory), and later also for the city of Munich (especially street cleaning and streetcar maintenance and cleaning).[35] The Lohhof flax retting pit and the Kammerer telephone factory, however, were considered essential to the war effort.[36] Foreign forced laborers, in contrast, made up a much more significant workforce. In July 1941, there were more than two thousand foreign workers in the BMW works in Allach alone.[37]

CARRYING OUT THE DEPORTATIONS FROM MUNICH

The tasks involved in organizing the transports and carrying out the deportations from Munich were divided up among the Gestapo headquarters in Munich, the Aryanization Office, the officials in the Munich Regional Tax Office, the employment office, and the Munich Food Office.[38] The tax office registered and secured the remaining assets of the deportees. The food office was responsible for the provisions for the transports, and the employment office was put in charge of the Jewish forced laborers.[39] The Gestapo headquarters received instructions from the RSHA regarding the schedule, size, and configuration of the transports. Local Gestapo offices then organized the actual deportations. As of December 1939, the Munich Gestapo was headed by Dr. Erich Isselhorst, who was succeeded in early 1942 by the jurist Oswald Schäfer. Johann Pfeuffer was in charge of the Gestapo's Jewish Affairs section, and he and his staff were feared.[40] Some midlevel officials, who arrested Jews in Munich, confiscated their last remaining assets, and packed them into the deportation trains, were particularly brutal and corrupt. Hans Grahammer, Gerhard Grimm, and Georg Gassner, all of them Gestapo men, faced serious charges in postwar trials, and many witnesses testified to crimes they committed, such as torture, beatings, robbery, sexual assault, and extortion with related threats of consequences. Also feared were not only Aryanization Office chief Hans Wegner, but also other members of his staff, including Franz Mugler, Ludwig Schrott, and Richard Westermayr.[41]

In Munich as in other cities, compiling the transport lists was the responsibility of the Gestapo. The Jewish community administration was forced to assist in the process. Based on the instructions of the RSHA in Berlin, the Munich Gestapo specified the criteria for the transports, which were prepared from an existing "file of Jews" of the Jewish community. For the first transport to Kaunas, for example, people under sixty-five who were fit for work but not currently working in a war-essential factory were to be selected. The Gestapo issued preprinted summonses to report for deportation for the IKG to distribute among those selected for a transport, which then had to be filled out and returned.[42] The Jewish community leadership was thus coerced into participating in the selection of those who would be "sent to the East." This task was done by the head of the Jewish community, Karl Stahl, and by Julius Hechinger, who was in charge of financial and legal affairs of the IKG before becoming head of the Bavarian district branch of the Reich Association, together with the executive committee of the IKG.[43] Hechinger and Stahl were themselves deported in 1942. Ultimately, the community officials also had to assist in carrying out the deportations themselves.[44] They carried the burden of assuring that the transport of their members would proceed smoothly.[45]

The willingness to cooperate was understandable in view of an overpowering and brutal adversary, but it also meant that individual members of the community became actively involved in the process of mass murder. In addition to the heads of the district branches of the Reich Association of Jews and the "liaisons" to the Gestapo, this also pertained to those in charge of the Jewish camps that were formally "self-administered." This system served in a most treacherous manner to force the Jewish community leadership to participate in the destruction process and, after 1945, for their actions to be construed as sharing responsibility for the deportations.[46]

The Eleventh Regulation under the Reich Citizenship Law of November 1941 declared all property of the deportees to be automatically forfeited to the German Reich because they were leaving the Reich and thus losing their citizenship. The Eleventh Regulation did not apply to those bound for Theresienstadt, as that did not involve a border crossing. Through the creation of the protectorate of Bohemia and Moravia in 1939, Theresienstadt was not considered as lying outside of Reich territory. In the case of Theresienstadt, therefore, the Law on the Seizure of Assets of Enemies of the People and the State was applied, and the deportees were formally dispossessed as enemies of the state.[47] The last valuables that Jews wanted to take with them were taken away at the "baggage check." Gerty Spies, who was deported to Theresienstadt, later said that "the plundered things were carried away by the basketful."[48]

In an operation codenamed *Aktion* 3, a newly established department in the office of the chief financial officer of the city of Munich evaluated and monetized the assets of the deportees. Securities were seized, apartments were cleared out and rented anew, and the personal property of the deportees was auctioned off.[49] What did the officials think would happen to the people whose apartments they cleared out and whose left-behind possessions they registered?[50] There were numerous auctions where Munich residents could acquire household items, furniture, dishes, and linens at very low prices. Did the new owners not ask whose belongings they had just acquired? Where did the former owners go? What fate befell them? There were obviously no thoughts of their return, and their possessions were also not forwarded to them. Exceedingly few people had any evident moral scruples in this regard. Even people who hid Jews in their homes obtained inexpensive "Jewish furniture." Marie Jalowicz-Simon, a young woman who had gone into hiding in Berlin, described a conversation she had had with her helper, who had just acquired some items: "'Do you think that's bad?' she asked diffidently. 'Those people have been taken away, and if I don't buy that piece of furniture, someone else will.' I said she was quite right, yet I felt a curious pang in my heart."[51]

THE MUNICH POPULATION AND THE DEPORTATIONS: REACTIONS AND KNOWLEDGE

How did the people of Munich react to the deportations that were going on around them? What could they know about the fate of those summoned to be "evacuated to the East"? How did they act toward neighbors and acquaintances whom they could observe from their windows as they were being picked up? Gerty Spies of Munich describes in her memoirs how she came home one evening in July 1942 and found her deportation notice in the mailbox. She was home alone, it was relatively late, and she longed to talk with friends about what lay ahead:

> The people on the first floor were always friendly. They still said hello, even now. Surely they would let me make a telephone call. My own phone had already been taken away. I rang the bell. I rang it again. . . . The man of the house opened. "Excuse me," I said, "I beg you to allow me to make a telephone call." He looked at me; he did not say a word—perhaps he thought I was ill-mannered? I had to explain, to win his heart. With great reluctance: "I—I will be taken away—with the transport—I—" Here the man shook his head, looked at me sadly, and closed his door. I ran outside. . . . I spoke to a stranger, asking him to give me some light in a telephone booth. He wanted to know why. I told him. He was alarmed, gave me some light, and fled.[52]

These lines tell of the not-wanting-to-know as well as the fear of coming into contact with those who were ostracized. Fear of denunciation certainly mixed with a reluctance to learn more about a fate that was doubtlessly perceived as bad.

Some people in Munich nevertheless followed very precisely what was happening. "From Camp Milbertshofen," wrote Gerty Spies, "where they kept us overnight and where they lightened our luggage by half its weight, a closed furniture truck took us to the train. On a side track, we were loaded onto the train. From the surrounding homes binoculars were turned on us. The train left."[53] The residents evidently understood that something unusual was taking place, and they followed the events closely. Even when the observers remained passive, their behavior cannot necessarily be interpreted as indifference.[54] Many neighbors must have witnessed entire families being picked up by the Gestapo and loaded with their meager possessions into vehicles disguised as furniture trucks. In most cases, these pickups went smoothly. Even if at first many Munich residents could not imagine that the deportees were being driven directly to their deaths, they must have suspected that something bad was going to happen to them.

The statement "We didn't know anything about it" was, as Peter Longerich, Frank Bajohr, and Dieter Pohl have shown, a defensive reflex mechanism of many Germans after 1945 in response to the question about what they knew about the Holocaust.[55] Even if the German civilian population had no precise information about the death camps, many people heard about the massacres by the mobile killing units. Soldiers on home leave reported what they had seen or done, and some had sent letters and photographs. Not only in Munich, but also in the rural regions of Upper Bavaria, people were well-informed about the

Gerty Spies (1962). Courtesy of the Leo Baeck Institute, New York.

mass murders. Author Friedrich Reck-Malleczewen, who lived on an isolated estate in the Chiemgau region, reported in his diary on October 30, 1942, about a conversation with a soldier he knew: "And H., with whom I philosophized today about man's inhumanity to man? He has just come back from the Eastern Front, and witnessed the massacre at K., where 30,000 Jews were slaughtered. This was done in a single day, in the space of an hour, perhaps, and when machine-gun bullets gave out, flamethrowers were used. And spectators hurried to the event from all over the city."[56]

Munich Jews also had such encounters with returning soldiers. When the son of Hugo Holzmann's neighbors came back from Russia deathly ill, he reported that he had seen numerous shootings of Jews with his own eyes.[57] The young man died a short time later. His parents pleaded with Hugo and his mother to comply under no circumstances with a notice of "evacuation to the East," and they offered to hide them if necessary with relatives in the countryside (which they then did; see chapter 7).[58] Munich Jews also had an extraordinary source of information that other communities did not: working together with the Jewish women from Munich at the Lohhof retting pit were seventy Jewish women from the Lodz ghetto who had come to Munich in December 1941.[59] They told about the generally horrible conditions in the ghettos in Poland. Walter Geismar later recalled that the Munich Jews initially rejected these stories as things that might happen to Polish Jews, but certainly not to German Jews. However, when Geismar's girlfriend, Ilselotte Nussbaum, who had worked in the rettery, was deported to Auschwitz in March 1943, she was sure that she would never see her boyfriend again.[60] Also, because no messages had arrived from the people deported in the first two transports, many Munich Jews felt confirmed in their intuitions. From the first transport to Kaunas, not a single sign of life ever reached Munich. And contact was also broken off with those deported on the second transport. "It has been fourteen days and we have received no news from our deportees from Piaski, and we no longer have any hope of seeing them again after the war," wrote Else Behrend-Rosenfeld, the manager of the Berg am Laim camp, in her diary on July 5, 1942.[61]

After a long period of uncertainty, short death notices arrived regarding the 193 patients from the Eglfing-Haar sanatorium who had been deported as early as September 1940. Rosa Hechinger, wife of the Munich Jewish community's legal advisor Julius Hechinger, was one of those patients. This therefore impacted the leadership of the Munich community directly. As previously mentioned, relatives had been informed that the Jewish patients had been brought to Poland and that they had died in a hospital in Cholm.[62] This also let people recognize that being brought to Poland did not bode well. News of Nazis murdering the sick reached the public in the summer of 1941.[63] Else Behrend-Rosenfeld later explained that around July 1942 it became clear to her that the deportations led to death.[64] As the camp manager, Behrend-Rosenfeld had a greater general understanding of what was happening than did other members of the Jewish community, and in the summer of 1942, there were many widely known indications that deportations to the East were tantamount to imminent death, even if people could not yet know the details. At the same time, mechanisms of denial and rationalization took effect among Jews who heard these stories, thus distorting their view of the murderous actions. In Berlin, too, by 1942 many Jews understood that deportation amounted to a death sentence, but some were still in denial about what "resettlement to the East" actually meant. Yet, in the capital the disturbing rumors were so widespread that even some seven-year-old children in an orphanage recognized their fate.[65]

The BBC had been reporting since 1942 in its radio broadcasts to Germany about the mass murder that was taking place.[66] In June 1942, the White Rose resistance group in Munich condemned the murder of Jews in Poland in its second flyer.[67] What the members of the White Rose knew, other Munich residents could also know. The many rumors about the forms of mass murder are evidence that the population at least suspected the fate of the deportees. Peter Longerich, Frank Bajohr, and Dieter Pohl agree that the "Final Solution" had become an "open secret."[68] Jews in hiding also heard of more than just massacres by the mobile killing units. Beate Steckhan, who lived in hiding at Walchensee, a lake in the Bavarian Alps, wrote that in late 1943, "rumors had made their way into the country indirectly via other countries"[69] about gas chambers and selections. In the course of the war, many Germans began presuming that the Allied air raids on German cities was revenge of the Jews for what the Germans had done to them. This interpretation is evidence not only of the internalization of Nazi propaganda that all-powerful Jews stood behind the Allies, but also a healthy dose of a guilty conscience.[70]

BETWEEN HOPE, RESIGNATION, DENIAL, AND REFUSAL: REACTIONS OF JEWS TO THE DEPORTATION NOTICE

As the manager of the Berg am Laim camp, Else Behrend-Rosenfeld had to deliver the first deportation notices to people in the camp in November 1941. In her diary, she reports extensively about the reactions of the recipients. The news of the upcoming deportation from Munich did not come as a total surprise to many, since mass deportations had been taking place from other German cities since October 15. Many took the news "calmly and with dignity" and tried to use the time until the transport to pack and do other travel preparations. Those who remained behind offered solace, and many gave their unlucky neighbors a portion of their food rations to take with them on their journey.[71]

As a reaction to the early deportations of Pomeranian Jews to Poland and Baden Jews to France, Jewish communities had begun sending aid packages to the deportees. In Munich, Else Behrend-Rosenfeld prepared numerous packages together with some friends and tried to mobilize additional relief efforts.[72] Although these early deportations were limited essentially to Jews at the margins of the German Reich, they put those remaining in Germany in a frightening wait mode, wondering when it would affect their own community. Else Behrend-Rosenfeld reckoned with further deportations. Others around her, on the other hand, hoped that these would remain isolated actions.[73] The mass deportations throughout the entire Reich then in fact began in October 1941.

As well-informed as Behrend-Rosenfeld was in her role as the Berg am Laim camp's manager, she was torn between a sober assessment of the situation and denial. When she heard rumors about the first deportation from Munich, she responded gruffly that the people were seeing "specters everywhere."[74] A few days later, she found herself compelled to distribute the deportation notices. After the first deportation from Munich, the situation calmed down again before news spread in March 1942 that another deportation was imminent. When Behrend-Rosenfeld discovered that she and the entire management were on the list, the task of delivering the notices was not as difficult this time, as she was able to say, "We're all going together."[75]

In making her own preparations for the transport, Else Behrend-Rosenfeld sewed a lethal dose of veronal tablets into the hem of her coat. Knowing that if worse came to worst she "could decide her fate for herself" gave her "comfort and strength."[76] She was lucky, as it turned out, and her name was cut from the deportation list at the last minute, since she was still needed to run the Berg am Laim camp. Many of the others decided not even to appear at the deportation collection point and to take their own lives instead. For the years 1941 and 1942, there were 133 documented suicides by Munich Jews.[77] Thus the number of suicides in Munich lay clearly above the number of attempts to flee. In other places as well, the number of suicides by Jews grew dramatically once the deportations began.[78] Taking one's own life was an everyday occurrence in Berg am Laim and Milbertshofen. In late July 1942, Behrend-Rosenfeld noted the following encounter with a police officer: "The officer from the homicide division of the criminal police, who after every suicide had to release the corpse for burial, told me the last time, with a somewhat unsuccessful attempt at a joke: 'You're my best customer, Doctor!' But with that he was simply attempting to hide the fact that this constantly growing number of suicides also touched him more profoundly than was usually the case."[79]

Sometimes the suicide was only feigned. In many cases in which people tried to evade deportation, a simulated suicide marked the beginning of the escape process. They announced their planned suicide in farewell letters to mislead the Gestapo. Forms of suicide were often announced that would make it difficult to search for a corpse. Some people mentioned plans to drown themselves in a river. This would gain them a little time to flee since the police first had to search for the alleged victim (see chapter 3). Others disappeared without a trace, as was the case with Else Behrend-Rosenfeld. On August 15, 1942, she removed the yellow star from her clothing and boarded a train to Berlin.[80] With that, she was one of the twenty women and men from Munich who decided to go underground between October 1941 and August 1942.

THREE

EARLY ESCAPES

Fall 1941–Summer 1942

THOSE WHO DECIDED IN THE fall of 1941 to evade deportation did so with prospects of a life lived in fear, deprivation, and isolation, and without any hope that the persecution would end quickly. At the time, a German victory against the Soviet Union appeared imminent and the United States had not yet entered the war. Anyone who in the fall of 1941 resisted the apparatus of persecution did so at the height of Nazi optimism for victory.[1] German Jews who fled before the early deportations had often acted spontaneously, as a direct reaction to having received their deportation notice, without having planned their flight beforehand or having made any precautionary arrangements. They fled at a time and in a situation in which their chances for a successful escape must have seemed slim. They resisted their deportation, not wanting under any circumstances to surrender to an unknown fate.

This chapter concerns Jews from Munich who went underground between October 1941 and August 1942, a period that included the first two mass deportations from Munich in November 1941 and April 1942, as well as the deportations to Theresienstadt from June to August 1942. During this period, a total of twenty escape attempts in Munich can be definitively confirmed. Seven of them took place in the fall of 1941 (prior to the first transport) and thirteen in 1942. Eleven people ultimately survived. On top of this comes an indefinite number of people who were brought to Switzerland by a Christian circle of escape helpers, but relevant information on this is too meager to allow for any precise figures.[2] Sketched below are the stories of eight Munich Jews who went into hiding under different conditions. The eight cases will then be analyzed from a comparative perspective to assess the situation of U-boats in different parts of Germany more generally.

IN HIS GIRLFRIEND'S COAL CELLAR

Sigmund W. came from a Jewish merchant family in the Franconian city of Bad Windsheim. He was a wine wholesaler and ran a successful business in Mainz in the 1920s. When the company started having difficulties, Sigmund W. decided to establish a second mainstay. He set up a wholesale business for medical incubators and, in 1931, moved his residence to Munich. The new company was doing well until the Nazis came to power.[3]

Sigmund W.'s former secretary and longtime confidante, Martha W., moved with him to Munich. In 1933, they successfully reregistered his business in her name, as she was not Jewish, and their shared apartment also officially belonged to Martha W.[4] The two, who were not married, were denounced in 1937 for "defiling the race" and arrested. Although both of them were released shortly thereafter and charges against Sigmund W. were ultimately dropped, Martha W.'s apartment on Perhamerstrasse in Munich-Laim came under Gestapo surveillance. Sigmund W. was taken in by various Jewish acquaintances. From then on, the couple met only secretly, mostly in the forest near Aubing, where Sigmund W. had paid for hunting rights up to 1937.[5] In November 1941, he received his deportation notice with instructions to report to the "Milbertshofen Jewish Camp."[6] His girlfriend later wrote that by that time, they had already had a dark suspicion that this marked the first step in a process that would ultimately lead to their deaths.[7] Sigmund W.'s incarceration in 1937–38 and the harassment he experienced left him convinced that there would be no escape.[8] As a result, he was determined to take his life, but his girlfriend—and later wife—convinced him to feign suicide and go into hiding.

Sigmund W. left a farewell letter declaring that he was going to commit suicide by jumping into the Isar River. In fact, however, he sought help from Otto W., his former game warden in Aubing, to whom he had already confided in 1937. Otto W. first brought his friend to lodgings in Türkenfeld, west of Munich. Then Sigmund W. went to friends in Rosenheim.[9] After about eight weeks, he secretly returned to the apartment on Perhamerstrasse. This is how Martha W. described their living conditions:

> [Sigmund] spent nights in our coal cellar in order not to be seen by the other building residents during an air raid, and so he wouldn't be discovered and recognized in the case of a direct hit by a bomb. We didn't find any peace during the day either, from time to time we were spied on . . . and then we would flee as it got dark, protected by our dog, into the forest in Aubing (Aubinger Lohe), where we spent days and nights on a camouflaged hunters'

> platform or in holes in the ground or we buried ourselves in freshly mowed seagrass laid out to dry.[10]

Many people in hiding in Berlin used forests as a place to spend the night, but this often led to raids, so they remained at risk.[11] There is no documented case of any other Jew in hiding in the Greater Munich area who hid for periods of time in the large forest areas outside the city.

In early 1945, the persistent tribulations and fear caused Sigmund W. to suffer a nervous breakdown and ultimately a stroke with one-sided paralysis, for which he received extremely insufficient treatment.[12] A French forced laborer helped carry him back and forth between apartment and cellar. Sigmund W. and Martha W. married in July 1945, after liberation. Sigmund W. died in 1952 after a second stroke.

Many questions regarding this case must regrettably be left open. It remains unclear why Otto W. helped, and the identities of the helpers in Rosenheim and Türkenfeld and of the French forced laborer are not known. It is conceivable that the couple had additional helpers, as otherwise their food supply would have been difficult to organize over such a long period. Neighbors might have helped out or known about them, which would better explain how Sigmund W. was able to live in the apartment building on Perhamerstrasse from late 1941 until May 1945 without being discovered. Even if the couple repeatedly hid out in the forest for days at a time, it is hard to imagine that no one took note of their coming and going. Especially in the spring of 1945, it would have been virtually impossible for a forced laborer to carry a seriously ill man back and forth between an apartment and the cellar without being noticed.

ASSISTANCE FOR A NEIGHBOR: FOR HER HE "DID EVERYTHING THAT A PERSON COULD DO FOR ANOTHER PERSON"

Stanislaus Hanisch not only risked his life to protect his Jewish neighbor Meta L., but he also joined the National Socialist Motor Vehicle Corps (NSKK) in order to drive around inconspicuously to scout out hiding places for her. Consequently, he had a denazification hearing after the war, but ultimately it was "determined in the evidentiary hearing with absolute unambiguity and clarity . . . that Stanislaus Hanisch did everything that a person could do for another person for this Jewish woman from 1938 to 1943," so he was not adversely affected by the denazification law.

In 1933, Hanisch, a carpenter, lived with his family in a small basement apartment in a building behind Munich's Viktualienmarkt. He was twenty-nine years old at the time and had been a member of the German Communist Party (KPD) since 1927. On May 6, 1933, Hanisch was interned in the Dachau concentration camp. He had been arrested not only because of his KPD membership, but also because he had hidden the state director of the Red Aid (*Rote Hilfe*) in Bavaria, Max Holy, for fourteen days in the home of acquaintances and in his own home.[13] German Red Aid had been founded in 1924 as a relief organization for politically persecuted Communists. It provided legal and financial support for incarcerated Communists, Social Democrats, and trade unionists.[14] Author Oskar Maria Graf was one of the most famous and active supporters of the Red Aid, and he and Max Holy were friends. In his memoirs, *Gelächter von außen*, Graf recalled that "all Nazis knew Max and hated him fiercely."[15] The head of the Red Aid, "nothing but skin and bones," was tirelessly "on the road with his motorcycle" to support various comrades.[16] Graf wrote about their last meeting before Holy was arrested: "I saw my friend Max Holy, half dead from exhaustion, race by on the street. He stopped and hurriedly spoke into my ear: 'You're going to the countryside, to Wasserburg?—Have a look around to see if we could find a safe farmer here and there to use as a refuge.'"[17] It never got that far. Oskar Maria Graf did drive to friends near Wasserburg, but Max Holy had to hastily find refuge in Stanislaus Hanisch's basement apartment. In April 1933, he was arrested as he was escaping to Austria.[18]

Stanislaus Hanisch paid for taking in his comrade with more than two years' imprisonment in Dachau. In July 1935, he was released from the concentration camp and returned to his apartment. There Meta L., a Jew, became his neighbor in 1938. Thirty-five at the time, she was divorced and had retired early because of hip trouble. She moved in with her widowed brother-in-law to do his housekeeping, as his wife (Meta L.'s sister) had died in 1931. Her brother-in-law had been incarcerated in Dachau concentration camp for a few weeks in November 1938 after the *Kristallnacht* pogrom. Meta's niece, who had been born in the United States and thus had US citizenship, then traveled directly to the United States to organize her father's emigration from there. Meta L. took care of her brother-in-law during that time until he successfully emigrated in 1940.[19] She and the Hanisch family evidently developed a friendly relationship rather quickly.

On October 31, 1941, Meta L. received a notice telling her to leave her apartment and report to the Milbertshofen camp for "evacuation to the East." Instead of complying with this summons, she attempted suicide. Stanislaus Hanisch brought Meta L. to the Jewish Hospital and picked her up three weeks later after she had recovered somewhat. Meta L. then went underground with the help of her neighbor rather than report to Milbertshofen.[20]

Stanislaus Hanisch contacted Josef Obermeier, a business friend of Meta L.'s brother, who was willing to take her in for a while. Then Hanisch took some of Meta L.'s clothing and her ID card and scattered them at the Isar River to feign a suicide.[21] The Obermeier family sheltered Meta L. until early March 1942, when Josef Obermeier was drafted into the Wehrmacht. A lot of the time she spent with the Obermeier family—including winter nights—was in an unheated woodshed that Stanislaus Hanisch had made as inhabitable as he could.[22] As previously mentioned, Hanisch had joined the NSKK to remain inconspicuous while scouting out hiding places for her. In early March, the two of them drove to the Bavarian Forest and then to Garmisch-Partenkirchen, finally ending up in Gröbenzell, where Meta L. found lodging for a few weeks. When forced laborers were quartered in the house, Hanisch brought her back to Munich, where she slept on the Hanisches' floor for a short time. One day the police appeared, asking the Hanisches about their neighbor's whereabouts. She could listen to the conversation since she had hurriedly hidden behind a curtain.[23] Meta L. had to disappear quickly. Her earlier domestic helper took her into her tiny apartment in Giesing for a few days.

In early April 1942, Meta L. was able to stay with Ilka Rodius, an old acquaintance, for a month. Ilka was married to Alfred Rodius, a Reich Railway worker who by no means rejected the Nazis. However, he also had a half-Jewish stepdaughter from his wife's earlier marriage and had nothing against having Meta L. stay with them.[24] Even after her divorce and her second marriage to Alfred Rodius, Ilka Rodius maintained friendly contact with the Jewish family and friends of her ex-husband, and she did not hesitate to offer refuge to a Jewish acquaintance from that time. Still, Ilka and Alfred Rodius did not live only with their three children, but also with Ilka Rodius's mother, and the space was very tight. For this reason, Meta L. stayed with the Rodius family for only a short time.

Stanislaus Hanisch had, meanwhile, found long-term lodgings for Meta L. He brought her to a teacher in Fürstenfeldbruck who lived with his niece, who was a cardiac patient, and a housekeeper in a mansion in quiet surroundings with a large garden. Meta L. lived there in hiding for three years. Stanislaus Hanisch had to continually beg that she be allowed to remain there.[25] The hosts let themselves be persuaded, and Meta L. was still in Fürstenfeldbruck when the war ended.

Both Meta L. and Stanislaus Hanisch remained in Munich after the war. The carpenter tried to return to normal life. He was recognized after the war as having suffered political persecution, and his denazification was a mere formality. Meta L. attested vis-à-vis various authorities to the fact that she had him to thank for her survival.[26]

When in 1941 Stanislaus Hanisch faced the decision of whether or not to help Meta L., he had already had considerable experience both with hiding a fugitive and in dealing with the Nazi apparatus of persecution. Of course, this also meant that he himself was seriously at risk. He was a Communist "repeat offender" and would have faced severe consequences had he been discovered. "Aiding and abetting Jews" did not necessarily lead to helpers being put in a concentration camp,[27] as the consequences varied greatly, but Hanisch would have had to reckon with being sent back to Dachau. He had risked his life for Meta L. When later asked why he did it, he responded succinctly: "I wasn't interested personally in the woman L. [name rendered anonymous]; we were just acquaintances. I did it all only to help someone who was facing annihilation because of her race."[28] Meta L. herself stated that he "was solely motivated by his Communist convictions."[29] There are no indications that he was politically active after 1945. Stanislaus Hanisch died in 1984.

THE REICH GOVERNOR'S "ADJUTANT"[30]

Rudolf V., a sales representative, was one of the first Munich Jews to venture going underground. He was helped by his non-Jewish fiancée, Maria H., in addition to an unidentified older woman from Berlin and the Catholic Caritas network in Stuttgart. He was helped also by his former boss, the Reich governor of Bavaria, Franz Ritter von Epp. The particularly tragic end of this case is that Rudolf V. died from a short but serious illness only months after having been liberated.

In July 1942, Else Behrend-Rosenfeld noted in her diary that, up to that time, four people living in the Berg am Laim camp had taken the risk of fleeing. One of them was probably Rudolf V. Behrend-Rosenfeld wrote, "The first was a younger man who had been scheduled for deportation at Easter. He was in Epp's Freikorps [Free Corps] during the period of the Soviet Republic in Munich. We assume that he was helped by former comrades."[31] Rudolf V. had been "promoted to reserve lieutenant in 1916 for bravery in the face of the enemy,"[32] and after the end of the First World War, as a member of the Free Corps Epp, he had been present both at the quashing of the Munich Soviet Republic and at the fighting in the Ruhr basin.[33] Rudolf V. had not only earned a wealth of war decorations, but had also been awarded the so-called Epp badge for particularly meritorious members of the Free Corps.[34]

Starting in 1925, Rudolf V., a convert to Catholicism, worked in Munich as a freelance advertising agent for a number of publishing houses. He disregarded all Nazi regulations and continued to practice his trade until 1941, although it was forbidden for Jews as of 1938. The trade licensing office took notice of the fact that he did not have a trade license in 1941 and, in the course of an investigation into the case, summoned him to appear.[35] By then, he had long since been forced out of his apartment on Leopoldstrasse and was living with his mother and an aunt in a "Jew house" at Richard Wagner Strasse 11.[36] Although it was an absolutely futile endeavor, he applied for a trade license in March 1941. This was immediately rejected, but he did not give up. With a letter in hand from the tradition-steeped Free Corps Epp, he sought special permission. In his petition, he requested that "the application of this good soldier, tried and proven despite his race, in the service of the German fatherland, be treated with particular benevolence."[37] The effort of his Free Corps comrades was also in vain. In November 1941, he was reported for working illegally and fined 100 reichsmarks.[38]

The "tried and proven good soldier" had, meanwhile, started doing forced labor, building the Milbertshofen camp, and he might have already been arrested before his conviction in early November 1941. His then fiancée, Maria H., declared after the war that Rudolf V. had been arrested and placed on the list for transport to the East. It was only thanks to the intervention of Reich Governor von Epp that her fiancé was crossed off the list, released, and permitted to move back in with his mother on Richard Wagner Strasse. From there, he was ultimately sent to the Berg am Laim camp.[39] Whether Epp actually did intervene for the release of his Free Corps comrade is not confirmed, yet it is not implausible. In addition to the June 1941 letter from the Free Corps Epp, which supported Rudolf V. unconditionally, Maria H. also reported that the contact between her fiancé and Epp had continued even after his time in the Free Corps. After 1933, Rudolf V. continued to serve as a lieutenant in the reserve, but a short time later, he was dismissed due to his "non-Aryan" descent. Informed that he could serve only as a regular soldier, he consulted with Epp on the matter. Epp ostensibly urged him at the time to take his leave, since "an Epp officer does not let himself be degraded."[40] Epp had already become a member of the Nazi Party (NSDAP) in 1928 and was a member of the Reichstag for the NSDAP. As Reich governor, he was one of the most prominent representatives of Nazism in Bavaria, but his priority was first and foremost loyalty to the men of his unit. His antisemitic statements have been sufficiently documented, but for Epp, Rudolf V. was not a Jew, but a national-conservative Catholic comrade with whom he had fought side by side against internal and external enemies. With respect to the internal enemies, Epp at least opposed what he euphemistically referred to in the 1930s as "*Schutzhaft-Auswüchse*" ("protective custody excesses").[41] Rudolf V. requested that not only Epp but also the Munich cardinal, Michael von Faulhaber, intervene to oppose his deportation. Consequently, the cardinal wrote a letter to Epp, but never mailed it.[42]

When in the spring of 1942 in the Berg am Laim camp Rudolf V. learned of the upcoming (second) deportation, he went underground. Maria H. reported further: "He then fled from Munich to Berlin and was hidden by a woman he knew, but now I can't remember her name. The woman was relatively old at the time and is no longer living. He stayed there in Berlin in a garden house, since he had to avoid being seen. He then attempted to flee to Switzerland but did not succeed. After that attempted escape he returned to Munich briefly and found shelter with acquaintances who could only put him up for a short time due to the danger that someone might see him and report him."[43]

From Munich, Rudolf V. made his way to Württemberg to the pastor Eugen Stöffler and his wife, Johanna, in Köngen, who were members of the so-called parsonage chain in Württemberg that offered numerous "non-Aryan Christians" shelter and support.[44] The Stöfflers referred him to the network of the Caritas Association in Stuttgart. The Baumeister family decided to take Rudolf V. into their home in Stuttgart-Vaihingen. From there, he moved from one accommodation to the next in the Stuttgart region.[45] All in all, fifteen people signed a confirmation after the war that they participated in saving Rudolf V. in Stuttgart.[46] His fiancée and friends and acquaintances from Munich supplied him as best they could with food ration cards and money. Among them was Hedwig Geng, herself a Munich Jew. She did not know Rudolf V. personally but had been asked by friends to help support him. Geng occasionally chipped in with money and food ration cards whenever she had something to spare.[47] In November 1943, Rudolf V. wrote a letter to Geng thanking her. He signed the letter only as "Rudolf V." and refrained from any personal salutation, since the Gestapo often read letters.[48] "Dear honorable friend," he wrote, "more than ever I think we must hold our heads up if we wish to bear in mind that we, especially, might have to face some difficult hours, but I trust completely in a compensatory justice and thus in the Lord."[49] Both of them nevertheless took a certain risk, as refraining from mentioning names might have raised suspicions. In January 1944, the support from Hedwig Geng dried up. She had been deported to Theresienstadt.[50]

After Stuttgart was liberated, Rudolf V. returned to Munich and finally met Hedwig Geng, who had survived Theresienstadt. She later reported on their meeting: "When I was brought back to Munich after the war and housed in the former Jewish nursing home, Herr V. [name rendered anonymous] visited me, to get to know me and to thank me for my support. He was beaming as he told me that he received the position of director of a DP camp. Three days later I received news that he had contracted a throat disease and died from it. Thus ended a years-long struggle for survival by him and his helpers."[51]

Rudolf V. died in December 1945, only days before he and Maria H. planned to marry. In 1959, his fiancée was retroactively awarded the legal status of a lawful marriage. The Bavarian State Compensation Office (Landesentschädigungsamt, LEA) set the date of the marriage at December 31, 1943.[52] Maria V. had been using her husband's last name since 1945.

Rudolf V. was an assimilated Jew who had converted to Catholicism and had fought on the front in the First World War. He had been a member of a nationalist Free Corps unit and could not believe that the Nazi race laws were also to apply to him. Believing he was more "German" than so many of his countrymen, he trusted that this would be taken into account and that he would be recognized as that which he definitely wanted to be: a German patriot and a member of the Nazis' "racial community (*Volksgemeinschaft*)." In this regard, Rudolf V. was similar to Rolf Grabower, the Jewish camp director of the Lohhof flax rettery. Like Grabower, Rudolf V. had access to high-ranking representatives of the Nazi regime, and both of them received help that made it easier for them to survive the persecution.[53] Grabower survived Theresienstadt, and his national-conservative patriotism was not diminished by the persecution he experienced: "We older ones loved this Germany in which we had grown up, and we also loved it when we were in Theresienstadt. I can still remember the words of a Jewish Free Corps fighter in Milbertshofen who was selected for deportation: 'If it were necessary again, I would do it again,' whereby he did not even imagine at that moment that we were not at all wanted."[54]

It is very likely that this Jewish Free Corps fighter, who would again "defend his fatherland on the side of his later murderers against the Communist threat of the revolution for the Soviet Republic in 1918–1919,"[55] was in fact Rudolf V. This might also explain why Rudolf V., like Rolf Grabower, wanted to participate in rebuilding Germany immediately following the war. His patriotism, too, was evidently unbroken. Perhaps it played a role that he had received assistance from a large group of Germans during the time of persecution. This made it possible for him, also like Rolf Grabower, to rationalize the period of persecution as a short, abnormal interruption to a German life, before he died in December 1945 as a result of that very persecution.

ESCAPE HELPER TB

In 1936, Edith S. worked as a volunteer caregiver in the children's home on Antonienstrasse in Munich. She was originally from Berlin, was divorced, and planned to emigrate to Britain with her son and her parents. She hoped that her vocational experience in childcare and pediatric nursing would improve her chances of securing a visa to emigrate. This is why in 1938 she took a job in a children's home run by doctors in Bad Kreuznach.[56]

After ten weeks in the children's home in Bad Kreuznach, Edith S. contracted a severe flu. She returned to Munich once she was feeling better, but had to remain under a doctor's care. Ultimately diagnosed with pulmonary tuberculosis, she was put in the Nordrach pulmonary sanatorium, a Jewish health clinic in the Black Forest, where she remained until February 1940.[57] Edith S.'s illness frustrated her plans for emigration, and her parents also did not emigrate. Nevertheless, in 1939, after the death of her ex-husband, she was able to send her son on a *Kindertransport,* an evacuation program to send Jewish children to Britain.[58]

When Edith S. returned from Nordrach to Munich in 1940, her apartment had already been confiscated. She lived for a while in a boardinghouse in the city. In late October 1941, she heard rumors about a first, imminent deportation from Munich. The illness from which she had just recovered offered her an escape, and she went back to Nordrach immediately. The pulmonary sanitorium gave her the opportunity to evade deportation, even though at the time she no longer showed any symptoms of the disease.[59] This was, however, a temporary refuge. Edith S. left Nordrach shortly before the sanitorium was closed in September 1942 and returned to Munich, where she was put in the Berg am Laim camp. Due to the difficult living conditions there, her tuberculosis returned. To avoid being deported to Auschwitz in March 1943, she fled to Berlin, where she spent a year in hiding.[60] Unfortunately, it is impossible to reconstruct the precise circumstances of her escape to Berlin, her living conditions there, and the identity of her helpers. All that is certain is that she returned to Munich in April 1944.

In Munich, Hugo Rothschild helped her with advice, money, and food ration cards. A fatherly friend, he was in a "privileged mixed marriage" and worked as a so-called legal advisor (*Rechtskonsulent*), since Jews were no longer permitted to practice law.[61] In the fall of 1944, Edith S.'s condition had worsened such that she underwent an examination in Munich's polyclinic and was admitted to the Schwabing hospital, where she remained unrecognized under the name Edith Berger. This did not go well for very long, however, and she was denounced in January 1945, arrested, and sent on the final transport to Theresienstadt.[62] She survived Theresienstadt, although gravely ill, and was finally admitted to the Munich-Harlaching hospital, where she remained until December 1946. In the years that followed, she repeatedly had to return to the hospital for inpatient treatment. Edith S. died in 1962 of tuberculosis. Her Jewish helper,

Hugo Rothschild, was also arrested as a result of the denunciation. He died in February 1945 in the Dachau concentration camp.[63]

SURVIVAL IN THE POLICE STATION

A mother with two daughters in the Berg am Laim camp wrote a farewell letter announcing their suicides in the Perlacher Forest. Else Behrend-Rosenfeld, who had noted the incident in her diary in July 1942, then had to go to the police station and file a missing person report. Because no bodies were found, Behrend-Rosenfeld assumed that the three women managed to escape to Switzerland.[64] It turned out she was wrong. The mother and two daughters who had fled the Berg am Laim camp were Paula Mayer and her adult daughters, Sophie and Lieselotte (Elisabeth Charlotte).[65]

The Mayer family had been put into the Berg am Laim camp in November 1941, where the father, Julius Mayer, died only a few months later. Sophie Mayer, a physician, and her sister Lieselotte, a singer, were conscripted to do forced labor in Berg am Laim for the Kammerer telephone factory. Paula Mayer, their mother, received her deportation notice in July 1942.[66] The sisters first decided to go with their mother, but then the three women changed their plans. While saying goodbye to Maria Letnar, an acquaintance, Letnar offered to help them.[67] She apparently knew people who would give refuge to the women. Paula Mayer and her daughter Lieselotte went to Rosi Fischer, a relative of Maria Letnar, at a farmhouse in the Bavarian Forest, where Fischer hid them in the attic. Hardly any further information is available regarding the living conditions of the two women. Hedwig Geng, an acquaintance of Sophie Mayer, could only report that one of the two women suffered from an unbearable toothache, but they did not dare contact a dentist.[68] In addition, their hiding place became increasingly unsafe, as bombed-out people started arriving from the cities. Lieselotte and Paula Mayer feared not only being found but also placing their helpers at risk. Desperate, mother and daughter threw themselves into the Danube River in the spring of 1944.[69] They were both declared dead after 1945.

Maria Letnar had sent Sophie Mayer to her sister Rosa and brother-in-law Paul Mayer (no relation to Sophie Mayer) in Lenggries. Paul Mayer was the police chief there, and their residence was in the building of the police department. Although numerous people, including SS personnel, went in and out of the police station, Rosa and Paul Mayer ultimately decided against bringing Sophie Mayer to a mountain cabin and instead hid her in their own apartment despite the great risk.[70] There were practical reasons for this decision. Over time, it would have been difficult to organize food provisions for a remote

Sophie Mayer (*right*), with her sister Lieselotte (Elisabeth Charlotte).
Munich City Archive (StadtAM), JUD-F-01-0009-SBM.

mountain cabin and too conspicuous. Once it had been decided that the Jewish fugitive Sophie Mayer would stay in the Mayers' apartment, their ten-year-old son, Günter, also had to be informed and sworn to absolute secrecy. Other parents in similar situations—understandably—did not want to take such a risk.[71] Thus, Sophie Mayer's survival was dependent on the mental discipline of a child and his ability to withstand such stress. For three years, the boy mentioned nothing to anyone about their long-term house guest.

Like almost all people in hiding, Sophie Mayer had no food ration cards, which meant that her helpers had to share their food with her. Rosa Mayer and Maria Letnar took turns going on hoarding missions to the farmers in the area to supplement their meager rations. It was easier to procure additional food supplies in rural areas than in a large city like Berlin or Munich.

The situation became particularly difficult for everyone involved when, only a few months before the end of the war, some bombed-out Nazis from a city were assigned quarters in the building.[72] Sophie Mayer's presence was evidently noticed at least once, as Paul Mayer was denounced anonymously. She was brought to another temporary hiding place just in time before the house was searched.[73]

Not only did Paul Mayer hide Sophie Mayer, but he was also in close contact with Otto Windeis, a farmer who led a small resistance group in the region. Mayer informed Windeis about imminent arrests, thus also protecting him. The police chief evidently also ignored instructions to arrest a Jew living in Lenggries and transfer him to Munich.[74] Regarding the village butcher's wife, who got carried away making anti-Nazi remarks, Paul Mayer blocked the investigation, although at the time he himself was already in danger of being taken into custody. Moreover, he helped Italian forced laborers who had fled their workplace in the final phase of the war to find a place to hide in the area.[75]

Paul Mayer had been transferred several times in 1934 for being politically unreliable, lastly to Lenggries. In 1936, he had participated in the Corpus Christi procession in an old uniform from the Weimar period, even though that was prohibited. The police chief had joined the Nazi Party in 1937, apparently on orders of Hans Däuwel, commander of the gendarmerie, who called on all gendarmerie officers who were not yet party members to join.[76] Mayer might have no longer been able to avoid joining the party without losing his position. It cannot be determined why he was allowed to join the Nazi Party, having already been deemed politically unreliable.

After the war, Paul Mayer, Rosa Mayer, Günter Mayer, and Maria Letnar did not boast about the help they had offered. Together with Otto Windeis and others, Sophie Mayer supported Paul Mayer in his denazification hearing, and she later wrote to Yad Vashem to ensure that her helpers were distinguished as Righteous Among the Nations (see chapters 9 and 12). After his successful denazification proceedings, Paul Mayer worked again as police chief. According to Sophie Mayer, he had acted out of "opposition to the Nazis and a sense of charity."[77] He died in 1976. After the war, Sophie Mayer resumed working as a doctor in Munich. She died in 1997, only four weeks before her hundredth birthday.[78]

ESCAPE FROM BERG AM LAIM

Else Behrend-Rosenfeld escaped in August 1942 from Munich to her sister Eva, who lived in Berlin with her non-Jewish husband. She had learned early that month that she would have to give up her position as camp manager in Berg am Laim and thus would no longer be able to do anything to help the remaining Jews there. She also feared being placed on the next deportation list since she no longer held an official position.[79] Shortly before her job in Berg am Laim was scheduled to end, she was physically exhausted, so she had a long weekend free and was permitted to leave the camp. She used the opportunity to go underground. Her escape was well planned by close college friends. They had checked out different escape plans, organized possible hiding places, and contacted Behrend-Rosenfeld's sister, who was protected by her mixed marriage.[80] The train ride to Berlin was risky, however, since Behrend-Rosenfeld had no identification to present if IDs were checked. A few days before her departure she noted in her diary: "Was I really the one who wanted to carry out this plan? I still couldn't imagine it! And what if it went wrong? The thought flashed suddenly into my head. I thought of an ID check on the train. If I didn't show enough presence of mind, I'd be lost! These and other thoughts tortured me constantly until Friday evening. I just did my work by rote. Terrible dreams tormented me in the little time I was able to sleep."[81]

She was lucky and the train was completely overcrowded, so there was no ID check at all. Once arriving in Berlin, she waited until dusk and then ran to the house of her relatives under the cover of darkness.[82]

After living in her sister's home for three months, during which she did not leave the house at all, Else Behrend-Rosenfeld and her helpers all showed marked signs of the stress caused by the situation. Her brother-in-law was so afraid that he couldn't sleep, and Behrend-Rosenfeld suffered from being a burden on the others.[83] Her girlfriends found a new refuge for her through an extensive network of friends and acquaintances. She moved in with Hans Kollmorgen, a factory owner, who needed a housekeeper. When Kollmorgen agreed to take her in, Behrend-Rosenfeld broke into tears of joy and relief. She was able to stay at Kollmorgen's from early December 1942 until mid-March 1943; at that time, he also took in other Jews in hiding. All told, he gave shelter to five people.[84] To relieve the burden on "Uncle Hans," which is how she called Kollmorgen, Behrend-Rosenfeld later moved in with friends, the Heilmann family. Ernst Heilmann, a Jewish former Social Democratic member of parliament, like his good friend Siegfried Rosenfeld, Else's husband (who had emigrated to England in August 1939), had been murdered in 1940 in the Buchenwald concentration camp. His Gentile widow, Magdalena, lived with their four (almost) grown children in Berlin.[85]

Behrend-Rosenfeld also managed to acquire false ID papers. Peter Heilmann, a son of Magdalena and Ernst Heilmann, had procured a clothing coupon through illicit trading issued in the name of Martha Schröder.[86] In the weeks that followed, Behrend-Rosenfeld also had a postal identity card issued in that name. The procedure was simple: friends would send a number of registered letters addressed to Martha Schröder, which Else Behrend-Rosenfeld accepted as Martha Schröder. She made an effort to start a conversation with the mail carrier to "get to know her." Carriers could legitimate people they knew for a postal identity card without their having to present documents such as ID cards or birth certificates. Behrend-Rosenfeld told the mail carrier that she had only recently moved there and that she often received registered mail, but in the future, she would not be able to accept it herself since she would be starting her new job. The mail carrier advised her to have a postal ID card issued, and she explained that she would only have to present a birth certificate. Behrend-Rosenfeld replied that she had been bombed out of her previous residence and had no access to her birth certificate. The mail carrier then said—as Behrend-Rosenfeld had been hoping—that she could confirm at the post office that she knew her by name, thus Behrend-Rosenfeld would not have to present her birth certificate.[87] Behrend-Rosenfeld then received a postal ID card issued to Martha Schröder. She was not the only Jew in hiding who obtained a postal ID in this way.[88] This identification card by itself was, of course, not a new identity. It only allowed the bearer to pick up packages and letters at the post office, but it could also be used as backup identification in lieu of an official identity card.

In June 1943, Else Behrend-Rosenfeld took the train from Berlin to Freiburg. The postal ID gave her a sense of security, even if it would not have stood up to a strict inspection. In Freiburg, she was taken in by the family of the journalist Edmund Goldschagg, who was a good friend of the Heilmann family.[89] She finally succeeded in escaping over the border to Switzerland in April 1944 (see chapter 8).

MUNICH, BERLIN, FRANKFURT, VIENNA: GENERAL CONDITIONS AND STRATEGIES OF PEOPLE IN HIDING AND THEIR HELPERS IN VARIOUS CITIES

Existing research on Jews in hiding has shown that the data varies on how many helpers were necessary to save a single person.[90] Nevertheless, a number of people were usually involved, even if regional differences are apparent. In Vienna, most U-boats were evidently supported by only two or three helpers.[91] Susanne Beer assumes a figure of at least five helpers per U-boat in Berlin, whereas Claudia Schoppmann and Beate Kosmala have concluded that up to ten helpers were usually involved and often even more.[92] Those who went underground early on tended to need more help than U-boats who were only in hiding for a short time. They had to change their hiding places, and numerous people helped supply them with food over longer periods of time. Staying in one hiding place for too long usually led to their being discovered, denounced, and arrested. In the cases of Meta L. and Rudolf V., it can be shown that about two dozen people participated in rescuing each of them.

Precisely in this regard, Sophie Mayer's survival is particularly unusual, as she did not change her location even once, and only very few people participated in caring for her needs. Sophie Mayer's case thus corresponds exactly to the common notions of life in hiding that many people associate with Anne Frank. Even if U-boats in Vienna had fewer hiding places and helpers available to them than their fellow U-boats in German cities, enduring for months or years in attics and hidden closets and receiving support from only a few helpers was more the exception than the rule.[93] Also in the case of Sigmund W., there was only one main hiding place, even if the Aubinger Lohe forest offered numerous places to find temporary refuge. Most likely, Martha W.'s neighbors noticed the presence of Sigmund W. but chose to turn a blind eye. This was not the case in the Schwabing hospital, where Edith S. was the victim of a denunciation. Sophie Mayer only barely avoided this fate. The problem of denunciations will be treated in depth in chapter 6, which addresses failed escape attempts.

Thoughts of suicide and flight lay close together. Sigmund W. and Meta L. had initially planned to commit suicide. Meta L. was saved, while Sigmund W. was dissuaded from his plans. In both cases, the suicide plans ultimately became flight plans. A feigned suicide was the first step in fleeing underground, but suicide was also a way out and the last resort if the situation in hiding became intolerable. In view of their situation, assimilated Jews in particular no longer felt bound to the religious commandment against suicide.[94] Like Else Behrend-Rosenfeld, who sewed veronal tablets into the hem of her coat (see chapter 2), it was also an option for others in hiding to be able to decide their fate for themselves. Another Munich U-boat, Siegfried B., carried a gun in order to be able to end his life at any moment.[95] A young woman who went underground in Essen later declared: "I always had enough medication with me, on my person, so that I could take my life at any time. That was the most important thing for me—that I would either get out of this inferno healthy or not at all."[96]

In their desperation, going underground was an interim solution that could be renegotiated based on the changing circumstances. Faced with the choice of suicide or flight, it was only of secondary importance that the prospects of success were dim. Paula and Lieselotte Mayer ended up in a situation in their hiding place in Lower Bavaria in which they no longer saw a way out. Their hiding place had become unsafe, the Gestapo was ostensibly on their tails, one of the two women was in unbearable pain, and it was impossible to call a doctor.[97] So they took their final escape to death; it was an end that many in hiding preferred to imminent arrest or deportation.

It is striking that with the exception of Sigmund W., everyone in hiding portrayed here left Munich. This was also the case for other early escapes that have not been dealt with in this chapter. Rudolf V., Else Behrend-Rosenfeld, and Edith S. all headed for Berlin when they fled Munich. The anonymity of the capital was obviously attractive, as they wanted to escape an environment in which they were known and recognized. In Berlin, they could immerse themselves in a large, heterogeneous population in which strangers did not attract attention. Personal contacts and known hiding places played an important role. Berlin U-boats usually stayed in the city, even if many of them shuttled back and forth between Berlin and other hiding places outside the city.[98]

Many U-boats from Munich favored a rural environment to a big city. Munich's environs, the pre-Alpine regions of Upper Bavaria, as well as remote villages in Lower Bavaria, were preferred destinations. People from Munich were familiar with these areas, but they were not known there. When Maria Letnar was suddenly confronted with the task of hiding three women, she decided to take all three of them out of Munich. Perhaps this decision was a result of her personal living and family situation, which did not offer any options to hide in the city. However, it is more likely that for Letnar and many others in hiding and their helpers, this was a very deliberate decision because the rural areas of Upper and Lower Bavaria promised better chances of survival. The issue of food supply was certainly crucial in this regard. To provide long term for a person lacking food ration coupons in Munich without attracting attention, many people had to work together or have particular supply sources. In the countryside, this was much easier.

It is true for all of the cases discussed in this chapter that those fleeing had contacts to people who were especially well positioned to help them. These contacts resulted in part from their respective living situations and in part could materialize by chance—a stroke of good luck—as in the case of Sophie Mayer. Meta L. had found an experienced helper who was resourceful and quick thinking, and who worked systematically. The actions of Stanislaus Hanisch and Meta L. corresponded most closely to the strategy that was widespread in Berlin, moving from one contact to the next, spending a few weeks here and there, mobilizing acquaintances from all social strata.[99]

Rudolf V. and Sigmund W. had non-Jewish girlfriends and therefore—as in the case of mixed marriages—"Aryan" families and a large non-Jewish circle of friends standing behind them. With Franz von Epp as a helper, Rudolf V. had someone from the highest ranks of the apparatus of persecution to count on. On the basis of Epp's inside knowledge and his personal loyalty to Rudolf V., he was able to prevent Rudolf V.'s early deportation. For her part, Else Behrend-Rosenfeld, as the manager of the Berg am Laim camp, had certain inside knowledge when she decided to flee in August 1942. She had been at all the deportations, she knew of the reports from Jews who had been deported earlier, and she came to understand their fate.[100]

In almost all the cases presented here, the motives of the Munich helpers seem to have been largely altruistic. Whether Else Behrend-Rosenfeld's helpers—a group of college friends who devised and organized the escape plans—the Mayer family, Rudolf V.'s Christian helpers, or the Communist carpenter Stanislaus Hanisch, apparently none of them demanded anything in return. Nevertheless, it cannot always be determined from the sources whether there were explicit demands, implicit expectations, or financial payments out of gratitude.[101] For both sides, it was not necessarily easy to speak in retrospect about that time. Some helpers needed financial support. Some survivors did not want to appear ungrateful and did not mention demands for payments. When Meta L. went underground, occasional smaller sums of money were in fact paid, but she emphasized that these were voluntary payments. Sophie Mayer also declared in her statement to Yad Vashem that she paid "3 marks per day of her own accord."[102] The support by largely altruistic helpers is remarkable. Precisely in view of the often very high number of helpers, many of the U-boats—especially in Berlin—were at some point faced with demands of a very varied nature, as we will see in chapter 4.

Jewish helpers were by no means unusual. These included Hedwig Geng, who supported Rudolf V. financially, and Dr. Hugo Rothschild, a partner in a privileged mixed marriage, who assisted Edith S. Else Behrend-Rosenfeld received help from her sister Eva. Jews in mixed marriages, their spouses, and their children could and did help in a number of ways. They offered temporary lodgings, held valuables and money in safekeeping, procured food and food ration coupons, and passed on additional contacts.[103] Not only in Munich, but also in Berlin, helpers were frequently non-Jewish relatives, in particular spouses in mixed marriages.[104] Susanne Beer came to the conclusion in her study of helpers of Jews that 27 percent of them supported Jewish relatives.[105] Among Jews living in mixed marriages were also people such as Franz Kaufmann in Berlin, who supplied many Jews in hiding with forged passports and food ration cards, or the doctor Benno Heller, who hid a number of Jews and procured hiding places for others.[106] It was much more dangerous for these people to offer aid than it was for non-Jewish Germans. Both Benno Heller and Franz Kaufmann in Berlin, like Hugo Rothschild in Munich, were sent to concentration camps and murdered. This in fact means that of those collectively deemed "silent heroes" or "good Germans" after 1945, many were actually "half Jews" or Jews living in mixed marriages. These groups, as well as non-Jewish spouses have, however, been excluded from the honors awarded to helpers.[107]

In contrast to the situation in Berlin, Munich helpers were largely recruited from social strata similar to those of the Jews they helped. Stanislaus Hanisch and Meta L.'s domestic help represent more the exception here. Most of those fleeing from Berlin were from middle-class families. The situation often required far greater social adjustments of them. Michael Degen and his mother were taken in for a while by an older woman whose three daughters worked at home as prostitutes.[108] Charlotte Lewinsky also lived with a prostitute.[109] Lothar Orbach also spent some time in a brothel and recruited additional helpers in a billiard hall frequented by cardsharps and shady characters, as well as people in hiding and foreign workers.[110] Many U-boats spent time living in bug-ridden slum dwellings and were for the first time in their lives confronted with bitter poverty, crime, and social neglect, but also with a willingness to help that many of them experienced precisely from these people living on the margins of society.

Thus, the early flights paint the following picture for us. Particular social contacts or living situations made it possible for a small group of Jews from Munich to go into hiding at the right time, before the major deportations took place. They could rely largely on altruistic helpers for support. The cases described here were unrelated to each other. With the exception of Lieselotte and Paula Mayer, the Munich U-boats went underground on their own. It was individual people who had the best chances of survival, and frequently it was single individuals who chose the path of going underground. One woman wrote, "I myself had little to lose, except for my life. When I went into hiding my son was already safe in England, my husband was dead, and my relatives had already been picked up."[111]

The contacts that were essential for survival could be activated spontaneously, as in the cases of Maria Letnar and Sophie, Lieselotte, and Paula Mayer. Here we must ask whether additional Munich Jews explored similar possibilities within their non-Jewish circle of friends and acquaintances, to the extent that they had any, prior to the deportations, but were disappointed, or whether they did not even try, or whether they refused support that was offered. Hedwig

Geng wrote in 1946 to her cousin's son about his mother's deportation: "I helped her pack, that most horrible task of removing a person at that age from the home and hustling her off to a gruesome uncertainty. I met Dr. Max every night; he devised the most adventurous plans to bring her away and was willing to make the greatest sacrifice in doing that, but your mother accepted nothing. She didn't want to jeopardize anyone. I can give you only one consolation: she carried poison with her in order to be able at any moment to put an end to it all."[112] In this respect, it is difficult to determine if additional Jews actually did seek help or if non-Jewish friends and acquaintances offered assistance in vain.

The cases discussed here refute the assumption that it must have been mostly young, healthy people who managed to evade deportation. This was by no means the case. Rudolf V. was forty-six years old when he fled; Else Behrend-Rosenfeld was fifty-one; and Sigmund W. was already sixty-five. Meta L. had serious hip trouble. Edith S. was even able to take advantage of the serious illness from which she had just recovered in order to evade deportation. She was forty-three at the time. Sophie Mayer and her sister were adult women, forty-five and forty-one years old, respectively, and their mother was elderly. Many of the Munich U-boats not discussed here were in their forties and fifties.

The cases generate a picture of the so-called typical U-boat from Munich as more likely female than male, living alone, and in the forty to fifty age group. This finding is consistent also with cases in Munich from 1941 to 1943 that have not been presented here. Of the twenty-seven known cases of Jews in hiding during this time period, only ten were male. The twelve U-boats who went to the Greater Munich area from elsewhere during this period were also largely female and older than forty. Among all of the Munich U-boats, the share of women comes to roughly 65 percent. Men of military age were hard to hide as they were more likely than everyone else to have their IDs checked in public. Rolf Themal, who had gone underground in Berlin, resolved the problem by simulating a war injury and making himself look much older than he actually was.[113] Others occasionally disguised themselves as women or borrowed Hitler Youth uniforms from friends.[114]

If this finding is compared with statistics on the age distribution of all known cases of German Jews in hiding, it shows that Munich was not an exception. The largest group throughout Germany was the forty-one to fifty age group at 22.5 percent, followed by the fifty-one-to-sixty-year-olds at 16.5 percent, and the twenty to thirty age group with 16.4 percent, while 8.5 percent were older than sixty. The proportion of women was a good 60 percent.[115] This finding can be explained in part by the fact that it was predominantly younger people and men who had emigrated before the war. This means that the Jewish population in

Germany in 1941 was already relatively old and that the share of women was significantly greater than 50 percent.[116] However, if we look closely, we can also see some differences. Although it is difficult to compare the figures for Munich to those for Berlin because the most recent statistics for Berlin comprise only those U-boats who survived the war, the U-boats in Munich were on average a little older than those in Berlin. In Berlin, most of the U-boats were in their thirties or forties.[117] The U-boats were the oldest in Vienna, as those fifty-one and older constituted the largest age group there, followed by the forty-one to fifty age group.[118]

In 1941 and 1942, at least twenty Jews went underground in Munich, seventeen of whom were facing imminent deportation. There are indications of additional cases, but for this time period, the actual number is likely not much higher, and one can assume at most twenty-five to thirty cases.[119] On top of these were a few others who went to the Greater Munich area and hid there for a time. In 1943, the number of Jews who fled the deportations in Munich dropped to single digits (see chapter 4). In this particular respect, the picture for this early phase in Munich is very different from that of Berlin. In Berlin, only 3 percent of all known U-boats had already gone underground by the end of 1941. Another 34 percent followed over the course of 1942 (most of them between October and December), and more than half of all those who went into hiding did so within the scope of the Factory Operation in February 1943.[120] Thus, the percentage of early flights in Munich was high since clearly more escaped in 1941–42 than in 1943. The figures are very telling, specifically as compared with Hamburg. Roughly 7,500 Jews were still living in Hamburg in September 1941, and only about five to ten of them attempted to evade deportation before June 1943 by fleeing.[121] There were far more in the Greater Frankfurt area, the Jewish community that had been the second largest in Germany prior to 1938. By late 1941, it had dwindled to 10,592 people, but on the eve of the deportations, the Frankfurt Jewish community was still about three times the size of the Jewish community in Munich. At least thirty of its members attempted to escape by the end of 1942.[122]

Jakob Sprenger, the Gauleiter of Hesse-Nassau, an antisemitic zealot even by Nazi standards, had aimed to make his district *judenrein* ("free of Jews") as quickly as possible. He pressured the Frankfurt Gestapo to implement his plans, which led to the deportation of the Frankfurt Jews being largely completed as early as the fall of 1942—that is, far earlier than in Berlin.[123] The only Jews remaining in Frankfurt after that point were Jews in mixed marriages and so-called *Geltungsjuden*. In Munich, the vast majority of Jews had also already been deported by August 1942, though in contrast to Frankfurt, there was yet another, final mass deportation from Munich in early 1943. Most fugitive Jews from Frankfurt also sought hiding places outside the city. They feared the "tenacity of the Frankfurt Gestapo" and its informers and denouncers.[124] The Frankfurt Gestapo also made use of Jewish informers. Together with Berlin and Vienna, Frankfurt was one of the three cities in the German Reich that utilized Jewish snatchers (*Greifer*).[125] Thus, the situation in Munch differed in some significant ways from that in other major cities. Further regional differences will be explored in the following chapter.

FOUR

THE CONCLUSION OF THE MASS DEPORTATIONS IN 1943

A Second Wave of Escapes?

SEVERAL THOUSAND JEWS IN BERLIN fled to evade the so-called Factory Operation, the major series of arrests leading up to the final mass deportations in late February/early March 1943.[1] In Munich, on the other hand, there were in all probability fewer than ten Jews who attempted to avoid the last major deportation from the Bavarian capital in March 1943. Of the roughly thirty-three thousand Jews who remained in Berlin in early 1943,[2] more than fifteen thousand were working as forced laborers in armaments factories.[3] Hence, the situation in Berlin differed substantially from that in other German cities. In some major cities, such as Frankfurt, the deportations had largely been completed. In others, there were still only small numbers of Jewish forced laborers, such as in Dresden (483), Duisburg (497), Munich (313), and Düsseldorf (673).[4] Only in Breslau (now Wrocław, Poland) did several thousand Jews remain, 2,400 of whom were forced laborers.[5] However, even though only a few hundred Jews still lived in Munich in early 1943, and the final mass transport included "only" 108 Jews from that city, the question nevertheless remains why, in contrast to Berlin, there was not a greater flow of Jews fleeing Munich at this time. In early 1943 in Berlin, "about one in three of those designated for deportation" did not report.[6]

EARLY 1943: THE FACTORY OPERATION IN BERLIN AND FINAL MASS DEPORTATION IN MUNICH

In the course of the Factory Operation, the remaining Jewish forced laborers and employees of the Reich Association of Jews in Germany throughout the German Reich were to be deported. Excepted from the deportations were only

Jews in mixed marriages and certain groups of *Geltungsjuden*, "half Jews" treated as Jews under the Nuremberg Race Laws. The Factory Operation was centered in Berlin, but final mass deportations also took place in other cities, such as Breslau, Dortmund, and Munich. The Nazi authorities in Berlin reckoned with numerous flight attempts. For this reason, the raids took place throughout Berlin without any prior announcement. As of February 27, factories were locked down (thus the name "Factory Operation"). The Jewish workers were arrested and brought to predeportation internment camps.[7] The journalist Ruth Andreas-Friedrich was a member of the "Uncle Emil" resistance group, which hid a number of Jews in Berlin. She noted in her diary: "Since six o'clock this morning trucks have been driving through Berlin, escorted by armed SS men. They stop at factory gates, in front of private houses; they load in human cargo—men, women, children. Distracted faces are crowded together under the gray canvas covers. Figures of misery, penned in and jostled about like cattle going to the stockyards. More and more new ones arrive, and are thrust into the overcrowded trucks with blows of gun butts."[8]

There were frequent comments by Berliners about the brutal treatment of the Jews.[9] The Factory Operation dragged on for about a week, and during this time, many people took advantage of the opportunity to flee. Rumors of the imminent raids had also leaked in the days prior. Many Jews had been warned by colleagues or foremen not to come to work.[10] Consequently, Joseph Goebbels, Reich Propaganda Minister and Gauleiter of Berlin, confided his displeasure to his diary on March 11, writing that "we therefore failed to lay our hands on about 4,000."[11]

Many of the Jews who had not yet been deported were well aware of the fate awaiting them. No news arrived from those already deported, and rumors about the actions in Poland were ever present. The Allied forces had been reporting in detail about the German atrocities as of the fall of 1942.[12] In December 1942, knowledge of the fate of the Jews was so widespread that Goebbels expressed his concern.[13] Any Jew who was still living in Germany in early 1943 usually had relatives who had already been deported. They had had to witness many times how parents, relatives, and friends were rounded up and put in the predeportation internment camps.[14]

In late February 1943, Nazi Germany had lost its aura of invincibility. Although an end to Nazi rule was not yet inevitable after Germany was defeated at Stalingrad, the hopes of Jews were raised that the Allies would win the war. Perhaps, some might have thought, it would be possible to survive in hiding until that time.[15] Even if those prospects were still not all that good, many

Jewish forced laborers considered it a better option than being deported to face death in the East.

In early 1943, the remaining Jewish forced laborers from Munich were also supposed to be deported, followed by the employees of the official Jewish community, insofar as they did not enjoy the protection of being in a mixed marriage.[16] Thousands of foreign forced laborers and prisoners of war had long been working in the major factories in Munich deemed vital to the war effort. The Jewish forced laborers worked mainly for the Kammerer telephone and battery factory, a relatively small business belonging to the brothers Rudolf and August Kammerer in eastern Munich (see chapter 2).

The final mass transport from Munich took place on March 13. No major raid was necessary since those to be deported were already in the Berg am Laim camp, which was to be liquidated. All Jews not yet living in the camp had been brought there beforehand, and then the camp was locked down and the inhabitants deported.[17] It is difficult to determine how rigorous the security measures in Berg am Laim were, but the deportations had been postponed a couple of days due to an air raid, which must have enhanced the opportunities to flee.[18]

In contrast to Berlin, there was no mass exodus in Munich prior to the last major transport in March 1943. In fact, only very few escapes have been documented for early 1943.[19] In addition to those who went underground in connection with the final major deportation in March 1943, more Jews went in to hiding over the course of 1943 and 1944 after having lost the protection of being in a mixed marriage through the death or divorce of the non-Jewish spouse.

The fates of four Munich Jews will be presented in the following sections. Siegfried B., the superintendent of the Milbertshofen camp, fled before he was to be deported to Auschwitz. Dr. Benno Schülein escaped with the help of old friends and the Kammerer brothers.[20] For their escapes, Albertine Gimpel and Max Bachmann had a circle of non-Jewish artist and writer friends on whom they could rely.

"MY CONSTANT COMPANION WAS MY REVOLVER"

As of 1937, Siegfried B. worked as an occasional driver and groundskeeper for the Jewish gymnastics and sports club in Munich. In March 1941, he was conscripted to help build the Milbertshofen Jewish camp. During construction, he fell from a ladder and suffered a severe concussion and a bruised liver. He was unconscious for a few days and spent several months in the Jewish hospital. The serious injuries could not be healed. For the rest of his life, Siegfried

B. suffered from serious liver damage.[21] When the Milbertshofen camp was completed, Siegfried B. became its superintendent. He was present at all the transports. Starting in August 1942, he had to work on the closing and liquidation of the camp, which, according to his information, continued up to March 1943.[22] Siegfried B. had a relationship with a non-Jewish woman, and they had a daughter. For this reason, he was prosecuted in 1942 for "defiling the race," but the case was ultimately dismissed.[23] After the war, Siegfried B. married the mother of his daughter.

When in March 1943 Siegfried B. learned that he had been slated for the transport to Auschwitz, he went into hiding. Consequently, Gestapo officer Hans Grahammer placed Siegfried B.'s brother, Julius, under severe pressure.[24] Grahammer gave Julius one day to reveal his missing brother's whereabouts or else he, too, would be deported on the upcoming transport.[25] Julius did not, in fact, know where Siegfried B. was hiding. A short time later, however, the camp director, Curt Mezger, was arrested and deported, ostensibly because he had helped Siegfried B. escape.[26] In the postwar trial against Grahammer, Siegfried B. denied vehemently that Mezger had helped him. In fact, Siegfried B. and Julius had presumed that the Gestapo wanted to get Mezger out of the way because he knew too much about Gestapo officers plundering the luggage of deportees.[27] The Munich Gestapo officers probably had in fact believed that Mezger had helped Siegfried B. and had wanted to use the case as a warning to others.[28] Mezger was deported to Auschwitz even though he had a mixed marriage. His case shows how quickly and arbitrarily so-called protection from a mixed marriage could be revoked by local Gestapo officers. Curt Mezger was transferred in January 1945 from Auschwitz to Mauthausen, where he was murdered in the Ebensee subcamp in March 1945.[29]

Siegfried B. later described his flight as follows:

> I had to spend the first eight weeks with a Sabbath Christian [*sic,* Seventh-Day Adventist]. There I had nothing but my bare life. All I had to eat was potatoes and salt. Once the uproar about my disappearance had died down and I could no longer endure this existence, I decided to risk everything and went to Mr. Franz Xaver Huber in Munich. . . . There I had more to eat, but the constant danger of being recognized was much greater. I also had to endure all the air raids out of doors. My life was always hanging by a thread and my constant companion was my revolver.[30]

Unfortunately, we know nothing more about the circumstances under which Siegfried B. lived with his hosts, nor about their reasons for taking him in. There were only very few Seventh-Day Adventists in Germany who were willing to support Jews.[31] Siegfried B.'s girlfriend, Maria S., probably also helped care for him. He survived the persecution and became an important witness in the postwar period during the proceedings against the Munich Gestapo officers who stood trial for unlawful personal gain, deprivation of liberty, bodily harm, and other offenses. These trials will be discussed in chapter 10.

OLD FRIENDSHIPS

The friendship between the Jordan and Schülein families began in 1913, when Benno Schülein opened his legal office in the building of the non-Jewish commercial councilor Otto Jordan Sr. on Perusastrasse. Jordan Sr. and his son ran a fabric store there. The lawyer Dr. Benno Schülein became the managing director of the Association of Bavarian Textile Retailers, and Otto Jordan Sr. served as chairman of the board. Over time, Otto Jordan Sr. became like a second father to Benno Schülein, and Otto Jordan Jr. became a close friend.[32]

Benno Schülein was forced to close his legal office in 1938. In November 1938, he was sent to the Dachau concentration camp. When he was released in December, the Jordan family took him in, as his apartment lease had since been terminated without notice. In the period that followed, Schülein took turns staying with various friends and acquaintances. When he went into hiding in March 1943, Otto Jordan Jr. and his wife Anny supplied him with food and money. Friends helped organize various hiding places for him and also took him in for periods of time. Schülein consequently spent Christmas and New Year's Eve 1943 with the Jordans. After the war, Benno Schülein declared that the Jordan father and son had only joined the Nazi Party because they hoped "to be able to keep me in my position and to protect me from the persecution."[33] Business interests had presumably played a role in this decision. It is also conceivable that they thought they had better options for maintaining Schülein in his position as managing director of the Association of Bavarian Textile Retailers if they were party members.

In addition to Otto Jordan Jr., Benno Schülein had other resourceful helpers: Rudolf and August Kammerer. Schülein had already met August Kammerer before the Nazis came to power. He was the Kammerer company's legal counsel and had a friendly relationship with both brothers. The company held on to Schülein as its lawyer until he was forced to dissolve his legal office in 1938. When in 1940 Schülein was conscripted to do forced labor, the Kammerer brothers hired him as their office manager.[34]

In March 1943, Schülein received his notice to report for deportation. He fled because he "did not want to suffer the same fate as his former associate Dr.

Josef Gunzenhäuser, who was murdered in Theresienstadt in 1942, only days after having been brought there."[35] Schülein later sketched his odyssey during the years that followed:

> First I spent a few days hidden by Frau Baier, wife of the Regional Court judge, and then by Dr. Hans Fetzer and Dr. Lothar Gerweck on Irnfriedstrasse. I then spent six weeks at Mr. Rudolf Kammerer's place in Denning [a suburb of Munich], where I had to stay in a darkened room for twelve hours a day. After that, I spent eight days in Geiselgasteig with Frau Mayor [*sic*] Bucher. When I was at risk of being discovered, I fled again back to Dr. Fetzer, from where I again went to Rudolf Kammerer in Denning on January 1, 1944. Since the Gestapo was on my tail, I had to flee yet again and managed to find refuge with an acquaintance, the present member of the Bavarian state parliament August Melchner, in Ottobrunn [a village just outside of Munich], as a stable hand and servant. I stayed there until I was liberated by the Americans when they came in on May 3, 1945. I was only able to persevere because my friends, Otto and Anny Jordan, provided me with what I needed. They alone knew about this.[36]

After the war, the financial auditor August Melchner was considered a co-founder of the Christian Social Union (CSU) political party in Upper Bavaria, although he was a member of the state parliament only for a short time, from 1949 to 1950. He died in 1967.[37]

Rudolf Kammerer arranged for Schülein to go into hiding. He organized the hiding place with his acquaintance Frau Baier and probably also the lodgings with Dr. Fetzer, who in turn knew Lothar Gerweck. This case illustrates the high proportion of couples in mixed marriages among the helpers. Fetzer's wife also worked as a Jewish forced laborer for the Kammerer company. Gerweck, as well, had a "privileged mixed marriage." His wife Ilse went into hiding with their daughters in early 1945.[38]

The greatest concern of Benno Schülein and his helpers were the denouncers. Otto and Anny Jordan's domestic worker had threatened to denounce them. Frau Baier explained later that Schülein had to leave her apartment suddenly "when a former tenant of mine . . . told me that he would have to—and he would—report to the police the fact that Dr. Schülein was hiding with me. Dr. Schülein, whom I informed immediately, of course, vanished from my apartment helter-skelter on the very same day at 8 o'clock in the evening. As far as I can remember he wandered around the Isar wetlands until he met Mr. Rudolf Kammerer that evening."[39]

At the Kammerers', Schülein had to remain silent the entire day, since the domestic help worked in the house and Rudolf and Siglinde Kammerer both worked during the day. They were very worried that the domestic help might hear sounds and report them to the Gestapo. In early May, Rudolf Kammerer's brother August was denounced by an employee of their company for hiding Schülein. Even though the denouncer, a mechanical fitter, had reported the wrong brother, it was certain that Rudolf Kammerer's house would also soon be searched.[40] Rudolf Kammerer helped not only his friend Benno Schülein, but also the jurist Dr. Fritz Kuhn, who had been a forced laborer for the Kammerer company since 1940. Kuhn was in a mixed marriage. In late 1941, Kuhn was supposed to be put in one of the Jewish internment camps. When Rudolf Kammerer heard about this, he set up a shelter for Kuhn in the basement of the factory and registered him matter-of-factly to the Gestapo as the night watchman for the Kammerer company. Consequently, Kuhn could return home to his wife in the evenings or, if necessary, spend the night in the company building.[41] Dr. Kuhn was a friend of Schülein and had probably already known Kammerer since before the war.

Building director Hans Günther had known the Kammerer brothers since the late 1920s. He worked for the company on a freelance basis after having lost his job with the city of Munich because his wife Margarethe was not "Aryan." Margarethe Günther was a forced laborer for the Kammerer company, but due to her poor health, Rudolf Kammerer let her work from home.[42] When she was scheduled for deportation in February 1945 within the final wave of deportations, Kammerer offered to hide her. Margarethe Günther did not accept his offer, but evaded deportation nonetheless by fleeing. Kammerer did not report her disappearance to the Gestapo until ten days later.[43] Kammerer also offered to hide Eduard Meyer, who was also in a mixed marriage, in 1945.[44] The vast majority of Jewish forced laborers working for Kammerer were in fact deported.

FAMOUS ARTIST AS A HELPER

When the deportation of the Jews of Munich began in 1941, Franz Herda had already helped a number of Jews, some of whom were total strangers to him. Before the war, someone he knew was denounced for "defiling the race" and was to be arrested. Herda hid him on short notice. When SA men knocked on Herda's door looking for the man, he told them that they "should go to hell" and put his acquaintance on a night train to Berlin that same evening.[45] When he heard about a Jewish craftsman who had been brought to the Dachau concentration camp for telling a joke about Goebbels, Herda went to the Gestapo and demanded that the man be released. He explained that these jokes were very popular among leading Nazis and he could offer a list of those who enjoyed hearing and telling such jokes. In such situations, Herda often mentioned that he had good connections to Hermann Göring. The craftsman was evidently released due to Herda's intervention.[46]

Herda did not invent the story about knowing Göring. In the First World War, he had served in Göring's flying squadron. Although he no longer had any contact to Göring, he was able to continually impress people by dropping Göring's name in conversations with Nazi officials. His self-confident manner at offices and government agencies might have come from the fact that Herda held a US passport, so he felt more secure than many Germans (at least until the two countries entered into a state of war in December 1941). He had a German father and an American mother and had been born in Brooklyn, New York, in 1897, but the family moved to Germany when he was still a child. After the First World War, he studied art and then settled in Munich as an artist.[47]

Through acquaintances, Herda met Albertine Gimpel, a Jew, in Munich in the mid-1930s. They became friends, and Herda promised Gimpel that he would help her if her situation in Nazi Munich became intolerable. When Gimpel received her notice in the mail that she was to report for the first transport to the East from Munich, she turned to Herda. When the bus that was picking up the Jews scheduled for deportation stopped at the "Jew house" where Gimpel lived, Franz Herda was waiting there, and he convinced the men that Gimpel had been struck from the transport list on orders of the Gestapo.[48] Gimpel was able to remain in Munich. In February 1942, she was put in the Berg am Laim camp and, after it was closed, in the building of the Jewish Community of Munich at Lindwurmstrasse 125.[49]

On May 13, 1943, the remaining residents at Lindwurmstrasse 125 were told to stay at home the following day.[50] Albertine Gimpel correctly presumed that another deportation was imminent. She had already been on the list for the transport in March 1943, but once again Franz Herda had managed to get her released "by twisting the facts," as she later wrote.[51] On the evening of May 13, Albertine Gimpel snuck out of the house and called Herda, who told her to wait for him in Luitpold Park at six o'clock in the morning. Herda presumed that the Gestapo was aware of his friendship with Gimpel, and he feared that they would soon come looking for her at his place, so he brought Gimpel to his friends, the Winklers. Eduard Winkler was also an artist. The Winklers were immediately willing to take Gimpel in. She stayed with them for several months.[52] Little by little, Albertine Gimpel started showing signs of the persistent stress. She later wrote about that time: "With every unexpected sound—and there were lots of them at the time in Munich—I was startled and expected to be discovered and arrested. Physical deprivation and the constant fear brought me down mentally and physically and I developed an acute nervousness."[53] When Herda was certain that the Gestapo would no longer look for Gimpel at his place, he brought

Albertine Gimpel, passport photo, ID card. Munich City Archive, DE-1992-KKD-1076-pb.

her to his studio on Gabelsbergerstrasse. By then, Max Bachmann lived there as well, whom Herda also protected from deportation.

Neither Bachmann nor Gimpel had food ration stamps, but Franz Herda received help from Rosa Marx, who owned a fabric store where Herda sometimes shopped. Rosa Marx lived with her Jewish husband, Justin, in a so-called privileged mixed marriage. She came from Lower Bavaria and had contacts there enabling her to trade fabric for food, which she made available for Munich Jews in the Berg am Laim, Milbertshofen, and Lindwurmstrasse internment camps. Her son, Richard Marx, took over the task of smuggling food into the camps, and he also provided food for Gimpel and Bachmann.[54]

When in May 1944 Albertine Gimpel's anxiety attacks became increasingly dramatic, Herda brought her to his daughter, Vera Manthey, in Umratshausen at Lake Chiemsee. Manthey lived there with her daughter on a farm. For her landlord, Manthey made up a story about a friend visiting from abroad.[55] From Umratshausen, Gimpel moved on to another friend of Franz Herda, the writer

Franz Herda in 1961. Private collection, courtesy of Christoph von Weitzel.

Friedrich Reck-Malleczewen, at the Poing estate near Truchtlaching in the Alz valley. Also near Lake Chiemsee, it was a remote area roughly ninety kilometers (fifty-six miles) southeast of Munich. Reck-Malleczewen was without a doubt one of the most colorful personalities in the German literary scene of his day.[56] He had first become known for his young people's and travel literature, but eventually also through the novel *Bockelson: Geschichte eines Massenwahns* (1937).[57] This satirical presentation of Hitler's rise to power, which Reck-Malleczewen had disguised as a story of Jan Bockelson, the "Anabaptist king of Münster," was not banned by the Nazis, as the censors evidently missed the subversive quality of the book,[58] but Reck-Malleczewen and his family were placed under observation by the Gestapo. This did not, however, keep them from taking in Albertine Gimpel. During the regular visits by the Gestapo, Gimpel had to run into the nearby woods and from there watch for the Gestapo vehicle to drive away before venturing back out.[59]

In December 1944, Friedrich Reck-Malleczewen was denounced, arrested, and imprisoned in the Dachau concentration camp. The denunciation, however, was not in connection to Albertine Gimpel's presence. Instead, Alfred Salat, director of Knorr & Hirth publishers, had denounced Reck-Malleczewen for "disparaging the German currency."[60] The two men had had an argument over the amount of royalties for a novel by Reck-Malleczewen. Dissatisfied with the publisher's offer, Reck-Malleczewen made a sarcastic comment about the reichsmark's dramatic loss in value and the high cost of living. After the writer's arrest, Franz Herda traveled to Berlin in hopes of taking advantage of his family relation to an officer in the Reich Security Main Office in order to get Reck-Malleczewen released, but to no avail. On March 10, 1945, Reck-Malleczewen's wife received news that her husband had died from enterocolitis in the Dachau concentration camp.[61]

Before his death, Reck-Malleczewen was able to send a letter to his wife, in which he implied that it would be better if Albertine Gimpel left the house. Irmgard Reck-Malleczewen nonetheless kept Albertine Gimpel in her home despite the acute danger for all involved. Franz Herda, for his part, did not know what else could be done. He had reached the limits of his network. "It was urgently necessary for me to change my lodgings, but that was not possible, as Poing was the last possible hiding place available for me," wrote Albertine Gimpel dryly about the final, most difficult months of her life in hiding.[62] Irmgard Reck-Malleczewen had to cope with the death of her husband, but despite the risk, she kept the Jewish woman in hiding until the end of the war.

Irmgard Reck-Malleczewen also knew that more than Albertine Gimpel was hidden on the Poing estate. Parts of her husband's diary were concealed in the barn and buried in the fields.[63] *Diary of a Man in Despair*, in which the author vented his entire hatred for Hitler, referring to the "Führer" with any and all imaginable obscenities, was published posthumously in 1947.[64] The work is not only a merciless reckoning with the Nazi leadership, but also with the society that endured the war to the end, in part fanatically and in part passively. Reck-Malleczewen was well aware that his words posed a great danger for him. "Heads roll for a bagatelle," he wrote in 1943, "and they roll especially fast because of aspersions cast on the Great General."[65]

Diary of a Man in Despair is a fierce broadside against the mass insanity, the bestial upstarts, and the marching hordes from the perspective of a "Bavarian landed gentry (*Junker*)," although the author was neither Bavarian nor a genuine Junker.[66] Reck-Malleczewen's feudal conservatism was expressed in his literary virtuosity. The value of his diary lies in his sharp powers of observation, in the presentation of everyday encounters with his fellow human beings, and in the biting irony with which he viewed Nazi society.

Alfred Salat, who had denounced Friedrich Reck-Malleczewen, was sentenced in 1948 to three years' imprisonment in his denazification proceedings.[67]

Salat was released rather quickly and joined the "Naumann circle."[68] This circle of former Nazis around Werner Naumann, undersecretary in Goebbels's propaganda ministry, included Wolfgang Diewerge, Werner Best, Friedrich Grimm, and Ernst Achenbach. The aim of the group was to undermine the Free Democratic Party (FDP) in the West German state of North Rhine–Westphalia and to reestablish old Nazis in positions of political leadership. The British put an end to this specter in 1953 when, exercising their Allied reserved rights, they arrested numerous members of the group.[69]

Franz Herda married Albertine Gimpel in 1948 and moved with her to New York. They could have attempted to marry earlier, as Herda was an American citizen. These marriages required authorization, but in some cases were successful.[70] It is not known why they did not try earlier.

When Albertine Gimpel went to Franz Herda's apartment in 1943, Max Bachmann was already hiding there, as previously mentioned. During the November pogrom of 1938, Bachmann had been arrested and had spent several weeks in the Dachau concentration camp. Starting in May 1941, he had been incarcerated in the Milbertshofen camp for five months, and he subsequently did forced labor for the Brettschneider company. For unknown reasons, he was supposed to be arrested in late June 1943, but he evaded arrest by going underground.[71] His non-Jewish wife reported his disappearance to the police and said that a suicide was likely. Bachmann was subsequently registered as deceased.[72] He was at first hidden by Franz Herda. When the house in which Herda lived was hit by a bomb, Bachmann fled into the Bavarian Forest, where he remained on the run, "moving from village to village and farmer to farmer," until he was liberated by American troops.[73] He initially financed his flight by selling valuables he still owned, such as jewelry. Later on, non-Jewish relatives gave him money.[74] Bachmann returned to Munich in 1945 and started to reestablish his livelihood. His struggle for compensation for the persecution he suffered is examined in greater depth in chapter 11.

JEWISH U-BOATS IN 1943

Varying Living Conditions and Courses of Action in Munich, Berlin, and Vienna

Why did only very few of the 140 Munich Jews whose names were on the deportation lists between March and June 1943 try to flee to avoid deportation, whereas there was a mass exodus of Jews in Berlin prior to the final deportation?

When thousands of people sought to go underground in Berlin in February 1943, there were forgery workshops and an underground market for lodgings, false identity documents, and food ration and clothing cards. Countless people had already gone into hiding, asking friends and acquaintances for help. This led to the emergence of comprehensive networks connecting the remaining Jews and their helpers, which were lacking in other regions. Saving Jews became a matter of conscience for many Berliners, or a spontaneous decision for others. People asked within their circle of friends who might be willing to take someone in for a few days or even longer. "Referral chains"[75] or "help chains"[76] thus developed through which those seeking help were referred to potential helpers. Emerging networks and individual helpers working independently of one another activated local and regional contacts, sought lodgings, and kept on the lookout for like-minded people. Helpers asked friends and relatives to offer up their ID cards to be forged; food ration cards were collected and counterfeited; contacts were used to gain access to official forms and printing facilities, as well as to traders on the illicit underground market. Although some—mainly Christian—aid networks had emerged in other parts of Germany as well (see chapter 7), these "referral chains" and coordinated efforts remained largely confined to Berlin.

Saving people in hiding had become a task for the organized resistance, and new resistance groups developed from actions to save those in hiding. A number of networks, such as the Uncle Emil group or the circle of helpers from the Confessing Church in Berlin-Dahlem, looked after Jews in hiding.[77] In the fall of 1943, the group of helpers around Hans Winkler, which called itself the High Stakes Savings Club (Sparverein grosser Einsatz),[78] and Werner Scharff's network together founded the Community for Peace and Reconstruction, which hid many people and also distributed flyers against Nazism.[79] Edith Wolff, a young Zionist, took on the task of taking care of many needs of the Zionist youth group Chug Chaluzi (Circle of Pioneers) in an attempt to save young Jews. Wolff was one of the founders of the group, which had formed during the Factory Operation. She scouted out hiding places and knew people who sold food ration cards and counterfeited identity cards. Through contacts to helpers in the Confessing Church, she had already procured a passport in 1942 for her friend Jizchak Schwersenz, who was the leader of Chug Chaluzi.[80] The graphic artist Cioma Schönhaus reworked ID cards that Franz Kaufmann, who was persecuted as a non-Aryan Christian, was able to procure on the illicit underground market.[81] Schönhaus's forgeries reached a level of perfection that assured the survival of many people.[82]

These activities intensified dramatically during the Factory Operation. "The Jews are disappearing in throngs," noted Ruth Andreas-Friedrich in her diary entry for December 2, 1942, and continued:

> Ghastly rumors are current about the fate of the evacuees—mass shootings and death by starvation, tortures, and gassings. . . . Any hide-out is a gift from heaven. . . . The Jakobs [the family of the dentist Dr. Hugo Jakob] have abandoned their apartment. For weeks now they have been living in a tumble-down tool shed. By turns one or two members of the family camp on our narrow guest sofa. . . . "We've got to get stamps, we've got to get stamps!" Frank urges [Frank Matthis, a doctor and friend of Ruth Andreas-Friedrich]. "I have a place for two to sleep tomorrow; for three the day after. Starting December 15 there's a good safe apartment available in Lankwitz."[83]

Many people helped without demanding anything in return. But many others viewed support for Jews in hiding as an opportunity for some bartering. The line separating the two groups was not a clear one. Even largely altruistic helpers sometimes received—or needed—some things in return. In Berlin in 1942–43, many people—including fanatical Nazis—saw an opportunity to earn some money in this way.[84] They received payment for hiding people or obtained a family's last pieces of jewelry in return for providing lodgings. Very high rents were sometimes charged even for short-term quarters.[85] Ever-present antisemitic stereotypes of the "rich Jew" may have encouraged these demands, and the antisemitic propaganda about Jewish fortunes ostensibly acquired unfairly and at the cost of the German people might have soothed many a guilty conscience.

In fact, more than a few Berlin U-boats worked in some way to earn their keep.[86] Others were lucky and still had access to money. Assets could be rescued through non-Jewish friends, and sometimes hidden Jews received payment from the people to whom they had entrusted their possessions for storage.[87] Such people were known colloquially as "*Verwarier*" or "*Aufbewarier*" ("custodaryans"), a play on words combining *Verwahrer* (custodian) and *Arier* (Aryan, non-Jew). Such custodaryans kept valuables and household items in safekeeping for Jews. This was a common occurrence; before being deported, Jews would often deposit their last remaining possessions with non-Jews they knew in hopes of retrieving them upon their return.

In a society marked by unlimited war and boundless shortages, there were no limits to the fantasy of the bartering. Marie Jalowicz Simon was referred by one of her helpers, Benno Heller, a doctor in a mixed marriage, to a former patient of his. For a fee, this former patient, a waitress, referred Jalowicz Simon to one of her guests, a Nazi director of a small company who was seeking a young woman to keep him company and run the household.[88] Jalowicz Simon was relieved that this deal did not involve sexual services, since the man had syphilis, though she had, in fact, been previously confronted with such a demand from some helpers—as did many other Jews in hiding as well.[89] Not only male helpers, but women, too, sought sexual contact with the men and women they hid.[90]

Some Berliners traded food ration stamps and clothing coupons, sold ID cards and passports, or acted as human smugglers. Nelly Orbach procured forged ID papers on the illicit underground market for her son and herself, and the marketeer gave her the address of a man who would take them in for a while. According to the marketeer, the potential landlord was not at all altruistic, but "very money hungry," thus many Jews had already passed through his place.[91] Others bought ID papers illegally that let them pose as French or Italian foreign workers.[92] One officer sold military papers for 4,000 reichsmarks each.[93] Lotte Bamberg paid an official in the armaments ministry who was willing to strike names from the deportation list for a fee.[94] Aside from contacts to non-Jews, financial means were especially important for opening up possibilities for Berlin U-boats. (Ideally, they would also look "like a Gentile."[95]) Many of them needed large sums of money for a prolonged life in the underground. A woman in Berlin reflected on this situation in a letter she wrote in 1946 to relatives abroad: "Of course I had the means, once we went wandering. But it was taking too long. We hoped back then that it would not last more than another six months. And then it turned into more than two years, and food was getting prohibitively expensive. And even the deepest well dries up."[96] In contrast to Berlin, money was secondary in Munich; appropriate contacts to non-Jews appeared to be much more important.

As compared with Berlin, the number of Jews still living in Munich was small, especially since most of Munich's Jews had already been deported by late 1942. Most Munich Jews were now living largely isolated from the non-Jewish population in the Jewish camps on the outskirts of the city. This was very different from the situation in Berlin, which also made it easier to monitor the Jews in Munich than those in the Reich capital. Because of their small numbers and isolation, little awareness of this group developed in Munich and no shadow economy emerged. There was no—or too little—perceived need. Also, the absence of a shadow economy was a factor that discouraged Munich Jews from going underground. False ID papers, no matter what quality, were difficult to procure in Munich,[97] so most Jews in hiding did not even attempt to obtain them. As the percentage of Jews remaining in Berlin with respect to the total population of the city was so much greater than in Munich, far more Berliners were confronted with the question of "Should I help?" than were the people of Munich. This was the case especially for the period of the factory raids in February 1943, when many Berliners witnessed the brutality with which Jews were loaded onto trucks and carted off.[98]

Many Berlin Jews had friends or relatives who had already gone into hiding or wanted to. This generated a certain dynamic, in which Jews who were considering going underground followed the example of other U-boats. Valerie Wolffenstein later wrote that the flight of others whom she and her sister knew encouraged them to venture such a step themselves.[99] The same was true for Auguste Bendheim.[100] Once Jews went underground, they could gain important information from other "illegals."[101] In contrast, the group of those who received their deportation notices in March 1943 in Munich might have felt that their fate was inescapable. Their family, relatives, and friends were already gone, and so most acquiesced in their deportation. The few Munich Jews who went into hiding in 1943 had altruistically motivated close friends or a partner or spouse on whom they could rely. Last-minute escapes might have also been prevented by the security measures in the Berg am Laim camp during the final major deportation in 1943. In Berlin, on the other hand, so many people attempted to evade the deportations in 1943 that one woman in hiding feared that many of them were not prepared for an "illegal" life and would endanger their helpers as well as other U-boats.[102] Many of the Berlin Jews who went underground at the time of the Factory Operation were arrested only a short time later, as far more U-boats were arrested in the capital city in 1943 than in 1944 or 1945.[103] Richard Lutjens therefore posits that those who avoided arrest in 1943 became increasingly adept at organizing their "illegal" life and avoiding being discovered and arrested.[104]

In this context, a comparison with Vienna is helpful, where in 1939 more Jews had still been living than in Berlin.[105] The destruction of the Jewish community in Vienna starting in 1938, after the German annexation of Austria, was pursued particularly "forcefully and radically," a practice that has been referred to as the "Vienna methods" or the "Vienna model."[106] In the fall of 1942, Adolf Eichmann, head of the Judenreferat, the Jewish Affairs Department IV B 4 in the Reich Security Main Office (RSHA), brought his former colleague in Vienna, Alois Brunner, to Berlin. Brunner had been the director of the Central Office for Jewish Emigration in Vienna. With his transfer to the RSHA in Berlin (and later to Greece and France), these "Vienna methods" were also applied in other regions. These "methods" also involved the use of Jewish collaborators as snatchers (*Greifer*), some of whom were also transferred from Vienna to Berlin.[107]

When Brunner and his staff left Vienna and headed to Berlin in October 1942, the mass deportations in Vienna had largely been completed. Nowhere else had they started as early as in Vienna. More than 1,500 Jews were deported to Nisko in 1939, and more than five thousand to Poland in early 1941.[108] Of the more than ninety thousand Jews who were still living in Vienna in 1939, barely eight thousand were still there in January 1943, most of whom were in mixed marriages.[109] Although smaller transports to Theresienstadt and Auschwitz did take place in early 1943, those in power felt that a Factory Operation like the one in Berlin was no longer necessary.[110] According to Hans Safrian, "by fine-tuning the 'Vienna Model' into merciless manhunts, they already completed the mass deportations from the Ostmark [Austria] at a time when even the expulsion bureaucrats in the capital of the Reich lagged far behind."[111] Based on the present state of research, more than 1,600 people lived in Vienna at least temporarily as U-boats. The number who survived must be assumed to be far lower.[112] Since the deportations there had started very early, many Jews in Vienna—and all of Austria—fled as early as 1941–42 rather than in 1943.[113] In this regard, a similar picture exists for Munich. Even if individual U-boats in Vienna managed to acquire false ID papers[114] and food and ration stamps on the illegal underground market,[115] structures like those in Berlin did not exist there. It is particularly striking that in Vienna, a large majority of U-boats spent extended periods of time in just one or two hiding places and had a small number of helpers.[116] Those in hiding could not change their hiding places multiple times through "referral chains" and networks. What was necessary in many cases—as in Munich—was "earlier friendships with non-Jews."[117]

AIR WAR AND FLIGHT: OPTIONS AND DANGERS FOR JEWS HIDING IN THE CITIES

Especially in Berlin, but also in other cities, many U-boats lost their hiding places and even their lives in the numerous air raids.[118] As the number of raids increased in the course of the war, so did this danger. The U-boats had to avoid the air raid shelters since they feared both ID checks by the air raid wardens and being recognized in the shelters by people they knew.[119] Those who nevertheless dared to enter the shelters often sought a particularly dark corner.[120] But while the air raids posed great dangers for Jews in hiding, they also opened up new courses of action.

The major air raids on Munich began late in the summer of 1942. Further waves of attacks followed on March 9–10, 1943, and then in September–October 1943. The heaviest destruction resulted from the days-long bombings by the

US Army Air Forces in June and July 1944.[121] The attack by the bombers of the British Royal Air Force on March 9, 1943, took place shortly before the last mass deportation from Munich. It interfered with preparations only to the extent that the scheduled deportation had to be postponed for a couple of days.[122] However, the air raids in March 1943 thwarted the flight plans of Ilselotte Nussbaum and Walter Geismar. Nussbaum worked for the Kammerer company and was supposed to be deported with her mother in March 1943. Her boyfriend, Walter Geismar, had been exempted from the deportation because he had the status of a *Geltungsjude*. He had planned to hide Nussbaum in a garden house of relatives in Giesing and from there to bring her to friends in Schrobenhausen. This was not possible, however, since the allotment garden in Giesing had been burned down a short time earlier in an air raid.[123] Ilselotte Nussbaum and her mother Olga were deported and murdered in Auschwitz.[124] There might have also been others who had their suitcases packed and were ready to flee, but who suffered a fate similar to Ilselotte Nussbaum's.

Franz Herda's artist studio in Munich was bombed out in July 1944. Hence, Max Bachmann also lost his hiding place. As bombs hailed down in the summer of 1944, he decided to leave the city and flee into the Bavarian Forest. Like Bachmann, Marion V., a woman in hiding in Munich, survived the air raids in 1944 outside the air raid shelters. She later wrote about this time:

> I remember that sometime in the summer I would lie down on the floor of the balcony to get some fresh air. Fear of being seen followed me everywhere. During the numerous air raids I remained in the apartment to avoid the nosey bodies. I crawled into a large wardrobe in the hallway. It shook back and forth during the air raids. One day the top floor of the building was set on fire from a hit and I heard the terrible crashing sounds as if all the housewives had thrown all their dishes and pots into the courtyard. In spite of everything those were my calmest moments, since I knew that no Gestapo man could show up right then.[125]

Others in hiding also expressed this brief feeling of relief, rest, and respite during the attacks.[126]

In Hamburg, many Jews took advantage of the chaos after the major air raids in July–August 1943 to go into hiding.[127] Many of those who fled were Jews in mixed marriages who feared that it was only a matter of time until they, too, would be deported. They mingled with people who had been bombed out, who had lost all their possessions. It is certain that among them there was at least one person who had escaped from the Fuhlsbüttel concentration camp as early as October 1942.[128] Although the Gestapo searched for them, at least forty-four Jews remained missing.[129] Buildings in ruins and half-buried cellars offered short-term refuge for people on the run.[130] In Berlin, Ilselotte Themal used the air raids on Hamburg as an opportunity to acquire false ID papers for herself and her husband. She mentioned an address on a completely bombed-out Hamburg street, explaining that her emergency housing in Berlin had also just been destroyed the previous night. She said that she and her husband had lost everything and her husband had suffered a severe nervous breakdown from the repeated bombing. She received papers and food ration stamps for two weeks.[131] Another woman in hiding in Berlin searched through corpses lying on the street following an air raid in hopes of finding ID cards that she could use to create a new identity for herself.[132] More than twenty people in Frankfurt used the air raids of March 1944 as an incentive to go into hiding. As in Hamburg, these were Jews in mixed marriages or those deemed *Geltungsjuden*.[133] In Dresden, Victor Klemperer and other Dresden Jews in mixed marriages took advantage of the air raids of February 1945 to flee. They had received notice to report for deportation only days earlier.[134]

The growing number of air raids made life in the major cities increasingly dangerous, but it now offered plausible explanations for people with unfamiliar faces and no identification papers. Many people had lost all their possessions and had fled to friends and relatives outside the cities. Lilly Neumark went into hiding during the Factory Operation, and her flight led her to a town in Thuringia in February 1945. There she learned that she could easily register an address with the police and receive food ration cards. She was not even asked for verification.[135] In Berlin after the bombings, Anna Drach wrote, "it somehow was easier to be out on the street, since so many people were bombed out and running around on the street with the last of their worldly goods. The police were no longer as interested in finding Jews as they were in finding deserters."[136]

AFTER THE MASS DEPORTATIONS: MORE FLIGHTS 1943–1944

Once the mass deportations had been concluded, Jews who had lost the protection of a mixed marriage either through divorce or the death of the non-Jewish spouse found themselves in the crosshairs of the Gestapo. Many of them had already been deported in 1942, especially if the marriage had been childless and considered nonprivileged. The deportations of these Jews from former mixed marriages intensified in 1943, and by December of that year, all Jews in dissolved mixed marriages, except those who had been in privileged mixed marriages and had underage children, were slated for deportation to Theresienstadt.[137] Thus in the second half of 1943 and in 1944, it was predominantly Jews from dissolved mixed marriages who went underground, as well as Jews in existing mixed marriages who feared an impending arrest. Also, as of 1944, non-Jewish husbands in mixed marriages and half-Jewish males (*Mischlinge*) were being brought to the Organization Todt (OT, named after its leader, Fritz Todt) work camps, thus more and more family members of people in these categories could also be found among those who fled.

With regard to the Jews who had lost the protection of a mixed marriage, it is striking that some already received their notice to report for deportation shortly after the death of the spouse or the divorce, whereas others remained undetected for months or even years. Some were not to be deported until February 1945. There were various reasons for this delay: arbitrariness and increasing administrative chaos; the protection offered by underage children who were considered first-degree *Mischlinge*; and the continuing use of forced labor. The complexity of this situation is illustrated by the following description of the fate of Elfriede Seitz and Else Gerlach, who went into hiding in 1943 and 1944, respectively, in Munich.

After Heinrich Seitz, a railway inspector, died in March 1943, only two months passed before his Jewish widow, Elfriede Seitz, received her notice on May 13, 1943, to prepare for deportation.[138] The Seitzes' daughter had emigrated to England in 1939. With the help of her artist friend Eugen Kubertzky, Elfriede Seitz fled to the home of a good friend of her husband, Alois Rauch, in Grucking near Erding (roughly fifty kilometers [thirty miles] northeast of Munich). Alois and his wife Maria ran a farm and a small inn there. Heinrich Seitz and Alois Rauch had known each other since the First World War, during which Rauch had served under Seitz, who had been a captain. They had remained in contact ever since. As late as the early 1940s, Alois Rauch had visited Heinrich and Elfriede Seitz in Munich, although he had already joined the Nazi Party in 1933.[139] When Elfriede Seitz showed up in Grucking in May 1943, the Rauchs took her in and at first hid her in a room. As it was not possible to keep this up very long, they passed Elfriede Seitz off as Alois Rauch's aunt. She then lived and worked on the farm as Maria Maier. When she became seriously ill in January 1945, her helpers decided to run the risk of her being discovered and took her to the hospital, where they also had her admitted as Maria Maier. They were lucky that no one asked any questions. Elfriede Seitz was treated and then returned to Grucking, where she remained until the area was liberated.[140]

In contrast to Elfriede Seitz, who lived alone, the Jewish widow Else Gerlach lived with her adult son Franz. Her non-Jewish husband, Ferdinand

Gerlach, had been a judge on the Reich court (*Reichsgericht*) before 1933 and had died in Munich in 1941. Else Gerlach was scheduled for deportation in January 1944. Her son Franz brought her to his fiancée's sister, who lived with her husband on a secluded estate near Assling (a village forty-five kilometers [twenty-eight miles] southeast of Munich). He told the Gestapo that his mother had gone to live with relatives in Cologne.[141] In addition to these two women, other Jews from Munich whose mixed marriages ended through death or divorce also went into hiding.

Starting in April 1944, non-Jewish husbands in mixed marriages and male *Mischlinge* were conscripted to do forced labor for the Organization Todt (OT), which was in charge of large construction projects.[142] At first these conscriptions proceeded rather slowly, but starting in the fall of 1944, men were called up throughout the Reich on orders of Himmler and brought to the OT work camps, many of which were in Thuringia (for example, Tiefenort and Clausthal-Zellerfeld). Others, especially those who had been called up early on, had to carry out fortification work behind the front lines in France or Holland, and some were assigned to forced labor locally, for example, in Hamburg.[143] The number of those conscripted varied from region to region.[144] A rather large group of men from Munich was put in the OT camp in Tiefenort and had to do forced labor in a salt mine. Walter N. recalled that he received a notice on October 13 instructing him to report to the Gestapo headquarters in Munich on October 19. Together with "roughly 120 men" between the ages of twenty and fifty, he had to board a train on the evening of October 19.[145] Walter N. described the situation: "The general mood was extremely gloomy; no one knew where the train was headed, and we had terrible premonitions."[146] Hans Armin Schrey was also brought to Tiefenort. Since he spoke of a transport of only about sixty people, it can be assumed that there were several transports from Munich. Schrey managed to escape from Tiefenort early in 1945.[147] In view of the imminent transfer to a work camp, many *Mischlinge* throughout the Reich went into hiding in 1944. They were not at all certain if they were truly "only" going to a forced labor camp, as rumors had long been circulating that *Mischlinge* were going to be treated the same way as Jews.[148]

One man from Munich who fled under these circumstances was Richard Marx, who went to Berlin in November 1944.[149] He had previously performed forced labor in a workshop that produced spare parts for airplanes. He had often been assigned the Sunday shift, during which he worked alone. Thus, he was able to write a letter on business letterhead without being discovered, stating that he needed to travel to Berlin for matters "essential to the war effort."[150] Richard Marx wanted to go to Vera Manthey, the daughter of Franz Herda, who had returned to Berlin from Upper Bavaria. The two of them lived with Vera Manthey's mother and later with an elderly woman in the Friedenau section of Berlin. In Berlin, Richard Marx suffered an appendicitis attack that required an operation. Luckily, he was able to disguise his true identity in the hospital in which he was treated.[151] In April 1945, he returned to Bavaria, again with a forged authorization letter, and remained hidden during the final weeks of the war on a farm near Moosburg.[152]

In the fall of 1944, in the Rhineland, in contrast to the situation in Munich and other parts of Germany, there were systematic arrests of *Mischlinge* and non-Jewish men in mixed marriages, as well as of the remaining *Geltungsjuden* and Jewish men and women in mixed marriages.[153] The wave of arrests known as the September Operation focused especially on the cities of Cologne, Düsseldorf, Essen, and Bonn.[154] As Maximilian Strnad has shown, this measure, which involved all of Military District IV, was carried out for reasons of military strategy. Jews and people related to Jews were considered security risks in view of the approaching front and were therefore to be removed.[155] In Cologne, mixed-marriage couples and their families received notice in mid-September to report to the Cologne-Müngersdorf predeportation internment camp. Some of the non-Jewish spouses were later released from the camp. From Cologne-Müngersdorf and other internment camps, people were deported to various OT labor camps, in particular Kassel-Bettenhausen and Lenne near Hannover.[156]

In light of this situation, there was a major wave of escapes in the Rhineland region during the fall of 1944.[157] In Düsseldorf, only about half of those called upon to report to the authorities actually showed up.[158] When the RSHA finally decreed that all Jews living in mixed marriages throughout the Reich were to be deported to Theresienstadt by February 15, 1945,[159] all of the Jewish spouses in mixed marriages in other areas also received deportation notices. Within the course of these final deportations in February 1945, numerous Jews in Munich and elsewhere went into hiding.

FIVE

EVADING THE FINAL DEPORTATIONS IN FEBRUARY 1945

IN FEBRUARY 1945, THE GESTAPO ordered that the remaining Jewish spouses in mixed marriages throughout the Reich be deported for "forced labor deployment abroad."[1] All the remaining *Geltungsjuden* were also threatened with deportation. Dozens of Munich Jews ignored orders to appear for transport to Theresienstadt and went underground. The wave of Munich Jews who fled thus reached its peak in early 1945. Nevertheless, in February 1945, eighty-three Jews were deported from Munich to Theresienstadt, fifty-three of whom were from Munich and the others from Augsburg.[2] Not only in Munich, but in other cities as well where deportation trains departed bound for Theresienstadt, numerous Jews did not comply with the call for them to report for deportation.

Jews who decided to go into hiding in early 1945 did so under very different conditions than those who had dared to take that step three years earlier. Germany's defeat was in the offing, and it was a matter of staying underground only for a limited period of time. The prospects were good for those avoiding deportation in this way. Based on all that had been heard about Theresienstadt, however, even if Jews reckoned with good chances of surviving there until the war ended, they could not know for sure what living conditions they would face or if they would survive until liberation. Victor Klemperer and many of the other Dresden Jews who were supposed to be deported in early 1945 were convinced that deportation "is without exception regarded as a death march."[3] The common decision to go underground was, therefore, not exceptional to Munich. In Hamburg, dozens of Jews evaded the deportations, and hundreds went underground in Berlin.[4]

There were substantial differences, however, in how the deportation orders were implemented throughout the Reich. Due to wartime destruction, hardly any further deportations left Berlin bound for Theresienstadt, and, in addition, large-scale arrests "with the remaining Gestapo personnel were barely possible in view of the widespread destruction, unremitting air raids, and increasingly unreliable transportation system."[5] There were also no further deportations from Vienna.[6] In this final phase of the war, a great deal depended on the zeal and capacities of local authorities to continue the persecution: "There could be differences even within one district: in one town, the majority of intermarried Jews could be deported, whereas in a neighboring city, a significantly smaller number had to join the transport."[7] A majority of the remaining Jews in Hildesheim were deported, whereas in nearby Hannover, only about 35 percent boarded the train to Theresienstadt.[8] Substantial numbers of Jews continued to be deported from Frankfurt and Leipzig.[9] In Breslau, numerous Jews in mixed marriages were forced to participate in a three-day foot march to the Gross-Rosen concentration camp in January 1945.[10] Up to the very end, there were great regional differences in how the deportations were conducted.

The percentage of Jews in Munich who were deported in early 1945 was lower than the percentage of Jews deported from other regions of the Reich.[11] The apparatus of persecution had been weakened, and the will to continue the persecution was not as strong as in the previous years. The feared Aryanization Office in Munich had been closed in the summer of 1943. Facing imminent defeat in early 1945, many Gestapo officers feared they would soon be held accountable for their actions. Some might have thought that a show of leniency could pay off in the near future.[12] At times this strategy worked; some of the Munich Jews deported in 1945 testified that the Gestapo man accompanying their train had treated them well and that they were able to go into a restaurant during one of the stops.[13] Despite the weakening of the apparatus, however, numerous notices to report for deportation were issued. In February 1945, two deportation trains left Munich bound for Theresienstadt. Among those deported were seriously ill women with their small children.[14]

In this situation, going underground seemed to many to be the better option. There are thirty-nine documented cases of Munich Jews who did so, but the actual number was probably higher. In early 1945, there were still 453 Jews living in Munich, fifty-three of whom were eventually deported.[15] Of the remaining four hundred, many never received a deportation notice, in part because mail delivery was no longer reliable or else because they were deferred from deportation.[16] So even if one assumes that the majority of the four hundred Jews who were not deported had either been exempted from deportation or had not received the notice, it seems likely that more than thirty-nine of them went underground.[17]

Some of the later escapes will be presented below, including what is probably the best-known story of an escape helper in Munich. For this reason, the cemetery caretaker Karl Schörghofer will be treated separately. He hid a whole group of young people, mostly children of couples in mixed marriages, on the grounds of the Munich Jewish cemetery.

GOING INTO HIDING IN THE CHAOS OF THE FINAL MONTHS OF THE WAR

Among Munich's Jews who went underground in early 1945 was the doctor Magdalena Schwarz. Schwarz had been divorced from her non-Jewish husband, Ludwig Schwarz, in 1937 and lived with her daughter in Munich. With her mixed marriage having been dissolved, her situation became difficult.[18] When all Jewish doctors had their license to practice medicine revoked in 1938, she was authorized, as a so-called treater of the sick, to continue to treat only Jewish patients (see chapter 1). After a conviction for "defiling the race," she was imprisoned in the Fuhlsbüttel concentration camp from May 1939 to January 1940.[19] As of 1941, she worked mostly as a doctor in the Berg am Laim and Milbertshofen camps. In 1942, she helped her friend Else Behrend-Rosenfeld escape to Berlin.[20] In addition to the fact that her daughter was considered a first-degree *Mischling*, her position as a doctor served to protect her until early 1945, since at that time there were only three Jewish doctors left in Munich.[21] According to her own testimony, in February 1945, she used forged medical certificates to get many other Jews released from the final transports before she finally received her own notice to report for deportation.[22]

In this situation, Schwarz received help from a colleague. Professor Kurt Schneider, chief physician in the psychiatry department of the Schwabing Hospital in Munich, hid her in the secure psychiatric ward for women. Schwarz wrote to her daughter from the hospital that she planned to commit suicide.[23] But she survived without being discovered. After liberation, she again worked as a doctor in Munich and cared for some of the Munich Jews who, like herself, had survived in hiding. In the postwar trials, she became one of the most significant witnesses against the personnel of the Aryanization Office and the Gestapo.[24]

Little is known about Schwarz's helper, Kurt Schneider. It cannot be determined how well he knew Schwarz and why he decided to help her. It can only be assumed that he offered assistance as a colleague and that he had an excellent opportunity to hide someone. Schneider left Munich after the war and took up a professorial chair in psychiatry at the University of Heidelberg.[25] In his

Magdalena Schwarz, ID card, 1939. Munich City Archive, DE-1992-KKD-3937-pb.

personnel file, coworkers referred to him as a serious, quiet, and modest man.[26] He was able to protect his psychiatric patients from the reach of the Reich Commissioner for Sanatoriums and Nursing Homes by repeatedly asserting that the psychiatry ward was not a sanatorium or nursing home, and the patients were not in need of long-term care, but instead were people with temporary, acute sicknesses.[27] He understood that patients transferred to a sanatorium or nursing home faced death in the Nazi eugenics program.

Cäcilie Langenwalter also received her order to report for deportation in February 1945. Together with her non-Jewish husband, the painting conservator Josef Langenwalter, she sought helpers who could hide her temporarily. In their desperation, the couple did not shy away from approaching strangers. Karl Rieger later testified that his daughter, who worked as a hairdresser, had been asked during a house call for a customer "if she knew of anyone who could hide a Jewish woman."[28] She discussed the matter with her parents, and a short time later, Langenwalter moved into the apartment that the Riegers shared with their daughter, who had been bombed out of her own apartment.[29] Langenwalter lived with the Rieger family for several weeks, but then changed her hiding place after the building the Riegers lived in suffered bomb damage.[30] Two weeks before the war ended, she moved to a colleague of her husband, an art dealer named Theodor Heller. The Langenwalters were passed off in the building as Herr and Frau Burger, who had supposedly lost their apartment and all their possessions in the bombings.[31]

Rosa Vetter received a call in January 1945 from an acquaintance who told her that the deportation of Jews in mixed marriages was imminent. The caller, architect Otto Roth (brother of the poet Eugen Roth), advised her to feign suicide and go underground.[32] Born in 1907, Vetter, a Munich Jew, had been living since 1933 with her non-Jewish husband in Traunstein, a small city one hundred kilometers (about sixty miles) southeast of Munich. She had been performing forced labor in a knitted goods factory since September 1942. "I did not want to suffer the same fate as much of my closest family—as my mother, three brothers, and one sister had died in concentration camps—so I followed the advice of Herr Roth," Rosa Vetter later wrote about her decision.[33] Her father, a furniture factory owner, Emanuel Weiss, had already died in 1925. Her mother, Jeanette Weiss, and her sister Julie had been deported to Theresienstadt. One brother had been murdered in Dachau.[34] It is not known where her two other brothers died. When had she last heard anything from a member of her family? Although in January 1945 she did not yet know with any certainty about the death of her relatives, she reckoned with the worst. It did not take long for Rosa Vetter to decide where she could find refuge. Her old friend Gisela Scherer from Munich and the friend's sister Josy Scherer-Hoffmann had already taken her in during the pogrom in November 1938. She had stayed with them for ten months and had not returned to Traunstein until shortly before the war started.[35] Six and a half years after the pogrom, the two sisters did not hesitate to hide Rosa Vetter again.

Justin Marx, a Jewish businessman, had met his future wife, Rosa Hörhammer, a Gentile from Lower Bavaria, at the Oktoberfest, and they had married in 1923.[36] Ten years later, in May 1933, the couple canceled the membership of their children—seven-year-old Elsa and nine-year-old Richard—in the Jewish community.[37] Since 1935, their two children had been considered *Mischlinge*. Their marriage was a "privileged mixed marriage." Justin and Rosa Marx's business, a shop for woolens and knitwear, had been registered under Rosa Marx's name since 1934.[38] They had done all this in hopes of protecting their family and their livelihood from Nazi persecution. Starting in 1938, Rosa Marx was continually questioned about suspicion of Jewish influence on their business, so the couple claimed that they were separated.[39] Richard Marx would secretly sneak his father into the apartment late in the evening and back out early in the morning.[40]

Starting in early 1941, Justin Marx had to perform forced labor. He first worked on the construction of the Milbertshofen barracks camp.[41] Starting in June 1941, he worked for the Weber painting contractor and was then transferred in August 1943 to the Centa Triendl company, which sold linens and mattresses.[42] When in January 1945 Justin Marx received a notice to report for deportation, he went underground. He hid with a communist working-class family in Neuaubing, a suburb of Munich.[43] He had another hiding place in Deisenhofen, at the southern periphery of the city, but while there, he was often secretly with his wife, who had been bombed out and was living with relatives in Munich.[44] Justin and Rosa Marx remained in Munich after 1945 and continued to run their woolens and knitwear business.[45]

Before going underground in early 1945, Siegfried Neuland, a Jewish lawyer from Munich, had already arranged a hiding place for his daughter Charlotte with Zenzi Hummel, his brother's former housekeeper, on a farm in Franconia.[46] He had lost the protection of having a mixed marriage because his wife, Margarete, had divorced him.[47] Neuland had been compelled to discontinue his work as a so-called legal advisor (*Rechtskonsulent*)—as Jews were no longer permitted to work as lawyers—for the rapidly shrinking Jewish community in February 1943. He was conscripted to perform forced labor for the Kammerer company. Neuland worked in the tinning department, and the extremely unhealthy work caused him to gradually lose his eyesight.[48] Walter Geismar, who also worked for Kammerer, later described Neuland's workplace as a "veritable hell."[49]

According to the recollections of his daughter, Charlotte Knobloch, Neuland went underground prior to the final deportations in 1945 with the help of Soviet forced laborers. He was then able to hide in the attic of friends in Gauting, a suburb of Munich.[50] These friends had already given refuge to him and his daughter during the pogrom in November 1938. In the final stage of the war, he needed treatment for his eye condition.[51] Neuland stopped working for the Kammerer company in April 1944,[52] presumably due to his poor health. It can no longer be determined how he came into contact with the Soviet forced laborers or whether he had gone underground prior to early 1945. It is also possible that the assistance Neuland received from Soviet forced laborers should be dated to the period in which they worked together for Kammerer and not to his time underground.

In late February 1945, after the last deportation trains had already left Munich, Neuland was evidently no longer able to postpone medical treatment. He later wrote: "Around February 25, 1945, I was operated on by Professor Dr. Meissner in the relocated eye clinic in Beuerberg."[53] No information is available about the circumstances under which he went from Gauting to Beuerberg or if he hid his true identity. The Munich eye clinic was evacuated during the war to the abbey of the Salesian Sisters in Beuerberg, a small town on Lake Starnberg. Located in the abbey at the end of the war were a military hospital, the Munich eye clinic, teachers and students of the Max Josef Stift (an academic high school in Munich), as well as a large number of nuns who had been taken in as war refugees and expellees.[54] Siegfried Neuland would later play a major role in rebuilding the Jewish community in Munich. He also represented numerous survivors as a lawyer in compensation matters.

POSSIBLE COURSES OF ACTION IN THE FINAL PHASE OF THE WAR: A GROWING WILLINGNESS TO HELP?

Many Jews who went into hiding late in the war remained in Munich (or, as in the case of Rosa Vetter, traveled there) rather than seeking to leave the city. This pertains not only to the cases presented in this chapter, but also to other Jews who went underground in February 1945.[55] This might have been dependent on individual opportunities for hiding, but in view of the frequent air raids on the city in the final months of the war, it is nevertheless surprising. However, the air war also opened up the chance for people in hiding to pass themselves off as "bombed-out national comrades." At the same time, some Jews still continued to flee to the rural areas of Upper Bavaria.[56] Others covered great distances. One woman found shelter with a friend in Stuttgart; another fled to Styria, in Austria.[57] Staying with non-Jewish relatives seemed too dangerous to many Jews, so in most cases, the support came from their circles of friends and colleagues and sometimes also from strangers. Both Siegfried Neuland and Rosa Vetter could rely on aid from people who had already supported them in November 1938. These bonds held out despite several years of state propaganda, persecution, and intimidation.

Were more people in Munich prepared to offer help in the winter of 1945 than in previous years? First of all, it must be kept in mind that only a small number of Jews had considered going underground in the fall of 1941. In the winter of 1945, this group was substantially larger, and therefore more people in Munich were faced with the question of whether or not they should help. Some spontaneously declared their readiness to offer assistance, such as the helpers of Cäcilie Langenwalter and the acquaintances of Harry Lisberger, who took in the young man and hid him in a storeroom.[58] The fact that Jews needed help must have been obvious to many people in Munich in the winter of 1944–45. Judith Hirsch was one of the Jews deported on February 22. Together with her father, she was sent to Theresienstadt. "No one looked at us; it was as if we didn't exist," she wrote about her foot march to the train station.[59] Even though a military officer at the station whispered a few encouraging words as he raced past, he appears to have been the exception. At that time, most people in Munich were focused on their own problems and their family's everyday survival.

As compared to families, it was easiest for childless adults to flee underground, as was the case with the Langenwalter and Vetter couples. In many mixed marriages, parents decided to go into hiding not for their own sakes but for the safety of their children. The parents often organized hiding places for the children even before they received a deportation notice (see chapter 7). If children in mixed marriages had been raised Jewish, they were deemed *Geltungsjuden* and were generally supposed to be sent to Theresienstadt in February 1945, most of them along with their Jewish parents, as in the case of Judith Hirsch. When a mixed marriage was dissolved, or when the Jewish parent was either deceased or deported, the non-Jewish parent was forced to watch how the *Mischling* children came into the crosshairs of the Nazis. Thus, many families were faced with the difficult decision of whether the children, or the Jewish parent together with the children, should comply with the notice to report for deportation, or whether it was possible to organize hiding places for multiple family members. Individual stories sometimes developed very differently within one family. In the case of a family consisting of two parents in a mixed marriage and three sons, the Jewish father did not receive a deportation notice, one son was seriously ill and therefore deferred from deportation, one son went into hiding, and the third son was deported to Theresienstadt.[60] Among those who went underground, there was also a large number of younger *Geltungsjuden* whose fates will be illustrated below.

MUNICH'S BEST-KNOWN HELPER: KARL SCHÖRGHOFER

There have been many retellings of the story of Karl Schörghofer, the "cemetery caretaker of Munich," ever since Kurt Grossmann introduced him as an "unsung hero" in 1957.[61] Schörghofer was the administrator, gravedigger, stonemason, and gardener for the new Jewish cemetery on Ungererstrasse (now Garchinger Strasse), and he protected at least six young Jews from deportation from Munich. Most of them wrote letters in the 1950s to Yad Vashem, the World Holocaust Remembrance Center, supporting efforts to honor the Schörghofer family. Although the case is relatively well known, not many details have been reported. Little has been written, for example, about the family's tragic fate after the war, and next to nothing has been written about

Schörghofer's involvement in Aryanization. Schörghofer hid all kinds of things at the cemetery: people, animals, food, cigarettes, religious objects, Torah scrolls, menorahs, gravestones, and even corpses. The cigarettes ultimately proved to be his undoing.

Born near Salzburg in 1879, Karl Schörghofer moved to Munich as a young man. In 1923, he started working at the Jewish cemetery, which became the center of his attention. Schörghofer gradually learned about the Jewish religion and came to know many members of Munich's Jewish community. His son, Karl Schörghofer Jr., was born in Munich in 1914 and helped his father at his job.[62] The cemetery also included a nursery with vegetable beds and greenhouses that Schörghofer had leased. Schörghofer's troubles started in 1933, when the Gestapo monitored his work suspiciously. When old gravestones were supposed to be confiscated for use as building materials, Schörghofer hid them against the rules. He was not willing to let his hearse be confiscated, and he was threatened a number of times with incarceration in the Dachau concentration camp. When the small Jewish communities in the region around Munich area were dissolved in the late 1930s, they sent religious objects, Torah scrolls, and menorahs to the Jewish cemetery to be buried there, but Schörghofer hid them instead.[63] Schörghofer also held in safekeeping religious objects that belonged to Jews who had emigrated. He was directly confronted with the suffering of the local Jews. When the suicide rate rose dramatically as the persecution intensified, Schörghofer had to bury more and more Jews who had taken their own lives out of desperation.[64]

In January 1944, Schörghofer saved Karl Vollmer, a Munich Jew, from deportation by hiding him on the cemetery grounds.[65] Vollmer had been arrested in October 1933 and spent several months in the Dachau concentration camp. The reasons for his detention are not known. In November 1938, he was again put in Dachau.[66] After his release in 1939, Vollmer was conscripted to work in the cemetery nursery. Vollmer had been in a privileged mixed marriage, but his wife died in 1942. In January 1944, he was scheduled to be deported to Theresienstadt, although he had a ten-year-old son to care for; at least for periods of time, the son was put up somewhere near Lake Chiemsee.[67]

In addition to Vollmer, some French prisoners of war might also have worked in the cemetery nursery.[68] Vollmer, however, was apparently the only Jewish forced laborer working there, which is an indication that Schörghofer had probably arranged his employment. In December 1939, Schörghofer acquired agricultural property in Riedmoos near Schleissheim, in the north of Munich, from Vollmer.[69] The sale was favorable for Schörghofer and unavoidable for Vollmer. From Schörghofer's perspective, he was able to protect a friend from persecution while at the same time achieving some financial gain from the measures of persecution, which he could not change.

In January 1940, Schörghofer and his wife Katharina intended to purchase property from Hermann Schülein, a Munich Jew, to set up another nursery. Schülein had owned undeveloped land in Perlach (in southeastern Munich) and was forced to sell this property, which had been divided into a number of plots. It is unclear if Schülein and Schörghofer knew each other, but as the sale was carried out through a realtor, it seems likely that there was no personal relationship between the two. The sales contract was never completed, however, because the city's General Building Inspector and the head of the Bavarian Peasants' League did not approve the sale.[70] The property was part of a site that was designated to become an industrial area.[71]

The Schörghofers did not want to accept this decision and hired a lawyer, who worded his complaint as follows: "Herr Schörghofer must provide for a family of six and his son is war-disabled and has been released from active military duty. The planned horticultural business is intended to secure a livelihood for the latter. Herr Schörghofer also wants to secure his own subsistence. Since his present nursery is located on the grounds of the Jewish cemetery, there is a danger that he will lose it in the near future due to a need for plots, which would more or less destroy his livelihood since he would lack the necessary land."[72]

Schörghofer could have lost the nursery grounds at the cemetery if given notice on his lease, which he might have justifiably feared due to his nonconforming behavior. In trying to convince the Nazi authorities, the lawyer's argumentation referred to the high mortality rate among Munich Jews, however, which could have resulted in the entire plot of land being needed for graves earlier than planned. Following the lawyer's strategy, dead Jews threatened the subsistence of a "national comrade," a scenario that could be prevented if the sales contract were authorized. The objection was not upheld, however, and the city of Munich ultimately purchased the property from Schülein.[73] Hermann Schülein committed suicide a short time later.[74]

In early 1945, the Schörghofer family took in Herta Neuburger, a twelve-year-old Jewish girl. Neuburger's father had died in 1941 as a result of imprisonment in Dachau. She and her siblings had a non-Jewish mother, but they had all been raised Jewish and thus registered as *Geltungsjuden*. Since the family regularly visited the father's grave, they were well acquainted with Karl Schörghofer. Josef Cammerer, who participated in the rescue effort, recalled, "I was supposed to go into her apartment, which he [Schörghofer] could not do himself, since he was known in the building, and tell her [Herta Neuburger] to leave the apartment immediately and, without leaving a note for her mother, to follow me to Karl Schörghofer Sr., who was waiting nearby. He said she knew him, so there was no risk involved; she could then decide what she wanted."[75]

Herta Neuburger did leave her mother a note, but all it said was: "See you after the war."[76] Schörghofer's youngest daughter brought Neuburger to an adult older sister, Martha Schörghofer-Schleipfer, on an isolated farm near Miesbach, a city south of Munich at the edge of the Alps, where Neuburger stayed until the end of the war.[77] Neuburger's brother Theodor (Ted) found a farmer in Oberaudorf, a village in the Inn valley near the Austrian border, who let him hide in the hay loft.[78]

In February 1945, Kurt and Rolf Kahn and the sisters Klara and Margot Schwalb sought refuge with the Schörghofer family. At the time the Kahn brothers were nineteen and twenty years old, respectively, and were classified as *Geltungsjuden*. Their father, Julius Kahn, was also on the list for the final transport to Theresienstadt. Kurt Kahn had worked as a mechanic in the Milbertshofen camp until it was closed, and he witnessed most of the deportations from Munich. After the camp was dissolved, he had to help carry luggage at the later deportations.[79] Margot and Klara Schwalb, also *Geltungsjuden*, were twenty and twenty-one years old, respectively, and had lived in the Berg am Laim camp. Their Jewish mother had been deported to Theresienstadt in 1942 because she had been divorced from her "Aryan" spouse since 1936.

After the war, Kurt Kahn described his escape:

> My brother and I, and Fräulein [Klara] Schwalb then tried to escape. We set up a hiding place in the Jewish cemetery on Ungererstrasse with the help of the gardener Scherghofer [*sic*] in a side room of the greenhouse.... One day the accused Gassner [Georg Gassner, Munich Gestapo officer], together with Herr Koronczyk [Theodor Koronczyk, Reich Association liaison to the Gestapo], came to arrest us. I jumped out of the window and was then arrested by Gassner. Gassner asked me who else was with me and I said that I was alone. Then Gassner went with me into the greenhouse and found Fräulein Schwalb hiding under a couch. He also found a letter of my brother's, which my brother had written a short time earlier to Fräulein Schwalb's sister, who was also in hiding. When Gassner saw that I was not alone, he took the fact that I had lied to him as a pretext to beat me.[80]

Rolf Kahn, for his part, managed to escape, but he soon returned to the cemetery. Klara Schwalb was also threatened with a beating, but she did not reveal her sister Margot's hiding place with the Osels, friends of the Schörghofers. Klara Schwalb had previously stayed with the Schörghofers and had also found refuge in Tutzing with the engineer Josef Cammerer, who was a good friend

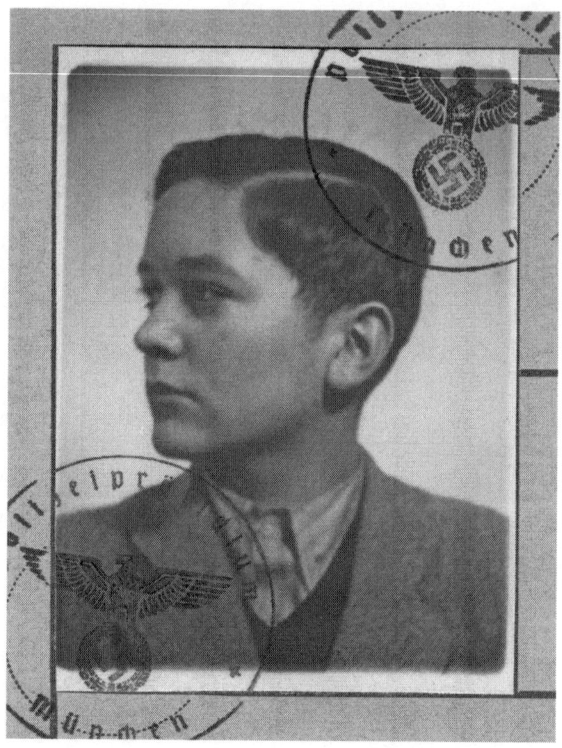

Kurt Kahn, ID card, 1939. Munich City Archive, DE-1992-KKD-1899-pb.

of Karl Schörghofer. This did not seem safe enough to her, however, so she returned to the cemetery.[81] After being arrested, Klara Schwalb was first sent to Stadelheim Prison and then to the Berg am Laim labor education camp for women. From there she managed to flee to her sister's hiding place.[82] Kurt Kahn was put in the Moosach labor education camp, from which he escaped on April 20. He returned to the Schörghofers.[83]

After Margot and Klara Schwalb had escaped, the Gestapo officers Gerhard Grimm and Eduard Fahlbusch appeared at the home of their brother. The young man was arrested and robbed of his last possessions. When he refused to reveal the hiding places of his sisters, he was beaten by Grimm. The Gestapo also wanted to charge him with listening to enemy radio broadcasts and with theft. His employer tried in vain to get the young man released. When the employer went to the Gestapo, he was told, "You won't get him back; he's going to the sausage machine."[84] A friend of the Kahn brothers and the Schwalb sisters was arrested and beaten with a leather whip after refusing to reveal the hiding place of his friends.[85] Franz Xaver Schwalb, the father, became a target of the

Gestapo, not only due to the disappearance of his daughters Klara and Margot, but also for "seditious talk."[86] The Gestapo officers cursed and beat him. Then they cleaned out his basement, where he had stored food, a bicycle, and various objects belonging to the Schwalb and Kahn families. Franz Xaver Schwalb was arrested, severely abused during his interrogation, and then incarcerated in the Dachau concentration camp.[87] There he was put in the typhus barrack. Surrounded by seriously ill and dying prisoners, Schwalb contracted the disease. Not until mid-June 1945 had he recuperated sufficiently to return to Munich.[88]

The Schörghofer father and son were arrested but soon released upon paying a fine of 800 reichsmarks. The cemetery nursery supplied large amounts of food for people employed in the war industry, which might be why the Schörghofers were spared being sent to Dachau, as had been threatened.[89] Despite the great risk, the Schörghofer family again took in the Kahn brothers, who lived at the cemetery until the end of the war. Many of the religious objects that had been hidden by the Schörghofers and which, in contrast to their former owners, had survived the war, were sent to the displaced persons camp in Feldafing.[90]

The admirable conduct of Karl and Katharina Schörghofer stands alongside the couple's (attempted) involvement in Aryanization. In the case of Karl Vollmer, one can surmise a "friendly Aryanization." In a letter of May 2, 1945, Vollmer thanked Schörghofer in very cordial, heartfelt words for the help and support received during the previous sixteen months.[91] There is less clarity about the relationship between Karl Schörghofer and Hermann Schülein and about the circumstances under which the former attempted to purchase part of the latter's landholdings. Schörghofer's merits in saving a number of people—and many religious objects—are absolutely undisputed. And yet, he had also been open to profit from Aryanization. From his perspective, he could not prevent Jews from being forced to sell their property. However, he also knew that he could do something to protect Vollmer and other Jews from the Nazi henchmen and was willing to do this. But somebody who offered assistance to some people despite the risk could nevertheless also pursue self-interest with respect to others.

At the old Jewish cemetery on Thalkirchner Strasse, as well, non-Jewish employees felt connected to Jews they knew. No burials had taken place there since 1908, but care of the grounds lay in the hands of a nursery business and the couple serving as caretakers. Werner Cahnman, who emigrated from Munich in 1939 and would later become a prominent sociologist in the United States, described Lina Angermeier, the wife of the caretaker, as the "brave administrator," who "went to the apartments [of Jews] with knapsacks full of food."[92] She regularly visited the Berg am Laim camp to bring food to the residents.

She protected the cemetery from neglect as much as possible, and, due to her attitude, she repeatedly ran into trouble with the Gestapo. In addition to multiple house searches, she had to endure having her gas and power turned off temporarily.[93]

Karl Vollmer died in 1947. Kurt and Rolf Kahn remained in Munich after liberation. Margot and Klara Schwalb sought their fortunes in the United States. Karl Schörghofer and his son, for their part, experienced considerable difficulties after the war because various items remained hidden on the cemetery grounds, including cigarettes intended for the illicit underground market. This part of the story of the Schörghofer family will be treated as part of Munich's postwar history in chapter 9.

EARLY 1945: WANING OF THE PRESSURE OF PERSECUTION?

The cases presented above show that it was still reasonable to be afraid of the persecuting Nazi authorities even in the final phase of the war. Not only did Karl Rieger clearly express such fear, but Rosa Vetter also continually emphasized the anxiety she felt while staying with the Scherer sisters.[94] Even if helpers and survivors sometimes dramatized the danger in their later accounts, many fugitives and their helpers were convinced, even in 1945, that they would be sent to Dachau if discovered. The Schörghofer case shows that their fears were not unfounded, as the danger proved to be real, even for non-Jewish relatives. Franz Xaver Schwalb, the non-Jewish father of Margot and Klara Schwalb, the two sisters who fled, was arrested and sent to Dachau. In another case, two "half-Jewish" women who refused to reveal their father's hiding place were arrested, beaten, and sent to the Berg am Laim labor education camp. The non-Jewish mother of Judith Hirsch was intensely pressured by the Gestapo in February 1945 to get a divorce. When she refused, she was conscripted to do forced labor. She had to wash streetcars with cold water in the middle of the winter, and the resulting damage to her health persisted for the rest of her life.[95] Heinrich Prölsdorfer, who was in a mixed marriage, exchanged a few trivial words with an English prisoner of war only a few weeks before the war ended. He was observed doing this by Ernst Poller, the Nazi Party local group leader for the vicinity around Danzig Freedom Square (Danziger Freiheit was the Nazis' name for Feilitzsch Square; it is now called Münchner Freiheit) in the Munich-Schwabing district, who then beat and arrested him. Prölsdorfer was sent to Dachau, where he died a short time later.[96] People who were seriously ill and small children were sent to Theresienstadt from Munich as late as February 1945.

There has not yet been a detailed examination of the Munich Gestapo, so it is difficult to say if or to what extent the behavior of the Munich Gestapo toward Jews in the final phase of the war differed from that of the Gestapo headquarters in other major German cities. In Cologne, in various cities in the Ruhr area, and in Kassel, for example, there were still mass shootings and public executions by the local Gestapo in the final phase of the war.[97] Prison inmates, foreign forced workers, real and alleged resistance fighters, and "deserters" were among those murdered, in addition to Jews.[98] In Düsseldorf, a hidden Jew was discovered shortly before Germany surrendered and was publicly hanged.[99] These highly visible murders may have contributed to the public appraising the danger of dealing with Jews, foreign workers, or "traitors" as being higher in early 1945 than it had been in the previous years.

The extent to which the discovery and deportation of the remaining Jews throughout the Reich remained a priority of the local Gestapo offices also has yet to be examined. It is certain that in many places Jews did not comply with deportation notices. According to the extant research, there tended to be fewer crimes committed by the Gestapo in the final phase of the war in southern Germany.[100] However, they did continue to take place there as well. In February 1945, for example, seven forced laborers from Poland and the Soviet Union were publicly hanged in the yard of the Munich Gestapo headquarters.[101] Denunciation, arrest, deportation to Theresienstadt, transfer to Dachau, and murder remained concrete scenarios threatening Jews who went underground in the winter of 1945.

In the final days of the war, Jews no longer fled to avoid deportation. By that time, it was concentration camp prisoners on death marches who attempted to escape from their guards. SS units forced prisoners from Dachau and its subcamps to march in the direction of Tyrol, and trains left Dachau and the Mühldorf subcamp heading south.[102] All in all, from April 23 on, at least twenty-five thousand prisoners were on the move from or to Dachau.[103] Along the train line from Mühldorf to Munich, thousands of mostly Jewish prisoners were initially left to their own devices near Poing on April 27, 1945, when the SS guards heard that the war was over. When it turned out that this news was incorrect, the guards initiated a bloodbath, loaded the prisoners who were still alive back onto the train, and continued on their way.[104] While the train was stopped, several prisoners managed to escape, including Gabriel Meltzer, a Jew, who was able to flee along with a French and a Polish prisoner. The three men were then hidden by Josef and Ursula Huber on their farm in Staudach (a district of Anzing, about twenty kilometers—twelve miles—east of Munich).[105]

Qiu Fazu, a physician from China who was the director of the makeshift hospital in Bad Tölz, a city south of Munich, told the SS to release a group of Jewish prisoners from Dachau, saying they had typhus. He was persuasive enough that the prisoners were put in his charge. He treated and hid them until the end of the war.[106] Additional acts of rescue in the final days of the war have been documented. In Ergoldsbach near Landshut, for example, where a train filled with prisoners from the Buchenwald concentration camp broke down, a group of locals hid thirteen Jewish prisoners in a barn until the end of the war.[107] It is, however, difficult to determine how many escapes succeeded as the result of spontaneous help from the townspeople.[108]

SIX

DANGERS AND FAILED ESCAPES, 1941–1945

Denunciation, Exploitation, Discovery, Illness

MOST ATTEMPTS TO AVOID DEPORTATION ended fatally. This chapter deals with the dangers facing Jews in hiding and with failed escape attempts. Betrayal, being recognized, ID checks, and losing one's cover generally led to arrest, deportation, and murder. Denunciation often followed financial exploitation by so-called *Judenfledderer*, "Jew fleecers," who posed as helpers to enrich themselves. Sickness or injury in hiding could also be fatal when it proved impossible to involve a trustworthy doctor. Moreover, in their profound desperation and fear of being discovered, an unknown number of Jews in hiding committed suicide.

It is difficult to estimate the survival rate of the U-boats.[1] Even if it cannot be determined with certainty how many Jews in hiding were caught in Munich, it is generally assumed that chances of survival were better in Munich than in Berlin. While this is likely, it is difficult to prove statistically. First of all, the figures for Berlin often do not take into account Jews in mixed marriages who went underground in the final phase of the war. The survival rate in this group was particularly high. The statistics for Berlin also do not include those Berlin U-boats who left the city, were liberated elsewhere, and then did not return to Berlin.[2] Finally, the numerous air raids and heavy fighting in the final phase of the war took the lives of many people in hiding in Berlin.

Jews in hiding were pursued more intensively in Berlin than in Munich or other cities. After all, several thousand Jews went underground in Berlin. Especially following the major wave of Jews going into hiding after the Factory Operation in February 1943, the manhunts increased considerably. As of March 1943, it was not only the Gestapo that was looking for them, but also the Jewish snatchers (*Greifer*), collaborators who were active in Berlin, Vienna, and (to a far lesser extent) Frankfurt.[3] There are no precise figures on how many Jews were caught by snatchers, but according to estimates, the figure may have been as high as one thousand.[4] Many snatchers were Jews who had previously been in hiding themselves, but were caught. They were promised that they and their families would be exempted from deportation if they helped locate other U-boats.[5] In the end, however, many of them were nevertheless deported. It was common practice for Jewish snatchers to be assigned to find specific people who had been denounced.[6]

Arrested Jews were pressured to reveal the names of other U-boats and helpers.[7] In the sometimes extensive networks of helpers and those they helped in Berlin, the arrest of an individual could suddenly severely jeopardize an entire group of people. When Dr. Franz Kaufmann, a Jew who was also a helper, was arrested after a denunciation led to a series of arrests, he had a notebook with him. The notebook entries made it possible for investigators to locate numerous members of his network.[8] This danger of a "chain of arrests"[9] was particularly great in Berlin.

For all these reasons, the ratio of surviving U-boats to those who were discovered was probably higher in Munich than in Berlin. In Munich, however, as in other parts of Germany, the actual figures of those who tried to hide but were captured will never be known, as many individual fates remain uncertain. In at least fourteen cases, escape attempts by Munich Jews ended fatally.[10] These also included people who died of illnesses or were driven to suicide out of desperation.

DEATH IN HIDING

> What are you to do if a person you are hiding in your apartment dies of heart failure one fine day? Are you to burn him in the oven, send him up in smoke, blow him out the chimney? What do you do with a corpse that hasn't been registered with the police? "We put it in our laundry basket, covered it with sheets, and carried it out of the house at night," we are told by acquaintances who suffered this particular embarrassment. "In the Tiergarten we dragged it out and put it on a bench." They smile distractedly; they are not pleased with their solution. For forty years, they have been respectable citizens.[11]

Here the journalist Ruth Andreas-Friedrich describes the situation of friends who had to deal with the sudden death of a Jewish woman they were hiding in their Berlin apartment. Together with Andreas-Friedrich, the friends were active in the Uncle Emil resistance group, which hid numerous Jews in Berlin and procured forged IDs for them.[12] They were now confronted with the task of either helping a dead person to inconspicuously "reappear" or helping a corpse to disappear.[13]

Not only members of the Uncle Emil group in Berlin were confronted with the situation of having an "illegal" corpse in their home. In Munich, the engineer Josef Cammerer faced the same dilemma. He decided against letting the dead person "reappear." In 1917, as a wounded soldier in a field hospital, Josef Cammerer got to know the student Gertrud Fröhlich. Fröhlich had signed up to volunteer as an aide. The encounter developed into a close lifelong friendship, evidently based largely on the profound religious faith of the Catholic Cammerer and the Jewish Fröhlich. After the war, Cammerer studied engineering and became a sought-after expert in the area of thermal and cold insulation.[14] Fröhlich stayed in Munich and married the chemist Walter Lustig. Cammerer and Fröhlich remained in contact. When the Nazis took power, Cammerer gave up his position as an adjunct professor at the Technical University of Berlin. He returned to Munich and set up a private research institute near the city, working on research projects for industry. Cammerer and the Lustigs saw each other almost daily during this period and also went on many outings together. As of 1938, Cammerer's institute was located in Tutzing, forty kilometers (about twenty-five miles) south of Munich on Lake Starnberg, a rather secluded area surrounded by forest. In the research building, Cammerer studied thermal insulation of walls.[15]

In the course of the pogrom of November 1938, Walter Lustig was arrested and then spent two months in Dachau. He was arrested again in the fall of 1939 and incarcerated for several weeks in Stadelheim Prison.[16] During this time, Cammerer attempted frantically, albeit in vain, to acquire emigration visas for his friends. After a short period of military service, Cammerer received a deferment in 1940 to study refrigeration warehouses for food storage in his research institute. Since his work was deemed essential to the war effort, Cammerer enjoyed certain privileges and special prerogatives; for example, outsiders—including local Nazis—were not permitted to enter his premises.[17] He managed to set up a branch office of his institute in Munich and to hire the Lustigs. In this way, Cammerer could protect Walter Lustig from being conscripted to forced labor. Lustig's state of health, however, had deteriorated to such a degree as a result of his imprisonment that he could hardly perform any tasks at all. Cammerer told the German Labor Front (DAF) that he needed Jewish workers for "especially unpleasant chemical experiments."[18]

Gertrud Lustig's health had also declined due to the hardship of persecution and out of concern for her sick husband. Walter Lustig died in early October 1941 and was buried in the new Jewish cemetery. This was how Josef Cammerer met Karl Schörghofer. After her husband's death, Gertrud Lustig's health continued to deteriorate.[19] Cammerer decided to hide her in Tutzing. For security reasons, it was no longer possible for her to say goodbye to her parents, the pharmacists Bernhard and Rosa Fröhlich.[20] The Fröhlichs' plans to emigrate to Cuba in 1941 failed at the last minute. One month after their daughter disappeared, Gertrud Lustig's parents received their deportation notices, and together they committed suicide. "My efforts to relieve her parents' lot were to no avail. They took morphine, which they had access to through the pharmacy they used to own," wrote Josef Cammerer later.[21] Their daughter Gertrud had predeceased them at Josef Cammerer's home in Tutzing.[22] Josef Cammerer had not known any doctor in whom he could have confided.

Josef Cammerer was now in the difficult situation that Ruth Andreas-Friedrich had described: What do you do if someone whom you have hidden illegally dies? The friends of Ruth Andreas-Friedrich lived in an urban apartment and had no choice other than to secretly remove the corpse from their home. Others faced similar situations. Two Berlin families suddenly confronted with the death of someone they were hiding dropped the body into the Spree River.[23] Frieda Jäger, who was seriously ill and in hiding in Vienna, instructed her daughter what to do in the case of her death: "I told her to put me in a sack immediately and crush my body with a hammer to break it up as small as possible so she could carry the sack away to the Danube without being noticed, so that good, dear Frau Richter [Frieda Jäger's helper] does not endanger her life through my death."[24] Paula and Lieselotte Mayer, Jews from Munich who were hidden in Lower Bavaria and who jumped into the Danube in 1944 (see chapter 3), might have chosen this form of suicide so their helpers would avoid such difficulties. One Berliner dropped his wife's corpse off in front of a police station—probably in hopes that the authorities would arrange for the unidentified body to be buried. He and his wife, who had cancer, had lived in hiding until she died.[25] Like Cammerer, this man later spoke of his feeling of helplessness in view of the fact that they had not tried to consult a doctor. And Marianne Ellenbogen, who had gone underground in Essen, explained succinctly, "God forbid anything happened and you needed a doctor."[26] Jews in hiding who ultimately dared to see a doctor or go to a hospital feared being discovered or revealing their identity while under anesthesia.[27]

Josef Cammerer decided to bury his deceased friend illegally. Together with a reliable employee, who kept silent, Cammerer dug out a grave under the sunroom of his residence in Tutzing. The snow was very deep, so an outdoor burial without leaving traces was out of the question.[28] A few months after Gertrud Lustig's death, Cammerer cautiously contacted—at first under a

Gertrud Lustig and Josef Sebastian Cammerer. Courtesy of the Leo Baeck Institute, New York.

pretext—the administrator of the Jewish cemetery in Munich, where Gertrud Lustig's husband had already been buried. Cammerer and Schörghofer came to know each other better. Trusting each other, they decided to bury Gertrud Lustig next to her husband, despite the risks. "In October 1943, Cammerer exhumed the corpse and transported it to the Jewish cemetery with the help of Karl Schörghofer Jr. in the dead of night, in his car along the autobahn, which had a lot of police and military troop traffic. Karl Schörghofer Sr. had already

Gertud Lustig's hiding place at Josef Cammerer's. Courtesy of the Leo Baeck Institute, New York.

dug out a grave next to Walter Lustig's. This is where Cammerer buried his friend."[29] After Gertrud Lustig's burial, Cammerer and Schörghofer remained in contact. In early 1945, Cammerer helped Schörghofer hide Herta Neuburger (see chapter 5).[30]

After the war ended, Cammerer took care of the formalities resulting from the death of Gertrud Lustig and her parents. He contacted Gertrud's brother, Hans Fröhlich, who was living in New York, and helped him collect the inheritance of his sister and parents. Cammerer also maintained the graves of Walter and Gertrud Lustig.[31] In 1946, Cammerer started studying theology and withdrew for several years to the St. Ottilien Archabbey. He had long felt a desire to devote his life to his faith, and he had discussed it with friends. His stay at the monastery apparently traced back to a promise he had made to Gertrud and Walter Lustig.[32] Cammerer was honored in 1976 as a Righteous Among the Nations. Cammerer himself thought the honor should be reserved for people who helped strangers in need. For him, the situation was different. "I don't know if an event that was so entirely determined by a great personal love falls under the duties of your office, which aims more to honor humanitarian ideas," he wrote in a 1963 letter to David Alcalay, director of the section for the Righteous Among the Nations at Yad Vashem.[33] Josef Cammerer died in 1983.

Gertrud Lustig was not the only Jew from Munich who died in hiding. As previously mentioned, Paula and Lieselotte Mayer committed suicide, as did the opera singer Margarethe Sterneck. Together with her husband, the acclaimed singer Berthold Sterneck, she had left Prague for Munich in 1923. Both of them were originally from Vienna and had converted to Protestantism.[34] They were actually scheduled to be deported with the last major transport in March 1943.[35] That never happened, however, possibly due to Berthold Sterneck's cancer.[36] It might also have been the result of a false entry in the file of Jewish community members. Berthold Sterneck was listed there as having a "privileged mixed marriage." In his first marriage, he had, in fact, been married to a non-Jewish woman with whom he had a son.[37] As a result of Sterneck's death in November 1943, his widow, Margarethe, a full Jew, received her deportation notice on January 17, 1944. Consequently, she fled to friends in Vienna and from there via Tyrol and Lower Bavaria to the vicar Dr. Margarete Hoffer in Schwenningen, a city at the eastern margins of the Black Forest.[38] Schwenningen was a major hub of the Württemberg "parsonage chain." From there, pastors Gotthilf Weber and Richard Schäfer, together with Vicar Hoffer, organized hiding places and escape routes to Switzerland.[39] One of Hoffer's charges was arrested at the Swiss border, through which the aid offered by the Schwenningen vicar became known to the authorities. Hoffer had to pay a fine of 600 reichsmarks.[40] That did not keep her from taking in Margarethe Sterneck, however, who was living in the parsonage under a false identity. A number of people in the town were privy to the secret.[41] In her desperation, however, Sterneck committed suicide only a few weeks before the end of the war. Margarete Hoffer later wrote, "On February 22, 1945, there was an air raid on Schwenningen and the following night, which I spent away from home with a sick woman who lived alone, she committed suicide with poison, out of fear that she could fall into the hands of the Gestapo if the building were to be damaged by bombs."[42] The suicide had to be registered with the police. Schwenningen's vicar was fortunate in that the investigating officer was a member of the Confessing Church and refrained from conducting an in-depth verification of the identity of the deceased person. Margarethe Sterneck was buried in Schwenningen under a false name.[43]

There were not only deaths, but also births in hiding, though none in Munich. Edith Hahn Beer gave birth to a child as a U-boat in Brandenburg.[44] She had excellent forged papers and had even married under her false identity. Marie Jalowicz Simon had become pregnant at the beginning of her life in hiding in Berlin and decided to have an abortion. She did not see any survival prospects for herself and a newborn child. Through a doctor she knew, she received medicine that triggered a miscarriage.[45] In occupied Poland, where many Jews in hiding survived for an extended period of time in larger, shared hiding places, women gave birth under extremely difficult conditions. For the mothers, the danger of infection was particularly great. The newborns had minimal chances of survival under these circumstances. Also, due to their crying, they were perceived by the adults as a danger to the entire group.[46]

FAILED ESCAPES: BEING DISCOVERED AND DENOUNCED

The following cases illustrate the different configurations and circumstances under which Jews who fled to or from Munich and elsewhere were caught. The fates of these people direct our attention once more to the varying local conditions. At the same time, they show that irrespective of the location of their hiding places, the greatest danger facing those who went underground and their helpers was denunciation. Information on failed escapes is frequently extremely sparse. Sometimes only the flight attempt itself can be verified, while the specific circumstances remain in the dark. For example, the statement "the Jew Renée (Irene) Strasser went fugitive prior to her scheduled evacuation" could be read in a declaration of June 21, 1944, to Munich's Chief Financial Officer (OFP).[47] She had evidently fled from Munich to Hungary, but the circumstances of her arrest and murder could not be clarified.[48]

From Wetzlar to Munich: On the Punishment of Helpers

Jewish spouses in mixed marriages were officially deferred from deportation until early 1945, but the situation in the Hesse-Nassau Gau shows that local agencies of persecution often disregarded the national regulations and even expanded the persecution, driven by their own ideological motives.[49] On the initiative of Gau leader Jakob Sprenger and the Frankfurt Gestapo, starting in early 1943, several Jewish spouses in mixed marriages were summoned, abused, arrested, and deported to the Auschwitz death camp by the Frankfurt Gestapo.[50] Sprenger had already distinguished himself regarding the unusually speedy deportation of the Jewish population. Once that had been completed in the fall of 1942, Sprenger's efforts focused on having Jewish spouses in mixed marriages detained. Several hundred people were arrested in these actions.[51] Against this background, the lawyer Elsie Kühn-Leitz decided to help Hedwig Palm, who had a mixed marriage. Palm had been ordered to appear before the Frankfurt Gestapo in May 1943. She was not the first Wetzlar Jew in a mixed marriage to receive such a summons, and the others had not returned. Kühn-Leitz later reported: "One evening Frau Gerke, an acquaintance of ours, came to us and said that the Jewish wife in the Palm family, an established optician family in Wetzlar, was in danger of being picked up. The family was despairing and considered whether they should kill themselves with gas or poison, or if there were a way to help the woman flee to her relatives in Switzerland. . . . I recommended that she find refuge with my very humanitarian aunt, Ella Bocks, in Munich."[52]

A few days later, Julie Gerke brought Hedwig Palm to Munich. Ella Bocks was the sister of the Wetzlar industrialist Ernst Leitz, and Elsie Kühn-Leitz was his daughter. Ernst Leitz, whose company was famous for manufacturing the Leica camera, had helped a number of Jews from Wetzlar emigrate before the war. Since the company had a few branches in the United States, Leitz was also able to refer them to jobs there.[53] After arriving in Munich, Hedwig Palm stayed with Ella Bocks for several weeks, from late May until early July 1943.[54] During that time, Kühn-Leitz and Gerke organized Palm's escape to Switzerland. Gerke traveled to Munich with a hiking map marked with the escape route, and from there they set off with Hedwig Palm toward the Swiss border. They had problems reading the map in the border area, however, and asked a stranger for help. He denounced the two women, who were arrested.[55] Ella Bocks was fined 300 reichsmarks for violating registration requirements.[56] Hedwig Palm spent several months in jail in Frankfurt and was then sent to the Ravensbrück women's concentration camp in November 1943. She probably died in the Uckermark concentration camp in March 1945.[57] Julie Gerke was sentenced to eight weeks in prison and was released in late September 1943.[58] Gerke, a member of the Nazi Party, testified in court that she had known Hedwig Palm for a long time and had "acted out of sympathy."[59] On September 10, Elsie Kühn-Leitz was questioned by the local Gestapo and subsequently imprisoned. She was released in late November 1943 from the Frankfurt police prison. According to her testimony, her father had paid a substantial sum to get her released.[60]

A failed escape could result in very different consequences for the helpers. Aiding Jews was not a formal statutory offense according to the German criminal code in the so-called Old Reich, the territory that comprised Germany up to 1937, and there was no uniform penalty.[61] Sometimes courts attempted to convict helpers on other, related criminal charges, such as "defiling the race."[62] Punishment for what the Nazis called "aiding and abetting Jews" (*Judenbegünstigung*) generally took place through the special courts established in 1933 and in particular through the Gestapo. The special courts (*Sondergerichte*) passed judgment on all sorts of resistance activity.[63] The Gestapo could impose orders for so-called "preventive detention" without any court ruling whatsoever. Especially starting in October 1941, when a decree of the Reich Security Main Office (RSHA) declared that "German-blooded people" who "publicly displayed friendly relations to Jews" were to be sentenced to such "preventive detention," the danger of imprisonment increased greatly.[64] Julie Gerke and Elsie Kühn-Leitz were sent to prison. Karl Schörghofer, who had hidden several Jews in the Jewish cemetery in Munich, had to pay a fine and was threatened with concentration camp detention (see chapter 5). Female helpers generally received more lenient penalties, but there are also examples of female helpers who paid for their support by being sent to the Ravensbrück concentration camp.[65] According to the present state of research, helpers of Jews in hiding were more severely penalized in Austria than in Germany.[66] A more precise differentiation of punishments based on regional practices would be helpful. Beate Kosmala has determined, for example, that penalties were particularly severe in the Wiesbaden area.[67]

As Kosmala has noted, "in the German Reich (in its 1937 borders), there were hardly any death sentences imposed for helping Jews. In contrast, German judges . . . in occupied Poland and the Protectorate of Bohemia and Moravia often handed down the death penalty. . . . However, these death sentences—which were highly publicized as a deterrent—were for the most part only imposed against Poles, Ukrainians, and Czechs."[68] In Germany, more important than deterrence was "the Nazi regime's wish to uphold the fiction of a functioning *Volksgemeinschaft*."[69] Cases in which "national comrades" (*Volksgenossen*) helped Jews were not favorable for the Nazi regime and for that reason were not supposed to be widely publicized.[70]

Escaping the "Lohhof Hell"[71]

Elisabeth Kühl, née Ganz, was born in Mainz in 1895. Her parents, Eugen und Margaretha Ganz, were Jewish businesspeople who had converted to Protestantism. Raised Protestant, she converted to Catholicism in 1919 to marry Karl Busemann. She and her husband had a daughter and a son before divorcing in 1928. In May 1933, Elisabeth Busemann was married again, this time to Herbert Karl Kühl. This marriage lasted only a few months, but the couple didn't divorce officially until 1940.[72] Elisabeth moved to Munich in 1940 or 1941 after her second divorce.

Elisabeth Kühl never identified as a Jew. She had been raised Protestant, had converted to Catholicism, and even claimed to have been a member of the Nazi Party for a short time. In a letter with which she applied for a passport in 1938, in order to obtain additional training to become a midwife in Switzerland (she had been trained as a nurse), she stated that she had joined the party in 1931.[73] Both of her husbands, Karl Busemann and Herbert Kühl, were Nazi Party members;[74] Herbert Kühl was already a member when he married Elisabeth in May 1933.[75] Elisabeth Kühl seemed not to understand that the Nazi race laws would in fact also be applied to her. In early 1942, she received a summary judgment fining her thirty reichsmarks, as she had not applied for an ID card including the middle name Sara, as all female Jews were required to do, until December 1941.[76]

At that point she was already doing forced labor at the Lohhof flax retting pit. On December 20, 1941, she was given the weekend off by Rolf Grabower, director of the camp, so that she could visit her son, who was about to be drafted into the Wehrmacht.[77] Without permission, she spent Christmas with relatives, but subsequently returned to Lohhof.[78] On March 15, 1942, Kühl fled the rettery, leaving behind a suicide note.[79] She was arrested in early May 1942 in Tösens, a small town in Tyrol, and a short time later was transferred to Innsbruck.[80] Tösens is in the triborder region on the Austrian border to Switzerland and Italy, so we can surmise that Kühl wanted to escape to Switzerland. She probably was not familiar with the area, nor did she have local helpers. On June 12, 1942, she was sent from Innsbruck to the Ravensbrück concentration camp. The last official entry for Elisabeth Kühl was from Auschwitz. A death certificate noted the date of her death as November 11, 1942.[81]

Father and Son on the Run

In the early 1930s, the Jewish physicist Dr. Oskar Cosmann was an esteemed scientist at the Kaiser Wilhelm Institute for Silicate Research in Berlin. He lost his position in 1933. His final scientific assignment led him and his family to Munich. The Cosmanns agreed to feign getting separated, presumably in hopes that at least his non-Jewish wife, Margarete Cosmann, would be permitted to continue working as a dentist and be able to support the family. The couple was formally divorced in 1937. Oskar Cosmann rented a room, but he secretly continued to live with his family.[82]

In 1940, Oskar Cosmann was conscripted to perform forced labor, including for a time at the Oldenbourg publishing company. In early August 1942, he and his twenty-two-year-old son Lorenz decided to flee to Switzerland. While Lorenz Cosmann traveled to Feldkirch (Austria) to familiarize himself with the border region, his father was preparing to flee, hiding with Gertrud Paulus, a friend of Lorenz.[83] Lorenz Cosmann was arrested at the Swiss border, and under torture he revealed his father's hiding place.[84]

On the morning of August 8, 1942, Gestapo officer Hans Grahammer entered Paulus's apartment, where he found Oskar Cosmann, still asleep. Grahammer beat him severely, swore at him, and arrested him.[85] Gertrud Paulus, who had already spent several years in prison for her Communist sympathies,[86] managed to flee to Margarete Cosmann and inform her of the events. Two days later, Margarete Cosmann went to the Munich Gestapo headquarters, where she hardly recognized her husband because his face had been so disfigured from the punches he had endured.[87] The Cosmanns' daughter had, meanwhile, found the father's bloody nightclothes and linens in Gertrud Paulus's apartment. Gertrud Paulus had not returned to her apartment, remaining hidden instead.[88] Gestapo officer Grahammer told Margarete Cosmann that her husband would be deported to Theresienstadt in two days. On August 12, 1942, Oskar Cosmann left Munich bound for Theresienstadt. His wife and daughter were not allowed to see him off at the train station.[89] On October 28, 1944, Oskar Cosmann was on the final transport from Theresienstadt to Auschwitz, where he was murdered.[90]

When Oskar Cosmann's son Lorenz was released from custody, he returned to Munich, where he joined a group of young rebels. His circle of friends can loosely be connected with the Swing Youth, nonconforming young people from middle-class circles who enjoyed listening and dancing to American swing music.[91] Some of them also produced political flyers and vandalized the sidewalk showcases of the Nazi *Stürmer* newspaper.[92] Lorenz Cosmann's friends partied, danced, and drank a lot. In this state, they also spoke disrespectfully about the Nazi Party leadership. When Margarete Cosmann's housekeeper was cleaning up after a Carnival party, she found not only empty bottles and young people sleeping on beds, sofas, and the floor, but allegedly also some pencil drawings of leading Nazis in distasteful poses. The housekeeper denounced Lorenz Cosmann and accused him of "defiling the race."[93] The author Eugen Roth had to appear at the questioning of witnesses, as he was Cosmann's tutor and had been present at the party. Roth vehemently denied that caricatures of leading Nazis had been passed around, and evidently none were actually found.[94]

Lorenz Cosmann was arrested in February 1943, at precisely the time when the Scholl siblings (of the White Rose resistance group) were also arrested in Munich. His mother later linked those arrests to Lorenz's. It can no longer be determined how far the contact went, but at least one member of Cosmann's circle, Franz Geiger, attended discussions at which members of the White Rose were also present.[95] Lorenz Cosmann was put in the Breitenau labor education camp. He tried to escape but was denounced, caught, and sent to the

Buchenwald concentration camp.[96] Lorenz Cosmann survived but was unable to find his bearings in postwar West German society (see chapter 9).[97]

Lorenz Cosmann, Elisabeth Kühl, and Hedwig Palm attempted to scout out or cross the border into Switzerland without any helpers and without knowing the border region, but failed. Others organized the border crossing on their own and successfully and safely passed into Switzerland.[98] Much depended on local conditions and chance. Whereas Hedwig Palm was denounced in the border region, Edith Dietz, a Jewish woman, was just as unfamiliar with the region but received valuable information about a hidden path across the border.[99] Those from Berlin who planned to escape into Switzerland had an advantage over people from Munich, as there were networks in Berlin that had good contacts in the border region. This meant that in Berlin it was possible to organize such an escape across the border beforehand.[100] This was not possible in Munich.[101]

Julius Hechinger, Financial and Legal Advisor for the Jewish Community

Quite a bit has already been written about Julius Hechinger, the legal advisor for the Jewish Community of Munich (IKG).[102] Hechinger was arrested after trying to flee and was brutally tortured by the staff of the Aryanization Office. He was then deported to the Auschwitz death camp on July 13, 1942.[103] The abuse that Hechinger experienced at the hands of Aryanization Office staff shows how that particular agency, working closely with the Gestapo, became the most vicious authority of persecution in Munich.[104]

Born in 1895, Julius Hechinger was a lawyer and a leading member of the Jewish community, in charge of financial affairs. When Alfred Neumeyer, head of the community, left Germany in February 1941, Karl Stahl assumed that position, with Hechinger as the community's legal and financial advisor. Neumeyer described Hechinger as an extraordinarily talented and clever official. According to Neumeyer, "The Gestapo admired him for his practical and flexible manner."[105] Hechinger served as the liaison to the Gestapo and, for that role, was consequently disdained by many Jewish community members. Neumeyer asserted that Hechinger nevertheless managed to achieve some relief for the Jewish community.[106] The animosity was understandable, as the leadership of the Jewish community was forced to participate in compiling the deportation lists, and Hechinger was perceived by other Jews as "privileged." The fact that he could derive no personal advantages from this supposed privileged status became apparent when he fell out of favor with the Aryanization Office.[107] In late March 1942, Hechinger was on the deportation list for the April 4 transport to Piaski. Also on the list were other Jewish community officials, including Hugo Railing, director of the Milbertshofen camp, as well as the entire administration of the Berg am Laim camp.[108] Karl Stahl tried to have the Jewish functionaries deferred from the deportation, succeeding only in the case of Else Behrend-Rosenfeld, who was removed from the transport list at the last minute.[109] Julius Hechinger evaded deportation by fleeing.

The circumstances of Hechinger's escape are mysterious, and the details will never be cleared up because the only extant statements—by Hechinger's successor, Theodor Koronczyk, and by the Aryanization Office staff and the Gestapo—are contradictory. It is likely that Hans Wegner, director of the Aryanization Office, personally had Hechinger's name placed on the deportation list, possibly on special orders from Gau leader Adolf Wagner.[110] It is conceivable that Hechinger, as an unwelcome witness who knew too much about the machinations of the Aryanization Office, was supposed to be eliminated. Theodor Koronczyk testified in retrospect that Hechinger had been placed on the list at the last minute and was not informed until the day of the deportation, by telephone, that he was to report for deportation in Milbertshofen. When Hechinger received the call from camp director Railing, he was at Lindwurmstrasse 125, the Munich Jewish community's official address at the time. According to Koronczyk, Hechinger immediately informed his colleague Karl Stahl about the call and said that he intended to go into hiding. Koronczyk stated that he had been present at this conversation and that Hechinger had asked him to find him a bicycle and meet him with it at the Bavaria Ring, a street close to Lindwurmstrasse. Hechinger then ostensibly left the arranged meeting place on the bicycle. A few days later, Hechinger supposedly turned himself in to the Gestapo voluntarily.[111]

Hechinger, however, had by no means been added to the list at the last minute. Already on March 21, Dr. Paul Eppstein, a member of the executive board of the Reich Association of Jews, had complained to the Reich Security Main Office, presumably upon the request of Karl Stahl, about the upcoming deportation of Hechinger and other functionaries of the Munich district branch the Reich Association.[112] The leadership of the Jewish Community of Munich and Hechinger himself hoped that their objection to Hechinger's deportation would be successful. But whereas Else Behrend-Rosenfeld's deportation was in fact deferred, the deportation notice for Hechinger was confirmed at the last minute, which would explain Hechinger's hasty and obviously totally unplanned escape. It can no longer be reconstructed where Hechinger spent those days in hiding. All that is certain is that he resurfaced several days later and was arrested. Hechinger was put in the Milbertshofen camp, where he was brutally mistreated by Aryanization Office officials and then deported to Auschwitz on July 13, 1942, where he perished.[113]

In postwar trials, the defendants from the Aryanization Office and the Gestapo accused Hechinger's successor, Koronczyk, of betrayal. Wegner, from the Aryanization Office, claimed that Koronczyk had known where Hechinger was hiding, had planned a meeting with him, and had then disclosed the meeting place to the Gestapo. Wegner himself said that he had heard this story from Gestapo colleagues during his internment.[114] At first glance, this story does not sound entirely far-fetched, as Koronczyk appeared to benefit from Hechinger's arrest and because after the war a number of Jews accused Koronczyk of denunciation. Why would Hechinger voluntarily turn himself in? Wegner's accusations were part of a particularly nefarious attempt to blame the Jews of Munich for the deportation and murder of Hechinger. Wegner and his staff claimed that Wagner had removed Hechinger from his position only as a result of numerous complaints from Munich Jews regarding the exercise of his duties and had placed him on the deportation list. According to the Gestapo men, they had even protected a Jewish woman whom Hechinger had reported for "defiling the race."[115] Hechinger was then supposedly arrested as a result of Koronczyk's denunciation.[116]

In their sadistic orgy of violence against Hechinger, the staff of the Aryanization Office forced their victim to keep running around the barracks of the Milbertshofen camp without a break. Hechinger had to clean out the latrines with his bare hands and was brutally beaten. Some of the Jews living in the camp were also incited to torture Hechinger. The officials in the Aryanization Office encouraged them to kill him.[117] They evidently presumed that it would be easy to spur the camp residents to acts of violence because Hechinger was unpopular. That was not the case, however. The residents followed the orders only as long as the Gestapo men were present.[118] Jews were supposed to participate in the excessive violence, because, as Beate Meyer and Maximilian Strnad have shown, the entire process of persecution always aimed to shift all or some of the blame for the events on to the Jews themselves.[119] The postwar trials against Hans Wegner and Franz Mugler, Hechinger's torturers at the Aryanization Office, will be discussed in chapter 10.

Julius Hechinger went underground on very short notice to avoid the transport to Piaski. He probably hoped that his disappearance and later reappearance would make his indispensability in the administration apparent and his deferment from the transport would be effected retroactively, as it were.[120] Theodor Koronczyk had not actively made an effort to obtain his predecessor's position.[121] Because he worked for Hechinger, he was well aware that the liaison could fall from grace at any time. The Munich Gestapo felt that with Koronczyk they would have someone who, from the perspective of the remaining members of the community, was not suited for the task and who was a weaker, timider person than Hechinger.[122] Hechinger's punishment served as a ritual of collective humiliation of the camp residents, who had to witness and participate in the abuse of Hechinger every evening.[123] It also served as a warning to all residents that attempts to flee would be punished severely.

Denounced and Deported, but Survived

Marion V., a Jew and a native Berliner, began her professional career as an actress. As a young woman, she had engagements at the city theaters in Bremen and Stuttgart. After the death of her first husband, who was Jewish, in 1915, she and her daughter Beate went to Munich, where she married Johann V., a Gentile, and gave birth to a son. Once her children were born, as Marion V. said later, she stopped acting and worked as a journalist.[124] She managed to make a name for herself as a fashion writer.

In 1934, her membership in the journalists' professional association was revoked, as it was for all Jews. This was tantamount to being banned from working in her profession. She tried to hide her Jewish background, claiming she had been adopted, but to no avail.[125] She then tried to earn her livelihood as a cosmetician in a hair salon, but was denounced as a Jew there and fired.[126] After receiving various offers from Swiss magazines, she moved to Switzerland. She divorced her second husband, Johann V., who had been an *Alter Kämpfer* (an "Old Fighter," i.e., someone who had joined the Nazi Party before 1933). His party membership was revoked in 1938 because he was married to a Jew. After the divorce, he applied for a new hearing, which was granted.[127] At the same time, however, he wrote to the Reich Office for Kinship Research (*Reichsstelle für Sippenforschung*) in support of his wife's claim not to be of Jewish descent. He also declared that he was the natural father of Marion V.'s daughter, Beate.[128]

Facing difficulties with the Swiss Foreign Police, Marion V. moved on to Italy to continue her work for the Swiss magazines. In Italy as well, it did not take long before she experienced difficulties, as she lacked a residence permit. Once the war started, her work situation worsened. Due to the years of hardship and agitation, Marion V. required medical attention. Faced with deteriorating health as well as professional and financial ruin, she tried to commit suicide. After her suicide attempt failed, she was admitted to a psychiatric clinic near Lucca for an extended period of time.[129] She returned to Munich after being released in 1941.

While Marion V. was in Italy, her petition to be classified as a non-Jew continued on its way through official channels in Germany. This was crucial not only for her but also especially for her two children. For daughter Beate, the recognition of Johann V's paternity and the clarification of whether her mother would be classified as a non-Jew were both significant matters. Beate K. had her own children, whose classification, in turn, also depended on that of their mother and grandmother. In Munich, Marion V. registered for a "genetic examination" at the anthropological institute of the University of Munich. From there, she was referred to the Reich Kinship Office (*Reichssippenamt*, formerly *Reichsstelle für Sippenforschung*) in Berlin, which declared in May 1942 that she was to be deemed a Jew.[130] Johann V. filed an objection to the decision and renewed his declaration that he was Beate K.'s father.[131]

In Munich, Marion V. lived at the home of Beate and Beate's children. When in January 1944 the Gestapo stood in front of their building with a deportation notice, Marion was able to hide at the last minute in a neighbor's apartment.[132] The neighbor had observed the arrival of the Gestapo from her window and had the presence of mind to quickly fetch Marion out of her apartment and take her into her own. Hermann B., an old friend of Marion, arranged longer-term quarters. He found lodgings for Marion with a friend of his, the lawyer Dr. Emil W.[133] Beate K., together with Hermann B. and his family, helped cover the costs and in particular helped to provide food.[134] Beate benefitted from a degree of protection provided by the *Mischling* status of her children. All went well for almost a year.

On December 16, 1944, the Gestapo came knocking at the door. Marion V. had been denounced, probably by neighbors who had noticed her presence. Marion V. was arrested and, after never-ending interrogations in the Wittelsbach Palace, the headquarters of the Munich Gestapo, she again attempted suicide. After several days in a coma, she awakened and was sent to the Berg am Laim labor education camp. From there she was deported to Theresienstadt on February 21, 1945.[135] She survived. Marion's daughter, Beate K., was also supposed to be deported with her children in February 1945, but according to an acquaintance, when the Gestapo men came to pick them up, they let her be because she was seriously ill.[136]

ROBBERS NOT HELPERS: "JEW FLEECERS" AND OTHER PROFITEERS

Assistance to Jews in hiding was often a transaction, and sometimes an unfair one. The U-boats often paid for their lodgings, food, and protection with service as a nanny or domestic help to a caring family or by contributing a share of the rent. But the transaction could also take the form of financial usury and sexual exploitation. The boundaries between these categories could be fluid.

Moreover, the agreed-upon arrangement often transpired to be a fraud or even a trap. Numerous people enriched themselves from the suffering of the Jews. The aid often turned out to be much more meager than promised. Forged papers were sometimes poorly made or never delivered. Hidden Jews were chased out of their lodgings much earlier than agreed upon. In extreme cases, they were even denounced to the Gestapo.[137]

The exploitation of Jews in hiding must be seen within the wider context of countless cases of fraud, theft, extortion, and other crimes aimed at taking advantage of the lawlessness of the situation and the desperation of the Jewish population. Especially in the aftermath of the November pogrom of 1938, forged visas and passports became more widely available, and fraudsters claimed to be able to get names crossed off deportation lists.[138] Richard Lutjens has discussed the case of Friedrich Wetzel and Dr. Walther Schotte, who fraudulently obtained almost 15,000 reichsmarks in 1941–42 in that way. They also deluded Berlin Jews into thinking they could obtain documents for legal entry into Switzerland and convert racial classifications from full Jew to half Jew.[139] Criminals pretended to be Gestapo officers, searched and plundered apartments, and raped defenseless victims.[140]

Numerous Berlin U-boats were deceived, robbed, extorted, or in some other way exploited by *Judenfledderer*, or Jew fleecers,[141] a term used colloquially by Berlin Jews to refer to people who usurped the last possessions of Jews before they were deported. One group among the Jew fleecers, were deceptive *Verwarier*, or "custodaryans."[142] These custodaryans kept valuables in safekeeping for Jewish friends or relatives. Among them, however, were also many who never considered returning the items entrusted to them.

The Jew fleecers had very little to fear since the victims were defenseless. If they wanted to, the fleecers could make matters worse with a denunciation. They did not reckon with the Jews ever returning. In most cases, this strategy paid off. There were many different forms of exploitation and fraud.[143] And there were many instances in which agreements regarding accommodations were not adhered to, yet the prepaid rent or the possessions of the fugitive Jews were kept.[144] Some U-boats were extorted to pay protection or hush money.[145] The wife of a military officer offered services to smuggle U-boats into Switzerland. As soon as Jews wanting to escape had paid several thousand reichsmarks, they were denounced to the Gestapo.[146] Because Jews fleeing from Munich could rely less on commercial forms of support, and because there were only a small number of Jews in hiding there, few cases of Jew fleecers are documented for that city. Even there, however, greed triumphed wherever the opportunity arose.

Margot S. worked as an English teacher in Munich, giving lessons to numerous Jews wanting to emigrate. The parents of the young single woman were able to emigrate in May 1939, but Margot remained in Munich. Starting in 1941, she had to do forced labor at the Lohhof flax rettery.[147] When in November 1941 she learned that the first deportation was imminent, she stopped going to work in Lohhof. By her own account, she had been warned by the Gestapo officer Eduard Fahlbusch.[148] Margot S. made an exonerating statement on behalf of Fahlbusch in 1947. She wrote that they had both been strolling in the English Garden, wearing sunglasses to conceal their identities, and he advised her "definitely to flee."[149] She did not mention how she had met Fahlbusch.

Margot S. followed his advice and found refuge with a friend, Wilhelm Eder. Also at this time she met a woman, Wally Cremer, in a Munich restaurant. Because Cremer's husband had English ancestors, and because Margot S., who had English relatives, could speak fluent English, the two women started a conversation. Cremer ultimately invited Margot S. to tea at her home. When Margot arrived, Wally Cremer offered her a temporary place to stay. According to Margot S.'s postwar account, she explained her situation to Cremer and showed her her ID card stamped with a J (for "Jew").[150] Margot S. moved in with Wally Cremer in the south of Munich a few days later, bringing all her remaining possessions with her.

A short time later, Margot S. traveled to Dresden, where she wanted to arrange a new hiding place for herself. After these efforts failed, she returned to Munich, but no longer wanted to stay where she had been previously. She told Cremer that she would be moving out and would soon return with her friend Wilhelm Eder to pick up her things. When Margot S. showed up at Cremer's a few days later, the police arrived after a short time and arrested her. Wally Cremer had denounced Margot S. during the latter's absence. At the police station, she had reported that a woman was living in her house under a false identity and that she was probably either an English spy or a Jew.[151] Cremer later claimed she had not known that Margot S. was Jewish, but rather that she had just wanted to determine who Margot really was, this woman who had been receiving mail from England and who had not wanted to register her address with the police.[152] After her arrest, Margot S. was transferred to the Munich Gestapo, where she spent two weeks in prison. Ultimately, the Gestapo officer Fahlbusch was supposed to bring her to the Aryanization Office on Widenmayerstrasse, but on a pretext and with the authorization of his superior, Johann Pfeuffer, he let her go alone.[153]

Margot S. immediately returned to the police station that had ordered her arrest and asked a policeman to accompany her to Wally Cremer's residence to demand the return of her possessions. Although it seems somewhat illogical that she would voluntarily return to the police in Pullach (who knew she was Jewish) shortly after escaping the Gestapo under extremely lucky circumstances, this detail is confirmed by statements by her and by the local police officer.[154] When she arrived with an officer at Wally Cremer's house, Cremer claimed that everything had already been picked up by a man she did not know. Margot S. then remained for another few days in Munich with friends of Wilhelm Eder, who also gave her money for a train ticket to Berlin, where she lived in hiding until the end of the war.[155] Margot S. eventually returned to Munich and started searching for her possessions. This postwar story will be treated in chapter 10.

There were fewer opportunities in Munich than in Berlin to make money by exploiting fugitive Jews. But like people all over Germany, many in Munich were not shy when it came to making a good deal at the expense of Jews and by profiting from the Aryanization and auctions of Jewish property. The latter was a common practice. We do not, however, know how common cases like that of Margot S. and Wally Cremer were. If Margot S. had not survived, her story would never have come to light. But we do know that hers was not an isolated case.

Otto and Anny Jordan, Benno Schülein's helpers, were extorted and threatened by their domestic help. As described in chapter 4, the Jordans hid their good friend Benno Schülein, a lawyer, for periods of time starting in 1943. They also supported him while he was hidden by other people. The couple's cook exploited this situation and started stealing systematically from the household once she learned that her employers were protecting and harboring a Jew. Little by little, valuables, linens, dishes, and food started vanishing from the apartment. The cook was friendly with an SS man whom she eventually also let spend the night in the Jordans' home. She threatened the Jordans that she would inform on them to the Gestapo if they reported the thefts. In 1943, the Jordans managed to get rid of the cook with the help of the labor office. While the cook was moving out, Anny Jordan had to watch her own household effects being hauled away by the box load.[156]

Eva Kobler, a *Geltungsjude* from Hamburg, received her summons to report for deportation to Theresienstadt in January 1944. She fled to Eduard Wolf and his wife in Munich. Wolf's first wife, Katharina, had been a close friend of Kobler's mother, to whom she had promised that she would take Kobler in should this become necessary. Although Katharina Wolf had since died, Eduard Wolf and his second wife, Anna, took Kobler in. A short time later, Wolf took away all of Kobler's possessions, saying that they had to be protected from the air raids. After a time, Kobler came under severe pressure by Wolf to follow the example of his first wife and commit suicide, arguing that Kobler would be arrested sooner or later anyway. When Kobler refused to kill herself, the Wolfs denounced her, although Kobler survived in prison.[157]

Many such cases of self-enrichment, betrayal, and theft are difficult to document, so even in cases where the victimized persons survived, charges were seldom filed. The survivors, relieved to have escaped death, and often ashamed of what they had gone through, saw no chance of holding the offenders accountable. For small swindlers who cashed in on their protection of Jews, and for Germans who did not shy away from robbing fugitive Jews of their possessions and then denouncing them, there were countless opportunities for self-enrichment from the desperate situation of the Jewish population. Even though there were far fewer cases of fugitive Jews who sought help in Munich than in Berlin, many, perhaps most, such cases never became part of the historical record due to the minimal risk for the exploiters and the fact that most of the victims were ultimately murdered. Very few cases led to criminal proceedings after the war. These will be treated in chapter 10.

ON THE DENUNCIATION OF THOSE IN HIDING AND THEIR HELPERS

The arrest of Jews in hiding often was the result of denunciations. In this context, two questions are of particular significance: (1) How widespread were denunciations of Jews in hiding, and how many U-boats and helpers were denounced by individuals in the general population?; and (2) What can be said about the practice of denunciations in Munich?

Regarding the first question, we do not yet have any systematic studies, but it is certain that a large percentage of those in hiding were denounced at one point or another. Based on the cases known to date, neighbors posed a particularly great risk.[158] Richard Lutjens has pointed out that survivor testimonies are replete with stories of U-boats who felt compelled to change their hiding places upon realizing that they were being observed. He has argued that "denunciation of illegal Jews was one of the Gestapo's most valuable tools."[159] Many cases of U-boats and helpers who were arrested show that the arrests were triggered by denunciations.[160] Many denunciations were made anonymously,[161] so we don't know anything about the denouncers and their motives. It was not only Germans who denounced Jews in hiding. In the Hessian village of Erbach, for example, a farmer was denounced by a Polish forced laborer who worked for him. The two had quarreled, and consequently the Polish worker denounced the farmer for hiding a Jew on his farm. The farmer eventually died in the Dachau concentration camp, but the hidden Jew was able to flee, making it safely to Switzerland.[162]

Also, very few conclusions can be reached regarding the question of what percentage of all denunciations were denunciations of Jews. In the Krefeld area between 1933 and 1939, there were about as many investigations stemming from denunciations of Jews as there were from denunciations of non-Jews. During the years 1940–45, 47 percent of the investigations resulted from denunciations of non-Jewish Germans, as opposed to 29 percent from denunciations of Jews.[163] Despite the continually decreasing size of the Jewish population through deportations, the percentage of investigations of Jews that were initiated due to a denunciation remained substantial. Denunciations by neighbors were in this case also relatively high.[164] The figures, which are estimates, can be understood to show that the Gestapo was more likely to introduce investigations against Jews, but they also indicate that Germans had fewer scruples about denouncing Jews than denouncing "national comrades" (*Volksgenossen*).[165] They might also indicate that Germans were sometimes fearful of the consequences of not denouncing a hidden Jew should the case eventually become known to the Gestapo.

As shown in chapter 1, the substantial number of Jews denounced between 1938 and 1941 is striking, also regarding figures for Munich. Even if the denunciations cannot be definitively evaluated quantitatively, thus precluding any far-reaching conclusions about the behavior of people in Munich regarding denunciations, the following can nevertheless be asserted. Denunciations can be documented in at least thirteen cases of Munich Jews who went into hiding or of U-boats from elsewhere who had gone to Munich. The actual number is probably higher. It must also be taken into account that between 1942 and 1945, there were no longer many people in Munich and environs who were confronted with the decision of whether or not to denounce a Jew. At the same time, it must be emphasized that many people were in a position to denounce but chose not to. Marie Jalowicz Simon was continually amazed by how many people in the building and the district in which she lived for a time were aware of her true identity.[166]

In Munich, as in other cities, neighbors represented a certain danger. Nevertheless, neighbors were by no means automatically denouncers. In the case of Sigmund W., who did not change his hiding place for a long time, it seems likely that neighbors noticed his presence but took no action. Marion V. was likely denounced by one neighbor and rescued by another. Domestic helpers sometimes reported the people they worked for, as in the Jordan and Cosmann cases. An employee of the Kammerer company denounced his boss as a "friend of Jews" (see chapter 3). Else Gerlach was repeatedly threatened with denunciation by the husband of her helper. He wanted to get rid of an inconvenient guest.[167] Eva Kobler was denounced by a supposed friend, and Margot S. by an acquaintance. In both of these cases, it was a matter of self-enrichment. In many cases, the identity of the denouncer could not be determined. Edith S. was denounced while in the Schwabing hospital. Rosa L. was denounced anonymously in a small village near Garmisch-Partenkirchen,[168] as was Sophie Mayer in Lenggries. Gerty Spies was denounced in 1941 because she and her daughter were visited by a non-Jewish young man. After the war, she reported that Ernst Poller, the Nazi Party local group leader, told her that "he had his informers" and she "could prepare herself for something" if he received any more reports.[169]

Older works on denunciation often posited the conclusion that a majority of the denunciations were made by women.[170] More recent research, however, has come to different conclusions based on local history studies.[171] Eric Johnson has written that in the Cologne/Krefeld area, "the typical denouncer was male, middle-aged, and middle class."[172] However, the statistics provided by Johnson merely show that in the Cologne/Krefeld area people under thirty, women, and the elderly tended to be less likely to denounce someone. A definitive trend cannot be derived from this information.[173] It is likewise not possible to draw conclusions from these findings as to what groups of people specifically denounced Jews or helpers of Jews since this was not examined separately.

Based on the cases from Munich presented here in which it was possible to determine the gender and social stratum of the denouncers, it can be said that Jews were denounced by people of all social strata—from aristocrats to domestic helpers, both male and female. Even though the findings are based on a relatively small group of people, they do validate Gisela Diewald-Kerkmann's argument that there was no typical personality type for denouncers.[174] Very different kinds of people, under various circumstances, had a variety of motives for denouncing Jews. And, also for very diverse reasons, others became helpers.

SEVEN

SPECIFIC GROUPS OF HELPERS AND THOSE THEY HELPED

Hidden Children and Church Aid

IN CONTRAST TO THE SITUATION in the German-occupied countries of Europe, in Germany itself relatively few Jewish children were hidden. In Berlin as in Bavaria, children comprised only a small group among the U-boats. Whereas numerous Jewish children in occupied Poland survived in monasteries and convents, this was rare in Germany.[1] Church aid nevertheless played a role in sheltering and caring for Jewish children in Germany as well. In most cases, however, church assistance was for adults and not young people. This chapter deals with hidden children as a specific group of U-boats, and with Christian helpers who often used their connections across the country to provide assistance. For the very small group of Jewish children from Munich who were hidden, it can be shown that their parents took them outside the city. Their escape routes led to remote rural regions of Bavaria, where they lived openly, albeit under a false identity, with host families. At the same time, there were also children from other parts of the country who traveled long distances as "illegal" U-boats with various way stations to Munich and Upper Bavaria, often with assistance from transregional Christian helper networks. Christian aid for Jews at the local level frequently operated within a network of widely dispersed helpers, providing fugitive Jews with both short and long escape routes throughout all of Germany.

SENDING CHILDREN AWAY

"It was very hard to say goodbye to my grandmother. She thought I didn't understand how threatening the situation was and tried to convince me that she was going on vacation and would be back soon and everything was just fine. But I knew all along that I would never see her again."[2]

This is how Charlotte Knobloch, née Neuland, described her farewell from her grandmother, Albertine Neuland, who was deported in July 1942. After her parents were divorced, Charlotte Neuland lived with her father and grandmother.[3] Shortly after her grandmother was deported, her father, lawyer Siegfried Neuland, arranged a hiding place for her. The girl was taken to her uncle's former housekeeper, Zenzi Hummel, on a farm in Franconia. She spent almost three years there and was passed off as Hummel's out-of-wedlock child.[4] For Charlotte Neuland, ten years old at the time, this meant losing her entire family little by little. She did not see her father again until 1945. Her grandmother, Albertine Neuland, was murdered in Theresienstadt in January 1944. As the long-serving president of postwar Munich's Jewish Community, president of the Central Council of Jews in Germany from 2006 until 2010, and vice president of the World Jewish Congress from 2005 until 2013, Charlotte Knobloch is certainly the most well-known person from Munich who survived the Holocaust in hiding.[5]

Children and adolescents were a minority among German Jews in hiding. Only about 12 percent were under fourteen years of age, and another 7.5 percent were between fourteen and nineteen years old.[6] As with the other age groups, most were in Berlin, where it was not unusual for a mother to go into hiding together with a child.[7] Sometimes entire families went underground and tried to survive in Berlin, at times together and at times separately.[8] Other parents thought their children would be safer alone and brought them to acquaintances, friends, or even complete strangers. In German-occupied areas, children were often sheltered in monasteries, where they were passed off as Christian orphans and raised Christian. Many lost their Jewish identity almost entirely. In Germany itself, there were only isolated cases of children being hidden in monasteries.[9] Beate Kosmala has traced this situation to the fact that there was no well-organized, strong resistance movement in Germany.[10] There was no systematic effort to shelter as many Jewish children as possible in Christian institutions. Also, many children had already been brought out of Germany through the *Kindertransports*, an evacuation program to send Jewish children to Britain.[11]

In Bavaria, the path taken by most hidden children led them to the countryside. There they could be accommodated while drawing relatively little attention. Their parents brought them to relatives in rural areas either as a precaution or because they had been bombed out. Hugo Holzmann, born in 1929, Hannelore Bach, born in 1931, Charlotte Neuland, born in 1932, and Bernhard K., born in 1936 (all in Munich), were children when the war started. Their Jewish fathers had married women who had either converted to Judaism before the marriage or had retained their Christian faith. A key factor in determining the status of the children within the Nazi racial hierarchy was whether the children were registered members of the Jewish community or whether they were raised Christian.

Hannelore Bach and Bernhard K. were raised Christian, and their mothers had not converted to Judaism. Their parents' marriages were thus "privileged mixed marriages," and the children, formally classified as first-degree *Mischlinge*, were in a better position than *Geltungsjuden*, such as Hugo Holzmann, who were raised Jewish. Charlotte Neuland was also raised Jewish by her grandmother, and her mother had converted to Judaism before marrying Siegfried Neuland.[12] Children six and older who were classified as *Geltungsjuden* had to wear the yellow star. Young *Geltungsjuden* were often deported along with their Jewish parent in February 1945.[13] *Mischlinge* did not have to wear the yellow star and were not designated for deportation.[14] However, this could have changed at any time, which many of the affected families certainly feared. The parents' first priority was to bring their children to safety. Many did not want to wait until they received their notice to report for deportation. *Mischlinge* were therefore hidden just as often as were *Geltungsjuden*, or so-called full Jews. Hugo Holzmann, one of these *Geltungsjuden*, was brought to an isolated farm in Lower Bavaria in January 1945, when he was fifteen.

Hugo Holzmann was born in 1929, the second child in his family. His mother, Anna Holzmann, had converted to Judaism in 1924, shortly before marrying Martin Holzmann, a Jewish textile vendor. When her husband died in 1935, Anna Holzmann was left to her own resources and lived with her two children, Herta and Hugo, in a small Munich apartment at Theresienstrasse 128. The building belonged to a Jewish couple, the Lewins, who had four daughters. Anna Holzmann decided in 1938 to send her fourteen-year-old daughter Herta to the United States, where she was to be adopted by a couple in Philadelphia. The Lewins also sent their three oldest daughters abroad. Only the youngest remained in Munich—Ilse Lewin with her parents, and Hugo Holzmann with his mother.[15]

In November 1941, the Lewin family was deported and murdered in Kaunas, Lithuania. Anna and Hugo Holzmann had not been able to say goodbye to their neighbors. This deportation was a traumatic experience for young Hugo. Not only his friend Ilse but also most of his classmates from the Jewish school had disappeared from one day to the next. A few weeks later, the school was closed.[16]

In April 1942, Hugo Holzmann was assigned to forced labor at the Buchner landscape nursery, where about a dozen Jews from Munich were conscripted.

Oskar Buchner had been an *Alter Kämpfer* (an "Old Fighter," someone who had joined the Nazi Party before 1933) and an SA man with good connections to the local Nazi Party leadership, so he could obtain cheap labor.[17] In late 1944, the building in which Hugo and Anna Holzmann were living was severely damaged in an air raid; in another air raid on January 8, 1945, the apartment was completely destroyed. Hugo and Anna Holzmann spontaneously decided to go into hiding. They left Munich only a few weeks before Hugo's deportation notice arrived. A neighbor, Frau Matschilles, had offered to let Hugo stay with her brother. Together with his mother and Frau Matschilles, Hugo Holzmann rode to Pilsting, a small town in Lower Bavaria, where he said goodbye to his mother, who then went on to her sister. Frau Matschilles and Hugo walked from Pilsting to a small hamlet nearby, where only the B. family and one other family lived.[18]

The B.s had thirteen children, but only the youngest was still living at home. The parents were willing to take in Hugo Holzmann, well aware that he was Jewish. The neighbors and their children also knew Hugo's identity. The oldest son in the B. family had deserted from an army punishment battalion and was a fugitive. He occasionally showed up secretly at his parents' home.[19] Hugo Holzmann stayed with the B. family until the end of the war. A few weeks after Germany surrendered, he rode back to Munich by bicycle.

In contrast to Anna Holzmann, Lotte Bach had not converted to Judaism when she married a Jewish man. Her daughter, Hannelore Bach, was raised Lutheran. Hannelore's father, Fritz Bach, was a self-employed textile wholesaler, and in 1939, he went without his family to the United States, where Lotte Bach had relatives.[20] Lotte Bach moved to her parents' home along with her daughter Hannelore. She did not yield to pressure from the Gestapo to divorce her husband. In this situation, former customers of her husband in the Munich environs were to become a great help to Lotte Bach. Not only did they bring her food, but they also found comforting words for her mother, who was visibly worried about her daughter. Lotte Bach regularly visited a farming family in the small town of Niederroth near Dachau (approximately thirty kilometers—about eighteen miles—northwest of Munich) and received food from them. They promised to take in Hannelore if necessary.[21]

In 1941, Lotte Bach deregistered her daughter from Munich and brought her to the Gailer family in Niederroth. Hannelore spent the next four years there, growing up together with Leonhard and Maria Gailer's six children.[22] Her true identity soon become an open secret in the village. Even the local group leader of the Nazi Party, who was also the village teacher, knew of Hannelore Bach's background. A visit by the Gestapo, which had heard rumors that a "Jewish child" was in the village, did not lead to any serious consequences. When asked why one of the children looked totally different from the others, Leonhard Gailer threw a fit: Visitors insulting his wife! He would not put up with that! The men from the Gestapo were immediately shown the door.[23] The Gestapo men probably let themselves be convinced so easily because Leonhard Gailer had been a member of the Nazi Party and various Nazi organizations since 1933. He was also the mayor of Niederroth.[24] Shortly before the war ended, Lotte Bach also sought refuge in Niederroth, so mother and daughter were there together when liberation came. In January 1947, they both went to New York to finally see Fritz Bach again after eight years.[25]

When Bernhard K. was born in 1936, he was the first child of Gustav K. and his wife Luise. Being raised as a Christian, Bernhard K. was classified a first-degree *Mischling*. His mother was Lutheran; his father, Jewish. Luise K. had another son from a previous marriage. According to the race laws, he was considered "Aryan." The family lived in Munich's city center. After being released from the Dachau concentration camp in December 1938, Gustav K. did everything he could to enable himself and his family to emigrate. In June 1940, Gustav and Luise K. finally received visas for the Dominican Republic, but they could no longer arrange the ocean passage. In December 1940, the consulate of the Dominican Republic destroyed all hopes of their leaving Germany once and for all. The letter Gustav K. received stated, "Our government has declared all entry visas authorized prior to July 5, 1940 to be null and void."[26]

Gustav K. had to do forced labor starting in April 1940. Having been referred by Pastor Stritter, who was friends with Gustav K., young Bernhard went to the preschool of the School Sisters of Notre Dame convent at Anger; his older half brother was drafted into military service. As the situation started becoming increasingly difficult, a neighbor—Kathi S., a waitress—was to become a protector of the family. At the time, Kathi S. was a childless, unmarried woman about fifty to sixty years old. Bernhard K. described her as an extremely resolute person, a typical Munich waitress. Kathi S. was a woman with an eventful life who did not care much for the social norms of bourgeois society. She now mostly cared for little Bernhard, who was treated with hostility by the neighborhood children, and often took him with her to her job at the Eberl-Bräu, an inn at Sendlinger Tor in the center of Munich.[27]

In August 1942, Gustav K.'s widowed mother was deported to Theresienstadt. She died there after only a few months, on Christmas Day 1942. Six months later, the family suffered another serious blow: Luise K.'s older son died in combat in Russia. Luise K. soon decided to go into hiding with young Bernhard. It is not clear whether the loss of her older son influenced her decision. Up to then, she could always mention to authorities that she had "an Aryan

Bernhard K. with Kathi S. Private collection, courtesy of Daniela Schmidl.

son in the field," which might have made her feel more secure. In any case, it was Kathi S. who then used her connections to various families in the Dachau environs to find a hiding place for Luise and Bernhard K. She then brought the mother and son to a farm of the L. family near Altomünster (a small city about fifty kilometers—thirty-one miles—northwest of Munich).[28]

The L.s were a strict Catholic family. Three sons were serving in the military, and only the then seventeen-year-old daughter helped the parents with the farmwork. Luise and Bernhard K. stayed in the *Austragshäusl*, a small house on the farm where the farmer would live after retiring and passing the farm on to his children. It was probably for religious reasons that the L. family was willing to offer refuge to strangers. Frau L. hoped to be rewarded by God for her good deed. Bernhard K. remembered that she insisted that he accompany her to church every day. The precise circumstances can no longer be reconstructed, but Gustav K. evidently managed to visit his family in secret on some Sundays. In early 1945, he hid on the farm to avoid the final series of deportations from Munich. Thus, the family was together when the war ended.[29]

Due to the persecution, Bernhard K. did not start school until the fall of 1945, when he was nine years old. The family returned to Munich. Emigration was no longer an option for Gustav and Luise K. Gustav K. was severely scarred from the hardship of the forced labor and the abuse he suffered in the Dachau concentration camp. He died in 1953, shortly before his fifty-ninth birthday. Kathi S. also died a short time after the war ended.

Like Hannelore Bach and Bernhard K., Ruth Schwink found shelter in the countryside, but her story of persecution ended tragically. Elisabeth Schwink, who had a mixed marriage, found refuge together with her teenaged daughter Ruth in Jachenau, a community near Bad Tölz in the Alpine foothills of Upper Bavaria. Mother and daughter lived there on a farm. All went well until they went on a hike to a mountain lake, Walchensee, with a friend of Ruth's on May 3, 1945, and were on the lookout for American troops. They came upon a group of SS men, who initially let them continue their hike. However, the SS men shot at the three women as they returned, evidently assuming they had sought contact with the American soldiers. Elisabeth and Ruth Schwink died in the barrage of gunfire, and the friend survived, although seriously injured.[30]

In all cases described so far, remote farms in Bavaria became refuges for children who were Jewish or half-Jewish. Some families had a personal connection to the individuals they hid; others were referred through friends, neighbors, or former domestic help. In a number of cases, there were religious motives behind the willingness to take in children.[31] Hopes that God would reward the good deed was of particular significance for families who had sons at the front.[32] It can certainly also be assumed that the parents paid a financial contribution toward the food for their children. For the mayor of Niederroth, Nazi Party membership and protecting Hannelore Bach were not a contradiction. It remains unclear, however, why this Catholic farmer had joined the Nazi Party.

The children who were hidden had to adapt to being in an unfamiliar extended family and usually had to hide their own identity. They were also compelled to adjust to a totally different way of life and often a much simpler existence.[33] Although the geographical distance to Munich was in many cases not all that great, the rural environment was nevertheless utterly alien to many city children. And even if they did not totally lose contact with their parents, the pain of separation and fear of loss were inevitable, all the more if they had already experienced one parent emigrating or the parents' divorce.[34] Small children in particular could interpret the separation from their parents as punishment for their own behavior. Others were only able to endure the loss by creating an emotional distance to their parents, whom they viewed as having abandoned them.[35]

It was not a matter of course for children to be received in their new environment with open arms. Often they were merely tolerated and treated accordingly. Franz Michalski of Breslau, for example, was nine years old when he and his younger brother Peter were given refuge in 1943 in a children's home of the Ursuline Order. As punishment for minor infringements, the nuns beat the boys. Franz later said that he was berated there as "Jew boy" and that other antisemitic insults were common as well.[36] In the Franconian village where Charlotte Neuland survived, she was known as the out-of-wedlock child of her helper. The ostensible stigma offered protection—nobody suspected that she was Jewish—but it also brought with it social ostracism. The children in the countryside, in particular, seemed to be comforted by contact with pets. A small cat became Charlotte Neuland's best friend, and Bernhard K. was very attached to an ox named Max.[37]

For many children in hiding, not only was the separation from their parents absolute, but they had to continually adjust to a new environment as they were often passed from one helper to the next. At the age of four, Denny F. started what would be a two-year odyssey throughout Germany, which also brought him to Munich. When Else F., a Berlin Jew, decided to go underground in January 1943, she separated from her son Denny in hopes that separate hiding places would increase their chances of survival. Whereas Else F. found refuge in changing accommodations with a good dozen helpers in Berlin, Denny traveled to Bavaria by way of Thuringia and Baden. His mother later had difficulty reconstructing the various stations he had passed through (and she probably did not even know of all of them). She reported that her son was first taken in by Eleonore von Trott zu Solz in Thuringia, and from there he went to Frau Schultz near Freiburg and finally to a baron in Gauting near Munich.[38]

The baron from Gauting was Otto Freiherr von Taube. The aristocratic author from Estonia had been a staunch Nazi in the early 1920s but had turned away from the party in the course of the Hitler putsch in 1923.[39] He expressed his disappointment in the novel *Das Opferfest* (*Feast of Sacrifice*) in 1923. "The author develops a nationalistic, ideologically dangerous sect through a fictitious figure, whose contours foreshadow the Nazi Germans of the 1930s and 1940s," wrote literary theorist Regina Mosbach about the novel.[40] In Taube's literary examination of Nazism, he parodied Nazi hopes of salvation as a religious-fanatical misdirection, in a way similar to that of Friedrich Reck-Malleczewen in *Bockelson*.[41] Taube withdrew into "inner emigration" in 1933, writing vicious poems in which he made fun of Nazi ideology and seeking comfort in exchanges with writer-friends.[42] In this regard, as well, there are parallels to Reck-Malleczewen. His friendship with resistance figure Adam von Trott zu Solz, who was eventually sentenced to death for his involvement in the plot to assassinate Hitler in July 1944, did not move him to join the Kreisau Circle conspirators. At the same time, Taube expected and hoped that the military leadership would liberate Germany.[43]

As Otto von Taube later reported, his wife Katharina received a letter in 1943 from her godmother, Eleonore von Trott zu Solz, the mother of Adam von Trott zu Solz. The letter stated that "she and her family had hidden a Jewish boy on their Imshausen estate near Bebra for an extended period of time. However, it was discovered in the very antisemitic village so she could not keep the child any longer and passed him on to a Protestant children's home in the Black Forest. There as well, however, the presence of the Jewish child in the home became known and he could no longer stay there either."[44]

Otto and Katharina von Taube took in the child themselves. The child only knew his first name, which he said was Toni. When Otto von Taube's sister, a devoted Nazi, came to visit, they had to entrust Toni/Denny to a good friend on short notice. Because the Taubes also feared that the child could soon be discovered, they turned to the Munich pastor, Leonhard Henninger, requesting that he find a new hiding place for the boy.[45] The cleric brought Toni/Denny to the Protestant orphanage in Munich, saying that he was a foundling from Hamburg.[46] Because the Gestapo had meanwhile started searching for Toni/Denny through an announcement in the Nazi newspaper *Völkischer Beobachter*, he was also brought from time to time to a children's home near Lenggries (a small town in the Bavarian Alps).[47] Over the long term, however, this meant that the boy had to be moved yet again. His journey ended with various families in Hamburg.

When Berlin was liberated in 1945, Else F. did not know where her son was. It took her several months to find out and to make her way to him in Hamburg. With the help of the authorities, she forced the release of her son. Else F. moved to Munich with Denny, and from there, she arranged their emigration to Uruguay, to where her husband had fled in 1939.[48] In 1949, Else F. and her son traveled to a country she did not know and to a husband she had not seen in ten years. Denny F., who as a four-year-old had been separated from his mother, went to a father he did not know. Many children who survived in hiding were, like Denny F., faced with new challenges after liberation, such as news of their parents' death or reuniting with parents they had not seen for years. This involved a clash of a wide range of emotions such as love, guilt, hate, helplessness, speechlessness, and pain, and it often meant moving to a new country. The social ostracism, forced denial of one's identity, and separation from members of their family left behind deep wounds.[49]

The fates and living conditions of children who survived in hiding in Germany have not yet been examined systematically.[50] It can nevertheless be said that their chances of survival were better than those of adults. Most of the hidden children from Munich who could be identified within the scope of this study survived. The survival rate of hidden children in Berlin was also high. Of the 3,600 known names of people who went into hiding in Berlin, three hundred were children, and only about fifty of them did not survive.[51] Also in the Netherlands, where all in all many more Jewish children were hidden than in Germany, the chances of survival were better than those of adults.[52] Church and Christian-motivated assistance for children played a role not only in the case of Denny F. In Berlin, there were other Jewish children who were first taken into parsonages and then passed on to other helpers.[53] The networks of Christian aid will be discussed in the second part of this chapter.

CHRISTIAN AID IN MUNICH AS PART OF NATIONWIDE CHRISTIAN RELIEF NETWORKS

Church assistance is the only aspect of the subject of flight and concealment in Munich that has been extensively studied. Although the available source materials are relatively sparse, there have been several publications on the subject.[54] The studies or relevant book chapters are often titled something like "Caring for the Jewish Christians,"[55] "Aid for Protestants Persecuted on Racial Grounds,"[56] or "On the Fate of Christians of Jewish Descent."[57] The Nazi race laws referred to Jews who had converted to Christianity, or who had been raised Christian, as "non-Aryan Christians." Regardless of their faith, they, along with practicing Jews and Jews who had rejected their faith, were all persecuted as Jews. The churches had an obligation to protect Protestants and Catholics, even if they were converts from Judaism. Through the sacrament of baptism, the Christians of Jewish origin had become full members of their Christian churches.[58] There was also a humanitarian and moral imperative to offer aid, beyond religious boundaries. Yet these distinctions posed fundamental questions. Whom did the Christian institutions address with their offers of assistance? Whom were they willing to help: Christians, people in mixed marriages, or practicing Jews? In fact, many of the church support centers for so-called non-Aryan Christians did not make distinctions between them and Jews, especially in the case of mixed marriages. There was, however, not necessarily unanimity regarding the question whether they should also help practicing Jews.

Church relief for Christians persecuted on racial grounds largely involved emigration advice, financial support, and family pastoral care. Probably best known in this area is the work of the Bureau Grüber in Berlin, named after its director, Pastor Heinrich Grüber, who assisted thousands of people starting in the summer of 1938.[59] The Bureau Grüber and its branch offices were based within the network of the Confessing Church, that is, the Protestant inner-church opposition to the German Christians, who fully supported Nazism. Until the arrest of Pastor Grüber and the closure of his office in December 1940, the Bureau Grüber and its branches arranged the emigration of an estimated 1,700–2,000 people.[60] Among Catholics, the relief organization of the Diocesan Authority Berlin (*Hilfswerk beim Bischöflichen Ordinariat Berlin*) was founded in 1938; it also was active in pastoral care, welfare, and emigration assistance, in particular efforts to send children away for their protection. Closely related to these efforts is the name Margarete Sommer, who was the managing director of the relief organization starting in 1941.[61] Though the focus was on Berlin, her organization worked throughout Germany, collaborating especially with the Catholic Caritas and the St. Raphael's Society, which advised prospective Catholic emigrants, and other aid organizations.[62]

One of the branches of the Bureau Grüber was the Aid Office for Non-Aryan Christians of the Inner Mission in Munich, where Pastor Friedrich Hofmann offered assistance starting in October 1938.[63] Bavarian State Bishop Hans Meiser had approved of the Aid Office and suggested Hofmann for the position. In January 1939, Meiser appointed Pastor Johannes Zwanzger to assist Hofmann.[64] Zwanzger was supposed to take over as director of the Aid Office. The State Church Council authorized 10,000 reichsmarks in November and another 10,000 reichsmarks a year later.[65] Enormous sums were sometimes needed for practical assistance. Zwanzger himself described the case of a man from Munich in a concentration camp, whom he had virtually "'bought' from the Gestapo for 5,000 reichsmarks"[66] to facilitate his release and subsequent emigration. Among Zwanzger's most resourceful helpers were Pastor Walter Hennighausen and Dean Friedrich Langenfass.[67]

Zwanzger also collaborated with the St. Raphael's Society and with the Caritas Association in Munich. August Kett, managing director of St.

Raphael's Society and Caritas, and Johannes Zwanzger were in close contact with Annemarie and Rudolf Cohen, both Quakers, who in the years 1938–41 had advised a total of 326 Munich Jews on emigration.[68] The Cohens maintained numerous contacts to Christians and Christian organizations elsewhere in Germany. They were supported in particular by international connections to Quakers and to representatives of Christian churches, especially in Britain. For example, the Cohens helped Siegfried Rosenfeld, Else Behrend-Rosenfeld's husband, emigrate to England.[69]

The Quakers tried to help Christians of Jewish descent, Jews, and persecuted people unaffiliated with any religion; the Aid Office and the St. Raphael's Society also refused to deny aid to Jews. The secretary general of the St. Raphael's Society in Hamburg protested the aid because he assessed it to be "useless and inopportune."[70] Munich cardinal Michael von Faulhaber also saw fundamental differences between Jews and non-Aryan Christians. Regarding baptized Jews, Faulhaber wrote in a letter to Cardinal Bertram that "the state can have the reassuring certainty that these are not Communists or Bolshevists." At the same time, he defended the right of the state to take action against "excesses of Judaism within its jurisdiction, especially when the Jews endanger the state order as Bolshevists or Communists."[71] As Andreas Wirsching has noted, the statement reflects Faulhaber's receptivity to antisemitic propaganda, and although Faulhaber emphasized the "right of non-Aryan Christians to be treated as Christians," he remained silent on the fate of the Jews.[72] In 1939, Faulhaber spoke out for the issuance of several thousand visas for non-Aryan Catholics so they could enter Brazil, taking advantage of his personal contact to the archbishop of Rio de Janeiro.[73] The selection criteria were very strict, however, and in the end, "only very few succeeded in emigrating within the scope of the Brazil Operation."[74] The cardinal had an adversarial stance toward some individuals and was receptive toward others. Dirk Schönlebe concluded that Faulhaber was "prepared, in isolated cases, to offer illegal assistance" to non-Aryan Catholics. At the same time, he was unwilling "to organize any large-scale assistance."[75]

With the closing of the Bureau Grüber in December 1940, the banning of the St. Raphael's Society in June 1941, and the end of Jewish emigration from Germany in October 1941, Christian relief shifted from being tolerated by the Nazis to being involved in illegal actions. Very few dared to take this step, but in Berlin and elsewhere, aid networks of Christians arose from circles of friends and acquaintances and maintained contacts throughout Germany.[76] Some of those involved had already known each other through the work of the *Hilfswerk* and the Bureau Grüber and its branches. There were also connections to the Kreisau Circle and the members of the group that participated in the July 20, 1944, attempt to assassinate Hitler. Members of the aid networks included pastors and members of the Confessing Church in Berlin, members of the Württemberg parsonage chain, Caritas staff, and sometimes also monasteries, Quakers, and local groups or loosely organized circles of helpers.[77] These connections also extended to Munich. It was easier for people who had converted from Judaism to the Protestant or Catholic faith, or for Jews in mixed marriages, to use these Christian aid networks. They were connected to the church communities and had Christian relatives and friends and, thus, access to their contacts. The following section will shed light on the members of these aid networks in Munich and will also address spontaneous assistance by individual church dignitaries.

In Munich, the Quaker couple Annemarie and Rudolf Cohen continued helping Jews after it had become increasingly difficult to emigrate. Annemarie Cohen worked in particular with Else Behrend-Rosenfeld, the manager of the Berg am Laim camp, organizing aid for those living in the camp and helping them deal with the prospect of deportation.[78] The two women remained in close contact even after Behrend-Rosenfeld had gone into hiding in Berlin. Cohen referred her to a Berlin Quaker for help in finding additional lodgings. Cohen later also located a mountain hut as a possible hiding place for Behrend-Rosenfeld.[79]

In addition to Annemarie Cohen, Luise Oestreicher, who was half Jewish, helped supply the Jews in the Berg am Laim camp with food and medicine.[80] Luise Oestreicher and her friend Maria Reis organized lodgings for Valerie and Andrea Wolffenstein, who ended up in Munich after fleeing Berlin.[81] Oestreicher was baptized Catholic and worked as a secretary for the Jesuit priest Dr. Alfred Delp. Delp, who had been directing a parish in Munich-Bogenhausen since 1939, was part of the Kreisau Circle around Helmuth James von Moltke and was arrested and executed as a member of the July 20, 1944, plot against Hitler.[82] Luise Oestreicher later recalled that Delp "in 1941 or '42, knew about a wonderful hiding place where an entire family was able to remain hidden throughout the entire winter and after that, in the spring, we trembled together until they made their way across Lake Constance into Switzerland."[83]

Luise Oestreicher was also a friend of Gertrud Luckner of Freiburg, who worked for the German Caritas Association. Luckner was arrested for helping Jews in March 1943 and put in the Ravensbrück concentration camp.[84] Since 1938, she had been supporting Jews through her connections throughout the country, organizing food and food ration cards and also scouting out escape routes to Freiburg and from there across the Swiss border. In addition to Luise

Oestreicher, her contacts in Munich included Alfred Delp, Else Behrend-Rosenfeld, and Rudolf and Annemarie Cohen.[85]

Youth pastor Leonhard Henninger, a cleric in the Inner Mission, was also an important contact point in the local network of Christian aid. Together with the director of the Protestant orphanage, he arranged Denny F.'s hiding place and sheltered a mixed-marriage couple, the Meyers, and their child for several weeks. Because of his help, Pastor Henninger repeatedly got into trouble with the Gestapo, though he was lucky in that the Gestapo officers on his case were well-disposed toward him (on this, see chapter 10).[86]

The Lempp circle played a key role in the Christian aid network in Munich. This was a Christian group around the publisher Albert Lempp, which included the professor Wilhelm Hengstenberg, the judge Emil Hochstädter, the pastor Karl Frör, the Swiss publisher Walter Classen, the pastor Hermann Diem (who did not live in Munich), and others. Diem was a close friend of Pastor Richard Gölz, a key member of the Württemberg parsonage chain, and the two of them kept hiding Jews, mostly from Berlin, in their parsonages. In a 1943 petition to State Bishop Hans Meiser, the Lempp circle condemned the stance of the Protestant church regarding the Jews.[87] Albert Lempp was the proprietor of the Christian Kaiser publishing house and bookstore in Munich's city hall. He had helped a Jewish employee in the bookstore escape to Switzerland in 1938.[88] Irmgard Meyenberg, a Christian of Jewish descent, lived in Lempp's apartment building on Isabellastrasse, where she was hidden in the apartment of Edith Holm.[89] The two women ran a book restoration workshop, which in 1933 had been transferred to Edith Holm, a Gentile, as the sole owner. After the Gestapo intercepted a letter from her father, Irmgard Meyenberg received a summons to appear in Wittelsbach Palais, the headquarters of the Munich Gestapo. She was supposed to report there two weeks later, but the Gestapo headquarters had been destroyed in the meantime by an air raid in April 1944. After that, she was left alone.[90]

Within the Lempp circle, it was the Swiss citizen Walter Classen in particular who helped people persecuted as Jews escape from Germany. Classen lived with his wife in Munich and ran the Ackermann art publishing company. At first, he helped Pastor Zwanzger, volunteering in the Aid Office for Non-Aryan Christians.[91] Classen was perhaps the only helper in Munich who had access to forged documents. He ostensibly had connections to officials who gave him blank forms, which he used for people wanting to flee.[92] Hermann Diem described Classen's activities as follows: "He sheltered escaped Jews in the Bavarian Oberland and at the same time organized an escape route via Austria and South Tyrol to Switzerland."[93] There he had contact to the theologian

Karl Barth. Diem participated in these escape operations. When the helpers in the border town of Nauders were exposed, Diem drove to the area himself in August 1943 to scout out a new escape route.[94] That was the last of the escapes in which they participated. Diem was drafted back into the Wehrmacht, and in late 1943, the Classens returned to Switzerland. It is unclear how many people Classen and his helpers were able to bring across the border and in what time frame, as there are hardly any surviving records about the network and their rescue actions.[95] An exception is the memoir of Beate Steckhan of Berlin, who published the story of her rescue.[96]

Beate Steckhan, a widow who was baptized Lutheran, was not brought to Switzerland. In December 1942, she embarked on a long journey throughout Germany. Countless helpers, mostly pastors or people connected to the Confessing Church, asked friends and relatives to take her in. These helpers in turn mobilized their friends and relatives so that a Christian relief network emerged that spanned all of Germany. Steckhan's Berlin helpers sent her to the Gölzes, members of the Württemberg parsonage chain in Wankheim near Tübingen and then further on to parsonages around Stuttgart. From there, she went to southern Bavaria, to Lake Walchensee and Garmisch-Partenkirchen, where she heard through Walter Classen that her hiding place with Pastor Kurt Müller in Stuttgart had been discovered.[97] Müller had organized various hiding places in Stuttgart for a whole series of Jews in hiding, including Hermann Diem's residence in Ebersbach, a small city east of Stuttgart. The Jews were supposed to register little by little as bombed-out refugees. These plans were foiled, as Diem presumed, through denunciations.[98] Beate Steckhan then went to Munich, where she, too, was denounced. She was able to flee in time, but she had to change hiding places very often since the Gestapo was on her tail. Via Berlin and the Brandenburg towns of Belzig and Buckow she returned to Munich, where Classen had arranged a hiding place for her in the Hotel Europäischer Hof, which was run by nuns. Gertrud Luckner also stayed there when she was in Munich.[99] Steckhan's flight continued to Ravensburg and Magdeburg and on to a countess in Prenzlau, where she was able to procure an ID card under a false name and remain until the war ended. This hiding place had been referred through the Munich dean Friedrich Langenfass.[100] In her account, Steckhan also mentions way stations in Karlsruhe, Heidelberg, and Königsberg.[101]

The story of Beate Steckhan shows how these aid networks developed and spread throughout all of Germany.[102] They extended from East Prussia and Pomerania to Brandenburg and Württemberg and down to the Swiss border.[103] Regional groups of helpers, such as the Württemberg parsonage chain or the circle around Walter Classen in Munich, then became parts of an interlocking system of networks of helpers.[104] Jews and non-Aryan Christians who were on the run, such as Beate Steckhan, Denny F., and Valerie Wolffenstein (see chapter 8), made it to Munich through these Christian aid networks. At the same time, Jews in Munich, such as Rudolf V., could leave the city with the help of this extended network of contacts and find refuge in other parts of the country (on this, see chapter 3).

Unlike Rudolf V., Irmgard Meyenberg, and Beate Steckhan, a majority of Jews in hiding in Munich found help that was not within the framework of such organized networks. By contrast, in Frankfurt, many people who went into hiding had one particular group of helpers to thank for their survival, though that group was, in turn, part of the larger interlocking system of networks. The Bockenheim network in Frankfurt around the physician Dr. Fritz Kahl and the pastor Heinz Welcke was a well-organized group of helpers, which ran a courier service and also included a talented forger.[105] Patients of Dr. Kahl supplied their doctor with food ration cards. Kahl and Welcke had contacts to the Württemberg parsonage chain, the Confessing Church in Berlin, and to Switzerland. The group managed to bring several people with forged IDs into Switzerland. One person was hidden in Vienna.[106]

Aside from the aid networks operating in Munich, ordinary clerics and nuns also tried to offer individual support. In late 1944, Pastor Josef Hahner turned to Cardinal Michael von Faulhaber, asking him for help in finding a hiding place for Gertrud Schaeffler. A chemist, Schaeffler was a baptized Jew who had lived in Munich-Solln until December 1944 under the protection of having a privileged mixed marriage. At that time, her husband and son were brought to a labor camp run by the Organization Todt.[107] Gertrud Schaeffler feared that her own deportation was imminent. Cardinal Faulhaber wanted to hide the woman in a convent and even procured a nun's habit.[108] Gertrud Schaeffler had reservations, however, fearing she would stand out immediately in a convent. Finally, Pastor Hahner took her in with the approval of the cardinal and hid her in the attic of the parish house.[109] He asked the farmers in the area for food. Although he told them the food was not for him, he could not tell them whom it was for, yet he received the support he needed. He then shared the secret with some women from the parish so Schaeffler would have someone to talk to now and then.[110]

In February 1945, Mother Superior Maria Medarda Hörterer of the English Ladies (Mary Ward sisters, Congregatio Jesu) hid Klara Mayr, whom she had not previously known. She passed her off as a convent sister in Blutenburg Castle,[111] where the English Ladies operated a rest home. Klara Mayr was not discovered when a raid took place there. Her family did not know where she had been hidden until the war ended.[112]

Pastor Hahner and Sister Medarda Hörterer were probably not isolated cases. There are indications that individual helpers were also active in other parishes.[113] In some instances, however, the information is not sufficient for reconstructing what actually took place. On the other hand, the number of cases that did not enter the historical record is probably not high because numerous efforts have been undertaken over time to locate church helpers, as is documented in many publications.

Once Christian relief was no longer tolerated by the Nazis, there were in fact only very few church dignitaries of both major churches who were still willing to continue their support. An example of this is the case of Karoline Borchardt, who was baptized as a Lutheran. The Nazis considered her a full Jew, and she could not rely on the protection granted mixed marriages since she was divorced from author Rudolf Borchardt.[114] Karoline Borchardt was supposed to be deported to Kaunas, Lithuania, in November 1941. Responding to this situation, a good friend of hers, the author Rudolf Alexander Schröder, wrote a letter to Dean Langenfass and pleaded with him to support Karoline Borchardt:

> A friend of mine said recently: "I would let her [Karoline Borchardt] sleep in the churches and sacristies." That is not possible offhand. But the word is evidence of a healthy sensibility and, once uttered, would *find an echo everywhere*. In the conversation with Pastor Hofmann I didn't find much of this sort of basic attitude. He brought up only the difficulties that would come with immediately offering lodging in a nursing home or some similar place, which in his opinion—and then also de facto—would make it impossible. As a civil servant, certainly, he was correct. The question for us Christians in such a *vitally* decisive time is whether the concept of impossible should perhaps be reevaluated. . . . It must be possible to make decisions on short notice that would spare the Church of Luther the disgrace before *all* people and—far more seriously—the horrible responsibility before the living God of the Epistle to the Hebrews, that it did not even find the *word* of protection and defense for the most impoverished and miserable of its members entrusted to it by the Lord our God. In Bavaria that would hardly mean an overwhelming number of souls that we would not want to help sell to Satan through silence. As far as I know, new conversions are forbidden in any case.[115]

There are several notable aspects of this letter. First, it suggests that even clerics who had exhausted all legal options to help were not willing to intervene to oppose the deportation of baptized Jews. Second, Schröder, too, explicitly referred only to baptized Jews although he had earlier—in November 1941—clearly outlined the fate of all those deported: "deportation to the hells of hunger and frost in the East."[116] Third, Schröder referred to fundamental Christian values, appealing specifically to the dean's conscience in an effort to mobilize help for his friend. At the same time, he seemed surprised that the church had not planned "at least something"[117] against the deportation of Christians. Dean Langenfass evidently left the letter unanswered.[118] A girlfriend of Karoline Borchardt managed to get her deferred from deportation in November 1941, but then in July 1942, Borchardt was deported to Theresienstadt and perished there.[119]

Pastor Henninger later emphasized that missionizing Jews was out of the question under the conditions of persecution. He wrote: "Even a four-year-old Jewish child who was entrusted by his Jewish mother . . . to a cleric who kept him hidden for a year when the child was being sought by the Gestapo was not missionized."[120] However, this was not the case everywhere. The Berlin Diocesan Authority *Hilfswerk* did in fact missionize some Jews in its charge,[121] but Christian organizations largely supported persecuted Christians. The cases of Gertrud Schaeffler, Klara Mayr, and Beate Steckhan involved persecuted Christians. This was also true of Rudolf V., who was hidden by the Caritas organization in Stuttgart, Margarete Sterneck, who committed suicide in a Württemberg parsonage, the sisters Valerie and Andrea Wolffenstein, and Anna Reinach, who succeeded in fleeing to Spain through her connections to the Beuron archabbey (see the following chapter). For some Christian dignitaries religion was irrelevant. Others distinguished between Jews and baptized Christians. In any case, it was largely "non-Aryan Christians" or spouses of Jews in mixed marriages who turned to church representatives for help. Many of them found dedicated helpers who knew of places to go throughout Germany. For many of these individuals, their illegal existence also meant they had to travel a lot. These journeys throughout all of Germany and also abroad will be discussed more closely in the next chapter.

EIGHT

TO AND FROM MUNICH

Regional, National, and Transnational Escape Routes and Connections

JEWISH U-BOATS IN NAZI GERMANY were often on the move. Along their escape routes, many of them traveled throughout the entire country. They covered countless miles by train, bicycle, or ship. This mobility will be examined in the present chapter, which traces the movements of U-boats to, from, and through Munich. Fugitive Jews went to Munich from the Rhineland, Berlin, or Vienna; others made their way from Munich to the Reich capital. The following sections will present the wide range of escape routes crisscrossing Germany and analyze the specific problems and challenges faced by the U-boats. Many attempted to reach neutral countries such as Switzerland, Sweden, or Spain, sometimes successfully. Numerous Jews from Munich who had emigrated in the 1930s, or had been expelled from Germany later, went underground in countries such as Poland, Italy, or the Netherlands. Individual cases illustrate the greater pan-European context of the persecution. Countless Jews traveled through multiple countries in Europe in their efforts to escape the Nazis, often needing to find a hiding place in an unfamiliar environment to avoid deportation.

ODYSSEYS THROUGHOUT THE GERMAN REICH: FINAL DESTINATION MUNICH

Valerie Wolffenstein wrote in 1947 that about one hundred people had participated in helping her and her sister Andrea survive in hiding.[1] The network of helpers stretched from Pomerania, on the Baltic Sea, to the Upper Bavarian town of Murnau, near Garmisch-Partenkirchen. From the very beginning, neither Valerie nor Andrea Wolffenstein remained more than a few weeks in any one place. Their flight led the sisters on an odyssey throughout all of Germany, ending with the Ammann family in Munich.

Valerie Wolffenstein was born in 1891 and her sister Andrea in 1897, both in Berlin. Their parents had been Jewish, but their mother turned toward Christianity, and the children were ultimately baptized.[2] Valerie Wolffenstein studied architecture and painting in Berlin and then worked for Dr. Edwin Redslob, the National Art Commissioner in the Ministry of the Interior;[3] she later became the secretary for art historian and architect Dr. Paul Zucker. When Zucker emigrated in 1937, she arranged the liquidation of his household and later became self-employed as an emigration consultant.[4] The two sisters delayed their own emigration in consideration of their mother, who was seriously ill. Their father had already died in 1919. When their mother died in 1939, it was too late for the daughters to emigrate.[5] Their brother Otto, who at sixteen suffered a serious illness and was permanently disabled, was a victim of the Nazis' mass murder of the disabled.[6]

Early in the summer of 1941, Valerie Wolffenstein started doing forced labor. She and her sister lived in tight quarters in overcrowded forced Jewish housing. After the Jewish landlady in their building went underground in December 1942, the two sisters decided to go into hiding as well. They were encouraged by the fact that the landlady had already taken the leap and because the Gestapo did not follow up that particular case with any further investigations. The sisters were urged by a number of friends to go underground, and in some cases the friends downright implored them to hide to avoid deportation.[7] There was no lack of offers of help for the two of them. As so-called non-Aryan Christians, they had good contacts to members of the Confessing Church in Berlin.

When they decided to go underground, Valerie and Andrea Wolffenstein were fifty-one and forty-six years old, respectively, and unmarried. Their parents and brother were already dead. In early January 1943, they left their apartment, announced their suicide, and departed from the Tiergarten suburban train station headed in different directions. Their paths crossed only occasionally over the subsequent two and a half years, but they were together in Munich when the war ended. Both Valerie and Andrea Wolffenstein stayed at first with friends in Berlin until they were able to procure forged ID cards. Valerie Wolffenstein later recalled: "The circles of the Confessing Church, especially in the Niemöller congregation in Dahlem, were unceasingly busy arranging forged IDs for Jews. Especially Dr. Franz Kaufmann, a lawyer, and Miss Helene Jakob [Helene Jacobs] distinguished themselves in this regard. They had found a young Jewish graphic artist in hiding who had become a first-class forger."[8]

Consequently, Andrea Wolffenstein became Charlotte Maly, and Valerie Wolffenstein became Edith Mailand. The real Edith Mailand was a Viennese language teacher who had passed her expired postal ID on to her friend Helene Jacobs so it could be used for this purpose. Andrea Wolffenstein traveled with her ID, which was an authentic ID card issued to Charlotte Maly, to a small town in Pomerania.[9]

Valerie Wolffenstein went to Bavaria. Her childhood friend Esther Seidel, who lived in Munich, had inquired confidentially with a nun whom she knew, Pia von Malsen, whether Valerie Wolffenstein could be hidden in a Bavarian convent. Pia von Malsen was seriously ill and lived in Haslach near Traunstein, a small town in the Alpine foothills in Bavaria between Munich and Salzburg. She planned for Valerie Wolffenstein initially to stay near Haslach with her friend Sophie Gasteiger, a farmer, and later to move from one convent to the next to avoid capture. The plan was not carried out, however, since a raid had ostensibly taken place at one of the convents. As a result, the women had to improvise, and Esther Seidel found an acquaintance in Munich, Rudolf Ammann, who was willing to take in Valerie Wolffenstein.[10] Ammann, a colleague of Seidel's husband, worked for BMW as an engineer.

Dr. Rudolf Ammann was born in Munich in 1894. He was the son of Ellen Ammann, a member of Bavaria's state parliament (*Landtag*), who had built up the Catholic aid services in railway stations (*Bahnhofsmission*) and, as a member of the Bavarian People's Party (BVP), had played a significant role in mobilizing her fellow party members against the Beer Hall Putsch in 1923.[11] Rudolf Ammann had been active in Quickborn, the Catholic youth movement, since 1920. Quickborn was a Catholic version of the Wandervogel back-to-nature youth movement, whose members neither drank alcohol nor smoked and who represented reformist ideas within Catholicism, especially coeducation. The organization was closely connected to Romano Guardini, a theologian from northern Italy who was the spiritual director of the Rothenfels am Main castle, the movement's Grail castle until it was confiscated by the Nazis in early August 1939. As of 1926, Ammann had been president of the Association of the Friends of Rothenfels Castle and worked closely with Guardini.[12] Rudolf Ammann and his wife Margaretha had six children and lived in Munich-Freimann, a suburban borough in the north of the city. Valerie Wolffenstein first stayed five weeks with the Ammanns and was to return there several times in the years that followed. The six children were never told her true identity. She was introduced as an aunt.[13]

From the Ammanns, Valerie Wolffenstein's journey brought her to a "half-Aryan" doctor's daughter in Murnau and then back to Munich to the empty house of a publisher who had been drafted. After that, she stayed in the Augsburg area, where she was taken in for a few weeks by Hertha Schnupp. Schnupp in turn brought Wolffenstein to a friend in Dillingen, where the Baroness of Recum hired her to be the nanny for her five children, despite not knowing Wolffenstein at all. From Dillingen, Wolffenstein moved on to the Guilleaume family, and then to the studio apartment of a Munich painter, and finally back to Wolffenstein's friend Esther Seidel, who had meanwhile moved to a village near Rosenheim. Now and then, Wolffenstein continued to spend extended periods of time with the Ammann family in Munich-Freimann. She was also a guest in Dillingen multiple times. From the summer of 1943 until liberation, Valerie Wolffenstein was on a restless odyssey that led her continually to new helpers who were total strangers. It was a network that expanded little by little—families who spoke to friends and women who confided in female friends. Many of the women who were spontaneously willing to take Valerie Wolffenstein into their homes were living on their own. Even when Wolffenstein was not staying with particular helpers, she continued to receive food ration coupons from them. There was a danger at times that the domestic servants of her helpers would become suspicious because she did not have any complete sets of food ration coupons. To safeguard Wolffenstein's assumed identity, therefore, it was imperative that the cook be presented with her expected share of those coupons.[14]

Andrea Wolffenstein left Pomerania in the summer of 1944 because her hosts had been forced to provide lodging for women who were supposed to dig trenches for the fight against the advancing Red Army. Via Berlin, Stuttgart, and Ulm, she made it to Munich, where she was also taken in by the Ammanns. Andrea Wolffenstein's forged papers enabled her to rent a room and register her address with the police.[15] This proved more difficult for her sister Valerie, especially since postal IDs were no longer accepted as provisional ID cards as of the fall of 1944. In February 1945, Margaretha Ammann was able to register Valerie Wolffenstein with the police. Ammann's two relatives from Silesia, who had fled to Munich without ID papers, thus became three. Wolffenstein still had no ID card, but at least she received food ration coupons.[16] A few months later, she and her sister were together when Munich was liberated.

When Rudolf Ammann was asked if he would take in a stranger to protect her from persecution, he immediately agreed. "We were very happy to take in Frau Wolffenstein, since we could finally do something to oppose the laws of the Nazi party. Also, we hoped to be able to save at least one human life from the party's rage,"[17] Ammann later said. In 1933, while still living in Mannheim, he had provided refuge to Alexander Schifrin, editor of the *Volksstimme*,

Mannheim's Social Democratic newspaper, hiding him in his own home until it was possible for friends to bring Schifrin to safety across the French border. Schifrin, who was from Kharkiv, was widely regarded as the "intellectual wunderkind of the exiled Mensheviks."[18] He had settled in Mannheim, where he worked for both the *Volksstimme* and the *Gesellschaft* journal. As a member of the Revolutionary Socialists in Paris, he managed to emigrate to the United States in 1940.[19] Ammann regarded such aid for strangers suffering persecution as neither a risk nor a burden. Quite the contrary, he felt honored that strangers would entrust him with their lives.[20] In 1947, Rudolf Ammann had to appear before a denazification tribunal (*Spruchkammer*) because he had joined the SA in 1933. That subject will be examined more closely in chapter 10.

Valerie Wolffenstein traveled often and was thus also visible in public, so she assumed a new identity for these situations. She became Edith Mailand of Vienna and had to be convincing in playing her role. She had an enormous number of helpers and was constantly adapting to get to know and deal with new people and to fit into their lifeworlds. In this regard, she was the absolute opposite of Sophie Mayer, who spent three years in one attic, hidden from the outside world and having contact only to the three people who cared for her during this period (see chapter 3). Valerie Wolffenstein covered hundreds of miles, while Sophie Mayer traveled none at all. Many U-boats had, like Valerie Wolffenstein, gone underground and then also resurfaced. Eva Guttmann traveled about two thousand kilometers (more than 1,200 miles) throughout Germany under an assumed name, but she spent all of the winter of 1944 in a tiny, unheated attic room, cared for by only a single helper.[21]

A large share of Jews who went underground traveled extensively. On a train, fear of inspections and interrogations was a constant companion. The traveling U-boats had various strategies for dealing with this challenge. Else Behrend-Rosenfeld sometimes wore a black mourner's veil covering her face; Edith Hahn Beer pulled her coat over her head and pretended to be sleeping; Marianne Ellenbogen preferred to travel by streetcar instead of train, since there were fewer ID checks on trams. On trains, she spent a lot of time in the restrooms. Else Krell gave an affable impression and talked a lot with her fellow travelers.[22] It was a great relief if the train was overcrowded, as inspections were then rare. Cioma Schönhaus felt it was safer to travel by bicycle; he rode from Berlin all the way to the Swiss border.[23]

Almost all Munich U-boats left the city. In Berlin, this was not the case, but even in Berlin, there were Jews on the run who sought temporary quarters in the countryside or abandoned the city permanently.[24] When considering the movements of U-boats between Berlin and the Greater Munich area, there was a substantial exchange: Valerie and Andrea Wolffenstein, Denny F., Beate Steckhan, and Eva Guttmann went to Munich or Upper Bavaria. Else Behrend-Rosenfeld, Margot S., Edith S., and Rudolf V., on the other hand, went (temporarily) from Munich to the Reich capital. Hans Krohn fled from Garmisch-Partenkirchen to Berlin, and from there he went, during the Factory Operation, to Munich, ultimately secretly returning to Garmisch-Partenkirchen.[25] David Ballhorn left Berlin in 1941 for Herrsching near Munich, where he was hidden by a business partner until mid-1943. Referred by a Munich wine dealer, he then traveled with Anton Viehböck, who ran a Tyrolean transport company, to Innsbruck. Since all attempts to get Ballhorn across the border to Switzerland had failed, he remained hidden with the Viehböck family until the war ended.[26] The Berlin artist Gertrud Zuelzer also spent several weeks in 1942 hidden in the Upper Bavarian town of Hohenpeissenberg before she and a friend attempted—unsuccessfully—to flee to Switzerland.[27]

In June 1943, the pediatrician Dr. Erna Rüppel of Solingen went to Munich. She had been living in hiding in Solingen and Düsseldorf before acquiring forged papers identifying her as the Croatian nurse Anna Marcus. With these in hand, she first set off for Leipzig and from there went to Munich. With her new identity, she received a position at the Red Cross hospital in Munich-Neuhausen and could live in the nurses' home there. As she was now officially a Croat, but could not speak Croatian, she was plagued until the end of the war by fear of being discovered.[28] It remains to be more systematically investigated how many U-boats from the Rhineland escaped to Upper Bavaria, but there are indications that Erna Rüppel was not an isolated case.[29]

There were also connections between Vienna and Munich. Edith Hahn Beer left Vienna for Munich in 1943. She received good-quality forged ID papers with the help of a genealogist and her friend Christl Denner, whom she resembled.[30] The genealogist explained to her what her friend should say when she reported her ID as lost to obtain a duplicate without raising suspicions. Since there were now two people registered in Vienna with identical ID papers, Edith Hahn Beer had to leave the city. She decided spontaneously on Munich.[31] She lived there withdrawn, but not in hiding. In Munich, she met her later husband, a Nazi Party member. A long time passed before she revealed her true identity to him. The forged papers withstood even the review necessary for the marriage, which took place in Brandenburg in 1943.[32] Hahn Beer survived without being discovered, though she was always careful not to say anything wrong and not to annoy her husband. When after 1945 Edith Hahn Beer reassumed her true identity, her husband responded aggressively, and the marriage broke up.[33]

All in all, as the historian Beate Kosmala has concluded, the great number of traveling U-boats makes it is difficult to determine the chances of survival for individual cities or regions.[34] A systematic analysis of the itinerant U-boats would nevertheless offer a multidimensional picture of people hidden locally, waves of escapes, escape routes, and transregional networks, thus also permitting a more nuanced set of conclusions about local conditions. It would also enable us to better analyze the chronological and geographical characteristics of escape within the broader framework of research on the deportations.[35] The U-boats fled to places where they had helpers and where their helpers had helpers. Moreover, there were additional advantages to particular locations, including both the remoteness of rural locations and the anonymity of major cities. On the other hand, it appears as though some rural areas were avoided by U-boats, while it was the specific conditions in Berlin (rather than the anonymity of any big city) that proved to be attractive.[36] Among those who traveled were also those who fled the country and had to hide abroad. People who tried to escape from the deportation trains should also be included here. With respect to Munich, up to now there has been no documentation of people who escaped from the trains. There has in fact been hardly any research on the extent to which such escapes took place on transports from anywhere in Germany.[37]

ESCAPING ABROAD, HIDING ABROAD

Numerous German Jews fled from Nazi Germany to other European countries, but the Nazis often soon caught up with them. Jews from Munich were among those who attempted to survive the persecution by hiding outside of Germany all across occupied Europe. In many cases, the escape failed. At least thirty-two Jews from Munich were arrested in France, and at least fifty-two in the Netherlands, and then deported "to the East."[38] Among the latter were the sisters Elfriede and Annemarie Goldschmidt, who had found refuge in the Koningsbosch convent near Echt before being deported to Auschwitz together with Edith Stein in 1942.[39] These people had mostly emigrated legally before being arrested abroad. Others had been expelled, including Jakob Littner, who was a Polish citizen living in Munich. However, there were also people who fled the country illegally. The following cases of Irma Ortenau and Jakob Littner are good examples, illustrating the extended escape routes taken by some Munich Jews, ending in the underground in occupied Europe. It is impossible to estimate how many Munich Jews—or generally German Jews—lived in hiding outside Germany, as Ortenau and Littner did. Many had left Germany long before deportations began, and the circumstances under which they survived or died abroad were not documented. The survivors did not necessarily return to Germany, making it all the more difficult to gather data systematically.

More than eight thousand German Jews fled to Italy between 1933 and 1941.[40] Among these were roughly four hundred from Munich, who sought either temporary or long-term refuge in Italy.[41] Some who are known include the Obarzanek, Engelhard, and Rauch families, as well as the siblings Irma and Erich Ortenau.[42] When the Germans occupied Italy in September 1943, the situation became extremely dangerous for them, as then came the deportation of Jews from Italy, which for many ended in the Auschwitz death camp. The Munich physician Irma Ortenau survived in hiding.

Irma Ortenau fled to Italy, the country of her childhood, where she had been born in Nervi, near Genoa, in 1905.[43] Her father, Dr. Gustav Ortenau, was a highly esteemed doctor; working as a spa physician, he practiced both in Bad Reichenhall and in Nervi, where he was the director of a sanatorium.[44] Irma Ortenau spent the first years of her life in Liguria, before she started school in Bad Reichenhall. After completing secondary school, she moved to Munich to study medicine. She passed the state examination in 1935 and then worked as a medical intern at the Heckscher sanatorium and research institute under Professor Max Isserlin.[45]

Over the next few years, Irma Ortenau constantly had to change her place of residence and work because Nazi shenanigans prevented her from practicing medicine.[46] Her father was forced to give up his medical practice in Bad Reichenhall once Jewish doctors were banned from practicing their profession in 1938. He and his wife, painter Adele Ortenau, emigrated to Switzerland.[47] A few months after their parents emigrated, Irma Ortenau and her brother Erich also decided to leave Germany.

In June 1939, Erich and Irma Ortenau set off from Munich by bicycle, headed for Italy. The siblings were lucky; they reached a small Austrian-Italian border station in South Tyrol and were able to cross without difficulty. They did not approach the customs house until the patrolling SS men had left for lunch. The border policeman turned out coincidentally to be a "former patient of their father."[48] They went to Trieste, the city regarded as the "gateway to Zion," where countless refugees were waiting for the chance to obtain passage on a ship to Palestine.[49] Erich Ortenau became one of them. Many local Jews in Trieste also felt compelled to leave their city when in September 1938 the Fascist government decreed the expulsion of all foreign Jews and revoked the citizenship of all Italian Jews who had been naturalized later than January 1, 1919.[50] Erich Ortenau made it to Palestine in 1940.

Erich's sister Irma continued to live legally in Italy on a tourist visa at first, working as a doctor for the Jewish community of Trieste.[51] Despite the Fascist expulsion decree of 1938, foreign Jews could still enter Italy on tourist or transit visas that were valid for three months. More than 2,400 foreign Jews did so between September 1938 and September 1939.[52] When Irma Ortenau's residence permit expired, she received an expulsion order.[53] Hers was not an isolated case; many foreign Jews now felt compelled to leave Italy or were in fact expelled, while others remained illegally in the country without a valid residence permit.[54] Irma Ortenau went underground, which at that time was still rather unusual in Italy.[55] Presumably she had experienced problems of some kind with the local authorities. Like all foreign Jews who were still in Italy at that time, from June 1940 on she was threatened with internment, but the authorities were unable to find her. The stations of her flight led her from Trieste to Naples and, via Brindisi and Milan, to Rome, where she was able to stay with friends for an extended period of time.[56] From there she returned for unknown reasons to Trieste. During this time, she had to rely on the support of some friends and countless strangers, as she had no food ration cards and thus very little to eat, and she was forced to hurry from one hiding place to the next. "For a few months she slept under the bed of her hosts," her friend Giovanni Savaldi later wrote.[57] Savaldi accompanied her on several stations of her flight.

On June 27, 1943, a month before the fall of the Fascist government, Irma Ortenau fled, together with Savaldi and Filippo Hirschl, from Trieste to Gorgo al Monticano, a village in the Alpine foothills in the province of Treviso.[58] Neither she nor Savaldi ever explained the immediate reason for them to flee; it is possible that they had been denounced. The situation of Jews in Trieste had worsened in general. As of 1941, more and more antisemitic violence occurred. In May 1943, a few weeks before Ortenau left the city, there was violent plundering of Jewish (and Slovenian) stores.[59] We do not know who helped the trio to hide. Michael Wedekind has argued that the area around Belluno had developed into a center of resistance to the Germans. Roughly 250,000 mountain troopers from the region had participated in the German campaign against the Soviet Union, and those who returned felt nothing but hatred and contempt for the Germans.[60] Irma Ortenau was in Gorgo al Monticano, only a few miles from the province of Belluno, so she might have benefitted from these local circumstances. From June to November 1943, she was hidden in a hayloft in the small town.[61]

With the establishment of the Italian Social Republic in September 1943 and the German occupation, the deportation of Jews from Italy began. The raid in Rome on October 16, 1943, marked the beginning of a series of manhunts in

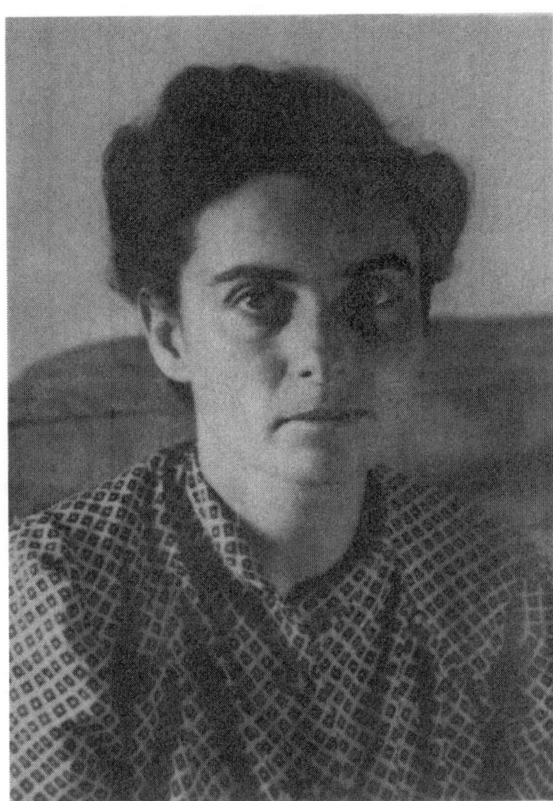

Irma Ortenau.
Munich City Archive,
DE-1992-JUD-V-0028-01.

larger cities such as Florence, Bologna, Turin, Milan, and Genoa. In the weeks and months that followed, Italian and foreign Jews were rounded up from apartments, internment camps, and hiding places and ultimately deported to Auschwitz from assembly points such as the San Vittore prison in Milan and the Fossoli camp.[62] In this situation, when countless Italian and foreign Jews were attempting to evade the Nazi henchmen, Irma Ortenau had already been on the run for a couple of years. On November 11, 1943, she left her hiding place in the Alpine foothills and set off for Rome.[63]

When on December 3, a few weeks after the major raid against the Jews, she arrived in Rome, the situation was very difficult for the Jews still in the city. The raid had claimed a total of 1,022 Jewish victims. The ghetto had been surrounded, and Jews had been systematically arrested in the early-morning hours and then deported directly to Auschwitz.[64] Wehrmacht soldiers then plundered the stores of the deportees. After the raid, however, the Germans had largely left it up to the Italian Fascists to search for Jews and arrest them.

The Italian collaborators, who were far more familiar with the city, were supposed to track down the hidden Jews.[65] Fascist gangs started manhunts for Jews and partisans. They were sometimes acting on racist grounds and sometimes out of pure avarice. Individual bounty hunters and Jew hunters working directly for the Germans were on the prowl to enrich themselves. Each Jew who was caught brought in between 3,000 and 5,000 liras, which was more than a month's wages.[66] Even neighbors and acquaintances occasionally participated in the hunt through denunciations.[67] Irma Ortenau, therefore, spent her first six months in Rome in a dark, damp basement.[68] She was in Rome on June 6 when the city was liberated and a short time later was reunited with her brother, who had joined a volunteer unit from Palestine that was fighting for the British in Italy.[69] Irma Ortenau returned to Munich in January 1947.

In contrast to the case of Irma and Erich Ortenau, who left Germany of their own accord, Jakob Littner's path to his hiding place began with an expulsion. Born in Budapest in 1883, Jakob Littner had moved from his hometown to Munich in 1912 along with his wife Katharina and their two children. Their marriage broke up in 1924, but Jakob Littner remained in Munich. Together with Christine Hintermeier, a Gentile, Littner ran a specialty shop for postage stamps. In February 1939, Littner was summoned to the police, who informed him that he had to leave Germany within fourteen days. Jakob Littner was a Polish citizen and had already been arrested in October 1938 and transported to the Polish border within the scope of the expulsion of Polish Jews from Germany (in Nazi jargon: October Operation or Pole Operation), together with roughly five hundred other Polish Jews living in Munich.[70] They were actually lucky under the circumstances, as the transport from Munich was sent right back from the Polish border.[71] In February 1939, however, Littner was forced to leave Germany. He traveled to Prague with a tourist visa, ten reichsmarks, and a small suitcase.[72]

Jakob Littner was surprised only a few weeks later by the arrival of German troops in Prague, and he was able to board a train to Poland at the last minute. Littner, who did not speak a word of Polish, found quarters in Krakow with the Jewish widow Janina Korngold, and the two became a couple. When Poland was invaded by the Germans in September 1939, Littner and Korngold fled eastward and ultimately became stranded in the small city of Zbarazh near Tarnopol in the General Government (now Ternopil, Ukraine), where they lived in the Jewish ghetto. There they witnessed mass shootings and were only able to avoid deportation to a death camp because they hid several times in a hole in the ground that Littner had dug under his house.[73]

Shortly before the ghetto was liquidated in the summer of 1943, Janina Korngold managed to find a Pole who, for a fee, hid them in a damp, cold crawl space under the basement of his residence.[74] Littner had money because Christine Hintermeier, the co-owner of his store in Munich, regularly supported him financially. In the chaos of the final weeks of the war, he knocked out a gold dental bridge to meet the demands of his helper. Jakob Littner and Janina Korngold were liberated in March 1944 by the Red Army. After they got married in June 1945, they returned to Munich and emigrated from there to the United States.[75]

Jakob Littner and Janina Korngold were two of about forty thousand to fifty thousand Jews who survived in hiding in occupied Poland. The number of Polish Jews who were still alive in the summer of 1942 and who attempted to evade deportation and murder is estimated at up to 250,000 people.[76] How and under what circumstances these people survived has recently attracted increased attention among historians.[77] Jan Grabowski has written the following in his study of the Dąbrowa Tarnowska (West Galicia) region: "For the Jews who survived the initial period after the liquidation of the ghettos, the choices of strategies of survival became more and more limited. Some were able to secure shelters in Polish houses. Sometimes they used false documents and tried to live 'on the surface,' among the gentiles, usually far away from their prewar residences. Both of these options required, however, substantial financial resources."[78]

Regular payments from Munich secured Littner's and Korngold's survival in the Tarnopol district. Apparently, Christine Hintermeier was able to send cash through registered mail to trusted helpers in Poland.[79] However, it was not only the financial support from Munich that saved Littner's life; it was also Janina Korngold, who, in contrast to him, spoke fluent Polish.

The story of the deportations from Munich still needs to be examined more closely with respect to the Eastern European Jewish inhabitants of the city. Even if the social divide between Eastern European Jews (so-called *Ostjuden*) and German Jews within the Munich population in the 1920s had largely been overcome,[80] the question remains how *Ostjuden* experienced the persecution and deportations from Munich and from Germany more generally. How many of them were expelled from Munich in 1939, as Jakob Littner was? How many fled back to their countries of origin? Regarding Munich Jews who went underground in or around Munich, it can be said that none of Eastern European descent could be identified. That was not the case in other countries. There were Jews of Polish origin such as the Obarzanek family who lived in hiding in Italy, Jakob Littner in Poland, and Ernestine Kalter and her daughter in the Netherlands.[81] Looking at the group of Munich Jews who fled to Italy, it is apparent that many of them had Polish citizenship and had to leave Munich as a result of an expulsion order in 1939.[82]

The escape routes discussed thus far in this chapter enabled Jews to go into hiding in Nazi-occupied countries. After 1941, the preferred destinations of those who did not go underground, but instead intended to cross the border to safety, were neutral countries, especially Switzerland. There was a small number of successful flights from Berlin to Sweden.[83] As previously shown in chapter 6, several attempted flights from Munich to the Swiss border failed. Only Else Behrend-Rosenfeld, who in 1942 first went from Munich to Berlin and then on to Freiburg, was successful. She was able to take advantage of a long-distance network connecting Berlin to the Swiss border region (see also chapter 6). The logistics of her crossing the border were organized by the group around Luise Meier and Josef Höfler. Behrend-Rosenfeld was dressed inconspicuously and traveling without luggage when she met her escape helper at the Singen train station using a code word. There she handed over an envelope with 3,000 reichsmarks and jewelry. Friends of hers had collected the money and valuables.[84] Two men then brought her to the Swiss border, though she had to go the final stage on her own. She fell down a slope and landed right in front of the Swiss customs house.[85]

There were also people in Munich whose contacts to the Nazi apparatus of persecution made it possible for them to escape abroad. Dr. Anna Reinach, a non-Aryan Christian, was able to flee to Spain in 1942 through her acquaintance with an SD agent. Reinach and her husband, the philosopher Dr. Adolf Reinach, had been baptized Lutheran in 1916. A year later, Adolf Reinach was dead. Like so many men of his generation, he had died in the trenches of Flanders.[86] After her husband's death, Reinach grew close to the philosopher Edith Stein, who had been a student of her husband. Having been introduced to Christianity by the Reinachs, Edith Stein converted from Judaism to Catholicism in 1922, and Anna Reinach (who had previously converted from Judaism to Lutheranism in 1916) followed suit and became a Catholic in 1923. Edith Stein, who later became a nun, was murdered in Auschwitz in 1942 and eventually beatified by Pope John Paul II in 1998.[87]

Anna Reinach moved from Göttingen to Munich, where her brother-in-law Heinrich Reinach had settled with his family. She remained in Munich even after her brother-in-law, together with his wife and children, set off for Brazil in 1938.[88] At that time, Anna Reinach became an oblate of the Benedictine Archabbey in Beuron, vowing to live according to the Rule of St. Benedict.[89] Her position at the abbey enabled her to live in Munich freely because the Prior of Beuron, Hermann Keller, was also an SD agent; he held his protective hand over Reinach and helped conceal her Jewish past.[90] In the archabbey of Beuron, people had expressed concern as early as 1938 about the future of the non-Aryan members of the monastery (including explicit mention of the oblates). Prior Keller reported that he had been commissioned to inquire about the situation with various offices to determine what was planned. His good connections, he implied, helped a number of persecuted members of the monastery before the start of the war.[91]

Anna Reinach was denounced in Munich in early 1942.[92] Keller procured the necessary documents for her to enter France. From there, he brought her to San Sebastian in Spain, where Reinach was able to eke out a living as a private teacher.[93] It is no longer possible to reconstruct precisely how the escape was accomplished, but Keller later spoke of "an adventurous story."[94] Edith Stein, for her part, had fled Germany in early 1939 for the Dutch Carmelite Convent in Echt. From Spain, Anna Reinach continued to try to arrange a way for Stein to escape from the convent in the Netherlands, but to no avail.[95] After the war, Reinach returned to Munich.[96]

In addition to Munich Jews who fled abroad or went into hiding, there were also Munich helpers who supported Jews while far from home. One of them was the Communist carpenter Ludwig Wörl, who spent more than a decade of his life in various Nazi camps.[97] Ludwig Wörl's story does not directly relate to Munich Jews or to Jews in hiding in Munich, but it does provide an example of helpers from Munich who came to the aid of people persecuted in camps or in German-occupied Europe. Among these, aside from Wörl, was Josef Meyer, who worked for the agricultural administration of the General Government in Poland, where he hid a number of Jews and supplied others with food.[98] It is important to discuss these cases because Ludwig Wörl and Josef Meyer were Munich citizens who were honored in the 1960s by Yad Vashem as Righteous Among the Nations and who therefore influenced both the public perception of Munich's helpers and the city's politics of memory. Thus, Munich's connections to the history of Jewish flight and of support for Jews extended well beyond the city of Munich to include helpers located elsewhere in Nazi-dominated Europe.[99]

Ludwig Wörl combined political resistance to the Nazi regime with aid for those suffering persecution, including Jews. In 1934, he had participated in the distribution of flyers informing the public about the dreadful conditions in the Dachau concentration camp.[100] As a result of this protest action, he was arrested and himself transferred to Dachau, where he worked as a paramedic in the infirmary. In 1942, Wörl and other paramedics were transferred to Auschwitz, ostensibly as a result of an intrigue against the Communists among the nursing staff. In Auschwitz, he helped fight a typhus epidemic.[101] As a non-Jewish German prisoner in Auschwitz, he became the infirmary's camp elder, and among the things he was able to do was forge selection lists, crossing names off and replacing them with names of people who had already been killed. He also arranged for Jewish doctors to move into positions in the camp that offered a degree of protection, and he helped some people escape when the camp was being liquidated. After 1945, Wörl once again lived in Munich, where he was honored for his actions.[102]

CONCLUSION: ESCAPE ROUTES AND PLACES OF REFUGE

Up to the end of the war in May 1945, numerous Jews from Munich decided to flee from the Nazis, most of them in February 1945, but also a substantial number earlier. A large majority of them did not remain in the city, but instead had multiple way stations while in hiding. At the same time, Jews from other regions of Germany who were living illegally moved in the opposite direction, going to Munich or to Upper Bavaria. This regional perspective therefore underscores the great geographical mobility of the U-boats. For many of them, flight meant movement—in some cases, constant movement—and adapting to new surroundings, strangers, and unforeseen situations. It is therefore impossible to determine the exact number of U-boats at any particular place, as many stayed at any one location only temporarily. The diversity of the experiences illustrated here is evidence of the abundance of different strategies of action among the U-boats.

Private quarters often served as places of refuge. These included ordinary apartments, houses, attics, backrooms, basements, remote farms, boats, weekend garden cabins, and company buildings. But some hiding places were also public spaces, such as bombed-out ruins, forests, fields, and cemeteries. Jewish cemeteries became refuges for U-boats, both in Munich and elsewhere. A mausoleum at the Weissensee Jewish cemetery in Berlin served as temporary, but safe, nightly quarters. U-boats slept in the most varied places, including parked cars, telephone booths, parking lots, and riverbanks.[103] In Berlin, some passed the time riding aimlessly through the city on streetcars. They visited restaurants to eat the daily special without needing ration coupons, and sometimes they went to the cinema or concerts to escape the dangers of reality.[104] They rode on trains to change their hiding places, to visit friends, or even to go on outings.[105] In areas close to the Swiss border, the mountains in clear view beyond the border became an object of longing for those who ventured to escape to another country.[106] All of this created a topography of life in illegality, of escape routes and public hiding places, of mental maps of cities and regions, and of secret addresses of helpers.[107]

A public life could also be a refuge. Many U-boats tried to live, at least temporarily, a fictitious normal life by assuming a false identity or telling a plausible story. The better the quality of forged papers, the freer they could move around within this fictitious normalcy. Forged papers made it possible for Anna Reinach to cross borders, for Edith Hahn Beer to get married, and for Erna Rüppel to work as a nurse. It was often primarily a matter of quickly adapting to a novel social environment or atmosphere. Marie Jalowicz Simon had lived for a while in Berlin in a rundown tenement in Berlin when she was punched one day by the forced laborer with whom she shared the apartment. With a face full of bruises, she did not at first dare to go out on the streets since she was afraid of attracting attention. However, she soon realized that her swollen face fit perfectly into her neighborhood and that she had become absolutely inconspicuous.[108] This was more difficult for U-boats whose forged papers identified them as foreign nationals or forced laborers. The Croatian nurse, the Italian or French foreign worker who spoke little Croatian, Italian, or French—in these cases even high-quality forgeries came with a high risk.

Even outside of Berlin, where options were limited, many U-boats succeeded in discovering increasingly diverse places of refuge, securing them from the outside and maintaining them. This could happen within one's own four walls or be organized from far away, as in the case of Jakob Littner, whose hiding place in occupied Poland was financed from Munich. But hiding places were not only a matter of mastering geography, as shown by the following concluding example.

Born in Munich, Rahel G. was the daughter of a non-Jewish German mother and a Jewish father from Belorussia. After her parents divorced in 1929, Rahel G. was raised by her mother, Gertrud G., who increasingly supported the Nazis. The mother was following the example set by her own father, who had already joined the Nazi Party before 1933.[109] As the family had belonged to the Jewish Community of Munich when Rahel G. was born, and as Rahel did not officially renounce her membership until 1939, she was deemed a *Geltungsjüdin* according to the Nazi race laws.

In August 1942, Gertrud G. was repeatedly summoned to the Gestapo for interrogation. They threatened to deport her daughter. Consequently, mother and daughter left the city and traveled aimlessly throughout Germany for several weeks.[110] While they were on the run, a lawyer they knew urged Rahel G. to marry a non-Jewish man from a neutral country, or one allied with the German Reich, as soon as possible.[111] Although marriages between *Geltungsjuden* and

"Aryan" Germans were prohibited, they were permitted with foreign citizens. How Rahel G. found a suitable groom remains her secret, but on November 25, 1942, a marriage between Rahel G. and a Spaniard took place in Munich.[112] With the marriage, the bride obtained Spanish citizenship and lived from that point forward in a so-called privileged mixed marriage. The couple left Munich together with the bride's mother and grandmother, settling in a small town in the Reich Protectorate of Bohemia and Moravia. Rahel G. was conscripted to forced labor, but she was spared deportation.[113] In 1945, she and her husband went their separate ways.

In receiving authorization to marry a non-German partner, Rahel G. succeeded where Marie Jalowicz Simon failed. Marie Jalowicz Simon had heard of this option in Berlin through "Jewish word of mouth" (so-called *Mundfunk*[114]) and even received the address of an apartment where several young Chinese men lived. She went there and explained that she wanted Chinese language lessons. The young men laughed and said they knew exactly why she had come, naming a very high sum as the price for an arranged marriage. The young men had evidently already received a number of similar inquiries. Marie Jalowicz Simon did manage to win the affections of one of the men, and marriage plans proceeded without a financial quid pro quo. However, because she did not receive the necessary documents, the wedding never took place.[115]

Most memoirs of Holocaust survivors come to an end with liberation in the spring of 1945. The research on U-boats has, similarly, also dealt only in isolated instances with the lives of former U-boats and their helpers in postwar Germany. The subsequent course of their lives and those of their helpers has generally remained unknown. The next chapter of this book will look at how the U-boats lived the next phase of their lives, how they dealt with the aftermath of the persecution, and how postwar society in West Germany, and specifically in Munich, perceived both the former U-boats as well as their helpers.

NINE

AFTER 1945

Reconstruction or New Beginning?

"VIEWS ON THE PROPER FUTURE for Jews in Germany inevitably reflected wartime experiences. Those who had survived underground, whose voices were more numerous and powerful in Berlin than elsewhere in Germany, tended to have both the most positive and the most narrow perspective. Often they were the most hopeful about the possibilities of reconciliation and cooperation for building a new democratic Germany. During the worst of the Nazi years, isolated in their hiding places, they had encountered primarily the best of the Germans."

This is how Atina Grossmann has summarized the atmosphere among the surviving U-boats in Berlin.[1] In occupied Berlin in the postwar years, Jewish survivors passionately debated whether Jews should emigrate as soon as possible or instead participate in Germany's reconstruction. Wasn't it a much more pressing task to help build a Jewish state? Was there even a future for Jews in Germany?

Numerous resurfacing U-boats tended in fact to remain in postwar Germany, even if they had conflicting feelings. Television host Hans Rosenthal was one of the most convincing advocates of staying and of reconciliation.[2] He said that his rescuers had "made it possible for me to live uninhibited in Germany up until today, after a time that was so terrible for us Jews. It has allowed me to feel German and to be a citizen of this country, without hatred. For these women risked their lives for me."[3]

Many saw it differently, perceiving their former helpers in a destroyed postwar Germany as isolated individuals in a society that was largely indifferent and often hostile. Heinrich Busse, who had gone into hiding during the Factory Operation in Berlin, determined with dismay that even among his former helpers, feelings of self-pity were rife in view of Germany's defeat, as was envy of the Allied support for the Jews. This reinforced his decision to emigrate. He resented what he saw as underlying antisemitism and self-stylized victimization precisely among the few who, despite great personal risk, had helped him and upon whom he had placed hopes for the reconstruction of a democratic Germany. From his new home in Britain, he felt it necessary to point out to former helpers that there were differences between the difficult conditions in postwar Germany and the horrific conditions in Auschwitz.[4]

With liberation in May 1945, the survivors came out of their hiding places, bid farewell to their helpers, and set off to rebuild their existence or plan a new beginning in another country. They did this in the context of a postwar society that was essentially focused on its own suffering and did not want to hear about the persecution and murder of the Jews of Europe, much less about its own responsibility for it. Small Jewish communities took form again in this postwar society. For some, life in these communities was an existence "in the waiting room" to emigration;[5] others felt obligated to rebuild Jewish life in Germany. The so-called non-Aryan Christians found themselves in an especially difficult situation. They had been persecuted as Jews, but after 1945 were not entirely recognized by Jewish communities and aid organizations and thus excluded from certain aid benefits.[6] Many struggled with conflicts of their identity and faith. The helpers also returned to everyday life. They were treated as ordinary Germans by the Allies, which meant they could not expect to receive any benefits or advantages because of the courage they had shown.

This chapter deals with those who survived in hiding, and with their helpers, in the period immediately following the war. What did the process of resurfacing look like? How did former U-boats decide whether to emigrate or to remain in Germany? With what specific repercussions from the time of persecution did those who survived in hiding have to struggle?

RESURFACING AND IMMEDIATE AID

The final weeks of the war were particularly difficult for the U-boats in Berlin. While the Battle of Berlin was raging, many of them lost their hiding places due to air raid damage and street fighting.[7] Leonie and Walter Frankenstein spent the last days of the war with non-Jewish Berliners in a U-Bahn (subway) station, which had been converted to an air raid shelter. During this time, they had neither water nor food.[8] Countless civilians died in these battles, certainly also including Jews in hiding.[9] Berlin U-boats were still arrested and executed as Jews, even in the very last days of the war, while others were shot and injured as "deserters" or "defeatists," without their Jewish identity being determined.[10] The long-desired liberation turned into a renewed flight for many female U-boats trying to escape sexual violence by soldiers of the Red Army. For Hans Rosenthal and his helpers, this situation meant a reversal of the relationship. Rosenthal now tried to protect the women who had hidden him from sexual attacks by Soviet soldiers.[11] Surviving Jews suddenly found themselves struggling with unexpected difficulties in credibly proving that they were Jewish. Rosenthal was almost shot by Russian soldiers shortly after liberation. He started wearing a yellow Jewish star again in order to be recognized as a Jew. However, Soviet soldiers had previously caught concentration camp guards attaching the yellow stars from the prisoners' clothing to their own. For this reason, they thought Rosenthal was an SS member and wanted to shoot him. An officer who just happened to pass by was able to clear up the misunderstanding.[12]

When American troops took Munich in late April 1945, they faced hardly any resistance. The few Jews who were in the city at that time experienced the war's end differently than the Jews in Berlin. Almost four hundred had survived in Munich as spouses in mixed marriages or as *Geltungsjuden*.[13] Jews who had been in hiding started resurfacing from all sorts of hiding places. Valerie Wolffenstein and her sister Andrea were in the city when it was liberated. "When the Nazi monster was finally brought down and the Americans victoriously entered Munich, I could finally breathe freely and resurface with my sister and start a new life,"[14] she wrote later. For most Jewish U-boats, regardless of whether they survived in Berlin, Munich, or elsewhere, one thing was certain: "It took some time . . . to get used to the fact that the situation of complete fear . . . had come to an end."[15] Many resurfaced in the countryside rather than in the city, in places such as Grucking near Erding, as Elfriede Seitz did, or in Lenggries, as Dr. Sophie Mayer did. The latter had been hidden "before the very noze [*sic*] of the Gestapo" noted an American GI, shaking his head, as the Munich doctor came out of her hiding place in the attic above the police station.[16]

There are very few extant personal accounts by Munich survivors about the period of resurfacing and the accompanying emotions. Berthold L. of Munich wrote about the first days of freedom after having endured twenty-six months in a closet: "I had totally forgotten how to move about in the outdoors, as I had to sneak around in house slippers if there were visitors. Half starved to death and emaciated to the bones, pale and tottering, I hung onto my wife's arm after the Americans entered Fürstenfeldbruck."[17] The accounts of people who had been hidden elsewhere show that many had to become reaccustomed to speaking normally and walking around, moving about freely. Brigitte Ungar-Klein described the case of a lawyer hidden in Vienna who had had to walk around on tiptoe to avoid making noise. It took a long time before he could again walk normally. Ungar-Klein also wrote of a singer who had lost her voice in hiding because she had only been able to whisper the entire time.[18]

They all required medical care, living quarters, and adequate food. Housing was extremely scarce, and whereas some survivors were able to stay with friends and acquaintances, many had to find a place to stay in the city. Like many others, Hugo Holzmann first went to the former Jewish retirement home in Munich, where a provisional Jewish administration issued identity papers and helped out in the search for housing.[19] Valerie Wolffenstein was not alone with her fear of whether she would even be acknowledged as having suffered racial persecution. She had no ID papers whatsoever to present, and she was not from Munich. In her case, it was serendipity that resolved her problem. In the retirement home, she ran into a childhood friend who could vouch for her; Heinz Guttmann had also been in hiding and, like her, had also made his way to Munich.[20]

Survivors returning from Theresienstadt also needed a place to stay. Some were initially also housed in the former Jewish retirement home, but conflicts developed, including over the distribution of resources. Hedwig Geng reported about her return to Munich from Theresienstadt:

> I was placed in a room with four other women. There were five steel bedsteads there, but nothing else. The directors were a couple [Dr. Neuburger and his wife]; he was Jewish and she was Gentile. There were also three Christian nurses and a Jewish doctor [Dr. Sophie Mayer] who had spent three years in hiding in an attic. We were still ordered and bossed around a lot by these people. The furniture, some of which was very pretty and comfortable, which had been donated little by little as charitable gifts, wandered first into the rooms of the nurses and the director. We never saw any of the donated food, such as beer, until by chance I heard about it from outsiders. The doctor had two rooms for herself as living space, plus a waiting room and a treatment room, while we continued to be crammed together like sardines.[21]

Within the Jewish community, people also helped each other out. For example, Hugo Holzmann and his mother sheltered an older man who had survived in hiding on a farm.[22]

When Hugo Holzmann rode a bicycle from his hiding place near Landau back into the city, he stopped at the Jewish cemetery on Ungererstrasse in the north of Munich:

> My first visit to anyone in freedom would be with my father. Herr Schoerghofer, the same caretaker as in older times, let me in. . . . And there

> was my father's grave[site]. A square headstone lying flat, I cleaned off the dirt and debris. MARTIN HOLZMANN, 1884–1934. Behind the stone, the red rosebush now grown wild. I talked to my father, I don't remember what I said. Tears rolling down my face, lately tears seem to come so easy, I didn't need to hold it all in anymore. . . . When I went back by the admin[istration] building Herr Schoerghofer came out and greeted me more warmly. He remembered me from five, six years ago when I came with my mother. He was genuinely happy that I had made it. He told me the story of Clairle [Klara] Schwalb and Kurt Kahn whom he had hidden [t]here.[23]

Hugo Holzmann knew Herta Neuburger, who had also been hidden by the Schörghofer family. The younger survivors celebrated their reunion, enjoyed the months after liberation, traveled to the mountains, and went swimming.[24] Sigmund W. and Rudolf V. made wedding plans with their partners. Many, however, were also severely scarred by the hardships of life in hiding.

Aid for the survivors, regardless of whether they had been U-boats or survivors of concentration and death camps, seemed to the survivors to have started out rather sluggishly. On June 26, 1945, Eduard Meyer, who had returned from Theresienstadt, appeared in the office of Munich's mayor and complained bitterly about the inadequate support:

> The fact is, neither I nor my other comrades who have returned in the last few days from Theresienstadt have received any support or aid from the officially announced registration center or any other agency that in any way corresponds to what we have been told everywhere and what we have also expected. My personal view, which would tend to agree with that of most of my comrades, is that we have not returned as impudent demanders who now expect to be received with a triumphal arch and chiming bells, but on the other hand we do not accept why we have to take the path of beggars, for whom the municipal administration could and should easily have shown us the way. After all, we are a group of people that has unfortunately dwindled.[25]

When Eduard Meyer complained at the city's welfare office, he was granted only the regular welfare payments. Meyer was even more incensed, however, that he had to sign a declaration stating that he would be liable for prosecution if he failed to report any financial assets, bank accounts, or other property. He bitterly characterized this treatment of a Jew, from whom everything had been taken, as "peculiar" and "unreal."[26]

To care for the Jewish survivors, the American military government set up a Support Committee for Those Affected by the Nuremberg Laws. It specifically helped Jewish survivors who had not been cared for as displaced persons (DPs) by the United Nations Relief and Rehabilitation Administration (UNRRA), and it supported Sinti and Roma as well. The assistance also explicitly covered non-Jewish spouses in mixed marriages and Jews who had converted to Christianity, that is, groups that were excluded by other aid organizations.[27] The support committee was the precursor to the Bavarian Aid Organization for Those Affected by the Nuremberg Laws (*Bayerisches Hilfswerk für die von den Nürnberger Gesetzen Betroffenen*), which was founded in early 1946.[28] In the initial postwar years, the Bavarian Aid Organization worked to relieve the most severe hardship for those who had suffered persecution. It awarded special payments to the needy, temporary pensions, health care, and small loans toward rebuilding a professional livelihood. It reimbursed doctors' and medical costs, and it even made items of everyday use available, such as clothing, shoes, soap, or heating materials.[29]

The Bavarian Aid Organization became a department of the State Commission for the Care of Jews in Bavaria, an agency established by the Bavarian state government in October 1945 to secure basic care for all Jewish survivors and to work out plans for compensation. Soon that agency, renamed the State Commission for Racial, Religious, and Political Persecutees, assumed the care of those who had suffered political persecution. The director of the State Commission, Auschwitz survivor Philipp Auerbach of Düsseldorf,[30] saw it as his task to serve as the "fatherly friend, as the 'primus inter pares' for his 'fellow sufferers.'"[31] He expended enormous personal energy in helping victims of persecution as unbureaucratically as possible and using unorthodox measures. He did not care if he violated regulations.[32] Auerbach saw the immediate aid as merely an interim measure until the actual compensation of victims of persecution took effect.[33]

The Bavarian Aid Organization also provided for converted Jews and people in mixed marriages, making no distinctions among groups of persecuted people in granting aid benefits. Nevertheless, Christians who had converted from Judaism found themselves somewhat at a disadvantage after the war ended. The American-Jewish Joint Distribution Committee (JDC, or Joint), for example, the most significant aid organization, supported only actual Jews among the survivors living outside the DP camps, thus cutting Christians of Jewish descent off from its aid.[34] The leadership of the Lutheran State Church had to be reminded that it was responsible for those cases. The following correspondence between State Commissioner Hermann Aumer (Philipp Auerbach's predecessor) and Bavarian State Bishop Hans Meiser shows what a hard time the church had in dealing with this group of people. On December 3, 1945, State Commissioner Aumer wrote to Bishop Meiser:

> Among the people I am caring for are a large number of Protestants. The Christmas celebration in 1945 is the first that they can celebrate once again as free people. Whereas the Jewish community, with the help of American organizations, can celebrate the holidays with its members, our Protestants have to rely on their church. This is not a matter of money, food, or clothing per se. I believe it is about showing these people that they who suffered so much through the National Socialist government are being remembered. The spouse not affected by the Nuremberg laws often suffered along with them and continued to support them. In the course of time this remembrance must ultimately find an expression in a material form.[35]

Meiser responded to this letter as follows: "I have received your reference to the members of our church entrusted to your care.... However, I have trust in you that you will make every endeavor to accept the so sorely afflicted community members of Jewish descent. During the last eight years we assigned a separate cleric for the pastoral and material care of those persons who fell under the Nuremberg laws, both in Munich and in Nuremberg, and spent substantial sums of church tax funds."[36]

Several aspects of this letter are notable. Meiser was completely content to leave care for the persecuted Protestants up to the state commissioner, describing them as a sort of "costly problem" for the church. At the same time, he sensed a certain need to justify his remarks, as he emphasized that his church had spared no expense in helping these people. Shortly after having received the letter, State Commissioner Aumer received a donation of 5,000 reichsmarks from the Lutheran State Church.[37] Whereas Pastor Grüber had already reestablished a Protestant aid office to care for the former Jews in Berlin,[38] it was initially only the Stuttgart vicar Fritz Majer-Leonhard (himself half-Jewish) and the Heidelberg district dean Hermann Maas, who, in addition to Grüber, launched similar initiatives.[39] In Bavaria, the Working Committee for the Lutheran Jewish Mission, founded in 1946, assumed responsibility for former Jews and people in mixed marriages, sending Sister Erna Unger to Munich in February 1947 to take up pastoral care efforts.[40] Pastor Leonard Henninger, director of the Association for Inner Mission since 1945, had expressed his approval of this undertaking. What did this care look like? Siegfried Hermle appraised what took place, saying that "a glance into the work log of Sister Unger shows that her activities shifted more and more toward 'missionizing

Jews.'"[41] The pastoral care was simply a means to an end in advancing the true aim.

In a letter of June 14, 1945, to the military government in Munich, Cardinal Michael von Faulhaber, the archbishop of Munich and Freising, offered to organize a bus to bring back the baptized Jews still in Theresienstadt and provide food for them.[42] Faulhaber's letter shows that he was aware that immediate aid for the surviving Catholics of Jewish descent was urgently needed. He was also willing, through the Caritas Association, "to do something for these severely persecuted and brutally abused Jews [*sic*]."[43] The aid offered by the Munich Caritas Association started only slowly. In late May 1946, a Catholic who had been persecuted as a Jew asked Anton Pollinger, the administrative director of the Bavarian State Caritas Association, when the Caritas's care for the Catholics of Jewish descent was to begin.[44] She indicated that Jewish persecutees received additional food rations via Jewish aid organizations and the official Jewish community, from which Catholics who had been persecuted as Jews were excluded. After a second letter, the woman received a food package, as did a second woman in an identical predicament.[45]

REESTABLISHING MUNICH'S JEWISH COMMUNITY

Many survivors participated actively in reestablishing the Jewish Community of Munich (IKG). It was officially founded anew on July 19, 1945, on Kaulbachstrasse. Dr. Julius Spanier, a doctor who returned from Theresienstadt, was chosen as president.[46] Aaron Ohrenstein, the new rabbi, moved to Munich in October 1945. Originally from Poland, he had lived for a long time in Berlin before being expelled to Poland in 1938.[47] At the first postwar Jewish New Year (Rosh Hashanah) celebration, the Torah scrolls and religious objects that the cemetery caretaker Schörghofer had hidden were used again.[48] In 1946, the Jewish Community of Munich already had 2,800 members, 796 of whom had been members prior to the war.[49] They had survived either as spouses in mixed marriages or in hiding in Munich and also included survivors of Theresienstadt as well as remigrants. However, a large majority of the members were new to Munich. In terms of numbers, the community was now dominated by Jewish displaced persons from Eastern Europe.[50] Rabbi Ohrenstein did a great deal to integrate the so-called *Ostjuden* (Eastern European Jews) into the community. The lawyer Siegfried Neuland, who served as Spanier's deputy and whose son-in-law came from Poland, also tried to create a balance.[51] Nevertheless, the postwar years of the Jewish Community of Munich were marked by cultural and ideological tensions.

Rededication of the synagogue on Reichenbachstrasse with General Lucius Clay as speaker, 1947. Munich City Archive, DE-1992-JUD-F-0536-21.

This was not only a matter of hegemony within the community, but in particular it was about whether an official Jewish community should be constituted long term in Munich at all. The Central Committee of Liberated Jews in the American Zone, founded in 1946, was dominated by displaced persons who were primarily concerned with organizing emigration. They had little understanding for those German Jews who wanted to reestablish Jewish life for the long term in Bavaria. Dr. Spanier attempted to limit voting rights within the Jewish community to those people who had already been members in 1938 to assure a leading role for the long-established German Jews.[52] The Jewish Community of Munich also did not want to join the Central Committee of Liberated Jews in the American Zone. Consequently, the Central Committee arranged that Munich's Jewish community not receive aid benefits from the Joint Distribution Committee (JDC). This did not change until early 1948, when the JDC ceased to distinguish between German and Eastern European Jews.[53]

It was not only the question of emigration versus remaining in Germany that divided the community into *Ostjuden* and German Jews, especially as there were also many among the latter who considered emigrating. On top of this came tension that had already existed prior to 1933. Long-established Munich Jews looked down upon the *Ostjuden*, whom they viewed as "unrefined" and suffering from a "lack of respect."[54] In the other direction, the accusation rang out that the established German Jews were "assimilated" and "ingratiating."[55] The share of orthodox Jews among the *Ostjuden* was considerably higher than among the liberal Jewish middle class in Munich.

Ideological trench warfare developed around whether the Jewish community should practice a "nationally defined" Judaism or if an assimilated exercise of religion was preferred, in which religion was largely a private matter.[56] Max Bachmann, who had survived in hiding, played a key role in the latter group, especially since he was concerned about the reputation of Munich's Jewish community in West German society. This was even more so the case after the legal proceedings against State Commissioner Auerbach and Rabbi Ohrenstein had given the community a good deal of negative press.[57] In 1952, Auerbach received a two-and-a-half-year prison sentence for crimes including bribery, extortion, fraud, and embezzlement.[58] The judge and state prosecutors all had a Nazi past, and the media reporting was one-sided and full of antisemitic stereotypes. Auerbach committed suicide in his cell on the very evening the judgment was pronounced. He was posthumously rehabilitated in 1954.[59] Ohrenstein was also charged in the trial against Auerbach, but he did not have to step down from his position.[60] In the 1950s, all of these questions and problems led to constant conflict within the Jewish community.[61] But for many Munich Jews, the first and most important question to be answered was straightforward: To go or to stay?

GO OR STAY?

"Salo, like I, was really very attached to Munich, we both had grown up in the city. But our love for the city and its people had been dirtied and besmirched by the Nazis. Separation for the sake of our own peace of mind was absolutely necessary."[62] Hugo Holzmann, who survived as an adolescent on a farm near Landau along the Isar River, and his friend Salomon Neuwirth, who had returned from Theresienstadt, did not hesitate at all; they wanted to emigrate. Herta Neuburger and Margot and Klara Schwalb, who had been hidden by the Schörghofers, sought their fortunes in the United States. Charlotte Neuland also wanted to go to the United States with her fiancé, Samuel Knobloch, but once she was pregnant, she could no longer endure a ship's passage. Thus their emigration continued to be postponed until the temporary postwar existence became a permanent condition.[63] It was first and foremost the generation of the fifteen- to twenty-five-year-olds among those who had survived in hiding who wanted to leave Munich to build a new life elsewhere.

For older people, the decision was more difficult, even if their closest family members were living abroad. Margot S.'s parents had been able to emigrate in 1939, but she went underground in Munich and ultimately ended up in Berlin. In 1946, she returned to Munich before setting off on an extended visit with her mother in Britain in 1948. "For me the situation is particularly ambivalent since my mother would of course love to keep me here, and the country, the people, and the customs are familiar, suitable, and favorable," wrote Margot S. from London to a friend in Munich in 1919. "But there is constantly this invincible love, yes almost passion, for the German homeland that almost cost me my life once already. And so I have been torn back and forth with my emotions; it is a situation that has already repeated three times for me."[64] Albertine Gimpel and Franz Herda went to New York together after they married, but they returned to Bavaria in 1962 (see chapter 12). Else Behrend-Rosenfeld had moved to Britain in 1946 to be with her husband and children, but after the death of her husband, she decided to spend half the year in Britain and the other half in Bavaria.[65]

A majority of surviving U-boats from Munich stayed in the city and environs. Did their experiences with their helpers influence their decision to believe in a future in Germany, as Hans Rosenthal claimed for himself? Other reasons appear to have been more significant. Most of the former U-boats were not young; rather, by the end of the war they belonged to the age group of the forty- to sixty-year-olds and had led an (upper) middle-class, assimilated existence. They wanted to reestablish themselves professionally and sought to return to their middle-class normalcy. Some of them were also too old or too sick to even consider emigrating. Dr. Irma Ortenau, Dr. Magdalena Schwarz, and Dr. Sophie Mayer (re)opened doctor's offices in Munich. Siegfried Neuland and Dr. Benno Schülein ran successful law firms. In 1946, Schülein became the deputy chairman of the Munich Bar Association.[66] Sigmund W. tried, together with his wife, to reestablish their store for medical incubators, despite his age (he was now seventy-five years old) and the fact that he was in a poor state of health.[67] With his daughter's help, Siegfried B. started his own business as a livestock dealer.[68] Siegfried Neuland became the head of the Jewish Community of Munich in 1952, succeeded for a short time in 1958 by Max Bachmann, who had also survived in hiding.[69] Of all the U-boats known to have survived in Germany, about half emigrated. Thus, throughout Germany, a higher percentage of former U-boats decided to emigrate than in Munich.[70]

For the younger adults among the U-boats, it was more difficult to get settled again after the war. In contrast to the older survivors, they had no jobs to which they could return, and consequently this might have reinforced many of them in their decision to emigrate. Many Jewish adolescents had only been able to complete the eight grades of primary school or had had to break off their schooling altogether since, from 1938 onward, Jewish schoolchildren were only allowed to attend Jewish primary and vocational schools, and after 1941 these, too, were closed. The Jewish training workshops (*Anlernwerkstätten*) were also closed in early 1942.[71]

Munich had numerous opportunities for vocational training and continuing education for displaced persons prior to their emigration.[72] This was aimed less toward being a comprehensive vocational training program and more toward learning skills that would facilitate DPs' finding jobs in their new homelands. Getting things going again proved difficult for many. Charlotte Knobloch was accepted to commercial school, but she also took private instruction to close some educational gaps.[73] How could people pick up where they had left off when they were teenagers who had not gone to school for a number of years? Even if the young survivors were able to complete vocational training in the postwar years, only in a minority of cases did it correspond to their original professional goals.

Lorenz Cosmann, whose attempted escapes from a labor camp of the Organization Todt and from the Buchenwald concentration camp had failed, struggled with a low income due to his lack of vocational training. He wanted to illegally supplement his salary as a timber dealer; after obtaining the names and addresses of US secret agents, blueprints, storage plans, and production plans for weapons through an acquaintance, he tried to sell them in the Soviet occupation zone. It never became clear where this all had come from and whether it was even really valuable or secret information at all, but the entire endeavor appeared to be carried out rather amateurishly. He was discovered and was convicted by an Allied military court of "criminal conspiracy in the service of the Soviet Union" and sentenced to two years in prison.[74] The reasons for his actions were certainly not only financial but also ideological. The *Spiegel* news magazine reported rather polemically on the case: "His father,

Professor Cossmann [*sic*] of the Kaiser Wilhelm Institute in Dahlem was killed in Auschwitz. His mother, Dr. Margarete Cossmann of Munich, couldn't make anything more out of the uneducated, untrained young man—who had been in various concentration camps since 1942—than what time itself had done with him. . . . When Hildegard of Leipzig [his accomplice] met the young man, he happened once again to be in need of money."[75]

Certainly, Cosmann committed a crime and was prosecuted for it. But he was not to blame for the fact that he had to spend his youth in various camps and consequently had neither vocational training nor a university education.

One of the young men from Munich who survived in hiding wrote in 1955 to the Bavarian State Compensation Office: "Despite constant, arduous attempts I have not been able to find a suitable job that allows me to support my family in an adequate, respectable manner. I am repeatedly told that my lack of training is the reason for my rejection."[76] For the lack of schooling, vocational training, or college studies, the survivors were granted a maximum of 5,000 deutsche marks as provided for in the Federal Compensation Law for damages to professional advancement. However, the money was not paid out until the 1950s, which was too late for most to acquire qualifications. The sum also did not correspond by any means to the economic damage suffered as the result of lack of training or education. Of course, many survivors of this generation did eventually build up careers and were professionally successful. But the lack of education and training made it much more difficult for many to continue where they had left off, and it had a lasting detrimental impact on their lives.

LONG-TERM HEALTH EFFECTS

In July 1954, Felix B. wrote the following to the Bavarian State Compensation Office: "Early in the summer of 1945 I met Frau V. in Munich on Leopoldstrasse. The vibrant colleague of the past had become a broken woman with gray hair. It was not only her physical state that shocked me, but almost more so her psychological condition. Her nerves were clearly in shreds and I vividly remember her faltering stories of the suffering she had gone through since 1933."[77]

The former colleague of Felix B. had been living in hiding in Munich. Felix B. had witnessed her futile attempts to regain a foothold professionally after 1945. "She could not free herself from her memories," he wrote about the years before his colleague fled abroad in an effort to escape her memories. There she had a nervous breakdown and ultimately returned to Munich, where she spent six months in a psychiatric clinic. She subsequently lived in a sanatorium. After being released, she told Felix B. about all that she had gone through in the previous years. "It moved me profoundly that she . . . was unable to heal,"[78] noted Felix B. in his statement.

Numerous U-boats suffered greatly in the aftermath of the persecution. Certainly, the things they went through were generally not comparable to the experiences of those who survived concentration camps. Those differing experiences also preoccupied former U-boats. Marianne Ellenbogen, who survived in the Ruhr region, said later to her biographer, Mark Roseman, "That was something I always feared when thinking of ending up in a concentration camp—how I would behave, whether I'd behave like a civilized human being, how long it would take before I wouldn't care anymore how civilized I was, and survival became the main thought, as it did for so many."[79]

Her biographer noted the following regarding this conversation: "The difference between camp survivors' memories and Marianne's was reflected in the quality of her testimony. Her flow of speech was not impaired by memory, as was that of some survivors. What she had to tell did not defy her capacity of expression."[80] But U-boats also went through traumatic experiences, and it took a long time before Marianne Ellenbogen could speak about what she had gone through. She emigrated to Britain, married, and had two children. For the children, their mother's past was apparent as an "unearthly heavy silence."[81] A neighbor of Marianne Ellenbogen told Mark Roseman how in the summer, when everyone had their windows wide open, "you could hear Marianne crying out loudly in German in her sleep."[82]

The medical records often mention a "complete breakdown of the nervous system" and severe depression. Not only those who had lived in hiding for a long time, but also some who did not go underground in Munich until early 1945 were later diagnosed with a complete nervous breakdown.[83] Even though only a minority of surviving U-boats from Munich exhibited health damage so severe that it was impossible for them to resume their everyday lives, the question remains what long-term health problems were caused by a life in hiding. To what extent were they even diagnosed and treated accordingly? This question was closely tied to the issue of compensation for health damages. No compensation was forthcoming if damages were not diagnosed or recognized. It should be noted that the state of psychological research in the late 1940s was inadequate for detection and treatment of the pathologies exhibited by Holocaust survivors. Not until the 1950s and 1960s did terms such as "survivor syndrome" or "concentration camp (or KZ) syndrome" become established to describe the pathology of the survivors.[84] Especially in Germany, it took a long time for a gradual shift in psychiatric practice to occur that led doctors and psychiatrists to recognize the suffering due to persecution as an illness.[85] Pathbreaking in this area was a 1964 study called "Psychiatry of the Persecuted," which documented in detail the health problems resulting from "extreme stress situations."[86] Although this study also contained case studies of surviving U-boats, whose ordeal was presented as almost as harrowing as that of concentration camp survivors,[87] it could be more difficult for this group than for the camp survivors to communicate the "extreme stress situation" and its consequences. Sigmund W. attempted to do just that in a letter to the Bavarian State Compensation Office:

> Even if I am among the few of those persecuted who had not been locked up in a concentration camp, a constant companion in my path of suffering, which was marked by much physical deprivation and hardship, was the fear of being discovered and of the accompanying consequences for my life. This fear did not leave my side for years, up to liberation, and is to a great degree the cause of my current suffering. Even if a constitutional predisposition might be presumed in the case of my suffering, it is irrefutable that the years of fear and the associated constant panic caused a possibly preexisting disposition to develop into such suffering, or worsened it to such an extent that it resulted in the stroke I had in February 1945. This terrible fear must be comprehensible even to anyone who was not in the situation at that time, if they bring to mind that it was already assumed at that time among the Jewish population that those who were deported were in fact killed. I was particularly reinforced in this assumption since I received no sign of life whatsoever from any of my Jewish acquaintances.[88]

Three months after writing this letter, Sigmund W. died from another stroke. For many adults, the worries about family members as well as the associated feelings of guilt presented a particular burden, since many U-boats had close relatives in concentration or death camps.[89] On top of that came a feeling that they were endangering others. Knowing that if someone in hiding was discovered, not only they, but also their helpers, were in the greatest danger placed a heavy burden on all U-boats.[90] The emotional tension could cause depression, anxiety attacks, nervous disorders, cardiovascular diseases, gastrointestinal diseases, and numerous other ailments.[91]

Although there have been numerous studies of the long-term health problems of Holocaust survivors, very few social scientists, doctors, psychologists, or historians have dealt with specific questions regarding the impact of living in hiding.[92] An exception is the impact of persecution on the further development of hidden children.[93] The psychoanalyst Hans Keilson, who examined the repercussions of traumatization on the development of child Holocaust survivors, coined the term "sequential traumatization," whereby he distinguished three phases of traumatization:

1. the initial phase with the events leading up to the persecution;
2. the time spent in a concentration camp or in hiding; and
3. the postwar period with all the difficulties attendant upon reintegration, etc.[94]

Keilson found that, for the further development of the children, their experiences directly following the persecution were particularly important: "The significance of the third sequence is determined by the quality of the foster environment, its ability to break the chain of traumatizing factors and so alleviate the entire process, i.e., the foster environment supplies the necessary support itself or makes a timely request for assistance and supervision."[95] At the same time, Keilson emphasized that the "findings . . . regarding the effects of traumatization were similar for the children who had been in concentration camps and for those who were in hiding."[96]

The social ostracism and the separation from family members left deep scars, but there was very little assistance in the postwar period to deal with the children's psychological harm. There were high hopes that young children in particular would forget the persecution they experienced or that they had perhaps not really registered what was happening. In the long term, reintegration into postwar society and a return to normalcy were the priority. Nobody was interested in hearing about the psychological damages, and the children could not describe them adequately.[97] Frau K. "attempted to raise her son, who was certainly not stupid, on her own," stated a staff member of the Bavarian Aid Organization succinctly about a client from Munich.[98] Bernhard K., the boy "who was certainly not stupid," reflected on the situation years later, as an adult: "At the time [post-1945] my father was financially, morally, and physically totally ruined and my own constitution can be confirmed by witnesses who are still alive (the farmer's wife and her sister) as appalling for a nine- to ten-year-old boy. In the subsequent period I suffered as a boy and adolescent very much under the past events and only from today's distanced perspective and adult maturity was I able to create a reasonable picture."[99]

Young survivors in particular were long left alone with their stories. This was true not only in Germany, but wherever survivors lived.[100] Those who were persecuted as *Mischlinge* were often confronted with the view that they had suffered relatively little or not at all. Feelings of guilt toward their murdered relatives played a significant role for this group of people.[101]

Regarding not only the survivors, but also the helpers, the question as to the long-term health repercussions of the emotional stress remains. To what extent did the tension and fear of being discovered cause psychosomatic illness, nervous disorders, anxiety, or cardiovascular diseases? Health problems resulting from the stress facing the helpers have not been taken into account or researched adequately. It can hardly be assumed that the helpers were not impacted in the aftermath. Mostly, however, they integrated themselves almost seamlessly back into the everyday postwar period. Josef Cammerer had to bury a beloved person in his own home and then exhume the body a short time later. His strong emotional bond to Gertrud Lustig, her suffering, and finally her death in hiding in his apartment, as well as the death of a friend, Gertrud's husband, and the knowledge that there was nothing that could be done for Gertrud's parents to keep them from committing suicide—all of this certainly left behind deep traces. After the war, he withdrew into a different world in the St. Ottilien monastery. The intensive correspondence over decades with Gertrud Lustig's brother, Hans Fröhlich, reflect Cammerer's profound love, grief, desperation, self-blame, and abysmal pain.[102]

Many other helpers also showed signs of the aftermath of the psychological hardship. The marriages of some helpers in Munich broke up. This was not necessarily directly connected to the emotional burden, but it is improbable that the psychological strain of the extreme, stressful situation had no influence on the married life of the helpers. Otto Freiherr von Taube, who together with his wife had hidden the four-year-old Denny F., described this most dramatically: "The constant agitation of those days because we had to hide the child, and the panic concerning my interrogation with the Gestapo—which had nothing to do with the mentioned case—is what I attribute to the fact that my wife started showing signs of paranoia, which got out of control in the Passion Week in 1944, developing into utter lunacy. She has been in an insane asylum since the spring of 1944."[103]

POSTWAR STRUGGLES

Concluding this chapter is the story of a helper who experienced great difficulties in the postwar period. The flourishing illegal underground market brought the downfall of Karl Schörghofer. To tell this story, it is necessary first to share some observations on Munich's postwar illegal markets, epitomized for many in Munich by Möhlstrasse in the Bogenhausen district: "It became famous overnight in 1945. Relief organizations and committees settled in the large mansions where prior to 1938 well-to-do Jews had lived. Expropriated during the Nazi period, they became the residences of high-ranking Nazis, such as Heinrich Himmler. These buildings were confiscated after liberation by the US Army and made available to the relief organizations. In short, Möhlstrasse formed the center of Jewish life within the city of Munich."[104]

Möhlstrasse, Munich, street scene and stores, 1949. Munich City Archive, FS-NL-RD-2014B36.

Small businesses, cafés, and restaurants sprang up around the offices of the aid organizations. And in between were street vendors hoping for customers. Möhlstrasse was popular among Munich residents, not only because of the wide selection of goods, but also because it offered an opportunity to shop on Sundays (which to this day is generally not permitted in Germany).[105]

Thanks to the support of the American Joint Jewish Distribution Committee (Joint or JDC) and the UNRRA, the Jewish DPs had access to sought-after goods such as cigarettes, chocolate, and coffee, which they could then sell on the illegal underground market. This alone filled many Germans with feelings of envy. In fact, all population groups and strata, German DPs, Americans, former forced laborers, and prisoners of war—they all participated in the underground market in some form.[106] For example, the Munich police president, Franz Xaver Pitzer, had to give up his position in 1949 due to his involvement in the illegal gold trade.[107] The illegal underground market was by no means limited to Möhlstrasse, a center of Jewish life, even though the Jewish DPs became scapegoats for the sprawling underground economy. The image of Jewish underground market commerce gave renewed life to old anti-Jewish stereotypes of profiteering and exploitative trading, mixing medieval anti-Judaism with the hateful tirades of the Nazi *Stürmer* newspaper. Shame about what had happened was expressed as finger-pointing accusations: the Germans viewed themselves as victims of Jewish illegal market criminals.[108] In Munich's Jewish community, members were worried about the new permutations of antisemitism. Those Jews who wanted to remain in Munich long term had an interest in not having the city's Jewish community associated with illegal market crime. The following case must be viewed against this background.

The cemetery caretaker Karl Schörghofer and his son had not only hidden people and religious objects on the cemetery grounds on Ungererstrasse, but they had also engaged in illegal butchering, not least to be able to feed the family and the hidden Jews. After the war, Schörghofer remained in contact with the Jewish survivors he knew, and he also came to know Jewish displaced persons. A DP named Lichtenstein asked Schörghofer in December 1947 if he could temporarily provide him with some storage space.[109] When Schörghofer granted his request, a group of DPs unloaded a large number of boxes. The contents turned out to be two million American cigarettes destined for Munich's underground market. Karl Schörghofer Jr. later testified that he had asked Lichtenstein if everything was legitimate, and Lichtenstein answered, "Yes, it's all okay with Dr. Auerbach." According to the testimony, Lichtenstein told Schörghofer that he would bring him "a written declaration from Dr. Auerbach about the things to be stored."[110] As soon became clear, everything was not okay. Karl Schörghofer Jr. later described the subsequent course of events:

> On January 5, 1948, at roughly 4 o'clock p.m., some men from the Jewish Community appeared, a certain Dr. Neuland and [Herr] Kahn. They explained that they had received a telephone call that cigarettes had been stored with me. I explained to the gentlemen that the cigarettes were here, and my father brought them to the cigarettes. Then the gentlemen explained that these were illicit trading goods. They also told me to lock the room and not to give the cigarettes to Lichtenstein. Later I was called to the Jewish Community, where I was told that it would be a major disgrace if it became publicly known that cigarettes were stored at the Jewish cemetery. I was also told: Do whatever you want with the cigarettes but get rid of them quickly and inconspicuously. On January 5, 1948, around 6 p.m., Lichtenstein showed up . . . and took the cigarettes to some location, but I don't know where.[111]

It is certain that the representatives of the official Jewish community had in fact visited Schörghofer. It is unclear, however, whether the words were uttered as reported by Schörghofer Jr. The concern is definitely understandable in view of an antisemitism that circulated under the guise of complaints about the illegal market activities of the DPs.

A few days later, the police appeared at the Schörghofers. They searched the premises and found two cows, two pigs, meat, leather, and large quantities of legumes and pasta.[112] According to the investigation report, Criminal Division Director Andreas Grasmüller had received a call from State Commissioner Philipp Auerbach that there were large quantities of American cigarettes stored in the buildings of the Jewish cemetery in Munich and that illegal butchering was also taking place there.[113] Subsequently, the cemetery grounds were searched, and Schörghofer Sr. and Jr., as well as an employee, were arrested. A short time later, a Polish Jew was arrested on Möhlstrasse in connection with the incident. The subsequent investigation on Möhlstrasse proceeded largely without any results. State Commissioner Auerbach pressured for complete clarification and prosecution of the perpetrators.[114] The owner of the cigarettes—possibly the same Lichtenstein who dropped them off and picked them up again—could not be identified, and the whereabouts of the cigarettes also remained in the dark. The case raised some questions that can no longer be answered. An illegal underground market delivery evidently got out of hand, which then reinforced the already existing tension between the DPs and the representatives of the Jewish Community of Munich. Auerbach had taken on the task of combatting the illegal market to counter the stigmatization of all DPs as criminals and the new fuel it was giving to antisemitism.[115] It remains open why he reported only Schörghofer and not Lichtenstein. Auerbach was not originally from Munich and knew neither Schörghofer nor anything about his aid to Jews during the Nazi period. Karl Schörghofer Sr. and his son ultimately had to stand trial.

On October 20, 1948, the second criminal chamber of the Munich Regional Court I, with Regional Court Judge Adalbert Gürthofer presiding, sentenced Karl Schörghofer Sr. to one year in prison and his son to ten months. Karl Schörghofer Sr.'s sentence was ultimately suspended to probation due to his age and poor state of health.[116] It was taken favorably into account that Schörghofer Sr. had helped Jews during the war. During the trial, the focus was solely on the facts of the case of illegal butchering. Assisting illegal market trading, of which the defendant had been accused during the interrogations, had been dropped. The cigarettes were never mentioned at all.

The *Neue Jüdische Zeitung*, a Jewish newspaper in Munich, reported in 1956 in a full-page article on "the old Gentile and the Munich cemetery."[117] The editor of the Yiddish-language paper, Marian Gid, found the "unpleasant aftermath chapter" to be just as newsworthy as Schörghofer's achievements and was very hard on the Jewish Community of Munich. The article claimed that "the then king of the Jews in Bavaria, Dr. Auerbach," together with "another prominent Jew," had sent the DPs to Schörghofer with the cigarettes.[118] Ultimately, the article continued, Auerbach reported the unsuspecting Schörghofer to the police when things got too risky for him.

Not only did Gid polemicize against Auerbach, who—as previously mentioned—had committed suicide in 1952 after being convicted of embezzlement in several scandalous proceedings; he also attacked the leadership of the Jewish Community of Munich. As Gid wrote, "But the administration of the Jewish Community of Munich at the time, including some who had 'privileged' status under the Nazi regime (due to their mixed marriages), had decided in April 1949 to dismiss him [Schörghofer] from his position as the faithful watchman and custodian of the Jewish cemetery."[119] Gid implied that things were easier for the "privileged" during the Nazi period, whereas Schörghofer put himself in danger to rescue Jews and religious objects. The article rebuked the community leadership for not having the courage after 1945 to defend Schörghofer. According to Gid, it was embarrassed and concerned about its reputation in mainstream society, resorting to sacrificing Schörghofer, who rescued Jews, instead of supporting him before the court. Polemical in tone, the accusation of "compulsively adapting" directed at the "over-assimilated" Jews was an old point of contention within Munich's Jewish community.[120] Gid's attack must be seen within the context of the conflicts regarding the election of the head of the Jewish community, which plagued the Jewish community in Munich in 1956–60. In the power struggle between Siegfried Neuland and Max Bachmann, the supporters of each candidate refused to recognize the election of the other, which led to years of legal conflict. In the end, Neuland won the new election in 1960.[121]

Karl Schörghofer Jr. was allowed to retain the lease on the nursery, which did not help him much because he was in prison. The incarceration threw the Schörghofer family into existential difficulties. Karl Schörghofer Jr.'s plea for clemency was ultimately granted.[122] Meanwhile, Karl Schörghofer Sr.'s health was deteriorating while he lived with his daughter in Miesbach. His marriage had broken up, and in 1962, Karl Schörghofer Sr. committed suicide. In 1967, Karl Schörghofer Sr., along with his wife, his son Karl Jr., and his daughter Martha Schörghofer-Schleipfer, were honored by Yad Vashem as Righteous Among the Nations.[123] Since December 2014, a commemorative plaque in the new Jewish cemetery has memorialized Karl Schörghofer.

TEN

POSTWAR ENCOUNTERS

IN HER SWORN STATEMENT FOR her helper, police commissioner Paul Mayer, written in 1946, Sophie Mayer stated the following: "If today I reflect on the fact that this man was a member of the party and will be lumped together with those criminals who wore the same party badge, I must say that this was not the case of a party comrade who did something good, but one of a brave man who was forced to wear a party badge. I could only wish that all those who did not join the party but faithfully supported the party line would have treated us persecutees as kindly as this man did."[1]

While there is extensive documentation of Paul Mayer's actions, there was also a great proliferation of letters of exoneration submitted to denazification courts that helped countless purportedly "deserving party comrades" mutate into resistance fighters or helpers of Jews. These letters, which came to be known as "Persil certificates," in reference to the German laundry detergent Persil, caused the number of supposed helpers to skyrocket after 1945.

Among the helpers, there were of course also people who, like Paul Mayer, did in fact help to hide Jews despite their membership in the Nazi Party or one of its associations. They, too, had to account for their actions in the postwar period in denazification proceedings. An obviously paradoxical case was that of the Communist Stanislaus Hanisch, who had spent a year and a half in the Dachau concentration camp. He had joined the National Socialist Motor Vehicle Corps (*Nationalsozialistisches Kraftfahrkorps*, NSKK) in order to drive around undisturbed to scout out hiding places for his neighbor Meta L. Consequently, his denazification proceedings were quickly brought to a close.[2] In other cases, the situation was more complicated. Police Commissioner Mayer, the engineer Rudolf Ammann, the businessman Otto Jordan, and the factory owners August and Rudolf Kammerer were all Nazi Party or SA members. In all these cases, the surviving U-boats supported their former helpers in denazification proceedings. In the case of the Kammerer brothers, however, although they were supported by Benno Schülein, who had been saved by them and later became their lawyer, other survivors viewed them as unscrupulous profiteers who had treated their forced laborers poorly.

For surviving Jews in Munich, the denazification hearings and postwar trials were an emotionally charged reunion with people with whom they had a wide range of connections: helpers, fellow U-boats, Jewish functionaries, Nazis, supposed helpers, and denouncers. These proceedings frequently did not take place until more than five years after the persecution had ended. They tore open old wounds and brought back painful memories. The testimony of Jewish survivors could be especially decisive for the classification of defendants in denazification proceedings. In addition to the denazification hearings, there were also trials against the persecutors. In Munich, state prosecutors investigated the staff of the Aryanization Office and the Gestapo on charges of extortion, deprivation of liberty, and bodily injury. Witness testimonies, transcripts, and sworn statements reflect not only judicial concerns but also individual perceptions, projections, and postwar interests, all with a chronological distance of five to ten years. This chapter will trace some of these "second encounters" in the denazification hearings and in postwar trials.

HELP FOR THE HELPERS

The engineer Rudolf Ammann, born in Munich in 1894, hid the socialist Alexander Schifrin in 1933 and the sisters Andrea and Valerie Wolffenstein, who were of Jewish descent, from 1943 to 1945 in his home (see chapter 8). Ammann had been active in Quickborn, the Catholic youth movement, since 1920. As of 1930, he was a member of the Center Party, for which he and his wife also worked in the election campaigns.[3] The Ammanns had lived in Mannheim until 1935 and then moved to Munich, where Rudolf Ammann worked as an engineer for BMW.

Rudolf Ammann had to appear before a denazification tribunal in 1947 because he had joined the SA in 1933. A short time later, he had also become a member of the German Labor Front (*Deutsche Arbeitsfront*, DAF) and the National Socialist People's Welfare (*Nationalsozialistische Volkswohlfahrt*, NSV).[4] Due to these memberships, he received what was called a "notification of atonement" in 1948 that imposed a fine of 1,000 reichsmarks and classified him in category 4, "followers" or "fellow travelers" (*Mitläufer*).[5] In a personal declaration, Ammann attempted to explain the reasons and circumstances regarding his SA membership. In a very awkwardly worded letter, he stated that he had joined the SA to protect his employer, the Josef Vögele company in Mannheim. According to Ammann, the company had been considered democratic and socially progressive and was a thorn in the side of the local Nazis. To improve relations between the company leadership and the city administration, and to assure the company's economic survival, leading employees (he was a senior engineer and authorized representative of the company) decided to join subsidiary Nazi organizations. Ammann even claimed to have hoped to be able to change something from the inside by becoming an SA member. In the aftermath of the Röhm affair, however, he abandoned this illusion and left the SA in December 1934. In 1935, the family moved to Munich, where Ammann joined the DAF and the NSV. As a BMW employee, Ammann was required to join the DAF. And Ammann said that he joined the NSV as a cover because a neighbor had warned him that he was considered politically unreliable for violating an ordinance regarding the display of flags.[6]

Ammann did not mention his assistance to Alexander Schifrin and Andrea Wolffenstein in his letter. He referred to Valerie Wolffenstein only once as a persecutee who could attest to his political stance. He mostly wanted to explain the reasons for his memberships in Nazi organizations. Ammann's statements were evidently not very convincing. He subsequently appealed his classification as a follower. In his comprehensive written justification, he described his attitudes during the Nazi period in detail. This time, he described in depth his help to Alexander Schifrin and Valerie and Andrea Wolffenstein, but he emphasized that Valerie Wolffenstein had pressured him to tell the story. The latter also assured in her own sworn statement that "there was not a trace of 'follower' in him and, what was more, he was prepared to pay for his attitudes with death."[7] The well-known theologian Romano Guardini, who had meanwhile become a professor at the university in Tübingen, also confirmed that Ammann "hated [National Socialism] and actively resisted."[8]

As a senior engineer at BMW, Ammann had, of course, knowingly put himself in the service of the Nazi armaments and war economy, even if in 1935 he still believed that there he could realize his dream of working in aeronautical engineering. As of 1943, Ammann apparently led a development department for piston engines.[9] The corporation had grown rapidly during the war years and profited greatly from using foreign forced laborers and concentration camp prisoners.[10] Ammann emphasized that he and a group of like-minded BMW employees had done everything possible to supply foreign forced laborers with food and clothing and to protect them from attacks. This group, he claimed, had also ensured that the main BMW plants were surrendered in April 1945 without a fight. Ammann explained that in 1944 he had rejected an offer to assume a directorship at BMW.[11] It could not be ascertained if he personally participated in the exploitation of camp prisoners or forced laborers.

In July 1948, Dr. Rolf (formerly Rudolf) Ammann was finally reclassified as "exonerated."[12] By that time, however, he had long since left Germany, as he had already been hired in the United States in September 1945, like so many German technology experts, to share his skills with the American armaments and aerospace industry. Ammann worked in the research department of the Wright Field Air Force Base in Dayton, Ohio. He maintained friendly contact with Valerie Wolffenstein.[13]

ADVOCATE FOR THE HELPERS

The businessman Otto Jordan was classified in April 1947 as "exonerated" by the Munich Denazification Tribunal. In December 1947, the Court of Cassation rescinded the judgment and petitioned for new proceedings, claiming that Jordan had been judged too leniently. Otto Jordan had joined the Nazi Party in early May 1933 and had also been a member of the National Socialist Flying Corps (*Nationalsozialistisches Fliegerkorps*, NSFK) and the DAF. The Court of Cassation judges did not want to accept Jordan's defense, namely, that he had protected his Jewish friend, the lawyer Benno Schülein, from persecution. They went so far as to claim that it was not even certain that Benno Schülein had suffered persecution. The case was therefore retried in March 1948. Benno Schülein, who served as Jordan's defense lawyer, was so incensed at the position of the Court of Cassation that he sent the following statement to the Munich Denazification Tribunal (*Spruchkammer*) VIII, which would be hearing the case:

> The Court of Cassation rescinded the judgment of December 22, 1947, on the basis of a justification that is not only legally erroneous but also lets it be recognized that the gentlemen who participated in preparing this decision either do not want to remember the time that lies behind us, or else they live in total ignorance of it. . . . The support did not lie in the fact that someone merely offered me a piece of bread; it consisted of providing housing, in providing active support in every respect. . . . All that is lacking here is that I'd still be referred to with "Israel" and the judgment be signed with "Heil Hitler." . . . I vigorously doubt whether the authors of the decision would have taken such actions as the involved person took upon himself, if they would have had the courage to conduct themselves in that way.[14]

After he had vented his anger, Benno Schülein explained again in detail how Otto and Anny Jordan helped him, noting that Otto Jordan and his father had become party members only because they had thought it would enable them to better protect him.[15] Ultimately, the denazification tribunal essentially followed Schülein's statements and confirmed the original judgment. Otto Jordan was then classified as exonerated.[16] We can assume that father and son did not join the party solely to protect Benno Schülein, but that business interests also played a role. It was therefore not entirely far-fetched for the Court of Cassation to question the story and seek a review. In this relatively early phase of denazification, at least a few of the tribunals attempted to apply fairly strict standards and avoid operating as "follower factories," as the historian Lutz Niethammer dismissively characterized them later.[17] The doubt as to whether he had in fact been persecuted was insulting to Benno Schülein, but the tribunal's skepticism regarding his helpers was conceivable in view of the wide circulation of "clean bills of health" (the so-called Persil certificates) documenting assistance supposedly given to Jews.

Dr. Benno Schülein also had to defend other people who had helped him go underground. In December 1947, the factory owner Rudolf Kammerer stood before the Denazification Tribunal VI in Munich in appeal proceedings. Kammerer had been a Nazi Party member since 1937. He was initially placed in category 4 as a follower.[18] The public prosecutor appealed the decision. Although Kammerer had faced a certain personal risk, he had nevertheless protected his friends Benno Schülein and Fritz Kuhn from persecution. At the same time, however, some forced laborers in his company testified that they had been mistreated by him. This evidence triggered the appeal proceedings.[19]

The engineer Kurt J. wrote to the denazification tribunal in September: "As compared with other companies, the treatment I received at that of A. and R. Kammerer was the *worst* and in particular I was greatly tormented by the foreman of the telephone factory."[20] Two women who were former forced laborers testified that they had requested part-time work from Kammerer because they had small children to take care of, but that this was gruffly denied.[21]

Hermann S. claimed in 1946 that he had been mistreated by Kammerer when he came late to work one day: "Kammerer walked up to me and did not give me even a moment to apologize. Instead he grabbed me by the collar and delivered a terrible blow to my face, yelling at the top of his lungs that he would call the Gestapo. He dragged me several meters through the factory hall and called me a dog and a scoundrel. Emotionally crushed and physically weak, with a terrible headache that I still suffer from to this day, I had to return to my workbench."[22]

Kurt J. and other former employees who had spoken negatively about the Kammerer company did not appear at the appeal proceedings despite being requested to do so. Some witnesses who had initially complained about their treatment changed their testimony in the appeal proceedings. Hermann S., too, now presented the situation in a different way. In 1947, he said on record that his wife had known Rudolf Kammerer since her childhood, so he, too, knew the Kammerer family. This was also the reason he had registered to do his forced labor there. All in all, the Jewish laborers had been very satisfied working for Kammerer, according to Hermann S. He then presented the conflict with Kammerer as follows:

> Kammerer was very agitated as he came up to my workbench and started reproaching me. I responded that I would like to tell him in his office why I was late. It was in fact because I wanted to look for a shelter in case of arrests. Herr Kammerer grabbed me by the collar of my work shirt and yelled out very excitedly: "Are you telling me what to do?!" And he gave me a hard slap. Then he took me with him by holding on to the collar of my shirt and said, "So now you'll come with me, you rascal; now I'll report you to the Gestapo." But after a few steps he sent me back to my workplace. The next day, after my wife had spoken with him, Kammerer called me into his office and said he was sorry that in his agitation he gave me, of all people, a slap, since I was his favorite and we should forget the whole incident. We shook hands and I promised not to hold a grudge.[23]

It is impossible to reconstruct the precise reasons for this change of heart. With the passage of time, perspectives often changed. Various witnesses testified that the psychological pressure of the frequent inspections of the factory and of the threat of denunciations had weighed heavily on Rudolf Kammerer and that because of this, he repeatedly lost his composure.[24] People from the Aryanization Office often came by to check if all the Jews were wearing the yellow star.[25] This sometimes led to tense situations and conflicts.[26] After 1945, Benno Schülein was vehement in expressing his opinion that the Kammerer brothers had fought for their Jewish forced laborers. He said he often witnessed how August Kammerer had "scuffled" with the Gestapo to get deferments for his workers from upcoming deportations, and he also noted that the Kammerer brothers in some cases had covered the fines that Jewish workers had had to pay for not wearing the yellow star.[27] The denazification tribunal also followed this argumentation and determined that "the person concerned . . . has verified by presenting numerous credible documents that he stood up for the Jews assigned to work in his factory in such a manner that went far beyond that which was permitted in the National Socialist regime."[28] Thus, Rudolf Kammerer was declared exonerated.[29]

In the proceedings against Rudolf Kammerer's brother August, a similar ambivalence is apparent. The court initially classified August Kammerer as a "lesser offender" (category 3). He appealed, and in 1948, he, too, was ultimately classified as exonerated.[30] In his case as well, there were contrasting witness testimonies. As stated in the reasons for the judgment, some former forced laborers reported of tantrums and abuses, while others underscored that Kammerer, despite all his unpredictability, had wanted to help the Jews in his company to survive until the war ended.[31] What ultimately assured August Kammerer of his classification as exonerated, however, was the fact that he could cite acts of resistance in which he had participated. These were expressly acknowledged in the reasons for the judgment: "The person concerned had been a member of a resistance movement since late 1943, for which he performed valuable services by passing on news about the broadcasting installations to be occupied and by making contacts to leading anti–National Socialist personalities. The activities of the person concerned for the church news service was active resistance. He often passed on important ecclesiopolitical news that was never to fall into the hands of the Gestapo from Munich to Vienna and Berlin."[32] It is unclear if concrete evidence confirming these actions was presented and what kind of news messages were involved, as only the judgments themselves are extant in the files.

It is uncontested that Rudolf and August Kammerer protected Benno Schülein, Fritz Kuhn, and several other forced laborers in their company from persecution. However, it is also uncontested that the Kammerer company profited considerably from the use of Jewish forced laborers. "The owners were previously rather broke and boosted themselves with Nazi orders," wrote Hedwig Geng, who had also worked for Kammerer.[33] Moreover, many people worked at the Kammerer factory under extremely unhealthy conditions. Siegfried Neuland lost his eyesight while engaged in tinning work, while other workers were totally unprotected and at the mercy of toxic acid fumes.[34] In March 1943, the company owners hid Benno Schülein and helped Fritz Kuhn. In the final phase of the war, they did much more to protect the remaining Jewish forced laborers—generally Jewish spouses in mixed marriages—from being deported. Tactical preparation for postwar life might also have played a role. Nevertheless, the Kammerer brothers assumed a great risk with their aid for Benno Schülein in particular. It was indeed not just a piece of bread that he was occasionally given, as the incensed lawyer later wrote. He had in fact spent many weeks living in hiding in Rudolf Kammerer's home.

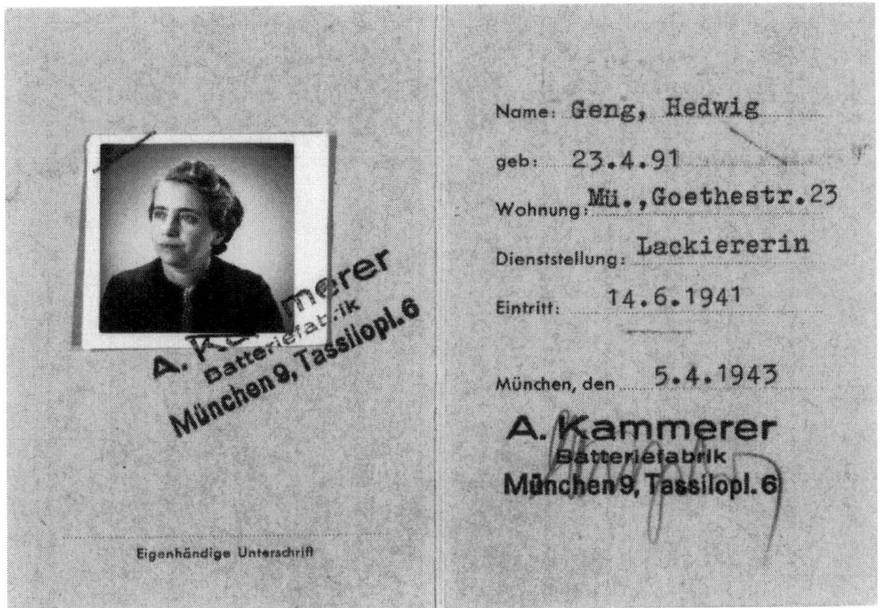

A. Kammerer
Batteriefabrik
München 9, Tassilopl. 6

Eigenhändige Unterschrift

Name: Geng, Hedwig
geb: 23.4.91
Wohnung: Mü.,Goethestr.23
Dienststellung: Lackiererin
Eintritt: 14.6.1941

München, den 5.4.1943

A. Kammerer
Batteriefabrik
München 9, Tassilopl. 6

Hedwig Geng's worker identification card from the Kammerer Battery and Telephone Factory. Courtesy of the Leo Baeck Institute, New York.

PENALIZING "JEW FLEECERS" AND DENOUNCERS

Many people made money from the suffering of Jews. They charged exorbitant prices, extorting and robbing both those in hiding and their helpers. In very few cases did these acts lead to criminal proceedings, and the stolen property was very rarely returned. Even if victims survived, they could generally not prove that the objects had belonged to them or their families or that the objects were not considered gifts at the time. The so-called Jew fleecers could assume that they would remain unpunished. To play it absolutely safe, some of them followed up their actions with a denunciation that led to the arrest and deportation of the already aggrieved party. Rarely did hidden Jews or their fleecers encounter each other in court after the war.

Margot S., a Munich Jew, was denounced and robbed by a supposed helper. She survived in a hiding place in Berlin and was determined to find her possessions and press charges against the woman who denounced her. When Margot S. returned to Munich in 1946, she started by going back to the home of Wally

Cremer, where she had lived briefly in 1943. Margot S. demanded the return of her possessions. When Cremer refused, she went to the police and filed a complaint against her former host. A house search followed, during which some objects that had belonged to Margot S. were discovered. Some of her possessions were also found in the home of Wally Cremer's sister. Margot S. did not want to let the matter rest, and additional possessions of hers were seized during a second search of Cremer's home. The Munich Local Court convicted Wally Cremer, the widow of a local court judge, of false accusations and embezzlement in 1947 and sentenced her to three months in prison. The judgment was confirmed in appeal proceedings on September 14, 1959.[35] The court considered it proven that "the defendant had evidently reckoned that Frau S. [name rendered anonymous], as a Jew, would sooner or later be arrested again and would perhaps disappear so that no inquiries about the whereabouts of her possessions would ensue."[36]

Wally Cremer also had to appear before a denazification tribunal. Her downfall was that she had denounced others in addition to Margot S. There were evidently no political reasons for the denunciations. Her political stance remained unclear to the end; she was never a member of the Nazi Party. She was initially classified in the group of "major offenders" and sentenced to three years in a work camp and the loss of all her assets except for 3,000 reichsmarks.[37] In the appeal proceedings, Cremer's sentence was reduced to two years in a work camp, 60 percent of her assets, and classification in category 2, "offenders."[38] Her case was one of very few after 1945 that managed to hold such "Jew fleecers" accountable for their actions. The Cremer case should also be seen within the context of other judgments, however. The chief of the Munich Gestapo, Oswald Schäfer, got off with a sentence of only two years in a work camp and confiscation of all his assets except for 5,000 reichsmarks.[39] Karl Fiehler, the Nazi mayor of Munich and an "Old Fighter," who had already joined the Nazi party before 1933, was also sentenced to two years in a work camp.[40]

Wally Cremer was not an isolated case. Denouncers received harsh penalties in the Munich denazification proceedings. A woman who denounced a Jew for making a disparaging comment about the Wehrmacht, for example, was classified in 1950 by the denazification tribunal as category 2, offender.[41] The housekeeper for the Cosmann family, Maria Spiegel, who had denounced Lorenz Cosmann for "defiling the race," was also assigned to category 2, offender, and put in a work camp for one year. Not until the appeal proceedings in 1950 was the sentence reduced to three hundred days of special work for the public good, but the assignment to category 2 remained.[42] Nazi functionaries successfully testified in court to having acted under orders, whereas denouncers were sometimes harshly punished for their independent actions.

Although in Munich the denazification tribunals did not spare denouncers, this was not the case everywhere. In his analysis of denazification in the American zone, which included Munich, Lutz Niethammer has written of the denazification tribunals' "failure" in the cases of denunciation.[43] The main problem in the American zone was that, in contrast to the situation in the British and French zones, American occupation forces did not authorize German courts to apply the Allied Control Council Law no. 10 in relevant cases.[44] Consequently, the following differences resulted in how cases of denunciation were treated: "CCL no. 10 was applied in the British and French zones for crimes such as denunciations because they were not explicitly mentioned in the German criminal code. In the American zone they were supposed to be treated either under existing criminal offenses, such as deprivation of liberty or false accusation, or through referral to the denazification tribunals."[45]

Consequently, in the American zone in particular, "most proceedings introduced because of denunciations" did not even come before a court, or in the few cases in which a trial took place, the proceedings were often discontinued.[46] However, the criminal prosecution of denunciation and its consequences also proved difficult in the other two Western zones. Although significantly more proceedings were introduced in those zones, there were also numerous dismissals, and at times, the state prosecutors and courts showed little interest in prosecuting denouncers.[47]

A PROMINENT HELPER'S DENAZIFICATION

Reich Governor Franz Ritter von Epp died in late January 1947 while incarcerated. Denazification proceedings against him nevertheless started in 1949, most likely because, having been a high-ranking representative of the Nazi state, there was a good chance that his classification as a Nazi offender would have led to confiscation of his assets.[48] Rudolf V., once a member of Epp's Free Corps, who had been warned by Epp and protected by him from persecution, was also dead. The public prosecutor demanded that Epp be classified as belonging to category 1, major offender. As the Reich governor in Bavaria and the Reich leader of the Nazi Party's Office of Colonial Policy, as well as due to his great prestige, which he had placed in the service of the party, Epp was a key representative of the Nazi state for the postwar prosecutor. His defense lawyers argued that he had opposed so-called protective custody excesses (*Schutzhaft-Auswüchse*) very early on, that he had helped people suffering under persecution, and that he had stood up for the rights of the church. They also said that during the war, Epp, who had joined the Nazi Party in 1928, had turned away from Nazism.[49]

A number of witnesses were heard who generally emphasized how Epp supported those "persecuted on racial grounds," but without giving any concrete examples. Epp's support for Rudolf V. was not brought up at all. It is certain that Epp did in fact help people suffering persecution, such as Rudolf V., whom Epp viewed primarily as an "old comrade." However, this does nothing to change the fact that Epp basically supported Nazi racial policies. His rabid antisemitism has been sufficiently documented.[50] Epp's attempts to curb the excesses of so-called protective custody does not mean that he categorically questioned the system of arbitrarily arresting political opponents, but only that he found the extent of it and the sadistic brutality in the prisons and concentration camps to be questionable. The denazification tribunal did not choose to follow the argumentation of the defense, which wanted to categorize Epp only as a follower since he had also maintained contact with resistance groups. Epp was ultimately placed in category 2, offenders.

In his reasoning, Presiding Judge von Dewitz stated the following:

> He was an ornament, so to speak, for the Nazi party. . . . His position as the Reich governor in Bavaria was simply a matter of prestige and in the opinion of the chamber his substantial annual salary from the party of 80,000 marks should be viewed as "compensation for services rendered." The *power* in Bavaria was exercised by the Gauleiter. . . . He was the classic example of those higher-ranked, active officers who had no political judgment whatsoever and did not or could not see what was going on around them, and who with their oath to Hitler felt connected to him unconditionally and exclusively, in any case stronger than to their people and fatherland. . . . The individual "help efforts" for those persecuted on racial or political grounds could not change anything about the overall picture of the person concerned.[51]

This judgment is certainly valid on most points, but the court endorsed the self-representations of many Nazi officers, according to which they had not perceived the horrible reality right before their eyes because of supposed blindness and naivete. In his notes from his incarceration shortly before his death, for example, Epp wrote, "I know that—I believe it was 1933—a concentration camp was established in Dachau. I do not know who commissioned this facility. In any case, as the Reich governor I was in no way involved in its construction. In 1933–34 I inspected the camp once. At that time, its spaciousness, which gave the prisoners air and light, and their varied outdoor activities gave me the impression of a modern prison facility. I could see nothing to criticize about the treatment. Later I never saw it again."[52] In fact, Epp helped his "old comrade" Rudolf V. and opposed the excesses of protective custody precisely because he had been informed of the harsh realities of places like Dachau. The "ornament"[53] of the movement was neither blind nor deaf, but in 1946, he had to prepare the lie depicting this version of the story.

THE HANGMAN AS HELPER? OR THE HANGMAN'S HELPER?

"The support I received continued for about a year and a half. It was not a lot but I must acknowledge it. He gave me meat ration coupons, bread, pasta, but neither clothing nor money. I must also report that Reichhart always hid me when there was something against Jews going on. . . . He also supported my family once I was already in Theresienstadt."[54]

With these words, Rudolf D. described before the Munich Denazification Tribunal the assistance he had received during the Nazi period from his friend Johann Reichhart. The Munich executioner and hangman, Johann Reichhart, who had carried out more than three thousand executions between 1924 and 1946,[55] had briefly hidden a Jew on several occasions and supported his family with food.

Rudolf D., a produce merchant, had been incarcerated for several weeks in the Dachau concentration camp in the wake of the pogroms on November 9, 1938. After being released in January 1939, he was conscripted for forced labor. Due to his privileged mixed marriage, he was initially protected from deportation, but in February 1945, he was ultimately sent to Theresienstadt. After liberation in 1945, he returned to Munich and resumed his work as a produce merchant.[56]

Two years later, in 1947, the executioner Johann Reichhart had to appear before the Munich Denazification Tribunal. Things did not look good for him. He had been a member of the Nazi Party since May 1937, had achieved considerable affluence from his occupation, and had pointedly denounced some of his drinking buddies. Several people said they had heard him say that "the Jews should be chopped up and fed to animals in the zoo."[57] Reichhart's denazification dossier conveys the image of a braggart with considerable egotism, a person whose party membership was due more to professional interests than to political convictions. Rudolf D. was an advocate for the former executioner, testifying that he definitely knew about Reichhart's earlier job, but could only speak the truth, which was that Reichhart had protected and supported Rudolf D.'s family during the entire duration of the war.[58]

The denazification tribunal found that Rudolf D. expressed such support only because Reichhart's son and Rudolf D.'s stepson had been playmates. Thus, the assistance could not offset Reichhart's antisemitism. With the decision of August 21, 1947, Reichhart was assigned to category 1, major offenders, and sentenced to ten years in a work camp.[59] In the appeal proceedings, Rudolf D. reiterated his testimony.[60] This time Reichhart was reassigned down to category 2, offenders, and his prison time was reduced to two years in a work camp.[61] As a result of a renewed appeal, the sentence was ultimately reduced to a year and a half.[62] With that, the executioner was nevertheless punished more harshly than many of the judges who had imposed the death sentences that he had carried out.[63]

The hangman as a helper—the story seems odd. In Rudolf D.'s compensation file there is no mention of the support he received from Johann Reichhart. Like all petitioners, Rudolf D. had to describe his whereabouts between 1939 and 1945 as precisely as possible, also naming witnesses who could corroborate his statements. Johann Reichhart was not mentioned anywhere. On the one hand, it was not absolutely necessary for Rudolf D. to mention Reichhart in his compensation application, and mention of helpers is missing in other files as well. Moreover, when Rudolf D. filed his compensation claim, he was in a poor state of health. That said, it cannot be ruled out that Reichhart, who claimed that he wanted to feed Jews to the animals in the zoo, had in fact helped Rudolf D. and his family.

On the other hand, it is also possible that Rudolf D. wrote a positive report as a favor to Johann Reichhart in 1947 and 1948 and that Reichhart intended to reciprocate in some way. Receiving a Persil certificate, or clean bill of health, from a Jew meant a lot. Hedwig Geng wrote about the situation in the Jewish rest home where she was quartered together with some Theresienstadt survivors: "First there is Frau Schülein from Dalmessing [Thalmässing, Franconia], a dear old lady, to whom the whole town now pilgrimages for certificates saying how friendly everyone was to the Jews. But she only says things that she can confirm."[64] More than a few Jews were willing to issue these certificates, sometimes out of gratitude, sometimes for a fee, and sometimes with a certain disdain.[65] Oskar Buchner had had a good dozen Jewish forced laborers working in his nursery. An SA man and Old Fighter, he contacted one of his former forced laborers, Hugo Holzmann, in the summer of 1945. Buchner let Holzmann know that he should come by and could work for him again and that he would pay him well. And if he could please sign a declaration that Buchner had treated all the Jewish forced laborers decently.[66] Holzmann did him the favor and demanded in return nothing but a large bouquet of flowers for his mother.

Some other Jewish survivors also signed. Oskar Buchner was classified in the denazification proceedings as a follower. The declarations by the Jewish forced laborers left a profound impression on the court.[67]

Rolf Grabower, a Jew and the former director of the Lohhof camp, spoke out after the war for Hans Heinrich Lammers, who had headed Hitler's Reich Chancellery, and Lutz Graf Schwerin von Krosigk, the Reich Finance Minister. These two had protected him from being deported on multiple occasions because they perceived him first and foremost as a German-National patriot and less as a Jew.[68] Grabower also certified that SA Obersturmführer Franz Mugler from Munich's Aryanization Office had "acted impeccably."[69] In Berlin, the Jewish community noted the following dilemma: "Even if Germans had been personally helpful in individual cases, such 'subjective' judgments did not take into account that the same people might very well have sent others to their death."[70]

How much weight should be given to support for an individual, for isolated gestures of humanity, or for "decent treatment" in the total evaluation of persons who now had to account for their actions as perpetrators? In discussing this question, Primo Levi refers to a passage in Dostoyevsky's novel *The Brothers Karamasov*. One of the main characters, Grushenka, tells the story of a single good deed. "A vicious old woman dies and goes to hell, but her guardian angel, straining his memory, recalls that she once, only once, gave a beggar the gift of a little onion she had dug up from her garden."[71] Consequently, God gave the vicious woman a chance to escape purgatory.

Levi found the story "revolting," as many evil people at some points in their lives show rare acts of kindness.[72] But for many perpetrators in postwar Germany, a single, however small, good deed was enough to receive a benevolent judgment from the court.

MEMBERS OF THE GESTAPO AND THE ARYANIZATION OFFICE IN COURT

In addition to the denazification hearings in Munich, between 1949 and 1954 there were also a number of proceedings against people who had worked for the Munich Gestapo and Aryanization Office.[73] Here as well it was about the extent to which mitigating circumstances and gestures of humanity could offset acts of contempt for humanity, brutality, and avarice. The public prosecutors investigated mainly on the set of facts that included "personal enrichment," "extortion and threats," "deprivation of liberty," and "bodily injury," in other words, the abuse of Jews.[74] However, these proceedings stood in the shadow of more sensational ones. In the focus of public interest was the trial of the two Munich Gestapo officers Oswald Schäfer and Richard Lebkücher for the murder of foreign forced laborers.[75]

In the investigations of Gestapo agents and Aryanization Office functionaries facing charges of deprivation of liberty and abuse of Jews, a number of Munich Jews were heard as witnesses. The questioning was based on the specific charges and revolved around the witnesses' personal experiences with the defendants. The U-boats and their family members and helpers were able to contribute significantly to presenting the case for excessive violence on the part of the accused, as well as for their bribability and self-enrichment. Gertrud Hirschauer (formerly Paulus) described how the Gestapo officer Hans Grahammer had dragged the sleeping Oskar Cosmann, who was hidden in her apartment, out of bed, beating him constantly, and how Grahammer had cursed at her and kicked her three-year-old child.[76] Margarete Cosmann confirmed the abuse her husband had suffered. Siegfried B. and other witnesses depicted the days-long brutal torture of Julius Hechinger by Hans Wegner and Franz Mugler, staff members of the Aryanization Office.[77] Siegfried B.'s brother described the great pressure under which he had been placed to reveal his brother's hiding place, having been threatened with deportation in his brother's stead.[78] Many also reported on corruption and enrichment during the deportations. Out of the ordinary was the case of Kurt Kahn, who was able to recover his stolen property from the apartment of Gestapo officer Georg Gassner in May 1945.[79]

In the denazification proceedings in particular, there were also positive, exonerating testimonies. Margot S. spoke out for the Gestapo officer Eduard Fahlbusch, stating that he had made it possible for her to escape and go underground. Fahlbusch had joined the Nazi Party and the SA in 1931, probably for economic reasons since he had been unemployed at the time. In 1937, he had been given a low-level position in the Gestapo. He said that he had believed the propaganda that promised him bread and work. In the judgment of March 16, 1948, Fahlbusch was assigned to category 3, lesser offenders, and had to pay a punitive fine of 500 reichsmarks.[80] In his denazification proceedings in 1948, some positive witness testimonies benefited him. Clearly in his favor were the letters of Margot S. and Leonhard Henninger, a pastor at the Inner Mission in Munich. Fahlbusch had also been entrusted with monitoring Henninger's sermons and had always forewarned him when visiting Henninger's worship services.[81] In addition to Margot S., another Jewish woman, Irmgard S., confirmed that Fahlbusch had helped her avoid deportation. She said that he had also slipped some food to her mother, who was deported to Theresienstadt.[82]

Fahlbusch evidently recognized his room for maneuver and knew how to take advantage of it in individual cases.

Some witnesses emphasized that Fahlbusch had shown a human side as the Gestapo officer accompanying the last deportation train to Theresienstadt, letting the deportees stop at a restaurant along the way.[83] This was, of course, problematic, since the experiences of people who were not deported until the very final months of the war yielded a distorted picture of what deportation had meant for the vast majority. These final deportations did in fact differ significantly from the deportations that had taken place from 1941 to 1943.

Rosa Baumgartner testified that the Gestapo officer Hans Ebenbeck had warned her prior to her deportation in February 1945 so that she could go into hiding. She also said that Ebenbeck had gotten rid of the file card for her son, who had been slated for internment in a work camp in October 1944.[84] Anna Westermayer explained that Ebenbeck had saved her life, crossing her name off a deportation list in June 1942.[85] Heinz Westermayer also spoke out for Ebenbeck, and not only because his mother had been deferred from a transport. In 1936, he had been denounced for making a political statement and then arrested. He said that Gestapo officer Ebenbeck had arranged for the charges to be dropped, resulting in Westermeyer's release.[86] Now and again, Ebenbeck, like Fahlbusch, had apparently taken advantage of his leeway for action. Both of them also received positive testimonies from church circles. Ebenbeck, however, also appeared as a tormenter. Erna Huber had been denounced for calling Hitler a "Kasperl," or clown. She attested to Ebenbeck's brutal and spiteful behavior.[87] Due to the exonerating statements by a number of Jews, Ebenbeck ended up being classified as a follower in his denazification proceedings.[88]

Some statements about former tormenters seem disconcerting from today's perspective. As previously mentioned, Rolf Grabower attested that the feared Franz Mugler had "acted impeccably."[89] Strict discipline had prevailed under Grabower as leader of the Jewish work detail in the Lohhof rettery. Grabower, who did not identify with Judaism, had demanded maximum effort from the conscripted women and had even reported "misbehavior" to the Aryanization Office.[90] To that extent, it is not surprising that Mugler had been content with him and had treated him "decently." Siegfried B., too, claimed that Mugler had not behaved nearly as badly as had his boss, Hans Wegner.[91] Gestapo agent Johann Pfeuffer was described by Siegfried Neuland as an agreeable person: "In my capacity at the time as a legal advisor I had dealt repeatedly with Department IIb [in charge of religious and Jewish affairs] of the Munich secret state police [Gestapo] on a wide range of matters from 1940 to roughly 1944, including deportation issues. Then head of this department was the defendant Pfeuffer, who as far as I could observe, worked in a quite humane and human manner. He was in any case a man who was in no way spiteful or brutal toward Jews."[92]

Other witnesses also exonerated Pfeuffer, testifying that he had been less brutal than his colleagues Grahammer and Grimm. Attempts to exercise fairness, to differentiate, or to acknowledge aid that individuals had received became a balancing act in which Gestapo men who had not been quite so brutal mutated into "decent guys." Johann Pfeuffer's denazification proceedings were adjourned in 1950, and in 1953, the proceedings against him were terminated.[93] After the preliminary investigations by the public prosecutor, no main proceedings were introduced against Pfeuffer at the Munich Regional Court I.[94] Thus, his role as head of the Department for Religious and Jewish Affairs from 1941 to 1943 never led to criminal proceedings.[95]

Magdalena Schwarz, who survived in hiding, claimed that "in no other city are there as many Jews left as in Munich."[96] Statements such as this could unintentionally have an exonerating effect and serve as an indication that the apparatus of persecution in Munich had operated more humanely than elsewhere. What she specifically meant to express was the satisfaction that many Jews had successfully resisted the deportations in the final months of the war, either going underground or simply ignoring the deportation notice to report. Magdalena Schwarz also emphasized that she was convinced "that the Gestapo officers and also the defendant Hans Wegner knew the fate awaiting those designated for deportation."[97] This was only marginally a subject in the proceedings, as the defendants tenaciously denied having known about the fate of the Jews. The discourse was largely reduced to the charges of "personal enrichment," "deprivation of liberty," and "bodily injury." In any case, based on witness testimony, it was possible for Hans Grahammer, for instance, to be sentenced in the Cosmann case to eight months in prison for bodily injury.[98] Hans Wegner, the notorious director of the Aryanization Office, was initially sentenced as a major offender in his denazification proceedings in 1948 to ten years in a work camp; in 1949, a judgment for two years in prison was handed down for "bodily injury in office."[99] In July 1950, Wegner was again convicted, this time for coercion. Including the previous two-year sentence, Wegner received a total sentence of five years in prison, whereby one year of detention and the remand time were also taken into account.[100] The Munich Regional Court I acquitted him in 1954 of the charge of bodily injury.[101]

THE "LIAISON" AND THE SURVIVORS

For many surviving Jews, a postwar reckoning with Jewish collaborators such as the snatchers in Berlin was very significant.[102] Right after the war, Lothar

Orbach, who had survived in hiding in Berlin, looked for a snatcher he knew, beat him up, and handed him over to the Soviet military administration.[103] The arrest of Stella Kübler-Isaaksohn, the most notorious snatcher, made headlines.[104] In Berlin and Frankfurt, the Jewish communities established courts of honor. Community members who in any way or form had inflicted harm on other Jews during the Nazi regime were called before them.[105]

In Munich, the surviving Jews projected their rage on one person in particular: Theodor Koronczyk, the last head of the district branch of the Reich Association of Jews and liaison to the Gestapo. His two predecessors, Julius Hechinger and Karl Stahl, had been deported and murdered. Other functionaries, such as Curt Mezger and Hugo Railing, were also dead. Dr. Julius Spanier, who had returned from Theresienstadt, was apparently not subjected to any sort of hostilities for the role he had played in preparing the deportation lists. Rolf Grabower, director of the Lohhof camp and later director of the male work details in Theresienstadt, was not a registered member of the Jewish community, though some people definitely had bad feelings toward him. An older Jewish man who had briefly been conscripted to Lohhof for forced labor referred to him as Franz Mugler's "compliant tool."[106] Even when former Jewish forced laborers remembered him with rancor, nothing came of the complaints. Grabower eventually became the chief financial officer of the city of Nuremberg.[107] The situation was different regarding Theodor Koronczyk. According to State Commissioner Philipp Auerbach, he had been part of the "Jewish Gestapo," and Auerbach was not alone in his opinion that, "as a Jew, Koronczyk will have to pay more heavily" for what he had done to other Jews.[108]

After 1945, Koronczyk had to account for his actions before the denazification tribunal. Numerous Munich Jews accused him of collaboration and betrayal. Koronczyk, as well as the denazification proceedings against him, have been thoroughly analyzed by Beate Meyer.[109] Her description of Koronczyk as a timid, utterly overwhelmed functionary, who was at the mercy of the arbitrary despotism of the Gestapo, is certainly correct. Koronczyk embodied, according to Meyer, "a problematic personal balancing act, a walk on the wire between anticipatory obedience, silence toward his fellow Jews, involuntary support for the Gestapo operations, and voluntary participation in some that he could not have prevented."[110]

The denazification proceedings against Koronczyk show how some survivors projected their experienced persecution onto the Reich Association and its representatives.[111] For many, Koronczyk became the collaborator par excellence, a friend of Munich's Gestapo men, a persecutor. Edith S. declared under oath that Koronczyk had recognized her while walking on the street, stopped her, and denounced her to the Gestapo as a Jew living in hiding.[112] The liaison was also accused of other denunciations: of having betrayed Julius Hechinger, his predecessor, and the Schwalb and Kahn siblings, who had been hidden by the cemetery caretaker Karl Schörghofer (see chapter 5).[113] Koronczyk vehemently denied these and other denunciations, and he also rejected accusations that he had extorted Jews and enriched himself at their expense. Some of these accusations were grave, such as that by Katharina Baerlein, who claimed that Koronczyk had told her daughter that he would protect her from deportation if she became his girlfriend.[114] Others in turn tried to exonerate Koronczyk, confirming that he had helped them and saved many people from deportation in the winter of 1945, although he had served at the whim of the Gestapo.[115]

The testimonies of the witnesses show that strong emotions were connected with the name Koronczyk. While Richard Riemer testified that Koronczyk had shown "satanic pleasure" in making the lives of Jews miserable, Oskar Maron stated that he was "shocked" by the display of resentment toward Koronczyk, who had been in a "terrible quandary."[116] In the end, the contrasting statements show that great sensitivity is needed when interpreting conflicting witness testimonies.[117]

Due to the various accusations of extortion and denunciations, and due to his participation in compiling deportation lists, Koronczyk was sentenced in November 1947 to six years in a work camp and seizure of his assets. His classification in category 1, major offenders, was confirmed in the appeal proceedings, but his prison time was somewhat reduced. Thus, the Jewish liaison, who was at the mercy of the Gestapo, received at first instance a barely more lenient penalty than Hans Wegner, the director of the Aryanization Office.[118]

Not until the case was reopened, as prescribed by the Court of Cassation, did the Munich Denazification Tribunal ultimately declare in 1948 what obviously had to be, namely, that the denazification legislation did not apply to Koronczyk and that the proceedings were, therefore, closed. The basis for the court's decision included testimony by the doctor Magdalena Schwarz, who exonerated Koronczyk. Like Edith S., she had also been hidden in the Schwabing Hospital, but at a later point in time. Magdalena Schwarz claimed that she had heard that a hospital employee had denounced Edith S. and that, due to his character, Koronczyk would not have been able to do such a thing. Because of this testimony, and also because of inconsistencies between the testimony of a Gestapo man and Edith S.'s statement, the charge of denunciation was dropped.[119] The court complained about "the somewhat spiteful accusations by some people" against Koronczyk. It also expressly condemned the conduct of the Gestapo officers who obscured the facts of the case and who, in their efforts not to incriminate themselves, did not tell the truth. In this, the presiding judge was correct. Moreover, in the proceedings regarding the arrest of Koronczyk's predecessor, Julius Hechinger, the Gestapo officers claimed numerous times that Koronczyk had betrayed Hechinger (see chapter 6). The strategy of passing on as much responsibility as possible to the Jews reached a cynical culmination when Hans Wegner, head of the Aryanization Office, claimed that Hechinger had been scheduled for deportation only as a result of efforts by leading members of the Jewish community.[120]

Koronczyk, too, could have fallen out of grace at any time, as his predecessor had, and he had been well aware of the fate that would have then awaited him. Somebody of greater moral fiber, who was more courageous and resourceful, might have exercised his duties differently, but, of course, there was a reason why precisely someone like Koronczyk had been placed in that position. In a treacherous system in which the persecutors made some of their victims into accessories, the persecuted were also to be shown that "you are no better than we are."[121] This applied to the liaisons like Koronczyk as much as to the Jewish Councils in the ghettos, Jewish kapos and *Sonderkommandos* in the concentration camps, and the snatchers in Berlin. In a certain way, Koronczyk's denazification tribunal continued this strategy. His conviction, too, was meant to demonstrate that "you were no better than we were."

ELEVEN

COMPENSATION FOR SURVIVING U-BOATS, THEIR FAMILY MEMBERS, AND THEIR HELPERS

IN EARLY JUNE 1953, META L. received a notice of denial in response to her petition for compensation. She had lived in various hiding places in and around Munich from the fall of 1941 until the end of the war. She applied for compensation for deprivation of liberty and for damage to her health resulting from her life in hiding. She was denied compensation on both counts on the following grounds:

> The petitioner has asserted a claim for compensation for wrongful imprisonment for the period from November 1, 1941, to April 30, 1945. She claims that she lived illegally during that period and has presented sworn witness statements to that effect. Based on the valid legal stipulations, only those have a right to compensation for deprivation of liberty who were persecuted under the National Socialist regime for reasons of political convictions, race, religious belief, or worldview, and in the course of that persecution were in political imprisonment during this period. Political imprisonment in accordance with the compensation law and the stipulations enacted for that purpose did not apply for the petitioner because she avoided imprisonment through an illegal existence. For this reason, compensation for the reported deprivation of liberty cannot be granted. At the same time, the declared damages to body and health are rejected since they resulted from the illegal existence.[1]

Many persecuted people who had gone underground experienced similar frustration when applying for compensation. According to the relevant law of the American occupation zone, the Law for Compensation for National Socialist Injustice, former U-boats were not entitled to compensation, and related claims were refused on absurd grounds. Legal flaws, loopholes, and overly formalistic thinking by administrative bodies often resulted in people like Meta L., who had suffered persecution, receiving bizarre notices of denial.[2] Their dangerous illegal existence in hiding was not recognized de jure as equivalent to imprisonment, and the resulting health damages were not brought into a causal relationship with the persecution they had endured. Those who had survived in hiding were, therefore, initially in a clearly worse position than the survivors of the camps. According to the notices they received, no persecution worthy of recognition had taken place.

The surviving U-boats experienced this lack of recognition for their suffering from non-Jewish Germans, from Jewish survivors returning from the camps, and from representatives of the occupying forces. "The 'illegals' who had survived in Berlin," Atina Grossmann has written, "found themselves on the defensive, prodded into protesting that they too had suffered, albeit in different ways than those who had actually been in the camps."[3] For Jews in Berlin, "the sometimes manic exhilaration of survival was severely tempered, therefore, not only by the loss of... 'everything,' but also by the growing awareness of how inadequately Germans, and even Allied authorities, relief agencies, and other Jews recognized, much less understood, their ordeal."[4]

In the following, the struggle for financial compensation for the surviving U-boats, their family members, and their helpers will be examined. When focusing on compensation for those who had gone underground, it should be kept in mind that a large share of former U-boats were older people (forty to sixty years of age).[5] In this respect, this group did not differ substantially from other German Jews who survived the Holocaust. In 1946 in Berlin, more than half of all German Jews were fifty or older.[6] However, those who had survived in hiding often had to wait much longer than concentration camp survivors did for their requests for financial compensation to be granted.

FINANCIAL COMPENSATION: THE LEGAL PROVISIONS

In late 1946, the State Commission for the Care of Jews in Bavaria was merged with the State Commission for the Care of Political Persecutees to form the State Commission for Racial, Religious, and Political Persecutees.[7] In the years directly following the war, the State Commission, under the leadership of Philipp Auerbach, was concerned with the immediate needs of persecutees (see chapter 9). Housing, employment, health, and convalescent care was organized by the commission.[8] Moreover, to reestablish their livelihoods, Jewish survivors enjoyed access to interest-free loans, which were to be paid back through the expected compensation payments at a later time.[9] The loans, also known as "Auerbach loans," were funded by denazification fines and were therefore regarded as "atonement payments."[10] Auerbach's efforts had some immediate impact: by 1947 his office had been able to arrange 1,400 jobs, support 750 new businesses, and enable 180 doctors to return to their profession.[11] One of the newly opened doctor's offices was run by a physician who had previously been in hiding.

An important legal basis for some of the assistance was the 1946 Law No. 35 for a Special Indemnification Fund, which was partially financed by atonement payments made by persecutors and seen as a stopgap measure until the passage of uniform nationwide compensation legislation.[12] "Damaged (*beschädigte*) persons"[13] and their families could apply on the basis of the pension law for up to eighteen months of benefits. The Special Fund law also provided awards to cover costs for health care, professional education and training, and setting up a business, as well as for allowances for victims of persecution facing acute financial distress.[14] It cannot be determined from the records whether surviving U-boats were disadvantaged relative to concentration camp survivors during this phase of immediate economic aid. The files instead tend to give the impression that small sums were awarded relatively quickly and unbureaucratically, which served to secure a minimum subsistence level. State Commissioner Auerbach, however, did not concern himself with balance sheets or bookkeeping, so the distribution of the funds was "not entirely transparent."[15]

At the time, the Stuttgart Council of States (Länderrat) of the American zone, under the supervision of the military government, was working out a uniform compensation law for the federal states within the American occupation zone. In August 1949, the Council of States ultimately enacted, with the approval of the military government, the Law for Compensation for National Socialist Injustice (Compensation Law), also known as the USEG (*Entschädigungsgesetz der US-Zone*). The USEG went into force in the federal states of Bavaria, Baden-Württemberg, Hessen, and Bremen.[16] Responsible for its implementation in Bavaria was the Bavarian State Compensation Office, which came out of the State Commission and was responsible to Bavaria's Ministry of Finance. It was under the direction of Philipp Auerbach until 1951. A uniform compensation law that was valid throughout West Germany was not passed until 1953.

According to the Compensation Law of 1949, anyone was entitled to compensation "who under the National Socialist regime was persecuted on grounds of race, religious belief, or worldview and consequently suffered damage to life, body, health, liberty, property, assets, or as regards economic advancement" (Sec. 1(1)).[17] Eligible to apply was anyone residing in the territory covered by the law on January 1, 1947, or who had died or emigrated prior to that date, but whose last residence had been within the applicable territory. The DP camps were expressly recognized as places of residence, thus incorporating Jewish DPs into the compensation law, although only those who had not emigrated by January 1, 1947.[18]

Pursuant to Sec. 15 of the Compensation Law (USEG), a prerequisite for compensation for deprivation of liberty was that the persecutee had to have been in political imprisonment. Political imprisonment was defined as "police or military detention, pretrial detention/remand, a penal sentence, concentration camp imprisonment, ghetto imprisonment, or assignment to a Wehrmacht penalty unit."[19] Survival underground in a state of illegality was not mentioned, which meant that Meta L. and others who had survived in hiding were not entitled to submit a claim. Helpers of people in hiding who had been imprisoned for their aid had a similar experience, as their motivation was not listed in Sec. 1(1) as a reason for their persecution. The compensation law was the result of Allied efforts to define and limit specifically Nazi forms of persecution. Before the war had even come to an end, a formula that would be used over the long term as a criterion for compensation claims had already emerged: eligible for compensation were people whose persecution had been on grounds of race, religious belief, or worldview.[20]

Moreover, compensation for damage to health as well as for death (referred to in legal jargon as "damage to life") could be refused to former U-boats since according to the USEG sections 13 and 14, damages to body, health, or life were only to be compensated when "in direct connection with persecution at the behest or with the approval of an office of the Reich, of a German federal state, . . . an office or official of the NSDAP [Nazi Party], or one of its divisions, . . . the persecutee was intentionally or recklessly killed or driven to death" or "received more than negligible damage to his body or his health."[21] With respect to the former U-boats, as the judge ruled in the case of Meta L., for example, damages to health were to be traced back to their having lived illegally, but it was deliberately ignored that the illegality was due to persecution.

The unfavorable treatment of those who had gone underground was not corrected until 1953, when the Federal Supplementary Law on Compensation for Victims of National Socialist Persecution (BErgG), the first unified compensation law for all of West Germany, was enacted.[22] It was already obvious when the law was promulgated in September 1953, however, that a revision would be necessary. This happened in 1956, when the Federal Compensation

Law for Victims of National Socialist Persecution (*Bundesentschädigungsgesetz*, BEG) was passed.[23]

In the text of the 1953 law, the following improvements were introduced for U-boats and their helpers. First, pursuant to Sec. 1(2), people who had taken a stand against the "morally unjustified—also due to the war—destruction of human life"[24] were made equivalent to political persecutees. The helpers were thus now treated as political persecutees. If they had been discovered and punished with imprisonment, helpers could assert claims for compensation. If, on the other hand, they had not been discovered, then they were not entitled to compensation.[25] Any health damages caused by deprivation and hardship were not compensated. Second, pursuant to Sec. 16(3), forced labor was recognized as deprivation of liberty to the extent that the persecutee had lived under "prisonlike conditions." (This was already the case in 1952 in Bavaria on the basis of a new implementation provision to the USEG.) According to Sec. 16(4), it was considered a deprivation of liberty "if within the territory of the German Reich as of December 31, 1937, the persecutee lived in illegality under prisonlike or inhumane conditions."[26] This entitled Jews who had gone underground to petition for compensation for damages to liberty, though only if they had hidden within Germany (in its 1937 borders). These restrictions were lifted in the BEG of 1956. Moreover, the revised 1956 version recognized the period during which persecutees had to wear a yellow star as a deprivation of liberty.[27] Third, damages to health, body, and life could now be interpreted as having derived from the deprivation of liberty. Persecutees received a pension only if their ability to work had been reduced by the persecution by at least 25 percent.[28]

The 1953 law formally removed the legal discrimination against the former U-boats. In practice, however, the survivors had to appeal notices of denial, submit new petitions, pay lawyers, and show a good amount of endurance in dealing with the compensation bureaucracy. On top of that came the fact that the absurdity of some of the reasons for denial made it difficult even to submit a new petition.

COMPENSATION IN PRACTICE

Meta L. did not accept the denial notice that she had received in response to her 1953 petition for compensation for wrongful imprisonment and instead lodged an appeal. In August 1954, a good year after her claim had been rejected, she was ultimately granted compensation, on the basis of the valid Federal Supplementary Law of 1953, for her illegal life during the period from May 1942 until the end of the war.[29] However, she had not gone underground in May 1942 but actually six months earlier. Between November 1941 and May 1942, the court argued, her living conditions had not yet become inhumane or prisonlike.[30] Only after again appealing the decision was she awarded compensation for wrongful imprisonment for the period from November 1941 to May 1942. In November 1955, a settlement was ultimately made with the Bavarian State Compensation Office.[31] Meta L.'s petition for recognition of damages to her health was also approved in 1955.[32] Until her death in 1978, she did not comment on what she had thought of her years of dealings with the authorities.

The compensation dossier of Edith S. includes several folders with extensive correspondence, a life story of petitions, medical certificates, transcripts, ordinances, and handwritten declarations, all of which ended in 1962. Up to only a few weeks before her death, Edith S. had written repeatedly to various offices, requesting minor amounts of money and a minimal increase to her pension and calling attention to incorrectly transferred payments. Edith S. had had tuberculosis during the war and had stayed in several hospitals under a false name until she was denounced in early 1945, arrested, and deported to Theresienstadt (see chapter 3). In 1948, she continued to possess medical certification confirming her complete occupational disability as a result of persecution, as her tuberculosis had improved only marginally. She was also severely visually impaired and lived alone in Erlangen.[33]

In August 1948, State Commissioner Auerbach granted her a monthly pension of 120 deutsche marks for three months. After an extension, the pension expired in June 1949, so Edith S. wrote to the Bavarian State Compensation Office on June 5:

> The owners demand back the borrowed, indispensable household goods, pillows, duvet, and chair, how should I replace them? . . . The linens, and clothing and underwear I acquired, just the smallest amounts urgently need to be supplemented. The mattress is miserable due to so much time bedridden that it needs to be replaced. How should I manage all this with less than DM 60 each month (after subtracting rent and health insurance)? You demand medical reports, witnesses for the persecutee ID, countless documents for the compensation, but no one gives me the money for it, or for the trips to the offices in Nuremberg and all the postage! (And also for the constant denazification inquiries referring to my Gestapo torturer, for all that postage I could buy milk or eggs!) . . . Help me at least by approving the most needed means to prevent further impoverishment![34]

Edith S. was granted compensation for damage to liberty in 1954, but only for the time she had spent in the Berg am Laim camp and in Theresienstadt. The time she had spent in hiding in hospitals in Berlin and Munich under a false name was not recognized because, according to the authorities, that period of living illegally had not been under prisonlike or inhumane conditions. Due to her severe tuberculosis, damage to health was recognized, but with only a 40 percent reduced earning capacity as of 1952.[35] A few years before she died, she requested anew that her pension be increased because her state of health had again deteriorated. Her correspondence with the authorities ended shortly before her death.

The cases of Edith S. and Meta L. show that from 1953 on, compensation benefits for forced labor and life in illegality were awarded de jure, but often only certain periods were acknowledged de facto as life under prisonlike or inhumane conditions. These restrictions gave the authorities discretionary leeway that was generally interpreted to the disadvantage of the petitioner. This can be confirmed also for numerous other Munich Jews who had gone underground.[36]

In late 1941, Margot S. had gone into hiding in Munich and was then robbed and denounced by a casual acquaintance who had given her housing for a period of time. She was able to flee and ended up living as a U-boat in Berlin. After returning to Munich in 1945, she challenged the injustice committed against her as best she could. She reported the denouncer and demanded the return of her possessions. Margot S. wanted to stay in Munich and resume working as an English teacher, although her mother, who had been living in Britain since Margot S.'s parents had emigrated in 1939, was in very poor health. Her father had died in the meantime. She did not apply for compensation until 1953, after returning from an extended stay in London. She limited her claim to compensation for damages to property and assets that had been taken from her deceased father, as well as to damages to her own economic advancement. The expected amount of compensation would suffice for her to get a fresh start in Munich. In a personal letter to the State Compensation Office, she explained, "I would like to expressly emphasize that I do not wish to make a monetary claim for forced labor, imprisonment, etc., as I am profoundly loath to receiving money for that which all the others working with me paid for with their lives."[37] In her long, eloquent letter she illustrated in detail her personal situation and her inner strife, referring to health and financial difficulties and requesting an unbureaucratic advance on the expected compensation benefits. Her petition was denied with the justification that she had already received advance payments of 2,000 reichsmarks in 1946 and then (after the currency reform) another 1,000 deutsche marks in 1952.[38] Her petition for compensation for assets taken from her deceased father was also rejected, as the listed claims (including the "Jewish Capital Levy" and "Reich Flight Tax," plus some special levies) did not fall under the Federal Compensation Law.

A year later, in 1954, Margot S. was so impoverished that she had to live for a short time in a shelter for homeless women.[39] She had no means whatsoever to have her acute health problems treated. Her lawyer made it clear to the authorities that she needed starter cash to cover rent for an apartment and medical treatment, which would enable her to resume working as an English teacher. Due to her financial hardship, she was subsequently awarded an advance of 1,000 deutsche marks toward the expected compensation for damage to her economic advancement.[40] Margot S.'s living conditions had not decisively improved by 1965, when her lawyer wrote: "She is living with an acquaintance where she sleeps on the couch in the living room and is dependent on financial support from friends."[41] Despite the adverse circumstances, she had resumed her work as an English teacher.

Margot S. gradually started exhibiting psychosomatic symptoms as a result of her suffering. She complained that even a simple knock at her door brought on heart palpitations, that she could not manage her daily life, and that she was confusing the past with the present. "Sometimes I have a complete blackout, and cannot remember anything; connected with my continually losing things, it happens much more frequently and frightens me because my whole existence is based on my head being fully intact," she wrote in 1968. "Luckily I have never had such a situation while teaching, but who knows how long everything will continue to go well? In any case it is often particularly difficult to appear as focused and cheerful as this profession demands."[42] In this situation, Margot S. ultimately applied for compensation for damages to health. However, because a doctor argued that her persecution-induced health problems should have subsided three years after the cessation of the persecution, it took until 1970 for her to win recognition of a 25 percent reduction in her ability to work as the result of persecution, which entitled her to a pension.[43] The extent of health problems among survivors was long underestimated, especially regarding the U-boats. And contrary to general expectations that even the persecutees shared, in many cases the health problems did not improve over time, but actually worsened.

Because Margot S. was certain that she would be compensated for the financial plundering of her father quickly and unbureaucratically, she had not concerned herself with legal clauses, guidelines, and petition deadlines, and she did not file for compensation for wrongful imprisonment. The Bavarian State Compensation Office's actions were legally correct, and it cannot be held responsible for the fact that Margot S. became severely impoverished in the postwar period. Nevertheless, it begs the question whether situations such

Margot S., ID photo, ca. 1938. Munich City Archive, DE-1992-KKD-3570-pb.

as hers could have been avoided through better advice and focused support. Could the responsible officials have informed Margot S. that it would have been advisable to petition for compensation on grounds of deprivation of liberty and damages to health? An agency that had to review thousands of petitions was likely too overwhelmed to engage in such personal support. In any case, many conflicts arose. For Margot S., it was perfectly clear that she was entitled to compensation, and she complained about the unfair, churlish treatment she received. The officials, on the other hand, rejected her accusation, asserting that the petitioner had not submitted required documents and verifications. They also insinuated—incorrectly—that she had never performed forced labor at the Lohhof rettery.[44] Consequently, two worlds collided: that of the overwhelmed, often inadequately qualified civil servants at the Bavarian State Compensation Office[45] and that of an isolated, somewhat helpless older woman who, in view of health and family problems, urgently needed individual advice to comprehend the legal framework and its consequences for her.

Denny F. had been separated from his mother, Else F., when he was four years old and then hidden in various places throughout Germany, including for an extended period of time in the Greater Munich area. After the war, Else F. and her son emigrated to Uruguay, where her husband had been living, as he had been able to leave Germany in 1939 (see chapter 7). In Uruguay, the family lived under difficult circumstances. As a junk dealer, Ludwig F. managed, barely, to keep the family above water.[46] From Uruguay, Ludwig F. applied for compensation for the still underage Denny on the grounds of deprivation of liberty. The petition was denied in February 1956 with the justification that Denny F. had not had to live under inhumane conditions. According to the bureaucrat responsible for the case:

> A life is not inhumane until, on top of the emotional overstress due to the imposed circumstances, there is also a physical and mental crisis situation that so significantly exceeds what is generally bearable and reasonable to expect, such that the minimum prerequisites for existence in the realm of our social order can no longer be guaranteed. Primitive and impoverished living conditions are not inhumane, not even for those who used to live better. As the mother of the petitioner stated, he was not together with her but rather with various families during this time, and was also housed in a Protestant orphanage in Munich as a foundling. As during this time the petitioner was living in neither prisonlike nor inhumane conditions, the asserted claim on the basis of damage to liberty is denied because the stipulations of Sec. 16(4) of the BEG have not been met.[47]

This decision was confirmed in 1959.[48]

Children in the underground were particularly disadvantaged because of the existing legal situation and the restrictive interpretation of the laws, as demonstrated by this case. What was to be understood as "inhumane conditions" in hiding lay within the discretion of the responsible agencies. In the case of Denny F., the Compensation Office assessed this requirement as not having been satisfied. But this misses the main point of what it means for young children to be separated from their parents for three years and to be passed from one stranger to the next. This was not taken into account at all. In addition, petitions for compensation for health damages in the case of children, such as Denny F., who on the surface appeared physically healthy, were usually not filed.

All in all, it can be said that from the very beginning of the legal compensation provisions in 1949 up until the implementation of the Federal Supplementary Law (BErgG) in 1953, the compensation legislation put those who survived in hiding in a worse legal position than those who survived in camps. Even after 1953, the period in which the persecutees had lived illegally was recognized either not entirely or not at all. If one considers that many of the surviving U-boats were already advanced in age, it becomes clear that, precisely in their senior years, members of this group could expect only minor compensation benefits.

It was often particularly difficult for family members of U-boats to receive compensation. Martha W. had hidden her husband, Sigmund W., and had shared both the meager rations and the emotional strain with him. She had been harassed by the Gestapo as of 1937 and detained for a short time. From November 1941 on, she had lived in constant fear of being discovered and had become utterly exhausted due to insufficient nourishment (see chapter 3). In 1961, Martha W. received notification that her health problems, which included a heart condition, were "constitutional" and not traceable to her persecution.[49] Martha W. also had to fight in court for her widow's pension as provided by the BEG. First she received notification that the death of her husband could not be attributed to persecution, but rather had been the result of his constitution and age.[50] In 1945, Sigmund W. had suffered a stroke as the result of the stress of living in hiding, which for obvious reasons could not be treated adequately. He had died in 1952 after a second stroke.

Luise K.'s experiences were similar to those of Martha W. After her family's effort to emigrate had failed at the last minute in 1939, Luise K., who was a Gentile, hid with her son on a farm, while her Jewish husband, Gustav, performed forced labor. Her husband joined them on the secluded farm in the final weeks of the war. Gustav K. was seriously ill when the war ended, and he died in 1953. When Luise K. filed a claim on the basis of her own health problems, she received a notice of denial, which was typical at the time. It said that her anxiety attacks could not have been caused by the persecution since it was her husband who had been persecuted and not her.[51]

The carpenter Stanislaus Hanisch had hidden his fellow Communist Party member Max Holy in 1933 (see chapter 3). After Holy was discovered, Hanisch had spent two years in the Dachau concentration camp. From 1941 on, Hanisch had arranged numerous hiding places for his neighbor Meta L. Although Hanisch received compensation for wrongful imprisonment for the time he spent in Dachau, it was not until 1973 that a pension was also granted for the health damage he suffered as the result of persecution.[52] Hanisch's support for Meta L. was irrelevant with regard to compensation law. It was immaterial whether the years of stress that this had caused continued to damage his health. He did not even mention this aid in his petition for compensation.

A final example clearly illustrates how compensation became the touchstone for how former persecutees were treated in postwar Germany. Max Bachmann had gone underground in 1943 and fled to his friend Franz Herda. After Herda's house had been seriously damaged in the Allied bombing, Bachmann moved from one hiding place to the next in Lower Bavaria (see chapter 4). Bachmann returned to Munich in 1945 and built up a livelihood again. He made a career as a diplomat, was active in the Jewish Community of Munich, and for a short time served as its head (see chapter 9). Bachmann, too, asserted claims for compensation; in addition to restitution of his house on Rosenstrasse, he also petitioned for compensation for deprivation of liberty and for the health damages he had suffered.

In June 1953, Bachmann received the following notice of denial of his petition for compensation on grounds of deprivation of liberty:

> According to the petitioner's own information he was put into ZAL Milbertshofen [Forced Labor Camp (*Zwangsarbeiterlager*) in Munich's Milbertshofen district] in May 1941 and was conscripted to work detail for the Brettscheider company in Munich from September 1941 until he went underground in June/July 1943. The period of his forced labor has been corroborated by a certificate from this company. There are no official documents or notarized sworn statements from witnesses about imprisonment in ZAL Milbertshofen. The time spent in this camp is not recognized as requiring compensation for wrongful imprisonment pursuant to Sec. 15(2) EG [Compensation Law], because according to the assessments made up to now of stays in this camp it did not involve a sustained deprivation of liberty as in other detention facilities. The petitioner was therefore issued an assessment notice only for the time he was imprisoned in the Dachau concentration camp from 10 November 1938 until 19 December 1938, in addition to the forced labor in connection with wearing a yellow star from 19 September 1941 until the end of June 1943. The asserted claims for imprisonment in ZAL Milbertshofen from May 1941 until 18 September 1941, as well as his time living illegally from July 1943 until the end of the war, must be denied. For the latter, compensation is presently not possible pursuant to the currently valid compensation law.[53]

Thus Bachmann received compensation for wrongful imprisonment for the periods from November 1938 to December 1938 (in Dachau concentration camp) and from September 1941 to December 1943 (forced labor). Forced labor (in connection with wearing the yellow star) was treated as equivalent to imprisonment pursuant to a new implementation provision of 1952, but this did not include time living illegally. Here the denial of the claim for the period that Bachmann spent in Milbertshofen is particularly absurd. In other cases processed around the same time (late 1952/early 1953), the camp in Munich's Berg am Laim district was expressly recognized as a forced labor camp, and the time spent there was regarded as "prisonlike" and compensated accordingly.[54]

In this regard it is not surprising that Max Bachmann reacted with anger, responding as follows:

> I would like to comment on the Notice of Partial Denial of June 17, 1953: . . . The fact that I was imprisoned in this Milbertshofen camp can be confirmed by your Mr. Vice President Heinz Meier. The desire to trivialize placement in this camp comes not without a certain humor. The daily visits by the SS hordes and the notorious fellows (such scoundrels cannot be referred to as "gentlemen"), [Franz] Muggler and [Hans] Wegener [*sic*], and the fact that from early in the morning until the evening heavy work was demanded—and this is the point—without any regard to physical fitness and health, made the time spent there alone a form of mental anguish. When, "according to the assessments made up to now," an agency evidently views a stay in Milbertshofen to be a summer retreat, then it is high time to rectify this incorrect judgment. Such decisions are not in conformity with the idea of compensation. In any case, I will never be content with this decision, although the material side of this claim is completely irrelevant.[55]

For Max Bachmann, who by then was over seventy, the battle against the injustices of the compensation legislation became a late-life task, which he pursued less in his own interest than out of a sense of fundamental responsibility to all those affected. To him, compensation meant the restoration of justice and decency. He and others, however, experienced it as "a mixture of ineptitude and unwillingness."[56] Bachmann used his position as the financial attaché at the German embassy in London to complain personally to the highest authorities about the practice of compensation.[57] He considered it a matter of fundamental values: justice, atonement, dignity, and respect. Bachmann had lived through the utter erosion of his bourgeois existence, which he arduously built back up after 1945. The indifference with which he was confronted regarding his legitimate claims underscored the lost social esteem and the lack of respect and empathy of postwar society for German and European Jewry. Max Bachmann died in 1966.

It might have been particularly bitter for Bachmann that Heinz Meier, vice president of the State Compensation Office, was someone who knew the Milbertshofen camp from his own experiences. But Meier was hopelessly overwhelmed in his position, as was fairly well known. Meier was neither a lawyer nor an administrative expert, and the only reason he received the position was that he had suffered persecution himself.[58] It was hoped that for that very reason Meier might show the necessary sensitivity for the office, which was not a bad idea per se. But it placed Meier and other former persecutees working in the area of compensation in a very difficult position, especially if they were newcomers to the field and lacked the necessary qualifications for the job. They were the ones who had to distribute the extremely limited financial means according to the legal provisions.

Officials at the Ministry of Finance were disillusioned, saying that "the constant complaints" about the Bavarian State Compensation Office could be traced back to the fact "that there were no senior officials in the management who were older, qualified, experienced, and with legal training, unlike in all the other federal states."[59] But it wasn't really all that simple. Massive complaints were also registered at the other compensation offices. This was due, on the one hand, to the experienced, legally trained officials who had been told by the Finance Ministry to save money, and, on the other hand, to the legislation, which created giant hurdles that the persecutees could often not overcome.

COMPENSATION FOR SURVIVING U-BOATS ACROSS GERMANY AND AUSTRIA

The situation in Bavaria was by no means unusual. In other parts of Germany as well, where different regulations were in effect until 1953, former U-boats were not treated any better. However, the problems were often of a different nature than in Bavaria. In the British zone, where Zonal Policy Instruction No. 20 regulated the initial compensation for the persecutees, benefits were directly coupled to the "camp imprisonment" criterion. There were, to be sure, informal instructions to stretch entitlement to compensation to all Jewish persecutees, regardless of whether they had been incarcerated in a concentration camp.[60] However, it was a different matter whether the local special assistance committees, which were responsible for assessing claims, always kept to the instructions. The first compensation regulations in the federal states within the British occupation zone took force in 1947, according to which persecutees or their family members could petition for compensation for health damage or for pensions for surviving dependents.[61] Here, too, damage to health or death was usually placed into the causal context of imprisonment, even though imprisonment was not necessarily a formal prerequisite. In 1949, a series of similar laws stipulating compensation for wrongful imprisonment followed in the federal states within the British zone. Having lived illegally was expressly recognized as worthy of compensation.[62] In practice, recognition of the persecution of U-boats varied from region to region. Marlene Klatt argued that the law in North Rhine–Westphalia was interpreted as narrowly as possible and that compensation for wrongful imprisonment was generally denied for time spent living in hiding.[63] In the Münster administrative district, living illegally was sometimes recognized.[64] Therefore, former U-boats in the British zone could formally petition for compensation for health damage as early as 1947 and for wrongful imprisonment as of 1949, but the denial rates differed by region. One can generally say that these laws were defined narrowly and, for the most part, interpreted restrictively. Also, because of the costs involved, the governments in the federal states were not interested in more generous regulations for the persecutees.[65]

After the Federal Supplementary Compensation Law was introduced in 1953, doubts were also expressed by the compensation agencies in North Rhine–Westphalia about whether petitioners had in fact lived under inhumane conditions during the time they spent underground. Marianne Ellenbogen received such a letter from the case officer responsible for her case in the Essen Compensation Office. She then wrote an enraged letter to her lawyer:

> I would have liked to hear what Herr Case Officer defines as "inhumane conditions in illegality"! Did you perhaps ask him that? Can he even put himself in the situation of being persecuted and pursued by the Gestapo and the criminal police, not having food ration cards or sufficient food and so being dependent on the good will of strangers, and existing trapped in limited quarters; not being able to leave the apartment during the day out of fear of being discovered and inevitably shot by the Gestapo; not being able to leave the apartment at night even to seek shelter from the continuing air raids in a basement.[66]

She was particularly incensed by the bureaucrat's question of whether she had still worn a yellow star after having gone underground. What a bureaucrat considered an essential question from the perspective of compensation law revealed to Marianne Ellenbogen nothing but boundless idiocy, as nobody would have seriously contemplated wearing a yellow star, and thereby making oneself recognizable as a Jew, while living underground.[67]

In Berlin, where a majority of U-boats had lived, there were different compensation regulations than in the American and British occupation zones during the immediate postwar period. In Berlin, the main committee for the Victims of Fascism (OdF) issued identity cards to persecutees. The main committee was part of the Department of Social Services of the Berlin Magistrate and could also approve immediate relief payments when necessary. Pension payments were possible in cases of occupational disability or for persons aged sixty-five and older.[68] In April 1946, the main committee published an informational brochure "Who is a Victim of Fascism?" which explained the guidelines for issuance of an OdF identification card. The main committee distinguished between "fighters against fascism" and "victims of fascism," the latter including the "victims of the Nuremberg Laws."[69] "Victims of the Nuremberg Laws" included Jewish concentration camp prisoners, people who had lived illegally, and *Mischlinge* who had been imprisoned in the labor camps of the Organization Todt (OT). People in so-called privileged mixed marriages were only recognized if they had been "subjected to particularly severe persecution."[70] This made those who survived underground and Jewish concentration camp survivors equivalent, but both groups were nevertheless formally "second-class persecutees" as compared with political fighters.

When Berlin was divided in 1948, support for the victims was also divided. In West Berlin, the new order led to the compensation law of January 1951, which essentially followed the pattern of the USEG of 1949.[71] However, it contained a substantial difference. According to Sec. 17(2c), life in illegality, to the extent that it took place under prisonlike or inhumane conditions, was made equivalent to prison.[72] The commentary to the law expressly noted: "We can only hope that in consideration of the serious emotional distress and the constant fear with which these people had to live, sometimes for years, that this term [i.e., life under inhumane conditions] not be interpreted too narrowly."[73] The extent to which this instruction was followed has yet to be examined. The commentary was written by the lawyer Ralf Loewenberg, who himself had survived as a U-boat in Berlin and who ran the compensation department in the Jewish Community of Berlin starting in 1949.[74] There was a relatively high number of people who survived in hiding in Berlin, a fact that was taken into consideration by the law.

In Austria, compensation for living illegally under inhumane conditions was first granted in 1961.[75] The recognition practice proved to be restrictive. Government agencies sought reasons to deny petitions. As part of this strategy, for example, information was requested from the neighbors of petitioners in an effort to determine whether their living conditions had been inhumane during their time in hiding.[76] The restriction stipulating life "under inhumane conditions" was struck in 1970, but another problem was that a minimum time period of six months of living in hiding was introduced as a condition for entitlement to compensation.[77] Thus, those who had to go underground in the final months of the war were excluded.

The history of compensation for U-boats and their families shows that compensation was frequently only available under difficult conditions. Limited knowledge of the compensation process often led persecutees to request the benefits to which they were entitled either too late or not at all. As compared with former camp prisoners, the U-boats were legally disadvantaged at first, but even later, when living in illegality was made equivalent to imprisonment, many petitions for compensation for the former were rejected if the agencies did not think the living conditions in illegality had been inhumane. Only in Berlin was it explicitly stated in the commentary accompanying the law that the decision was to be made in the interest of the persecutees.

The practice of compensation did not contribute to restoring the social dignity that the persecution had damaged. In some places, it was claimed that compensation showed the Jews that legal security in Germany had been reestablished.[78] On the one hand, this is correct, and many persecutees demanded their rights and did not let up. On the other hand, their actual experiences are also evidence of their powerlessness and their confrontation with a feeling of "unwillingness," as Max Bachmann put it. It ultimately came down to how the victims were treated. Not only were their material needs and legitimate claims often denied, but also their expectations of decency and respect, something with which they were all too familiar from the period of persecution. For many, this was more painful than the material shortcomings of compensation.

TWELVE

U-BOATS AND THEIR HELPERS IN POSTWAR GERMAN SOCIETY

THE PAINTER FRANZ HERDA, TOGETHER with some close friends, had hidden his fiancée, Albertine Gimpel, from 1943 to 1945, saving her from deportation. After the war, they married and emigrated together to the United States. In New York, Franz Herda met the journalist Kurt Grossmann, who had fled to the United States via Prague in 1933. Starting in 1951, Grossmann published stories in the German-Jewish *Aufbau* newspaper about people who had helped Jews. He wanted to pay public tribute to these few courageous people, whom he called "unsung heroes."[1] Franz and Albertine Herda told Grossmann their story. Herda did not expect any sort of recognition from Germany for the solidarity he had shown to the victims of persecution. Quite the contrary, he cheerfully explained to Grossmann: "By the way, if Aryan members of my species insist on being offended by my stories of support, then let me call out to them today the succinct saying of Götz von Berlichingen."[2] The saying Herda diplomatically avoided quoting: "They can kiss my ass."

Herda did not harbor any illusions that postwar German society would celebrate him as a "hero." When he returned from New York to Upper Bavaria with his wife in 1962, he did not make an issue of his help to Albertine Gimpel and Max Bachmann. The other helpers in Munich acted similarly. In a society whose members viewed themselves collectively as victims of a criminal regime, in which individuals had ostensibly been powerless to resist, nobody wanted to hear anything that would rock the boat regarding this conception of history.

Most helpers did not want their stories about assisting hidden Jews to turn them into outsiders in mainstream postwar society. Many said nothing about what they had done, and they had good reason to act that way.[3] The family that had hidden Charlotte Knobloch was threatened when it became known that the child who had grown up with them on the farm in Franconia was not the out-of-wedlock daughter of Zenzi Hummel, the farmer's daughter, but was in fact a Jewish girl.[4] This was not an exceptional incident. Klara Begall, a helper in Berlin, received an anonymous death threat in 1947.[5] The reactions were, of course, not always so extreme, but the helpers proved unpleasant to postwar society. Honoring them would have meant that Germans would have had to critically examine their own inaction and confront their shame over what had happened.[6] The survivors also felt this way. A Frankfurt woman refused to reveal her hiding place and the names of her helpers for a long time after the war out of fear that this could cause them problems.[7]

Many surviving U-boats just wanted to return to their daily lives, as Mark Roseman has put it, "to prevent the past from taking control of the present."[8] Others had little inclination to remember the people who had helped them, as they had also been exploited, beaten, humiliated, or sexually abused by them. In 1945, Marie Jalowicz Simon of Berlin deliberately wanted to distance herself from the conduct and manners to which she had become accustomed in the social milieu in which she had been forced to immerse herself.[9] Many were also plagued by feelings of guilt in light of the dead members of their family. Like Dr. Sophie Mayer, many were the sole survivors of an entire family.

In Sachenbach at Lake Walchensee, a memorial plaque commemorates the fates of Elisabeth Schwink and her daughter, who were murdered there by SS units from Bad Tölz in the final days of the war. The two women were not killed because their Jewish background had become known, but because the SS presumed they had attempted to contact the advancing American troops. Elisabeth Schwink, who had been in a mixed marriage, had withdrawn with her daughter to the seclusion of Jachenau, a small village near Sachenbach, to avoid being deported (see chapter 7). The plaque for the two women (see below) reads: "In pious memory of Elisabeth Schwink and her daughter Ruth, who left their lives at this site as victims of the war on May 3, 1945. Forgive us our trespasses as we forgive those who trespass against us."[10] With that, Elisabeth and Ruth Schwink are enshrined in local memory as German war victims. Their fates were adapted to correspond to the version of history prevalent in the region and the broader society. It is telling that there is no mention of the German murderers, namely the local SS units. It was Elisabeth Schwink's (non-Jewish) husband who had the plaque installed.[11]

When Else Behrend-Rosenfeld published her diary of the Nazi period in 1945, she was the first U-boat to decide to make her experiences accessible to a wide audience. The diary, which was first published by a Swiss publisher under the title *Verfemt und Verfolgt. Erlebnisse einer Jüdin in Nazi-Deutschland, 1933–44*

Memorial plaque commemorating the fate of Elisabeth Schwink and her daughter Ruth near Sachenbach (Upper Bavaria). Private collection of the author.

(Ostracized and Persecuted: Experiences of a Jewish Woman in Nazi Germany, 1933–44), was subsequently published in Hamburg in 1949 as *Ich stand nicht allein: Erlebnisse einer Jüdin in Deutschland, 1933–44* (I Was Not Alone: Experiences of a Jewish Woman in Germany, 1933–44).[12] The new title was intended to appeal to Germans. Germany was no longer equated with Nazi Germany. Behrend-Rosenfeld told about the "other Germans," rejecting the thesis of German collective guilt.[13] Max Krakauer also wrote his memoirs to express his personal gratitude to his helpers.[14] The Berliner Ruth Andreas-Friedrich published her diary *Berlin Underground, 1938–1945* in early 1947—in New York, not in Berlin, where she had been a member of the Uncle Emil resistance group during the Nazi period and had sheltered a number of Jews. The German edition, *Der Schattenmann*, appeared shortly thereafter in Berlin.[15] The memoirs of Behrend-Rosenfeld, Andreas-Friedrich, and Krakauer were not reprinted in Germany until the 1960s or 1970s.[16] In the 1950s, very few people were interested in hearing stories of persecution and resistance in Nazi Germany.[17]

In 1957, Kurt Grossmann published a book containing the stories of the unsung heroes that he had been collecting since the end of the war. It contained twenty-eight accounts of German helpers as well as some short reports he had received by mail.[18] Among the stories in the volume were those of Franz Herda of Munich, referred to by Grossmann as "the Scarlet Pimpernel,"[19] the cemetery caretaker Karl Schörghofer, as well as Sophie Mayer and Karl Rieger.[20] Sophie Mayer reported on how she was rescued by Paul Mayer; and Karl Rieger told of how he and his wife hid Cäcilie Langenwalter in the final months of the war. The book also contained several anonymous letters because certain helpers did not want their names to appear in print.[21]

In the early 1960s, the helpers received greater media attention when—during the trial of Adolf Eichmann in Jerusalem and the Auschwitz trial in Frankfurt—attempts were made to publicize the stories of "positively connoted counter figures"[22] to show that there were also "other Germans."[23] As Kobi Kabalek has argued, in 1979 the lack of "positively connoted counter figures" was widely noted in the German response to the American TV mini-series *Holocaust*. The series, which portrayed the Holocaust on West German television as a family story, brought lasting change to the public discourse and the politics of the past in Germany,[24] but it also attracted criticism in the country for depicting too few "good Germans."[25]

HONORING THE HELPERS

Despite growing interest in the rescue stories in West Germany, a special distinction for the helpers was established only in Berlin, where most of the rescues had taken place. After Grossmann's stories of the unsung heroes were published in 1957 by a West Berlin publisher, the Jewish Community of Berlin wanted to offer an award to honor this group of people.[26] In collaboration with West Berlin's Senator for Interior Affairs Joachim Lipschitz (SPD), the tribute to the unsung heroes was introduced. Lipschitz himself had survived in the underground. In November 1958, nineteen people in West Berlin were honored as unsung heroes. Honorees who were considered poor also received financial benefits.[27] Two years later, on Lipschitz's initiative, a "law for honoring altruistic Berlin residents who offered help during the Nazi period" was passed.[28] In the German press and in emigrant newspapers, calls were published to locate people deserving of this honor. By late 1963, 1,525 applications for the honor had been submitted to the Berlin Senate. A total of 738 people received recognition pursuant to the 1960 Berlin law.[29] The selection criteria were very strict. Those to be honored had to have residency in Berlin and had to have helped "altruistically and to a substantial degree."[30] In the years that followed, Berlin's Jewish community and various organizations of victims of Nazi persecution advocated extending the Berlin law to other federal states in Germany, but not a single one declared its willingness to take that step.[31] Also at the federal level, a request in 1967 by the Working Group of Persecutees' Associations was rejected by Federal Chancellor Ludwig Erhard with a reference to the stance of the governments of the federal states.[32] The Federal Finance Ministry, in particular, feared that the honor "could be interpreted as acknowledgement of an entitlement to material compensation."[33]

At the time when the first unsung heroes were being honored in West Berlin, Yad Vashem, the World Holocaust Remembrance Center in Israel, designated the first Righteous Among the Nations. When Yad Vashem was founded in 1953, the honoring of people who had supported Jews was laid down as one of the purposes of the institution. To this end, Yad Vashem set up a committee of thirty-five members, which to the present day decides on who should be accepted into the circle of the Righteous Among the Nations.[34] In Jerusalem, as in Berlin, the main criterion remains the altruism of the helpers.[35]

Ludwig Wörl, a carpenter from Munich, was the first person to receive this distinction in 1963.[36] Wörl had been deported to Dachau as a political prisoner in 1934; from there, he was transferred in 1942 to Auschwitz, where he worked in the infirmary barracks and did all he could to save Jewish prisoners from death (see chapter 8). Only one year after Wörl's recognition, another Munich resident, Werner Krumme, was honored by Yad Vashem. Like Wörl, Krumme had been both a persecutee and a helper. In his former hometown of Breslau (today Wrocław in Poland), Krumme and his Jewish wife Ruth attempted to help relatives of the latter, the sisters Anita and Renate Lasker, to escape to France. When the plans failed, all four were deported to Auschwitz, where Ruth Krumme was murdered. As a non-Jewish German prisoner, Werner Krumme received a privileged position through which he was able to protect Jewish prisoners, arrange better working conditions for them, and falsify transport lists.[37] After the war, he lived in Munich.

When the city of Munich heard that Yad Vashem was honoring several Munich residents, the city government considered giving them an award from the city as well. City Director Andreas Kohl discussed the idea with Werner Krumme, who was not only one of the Righteous from Munich, but also chairman of the Working Group of Bavarian Persecutees' Organizations. Kohl also suggested that Krumme ask the Bavarian minister president whether the Berlin provision for "honoring citizens who altruistically helped people suffering persecution during the Nazi period" might be adopted in Bavaria.[38] Although the Bavarian state government had already rejected a similar proposal from the persecutee organizations in 1960, the city leadership now turned to the state government in 1965, requesting a new review. In January 1966, Mayor Hans-Jochen Vogel received a rejection from Ministry Director Fritz Freudling of the Bavarian Ministry of Finance. The ministry had, apparently, not bothered to discuss the proposal a second time. In his rejection letter, Freudling simply copied the lines that the Bavarian state government had sent to the Working Group of Representatives of People Persecuted on Political, Racial, and Religious Grounds six years earlier in 1960. The following could be read therein:

> Your suggestion presented to Herr Minister President, to honor in Bavaria, similar to Berlin, those citizens who during the National Socialist period altruistically helped persecuted people, was reviewed in detail. There is no doubt that people who followed their conscience and heart during the rule of the National Socialist demon, and did not refuse to help the afflicted and the persecuted, deserve our appreciation and respect. However, I do not believe that this behavior, which belongs to a hidden human area of lofty values and noble impulses, should be acknowledged in a material form. Any other form of external tribute also seems not to be entirely appropriate; at most it could be considered with respect to suitable cases to suggest that particularly deserving persons be awarded the Federal Cross of Merit. Moreover, I share the opinion of the Interior Ministry for the state of Lower Saxony that public recognition of the merits of this circle of people alone under certain circumstances would lead to their assuming a preferential position as opposed to active resistance fighters, who as a rule faced greater dangers and

> deprivation, and who, if they were lucky enough not to be discovered, could expect no compensation at all from any agencies, even if they are presently in dire straits. It must also . . . be expected that citizens in the Soviet occupation zone, for instance, who helped someone oppressed by the regime there and now had to flee to West Germany, would make reference to an analogous application of such a provision.[39]

The reference to the Soviet occupation zone was absurd, as it was precisely the city at the front line of the Cold War, Berlin, that had no problem with the tributes. The argument that resistance fighters (to the extent that they had not been discovered and punished) could not reckon with either a medal or financial benefits was used here as a kind of defense shield. The government had no interest in recognizing certain groups of resistance fighters—certainly not Communists or someone like Georg Elser—or people who helped Jews.[40] One factor emphasized by the federal finance minister also certainly played a key role here, namely the fear that such recognition could lead to further demands for compensation.

The mayor of Munich regretted the decision. The city of Munich, meanwhile, resolved to honor people from Munich who were recognized by Yad Vashem with the "München leuchtet" (Munich shines) medal. This medal has been awarded since 1961 to people who have "rendered great service to Munich."[41] On the list of people to be honored in 1966 were Werner Krumme and Ludwig Wörl, in addition to Josef Meyer, who had worked for the agricultural administration in a small town in Galicia, where he hid numerous Jews and supplied them with food, and Karl Schörghofer, the cemetery caretaker in Munich (who was already deceased by that time).[42] Meyer was honored by Yad Vashem in 1965, and Schörghofer's recognition process was underway. In addition, Lina Angermeier, the administrator of the old Jewish cemetery on Thalkirchnerstrasse, and a Frau Schulz of the city of Munich were to be honored.[43] The latter had cared for Jewish graves during the Nazi period. Lina Angermeier had kept the cemetery from neglect and supplied Munich Jews with food, which was cause for the Gestapo to repeatedly threaten her.[44]

Josef Meyer expressed his thanks for the congratulatory letter from the city of Munich on the occasion of his award from Yad Vashem with these words: "I am all the more pleased about the participation of my hometown Munich since my actions at the time have so far met with little official interest, although they were the primary prerequisite for German foreign policy per se."[45] It was precisely Germans like himself, Meyer likely wanted to stress, who contributed to the fact that West Germany, despite the Holocaust and the war of extermination, had been accepted into the international community after 1945.

Even if Meyer might have overestimated his significance, his distinction by Yad Vashem in 1965, when Israel and West Germany were establishing diplomatic relations, certainly set a positive accent.

In 1966, Ludwig Wörl also received the Leo Baeck Prize awarded by the Central Council of Jews in Germany.[46] Although the press reported extensively on Wörl's accolades, and Mayor Vogel praised him as "courageous, just, merciful, humane,"[47] his Communist background was completely ignored.[48] Wörl was, in fact, under observation by the Bavarian State Office for Protection of the Constitution.[49] The secretary general of the Central Council, Hendrik G. van Dam, emphasized in his laudatory speech for Wörl that it was an urgent task of West Germany to officially recognize people who, despite the risks, had taken action to rescue Jews.[50] But the appeal to the federal government or the state governments to follow Berlin's example by introducing an initiative to honor these helpers was to no avail. In the end, the federal government could only agree that deserving helpers be honored with the Federal Cross of Merit and, if needed, be granted financial support.[51]

In 1967, Josef Cammerer and the Schörghofer family were honored as Righteous Among the Nations, followed in 1969 by Maria Letnar and Paul and Rosa Mayer and, in 1972, by Gisela Scherer and Josy Scherer-Hoffmann. In all of these cases, it was the Jews or their families who were saved who pushed for these tributes. Even if the former U-boats did not seek public attention for themselves, they wanted their helpers to receive this honor. In 1966, Sophie Mayer wrote to the Israeli ambassador in Germany to submit a report on how she was saved. She had read in the newspaper about several helpers being honored by Yad Vashem.[52] In her letter, she explicitly emphasized that her three helpers had all acted out of charity and a staunch opposition to Nazism and that none of them had pursued any financial or other personal interests whatsoever. It was also telling that Sophie Mayer wanted to see her helpers honored but was very cautious that her name not become publicly known.[53] Rosa Vetter wrote to Yad Vashem and Munich Mayor Hans-Jochen Vogel multiple times within a period of several years and collected further witness testimonies and evidence to document the willingness of her friends, the sisters Gisela Scherer and Josy Hofmann-Scherer, to help. In connection with the nomination of her helpers to be honored by Yad Vashem, she even spoke of "compensation" for her friends.[54]

The West German press reported on Germans being honored as Righteous by Yad Vashem, and in Munich, the local press was present at the "München leuchtet" (Munich shines) award ceremony. Whereas the *Bild Zeitung* tabloid limited the news about Gisela Scherer and Josy Scherer-Hoffmann to a tiny article without a photograph, the *Süddeutsche Zeitung, Abendzeitung, tz,* and *Münchener Jüdische Nachrichten* (Munich Jewish News) devoted more space to the story, including a large photograph of each of the sisters receiving the certificate.[55] The *Münchener Jüdische Nachrichten* described how the women had hidden their friend Rosa Vetter in their apartment even though a devoted Nazi had been present in the building. The photos show two elderly, seemingly frail women smiling at the readers.

All in all, among surviving U-boats from Munich, only a small number recommended their helpers for distinctions, even though in Munich a majority of the helpers had acted out of largely altruistic motives. The reasons for this were probably varied. Either contacts had broken off, the tribute was rejected by the helpers, the survivors were ill or deceased, or they were not aware of the tributes. All these reasons might explain why certain helpers did not receive official recognition. At the same time, conflicting feelings of the survivors toward the helpers certainly also played a role. Assisting them in denazification was one thing, but having them receive an award was another. The relationship between helpers and those they helped was often difficult, and, generally, very few survivors wanted to write about it in detail. Many memories had been repressed.[56] The "altruistic support" criterion was not always applicable or meaningful. Complex relationships could not always be clearly described as either self-serving or altruistic. Somebody might have been altruistic in helping some Jews but could very well have pursued selfish aims when dealing with others. The problems involved in documenting altruistic support still exist today and have become even more challenging due to the passage of time.

INVITING THE SURVIVORS TO VISIT THE "CITY OF HELPERS"

On January 19, 1960, the Munich city council was asked by the parliamentary delegations of several parties, including CSU, SPD, and FDP, to approve a catalog of measures aiming to fight racism and xenophobia. The multipartisan motion contained three steps:

1. The Department of Schools shall be commissioned to expand the international teacher and student exchange to include Israel and to ensure that instruction on contemporary history in the public schools intensifies treatment of the absurdity of antisemitism.
2. The Department of Arts and Culture shall be commissioned to develop a cultural exchange program with Israel.

3. Former Munich residents, or their descendants, who had to leave Munich because of their Jewish faith or their race shall be invited by the state capital to be guests of the city.[57]

This motion was triggered less by specific events in Munich than by a series of antisemitic attacks in West Germany between 1958 and 1960.[58] The motion was passed "in rare consensus"[59] and led in 1961 to the establishment of a visitors' program for former Munich residents, who could visit their former hometown at the city's expense. This was intended as a way to inform the emigrants about recent developments in the city. Ten visitors were to be invited each year to spend two weeks in Munich. The city would cover the costs of accommodations in a Munich hotel as well as a program including concerts, museum visits, and city tours, but the travel costs were to be paid by the participants themselves. To publicize the program, the Munich city council placed advertisements in New York's *Aufbau* newspaper as well as other Jewish newspapers in the United States, Britain, Israel, and Switzerland. The former Munich residents were requested to "send a sign of life" and contact their former hometown.[60]

This tentative beginning developed over the following years into a successful visitors' program. The Bavarian state capital was the first German city to initiate such a program, thereby assuming a pioneering role in West Germany. Little by little, other cities took up the idea after receiving requests from former citizens who had heard of the program in Munich.[61] The offer was addressed to all Jewish emigrants who had once lived in the city. It was therefore available also to Jews who had survived in hiding and then later emigrated.[62]

Between 1961 and mid-1965, a total of 425 former Munich residents expressed interest in visiting their erstwhile hometown, and 103 did in fact make the trip. With that, substantially more people took advantage of the offer than the city had expected. It is not known, however, how many former Munich residents knew about the program but deliberately decided against a visit.[63] It is especially interesting to see how the city of Munich presented itself within the framework of this visitors' program. The Press and Information Office of the city of Munich published a brochure in 1965 titled "Heimweh nach München" ("Homesick for Munich"), which was sent to potential visitors. The brochure also served as an information source to accompany the visitors' program. The text was authored by Gerd Thumser, then "City Hall reporter" for the *Münchner Abendzeitung* newspaper.[64] "Homesick for Munich"—the title as well as the content of the brochure appealed to the "emigrants' longing for Munich," to their conflicting emotions, and to their "painful loss of homeland."[65] The longing for the "imaginary" Munich[66] and the bonds with one's homeland were the focus of the text, underscored with pictures of the landmarks of the city and a poem by Shalom Ben-Chorin, an emigrant from Munich who settled in Israel.[67] Munich, that was "the rustling chestnut trees," "the light of the nearby south," and the "slender towers," as Ben-Chorin wrote.[68] In the name of the Jewish Community of Munich, Dr. Hans Lamm contributed a welcome address in which he emphasized the rebuilding and the revival of the Jewish community and its institutions.[69] Lamm had emigrated in 1938 but returned to Germany after the war, where he first worked as an interpreter for the Nuremberg trials. After completing his doctorate, he was responsible for cultural affairs for the Central Council of Jews in Germany. In 1961, he moved back to Munich, and in 1970, he became president of the Jewish Community of the city.[70]

The brochure separated the longing for Munich from the chapter on the "years of shame," that is, on Munich during the Nazi period. As if it were possible to clearly separate the two themes, this chapter briefly outlined the persecution of the Jews. The description of those events, rendered exclusively in the passive voice, seems strange from the perspective of later decades. The author, Gerd Thumser, concluded with this assessment: "Especially in Munich there are countless signs of the help the 'Aryan friends' gave their desperate fellow citizens. They helped them send charitable 'love' packages; they went shopping for them. The love was stronger than the terror. And it makes a fresh start possible after the years of shame."[71] The reference to non-Jewish helpers is placed in a key position at the end of the chapter on the persecution. At the same time, the examples given do not justify the dramatic conclusion that in Munich "the love was stronger than the terror."[72] The statement that "especially in Munich there are countless signs" of help implies that residents of the city did more for the Jews than Germans in other places. This perception can also be discerned in the contemporary self-presentations of other cities.[73] "Munich—City of Many Helpers": in 1965, the city's Press and Information Office reached out to those who had been expelled and persecuted with that sugarcoated image. This self-presentation was perhaps influenced by the fact that a number of Munich residents were honored at about the same time by Yad Vashem as Righteous Among the Nations (although the names of the Righteous were not mentioned in the Munich brochure). Hamburg is an example of a city that adopted a different tone when reestablishing contact with former residents. One-time Hamburg residents were sent a memorial book of the city's Jewish victims.[74] Not until 2003 did Munich publish the first volume of its own memorial book containing the biographies of Munich's Jews.[75]

The self-celebratory tenor was also reflected in a comprehensive report by the daily newspaper *Süddeutsche Zeitung* about the invitation program. The article was written by the journalist Karin Friedrich, who together with her mother, Ruth Andreas-Friedrich, had supported numerous Jews in hiding as members of the Uncle Emil resistance group in Berlin.[76] She quoted a number of visitors extensively, who told about the help they had received from non-Jews in Munich. They spoke of former neighbors who had helped "up to the last minute" (although it was not clear whether they were referring to emigration or deportation) and of a strict Catholic family "that insisted—and asserted itself against some Nazis in the building—that my seriously ill and unconscious mother be carried down to the public air raid shelter."[77] "And there was the house caretaker—a party member, but a decent man—who with his own hands carried Mama on the stretcher into the cellar and, when a dumb leader in the Nazi women's organization objected, retorted that Mama is Jewish but she has lived in our building for decades and is a dear, good woman."[78] The article closed with a quotation from a letter from Ernst W., who lived in Italy: "When I now think of the horrors back then, what predominates is the belief in the good that I experienced."[79] It was, of course, understandable that former Munich residents who returned to the city as visitors would want to revive their positive memories. It is also understandable that Karin Friedrich wanted to focus on the positive experiences that individual survivors had had with non-Jewish Germans. All in all, however, what resulted was a report on a city of helpful neighbors during the Nazi period.

It could also be read in Munich's official brochure that the city "wanted to make a very, very serious effort, above and beyond material compensation, also to make reparations at a human level."[80] There was much talk in 1960s Munich about humane, moral reparations, and corresponding aspirations certainly also existed. Mayor Vogel traveled to Israel for two weeks in 1964, and the aforementioned visitors' program, the first of its kind, should be acknowledged as a serious gesture. Moreover, the subject was indeed very important to many Munich city council members and employees of the municipal government.[81] Remigrant Hans Lamm confirmed this point in his welcome address in the brochure: Munich is "genuinely committed . . . to show . . . that a new spirit" has found its way into the city.[82] At the time, there was international criticism of the sluggish judicial response to Nazi crimes, the inadequacy of denazification, and the continuation of Nazis in important offices and agencies. West German compensation legislation, to put it diplomatically, did not have the best reputation. For this reason, Munich wanted to send a signal that the city took German-Jewish reconciliation seriously. With reference to reconciliation, the city assumed a very active role, but the record of the municipal administration in the persecution of the Jews during the Nazi period, including the economic plundering of the Jewish population, the conscription of Jewish forced laborers, and the carrying out of deportations, was not mentioned at all.

In his welcome message for the "Homesick for Munich" brochure, Mayor Vogel wrote: "But building the bridge to all those who were expelled from their old hometown of Munich by hate and agitation needs time and trust. If it was possible to bring the 1972 Olympic Games to Munich, this is an expression of the world's trust in the city's new spirit that is inspired by the firm commitment to overcome the past."[83] Munich was not only the designated host of the 1972 Olympic Games; it was also an up-and-coming business location. And, as Lina Nikou has shown, Mayor "Vogel aimed to improve the city's reputation abroad, to generate positive publicity for the city (in order to promote local tourism), and . . . to gain moral recognition for his efforts to deal with the Nazi past."[84]

Mayor Vogel was strongly supported by Hans Lamm, whose full-page article in the Jewish newspaper *Münchener Jüdische Nachrichten* in 1966 concluded that "we [the Jewish community] believe that no other German city has dealt so comprehensively, so systematically, so resolutely, and especially so genuinely, to remove the guilt and the shadow of the past."[85] Lamm also praised the "free spirit" that, "in this cosmopolitan city with a heart," is now looking ahead to the Olympic Games.[86] He had suggested the article and discussed it beforehand with Mayor Vogel, and the city's Press and Information Office made materials available to Lamm to help prepare the article.[87] Lamm thought "an essay about the ways in which the state capital supported the victims of Nazi persecution could probably contribute to reducing misconceptions and bias against our city that exist throughout the world." For this reason, the article was also to be translated into English and sent "to all the Jewish newspapers in the world" even "before the Olympic Committee's decision on Munich's application."[88] Lamm's attitude corresponded to what Anthony Kauders has referred to as "an exchange of gifts between the representatives of the Jewish Community and the West German elites."[89] The Jewish communities helped West Germany achieve international standing, and in return they expected respect from the West German political class.[90] This was true at both the national and local levels.

In the fall of 1957, Lamm had founded the Ner Tamid (Eternal Light) publishing company in Munich so that Germany would again have a publisher of Jewish literature.[91] In 1958, one of the first books he published was *Von Juden in München*, his book about the Jews of Munich.[92] It was important to him "in the twenty-fifth year after Hitler seized power and the twentieth year after the Munich synagogue was destroyed, to offer an image of what once was."[93] Lamm had collected an impressive number of articles that were intended to foster an appreciation of "the peculiar and perhaps unique atmosphere of Jewish life in Munich in the nineteenth and twentieth centuries."[94] The city of Munich covered the printing costs.[95]

Only a few articles in the volume dealt with the persecution and annihilation of Munich's Jewish community,[96] but interestingly enough, the volume did contain several stories taken from Kurt Grossmann's collection about people in Munich who had survived in hiding.[97] With its focus on the rescue of Jews in Munich, the book had set a thematic accent that was echoed in the official self-presentation of the city of Munich a few years later. This impression was corrected somewhat in the 1982 edition with the addition of an article by Baruch Ophir and Falk Wiesemann on the destruction of the Jewish community in the Nazi years.[98] Despite the sincerity of such efforts, the city's self-presentation diverged considerably from its actual endeavors to process the past. There was, for example, no memorial in Munich for the murdered Jews or for the destruction of the Jewish community, but only a busy location on the edge of the old city center that was (and still is) named "Square of the Victims of National Socialism."[99] A small, temporary memorial stone dedicated to all victims of Nazism was erected there in 1965. It was supposed to be replaced by a memorial at the planned cultural center (*Volksbildungshaus*). However, that structure, projected for the grounds of the former Wittelsbacher Palace, never came to be, so the plans for a memorial were also put on hold.[100]

A stone monument was first dedicated to memorializing the fate of the Jewish community in 1969. It marks the former location of the main synagogue in Munich, which was demolished in June 1938. It also commemorates—in meager words—the November pogrom. When the memorial stone was unveiled, Mayor Vogel held a speech in which he recalled the fate of the Jewish community, whose members had been "hunted, persecuted, ostracized, robbed, incarcerated, and finally killed."[101] Vogel's sincere, frank words thus stood in odd contrast to the small number of sites of remembrance in his city. The deportation of Munich's Jews was not memorialized in the cityscape until the 1980s, and then it was only on the outskirts of the city. A monument by the artist Alois Lippl was erected at the site of the former Milbertshofen camp in 1982, followed by another one in 1987 at the Sisters of Mercy convent in Berg am Laim.[102] With these, the public commemoration of the murdered Jews from Munich remained at a minimum until the early 1990s.

The end of the Cold War and the concomitant increase in scholarly focus on the Holocaust led to a broader public perception of Nazism and Nazi crimes. Since then, much has taken place in Munich regarding the scholarly

Monument commemorating the destruction of Munich's main synagogue in 1938, at the former location of the synagogue in the center of Munich. Private collection of the author.

examination of the city's history, the Jewish community during the Nazi period, and the local culture of remembrance and commemoration. With the erection in 2006 of a new main synagogue, a Jewish cultural and community center, and a Jewish Museum at Jakobsplatz, very near the city's center, Jewish life in Munich became visible again. Munich's Documentation Center for the History of National Socialism opened its doors in 2015, presenting the stories of some Munich U-boats and their helpers to a wider public. In 2013 and 2014, additional helpers from Munich and Upper Bavaria were recognized by Yad Vashem as Righteous Among the Nations. They included Franz Herda, Vera Manthey, Eduard Winkler, Sophie Gasteiger, Alois and Maria Rauch,

Friedrich Reck-Malleczewen and his wife Irmgard, and Stefan and Therese Steinbacher.[103] Karl Schörghofer was honored in December 2014 with a commemorative plaque at the Jewish cemetery. However, as this book appears in 2022, there is still no public memorial for the murdered Jews of Munich.[104]

In Berlin, a Memorial to the Murdered Jews of Europe was completed in 2005. Three years later, the German capital saw the opening of the Silent Heroes Memorial Center, where Jews who lived in hiding during the Nazi period, as well as their helpers, are remembered.[105] Survivors who had not previously wanted to speak or write about their experiences now began to publish their memoirs.[106] Margot Friedlander, who went into hiding in Berlin and survived Theresienstadt, not only wrote about her experiences, but moved from New York back to Berlin in 2010 to tell her story.[107] There was also growing interest in hearing the life stories of Hanni Lévy, Inge Deutschkron, and other surviving Berlin U-boats.[108] A number of these Berlin stories have also meanwhile been filmed. Most recently, in 2017, the film *The Invisibles* opened in movie theaters. It was based on the experiences of four Berlin Jews: Cioma Schönhaus, Hanni Lévy, Eugen Herman-Friede, and Ruth Arndt.[109] Because the commemoration of German-Jewish U-boats has largely focused on Berlin, it is not representative of a complex historical reality that was shaped significantly by regional factors.

CONCLUSION

FLIGHT AND LIFE IN THE underground were essential elements of the history of the deportation of German Jews. Thousands of people from a largely impoverished, aging Jewish population risked flight, thereby defying the intentions of the Nazis and hoping to avoid the fate of deportation and murder. Most of the escape attempts took place in Berlin, where roughly 40 percent of all Jews still remaining in Germany were living when the deportations began in 1941, but there were also many Jews in other German cities who fled or attempted to do so. The escapes took place under greatly varied local conditions. In Berlin, more than fifteen thousand Jewish forced laborers were excluded from deportation until early 1943, whereas the deportation of Frankfurt Jews had already been largely completed by late September 1942. In Munich as well, there were only a few hundred Jews still living in the city in 1943. Most of the escapes in Berlin took place during the Factory Operation in February–March 1943, whereas in Munich, the multiple waves of escape followed a different chronology. Although the percentage of escape attempts in Munich was higher in 1941–42 than in 1943, a major wave did not come until February/March 1945, shortly before the war ended, when Jewish spouses in mixed marriages were deported.

Regional differences led to differing experiences of flight and hiding, which were shaped by a multitude of factors and circumstances. In Berlin, relatively more Germans encountered the hardships of U-boats than elsewhere. Individuals sometimes spontaneously offered to help, and groups of helpers were able to form. Other Berliners saw the opportunity to capitalize on this situation, and often both motives—altruism and greed—came together. Thus, a widespread market emerged in Berlin for food ration cards, lodgings, forged documents, and the services of human smugglers. Sufficient demand and time existed for the necessary structures to develop. Many Jews followed the example of friends or relatives who had gone into hiding earlier when deciding to become U-boats themselves. The anonymity of the large metropolis offered favorable conditions to "submerge." That is why there was such a massive wave of flight in February 1943. The apparatus of persecution reacted by intensifying search efforts. Jewish snatchers were put to work tracking down U-boats, and Gestapo inspections and raids were increased. Consequently, the number of failed attempts to flee was also relatively high.

In Munich, the situation was different in a number of respects. Jews there decided to evade deportation relatively early on, frequently together with non-Jewish helpers. Existing contacts and particular life situations often facilitated the process of going into hiding. In contrast to the situation in Berlin, most helpers had largely altruistic motives, even though this cannot always be ascertained with absolute certainty. Because the actual number of escapes was rather low, no "infrastructure" for U-boats developed in Munich, and there was also no domino effect as there was in Berlin. There were no significant escape attempts among the last handful of Jews scheduled to be deported in March 1943. They had been ghettoized in a camp at the outskirts of the city and were therefore easier to control. Moreover, most of their fellow Jews had already been deported, and for those who had no direct helpers in their circle of friends, there were no known places to hide and no good prospect of success. For this reason, there was no major wave of Jews going underground in Munich until the Nazis initiated the deportation of Jewish spouses in mixed marriages in February 1945.

In Berlin, it was possible to pay for lodgings, food ration cards, and forged identification documents. Money played no decisive role in Munich, where going underground successfully was based more on having motivated helpers, inside information, and specific individual circumstances that could be exploited. For example, it was possible to take advantage of having just recovered from tuberculosis, as illustrated by the case of one woman who was able to withdraw into a pulmonary sanatorium and thereby temporarily evade deportation (see chapter 3). Something that all U-boats had in common, regardless of where they were, was a dual strategy in which suicide was always considered a last resort in response to the ever-present danger they faced. Some Jews in hiding carried lethal doses of sleeping pills in case arrest and deportation became inescapable.

In Munich, U-boats were most likely female and middle aged. Across Germany, the percentage of female U-boats was 60 percent, while in Munich about two-thirds were women.[1] Although it is difficult to compare the figures for Munich to those for Berlin because the most recent and most detailed statistics for Berlin comprise only those U-boats who survived the war, the percentage of female U-boats in Munich was somewhat higher than in Berlin, and they were slightly older than those in Berlin.[2] Except for a small number of children, the majority of Munich's U-boats were in their forties and fifties. In fact, about half of the Munich U-boats had been born before 1900. This age structure corresponds to the findings for Vienna, where most U-boats were also in their forties and fifties.[3] Munich U-boats were predominantly assimilated Jews. Most of them had non-Jewish spouses, partners, close friends, or a non-Jewish parent. Many of them were Protestants or Catholics who had converted from Judaism but were still Jews according to Nazi racial laws. These so-called non-Aryan Christians who were persecuted as Jews formed a distinct group among the persecutees. With respect to Munich, it can be shown that it was mostly Christians with a Jewish background who could take advantage of Christian rescue networks.

Despite directives from the Reich Security Main Office (RSHA) that were valid throughout the German Reich, there were sometimes considerable regional differences in the persecution of *Mischlinge* and persons in mixed marriages. In Frankfurt, some Jewish spouses in mixed marriages were arrested and deported as early as 1943. Entire families of mixed marriages were arrested in many cities in the Rhineland in the fall of 1944, with the Jewish spouses and children then sent to work camps. When some cities, such as Vienna, planned to deport the Jewish spouses in mixed marriages in February 1945, the deportations never took place because the war was nearing an end, while in other cities, such as Munich, transports still left for Theresienstadt. In general, the categories of *Mischling* and mixed marriage provided very tenuous protection up to February 1945. It is not surprising that research findings for Munich and other cities show that many people did not wait for a deportation notice but went into hiding preemptively, especially if a favorable opportunity presented itself. With respect to Munich, it is striking that a number of children who were deemed first-degree *Mischlinge* (so-called half Jews) were hidden by their parents even though they had been excluded from the deportations. Sometimes Jewish spouses in mixed marriages sought refuge, along with their children, in the rural seclusion of villages and farms in Upper Bavaria.

The air war over Germany profoundly influenced regional and local conditions for escape, as well as the behavior of those who fled. As we have seen, heavy air raids on Frankfurt and Hamburg in 1943 and 1944 facilitated mass escapes. Especially in Berlin, however, an unknown number of U-boats fell victim to the many bombing raids. Many did not dare use the public air raid shelters. In Munich as well, some U-boats endured the air raids outside of the shelters. Some were also bombed out of their lodgings, and some escapes became impossible when hiding places were destroyed. The extent to which options to flee were opened up or thwarted due to the air war in the especially heavily bombed Ruhr region has not yet been systematically examined.

Not only such wartime factors and regional differences determined the diversity of experiences among the U-boats. The experiences of people going underground to, from, and within Munich show how varied the circumstances could be even at a local level. Whereas the physician Sophie Mayer remained hidden in one single hiding place and was cared for, for years, by only a few helpers, other U-boats traveled hundreds or even thousands of miles during their time in hiding. In fact, cases such as that of Sophie Mayer were the exception. The famous example of Anne Frank has contributed to the emblematic image of enduring for years in a tiny hiding place becoming associated with Jews in hiding.[4] As a rule, however, U-boats had to change hiding places frequently. Consequently, many of them were very mobile. Some moved to the countryside, in part because of the air raids over the cities. Some went to areas outside Munich or to Lower Bavaria, and others fled over long distances, for example, from Munich to Berlin or in the other direction from Berlin to Upper Bavaria. Some U-boats used Munich as a way station, staying there only temporarily. And some Jews from Munich fled to safety abroad in neutral Switzerland or went into hiding in German-occupied countries.

Unlike the situation in Berlin, there were few U-boats in Upper Bavaria who were able to "resurface" at least temporarily with a new identity. Those who assumed a false identity had generally come to Munich or Upper Bavaria from elsewhere. Forged papers were extremely hard to procure in Munich. There was a small group of helpers around Walter Classen, a Swiss publisher, who were able to do this. Classen and his acquaintances, who managed to bring a number of people to safety, formed the only organized group of helpers in Munich that is currently known. In Berlin, on the other hand, there were a number of organized helper groups. Large, closely knit networks, of course, meant greater dangers if a member was arrested.

A minority of Germans helped the U-boats, and a minority denounced them or collaborated with the Nazis. The vast majority of people in Munich, and of Germans in general, had nothing at all to do with U-boats. Nevertheless, more Germans had some form of contact with those in hiding than has been recognized to date. In addition to denouncers, there were also profiteers, who enriched themselves in a variety of ways from the plight of the U-boats.

Potential denouncers at times monetized their silence. Hiding places were paid for in advance and then sometimes could not be used. Supposed helpers denounced their "guests" and kept their possessions. This form of Aryanization, which has not been researched sufficiently, must be viewed within the context of the social history of looting and deportation. This process was shaped not only by various state institutions but also by the actions of numerous ordinary Germans who reacted in one way or another to everyday conditions under Nazism. There were people who knew about the U-boats and protected them with their silence. These included neighbors, coworkers, and non-Jewish family members, as well as indirect helpers—people who occasionally passed along money or food ration cards, friends who passed along news and messages or scouted out potential quarters, and relatives who donated money.

There were numerous different kinds of people among the helpers in Munich: pastors, Communists, factory owners, housewives, artists, prostitutes, and nuns, to name a few. Not all of them were German citizens. Despite the diversity of these groups, it is apparent that U-boats and their helpers came largely from the middle class and often knew each other from before the war. Some helpers were Jewish or had one Jewish parent, that is, a substantial number of silent heroes were not "Aryans" but rather were victims of persecution themselves. Non-Jewish spouses in mixed marriages also played an important role as helpers. These groups have long been denied any sort of acknowledgment because their support has been viewed as self-evident. In contrast to the situation in Berlin, the Munich U-boats seldom encountered helpers from social strata different from their own. For many U-boats in Berlin, going into hiding meant submerging into unfamiliar social environments, such as run-down slums or provincial petty-bourgeois milieus.

When we consider the number of people in and around Munich who had some relationship to Jews in hiding—as providers of shelter or food, as denouncers, or as plunderers—then the complexity of the group referred to collectively as "bystanders" becomes apparent. Some bystanders benefited in smaller or greater ways; some were betrayers, and some were helpers. In the broadest sense, they were (more or less active) witnesses to persecution, which is to say that they were a large and heterogeneous group of social actors.[5]

Frank Bajohr and Andrea Löw have suggested that the category of bystanders might be subdivided into several distinct subgroups including beneficiaries, opportunists, helpers, spectators, and supporters. But, as they point out, the usefulness of such an exercise would be limited: "These [more narrowly defined] categories would enable us to take a more nuanced approach in the analysis of social behavior. Yet a possible objection to their use is the static character of all these terms. Under the intense and ever-changing pressures of violence, war, and occupation that prevailed in the Nazi era, people's positions could change from moment to moment: they were seldom fixed."[6]

The boundaries between perpetrators, victims, and bystanders were not always clear. The notorious Berlin snatchers were both victims and perpetrators at the same time.[7] There were perpetrators who helped out in isolated situations, while there were helpers who abused, exploited, extorted and threatened the people under their protection. In Berlin, the gray zone was much wider than in other cities. A broad and nuanced spectrum of behaviors was determined by a multiplicity of factors. These included the specific dilemmas and plights with which numerous individuals were confronted. Additional factors were greed, corruption, naiveté, and a range of (often shifting) personal emotions such as fear, hatred, jealousy, spontaneous sympathy, and a desire for revenge.

About 20 percent of Jews who survived the Holocaust in Berlin saved themselves by going into hiding. Another 23 percent survived in concentration and death camps, while 57 percent were saved by having a mixed marriage.[8] Berlin, however, was not a precisely delineated space, and such statistics generally do not take the transregional and transnational dimension of flight and hiding into account. The figures nevertheless show that surviving U-boats, at least in some parts of Germany, constituted a distinct group of German survivors of the Holocaust, something that has not been sufficiently reflected in scholarly or popular understanding of the Holocaust.

Even if in Munich, and generally anywhere outside of Berlin, this group was small, the postwar experiences of these survivors are part of the social history of the Holocaust. The survivors had to struggle with health problems resulting from their particular experiences and, especially in Munich, showed little inclination to emigrate. This had less to do with their experiences with "other Germans" than with factors relating to age, occupation, and social integration. As we have seen, Hans Rosenthal, who attributed his decision to remain in Germany after the war to the experience he had had with "good Germans," was an exception (see chapter 9). A majority of Munich U-boats who survived came from the assimilated middle class. Most of them were not young, but already advanced in age. They wanted to return to an everyday life with which they were familiar and hoped to resume working as they had before the persecution began; and some were too old or infirm to even consider emigrating.

Surviving U-boats were disadvantaged from the very beginning with respect to financial compensation for the persecution they had endured. And even when this formal legal discrimination was lifted in 1953, the legal texts left judges and case officers enough maneuvering room to deny them compensation on the grounds of deprivation of liberty. Not until the late 1960s was there a rethinking and a delayed or retroactive acceptance of petitions for compensation. This was tragic for the surviving U-boats, many of whom were already advanced in age at the war's end in 1945. After the initial aid received during the immediate postwar years, they required additional assistance in old age, which they were rarely awarded in the early 1950s. Consequently, some Munich U-boats became impoverished in their old age, usually in connection with illness. Only in Berlin, where a large number of surviving U-boats were visible in politics and the public sphere, did the city administration take into account the specific situation of this group in the early phase of compensation. Financial compensation was merely one of several issues for many former U-boats. There was also an emotional dimension to the question of compensation: the reestablishment of esteem, dignity, and respect.

For a long time, neither helpers nor survivors were subjects taken up by a broad public in West Germany. As we have seen, only in Berlin was official recognition of the helpers politically possible and socially acceptable early on. In Munich, attention to the helpers emerged a good deal later and remained more limited. Not until 1963 did the Munich city council resolve to honor Munich helpers with the *München leuchtet* (Munich shines) medal. Nevertheless, the city administration under Mayor Hans-Jochen Vogel made an effort toward reconciliation by launching the visitors' program for Jews who had emigrated from Germany, an initiative that was later copied by other German cities. There was an additional dimension to the visitors' program and the honoring of the helpers: In presenting its Nazi past, Munich portrayed itself as a "city of helpers," where many people had shown solidarity with Jews. This was part of a broader rebranding effort in which Munich depicted itself as a "cosmopolitan city with a heart" that had left behind its past as capital of the Nazi movement and now stood instead for tolerance, open-mindedness, and reconciliation with the victims of Nazism.

Even if hardly anyone was interested in hearing stories of surviving U-boats and their helpers in postwar Germany in the 1950s, eventually family stories of the war years were passed down to the younger generations, creating a "cumulative heroization" of the generation of the grandparents,[9] in which stories of grandparents who had helped Jews played a major role. "Grandpa was not a Nazi [after all]," but rather had attempted, against all odds, to support Jewish friends, neighbors, or even strangers.[10] Family stories were told in which the "helpful grandparents" became key figures in the collective memory of the generation of the grandchildren.[11] Indifference, betrayal, and greed were mentioned in these narratives as rarely as they were mentioned in the public presentation of the local history of Munich and other cities. When *Schindler's List* opened in German movie theaters in 1994, many Germans identified with the hero, the "good German" character of Oskar Schindler.[12] Over the course of time, the number of "perceived helpers"[13] in the collective memory of Germans grew well beyond the actual number of Germans who had actually helped Jews in hiding in any way whatsoever. This was true not only for Munich.

NOTES

INTRODUCTION

1. Affidavit by Dr. Sophie Mayer, May 15, 1946, StAM, SpkA, K 3643, Mayer, Paul.

2. Silent Heroes Memorial Center, *Resistance to the Persecution of the Jews*, 1. These numbers are estimates. The number of ten thousand to fifteen thousand Jews in hiding, which was provided in the German edition of this book (based on Schoppmann, "Rettung von Juden," 114), has been corrected downward by the Silent Heroes Memorial Center. Susanne Beer's estimate of seven thousand individuals is much lower; see Beer, *Banalität des Guten*, 114.

3. "Living illegally" became a common expression, also used by survivors, and I will occasionally use it as they did to refer to the time Jews defied instructions for deportation and lived in hiding. However, it should be kept in mind, as Richard Lutjens indicates, that adopting the term "illegals" or "illegality" may appear to continue the criminalization sought by the Nazis. On this, see Lutjens, "Vom Untertauchen," 53.

4. Up to five thousand may have survived. Croes and Kosmala, "Facing Deportation," 97.

5. Schoppmann, "Rettung von Juden," 115; and Benz, "Juden im Untergrund," 25.

6. Kosmala and Schoppmann, "Zwischenbilanz eines Forschungsprojektes," 21.

7. Statistics cited in Croes and Kosmala, "Facing Deportation," 115, 124. Most recently, Richard Lutjens has made the case for a figure of "approximately 6,500" Jews hiding in Berlin. Lutjens, "Jews in Hiding," 268.

8. This point has been made by Richard Lutjens, who argues that living in hiding is actually a "misnomer." Lutjens, *Submerged on the Surface*, 4–6. On the use of the term "U-boat," see ibid., XIII, 2.

9. Benz, "Juden im Untergrund," 23. On the snatchers (*Greifer*), see Tausendfreund, *Erzwungener Verrat*.

10. Bonavita, *Mit falschem Pass*, 175.

11. Meyer, "A conto Zukunft," 229.

12. In the course of my research, I was able to document seventy-seven cases of Jews who went into hiding in the Greater Munich area. On top of that, I gathered more or less vague information about further cases for which no names could be determined. There were also

at least fourteen people who went to Munich and/or environs after fleeing other areas. If we assume that about 30 percent of all cases never became known, we obtain the figure of 110–120 U-boats.

13. See also Schrafstetter, "Geographies of Living Underground." On geographical Holocaust research, see Knowles, Cole, and Giordano, eds., *Geographies of the Holocaust*; Cole, *Holocaust Landscapes*.

14. Friedländer, *Nazi Germany and the Jews*, vol. 1, 2.

15. Friedländer, ibid., defined his aim as follows: "The present study will attempt to convey an account in which Nazi policies are indeed the central element, but in which the surrounding world and the victims' attitudes, reactions, and fate are no less an integral part of this unfolding history."

16. On the term "bystander," see Hilberg, *Perpetrators, Victims, Bystanders*, xi–xii.

17. According to the Nuremberg Race Laws, people with three or four Jewish grandparents were classified as "full Jews." "Second-degree *Mischlinge*" had only one Jewish grandparent, and "first-degree *Mischlinge*" had two. Neither group of *Mischlinge* had to wear the yellow star, but they were subject to various persecution measures. Some first-degree *Mischlinge* were conscripted to do forced labor starting in the spring of 1944 and deported to work camps. Among the Jewish *Mischlinge* were also so-called *Geltungsjuden*, which means they were legally considered Jews. According to the Nuremberg Race Laws, certain *Mischlinge* were treated as Jews (a) if they were married to a Jew; (b) if they were a member of a Jewish religious congregation (for both, the cutoff date was September 15, 1935); (c) if they were born after July 31, 1936, to one Jewish and one non-Jewish parent who were not legally married, referred to by the Nazis as a result of "racial defilement" (*Rassenschande*); or (d) if they were children of a mixed marriage (according to its Nazi definition) that started (illegally, usually abroad) after September 15, 1935. The term *Geltungsjude* gained currency to refer to these people. The categorizations were contradictory, and the classifications were often arbitrary. On the situation of mixed marriages, *Mischlinge*, and *Geltungsjuden*, see Meyer, "Jüdische Mischlinge"; Strnad, *Privileg Mischehe?*; Kaplan, *Between Dignity and Despair*; Von der Heydt, "Wer fährt denn gerne mit dem Judenstern."

18. See chapter 2 and Von der Heydt, "Wer fährt denn gerne mit dem Judenstern."

19. Baumann and Heusler, *München arisiert*; Detjen, *"Zum Staatsfeind ernannt"*; Heusler und Weger, *"Kristallnacht"*; Löw, *Die Münchner*; Macek, *Ausgegrenzt*; Selig, *Leben unterm Rassenwahn*; Selig, *"Arisierung" in München*; Strnad, *Zwischenstation "Judensiedlung"*; Strnad, *Flachs für das Reich*.

20. The German Resistance Memorial Center, Silent Heroes database. For information on the database, see Kosmala and Schoppmann, "Überleben im Untergrund," 20–21. StadtAM, database of the Biographical Memorial Book of the Jews of Munich, 1933–1945. This database is partially online; see StadtAM, Biographical Memorial Book of the Jews of Munich, 1933–1945, last accessed February 24, 2022, https://gedenkbuch.muenchen.de/index.php?id=gedenkbuch&no_cache=1. Ilse Macek and Adi Trumpf (Gegen das Vergessen—für Demokratie e. V. [Against Oblivion—For Democracy] in Munich) and Andreas Heusler of the Munich City Archive had already compiled information about some individuals who had gone underground, which they generously made available to me.

21. On the significance of keeping a diary for Jews in hiding, see Garbarini, *Numbered Days*, 105–7, 158–59.

22. Behrend-Rosenfeld, *Ich stand nicht allein*. The diary was annotated and republished by Erich Kasberger and Marita Krauss, together with the notes of Behrend-Rosenfeld's

husband, who was able to emigrate to the UK in 1939, as Behrend-Rosenfeld and Rosenfeld, *Leben in zwei Welten*. It has just been published in English translation as *Living in Two Worlds*. The unpublished memoirs of Hugo Holzmann on his flight and survival are located in StadtAM, Judaica, Mem. 22, Hugo Holzmann, *Woman Courageous: Autobiography of Hugo W. Holzmann*. I would like to thank Hugo Holzmann, who made a digital version available to me for my research.

23. Particularly valuable in this context was a list of the members of the Jewish Community of Munich, presumably from 1943, titled "transport lists from the Gestapo–Munich area," 1.2.1.1./11194608–11194735, ITS Digital Archive, Arolsen Archives. They can also be found in the ITS Digital Archive of the USHMM. These are unfortunately incomplete; the letters A–F are missing. Recorded as "Transportlisten aus dem Gestapo Bereich München," this list was known by the UNRRA authorities in 1946 as "Gestapo-Liste" (Gestapo list); it was probably administered by Theodor Koronczyk, the director of the Bavarian branch of the Reich Association of Jews in Germany. See Strnad, "Die Deportationen aus München," 79. I would like to thank Maximilian Strnad for calling my attention to this list. The list of survivors published in 1945 by the New York newspaper *Aufbau* was also a key source; LBI, *Aufbau*, August 24, 1945, "Juden in München, Rückwanderer, Dritte Liste," last accessed March 19, 2022, https://archive.org/details/aufbau.

24. "Transport lists from the Gestapo–Munich area," 1.2.1.1./11194608–11194735, ITS Digital Archive, Arolsen Archives and USHMM.

25. On the problems associated with the sources, see also Lutjens, "Vom Untertauchen," 60–61; Seligmann, "An Illegal Way of Life," 330–32.

26. Statistics as of January 2021: Yad Vashem, "Names and Numbers of Righteous Among the Nations," last accessed February 25, 2022, https://www.yadvashem.org/righteous/statistics.html.

27. Yad Vashem, "The Righteous Among the Nations: how to apply," last accessed February 25, 2022, https://www.yadvashem.org/righteous/how-to-apply.html.

28. Benz, "Überleben im Untergrund," 670–71.

29. Benz, "Juden im Untergrund," 46.

30. On the postwar silence of survivors and helpers, and on the honoring of helpers, see Riffel, *Unbesungene Helden*.

31. See ibid., 248; Kabalek, "The Rescue of Jews," 253–54, last accessed February 24, 2022, https://libraetd.lib.virginia.edu/public_view/x633f123t.

32. Beer, *Banalität des Guten*, 321–22; Kabalek, ibid., 224–27.

33. See Welzer et al., *Opa war kein Nazi*, 67–69, 101–3, 149–50.

34. Figures cited from Kabalek, "The Rescue of Jews," 323, last accessed February 24, 2022, https://libraetd.lib.virginia.edu/public_view/x633f123t.

35. On this, see Benz, "Solidarität und Hilfe," 9–10; Kabalek, ibid., 321–26.

36. See, for example, *The Pianist* (2002), based on the memoirs of the Polish-Jewish pianist Władysław Szpilman about his survival in hiding in occupied Poland, and *In Darkness* (2011), based on the recollections of Krystyna Chiger of Lvov/Lviv (*In the Sewers of Lvov*, by Robert Marshall), who survived there with a group of Jews in the city's sewer system.
The German television film *Nicht alle waren Mörder* (*Not All Were Murderers*) (2006) by Jo Baier is based on the experiences of the actor Michael Degen, whose memoirs of the same name were published in 1999. In 2013, *Ein blinder Held. Die Liebe des Otto Weidt* (*A Blind Hero—The Love of Otto Weidt*) about the blind industrialist Otto Weidt of Berlin, who hid a number of Jews and traveled to Auschwitz to inquire into the situation of one of his employees whom he had grown very close to, aired on German television. The 2017

docudrama by Claus Räfle, *The Invisibles,* was shown in German movie theaters and on German TV. A subtitled version was released internationally. This film is about four young Jews who went into hiding in Berlin.

37. Hans Rosenthal's biography was published in 1980; Rosenthal, *Zwei Leben in Deutschland* (*Two Lives in Germany*). However, the story of Hans Rosenthal's survival in Nazi Berlin did not receive wide attention until after his death in 1987.

38. See, for example, Behar, "Versprich mir"; Lewyn, *On the Run*; Friedlander, *Try to Make Your Life*; Jalowicz-Simon, *Underground in Berlin*.

39. On the role of Inge Deutschkron (1922–2022), see Kosmala, "Gedenkstätte Stille Helden," 175–76. See also Deutschkron, *We Survived* and Deutschkron, *Outcast*.

40. See Gedenkstätte Stille Helden, "The Silent Heroes Memorial Center," last accessed February 24, 2022, https://www.gedenkstaette-stille-helden.de/en/memorial-center/. On the origins of the term "silent heroes," see Riffel, *Unbesungene Helden*, 11.

41. The seven volumes in the series *Solidarität und Hilfe für Juden während der NS-Zeit* appeared between 1996 and 2004. They include numerous country reports on occupied Europe, specific case studies, and a separate volume (vol. 5) on Germany; Kosmala and Schoppmann, *Überleben im Untergrund*.

42. Among them most importantly, Benz, *Überleben im Dritten Reich*; Schoppmann, "Die 'Fabrikaktion' in Berlin"; Croes and Kosmala, "Facing Deportation"; Tausendfreund, *Erzwungener Verrat*; Riffel, *Unbesungene Helden*.

43. The database is administered by the German Resistance Memorial Center, where the Silent Heroes Memorial Center is located. See Kosmala, "Gedenkstätte Stille Helden," 175, 210.

44. Roseman, *A Past in Hiding*; Roseman, *Lives Reclaimed*; Lutjens, *Submerged on the Surface*; Lutjens, "Jews in Hiding in Nazi Berlin"; Beer, *Banalität des Guten*; Düring, *Verdeckte soziale Netzwerke*.

45. Beer, *Banalität des Guten*; Düring, *Verdeckte soziale Netzwerke*; Roseman, *Lives Reclaimed*; Giesecke and Welzer, *Das Menschenmögliche*.

46. Ungar-Klein, *Schattenexistenz*; Grabowski, *Hunt for the Jews*; Paulsson, *Secret City*; Engelking, *Such a Beautiful Sunny Day*; Michmann, *Hiding, Sheltering, and Borrowing Identities*; Moore, *Survivors*.

47. Lustiger, *Rettungswiderstand*.

48. Wette, "Vorwort," 13.

49. See, for example, Löwenthal and Von zur Mühlen, *Widerstand*; Müller, *Widerstand*; Van Roon, *Widerstand*; Steinbach and Tuchel, *Widerstand* (1994). Peter Steinbach and Johannes Tuchel's edited volume *Widerstand gegen die nationalsozialistische Diktatur*, published in 2004, was the first comprehensive work on resistance in Nazi Germany to devote significant space to "rescue as resistance" in a section on Jewish resistance and aid to the victims of persecution: Borgstedt, "Hilfen"; Wette, "Rettungswiderstand."

50. Hilberg, *The Destruction of the European Jews*, 21–28. For Lustiger's fierce attack against Raul Hilberg, see *Der Spiegel*, "Täter, Opfer, Zuschauer," February 15, 1993, last accessed February 24, 2022, https://www.spiegel.de/politik/taeter-opfer-zuschauer-a-dd3ed3cd-0002-0001-0000-000013681126.

51. See, for example, Kwiet and Eschwege, *Selbstbehauptung und Widerstand*, 141–94. Most recently, Wolf Gruner has examined acts of nonconformity by the Jews of Berlin; see Gruner, "Open Protest." His analysis is based on a broad definition of the term "resistance"; ibid., 18. For literature on how to define resistance, see Kershaw, *Opinion*; and Peukert, *Volksgenossen*.

52. Wette, "Vorwort," 15.

53. Many book titles refer to *heroes* and *rescuers*: Wette, *Stille Helden*; Grossmann, *Unbesungene Helden*; Wette and Bald, eds., *Zivilcourage*; Wette and Haase, *Retter in Uniform*; Silver, *The Book of the Just*.

54. This has already been discussed in Schieb, "Nachwort," 220–21; and Enzenbach, "Problematik," 243–44.

55. See also ibid., 252–53. Various attempts have been made to work out a prototype of an altruistic personality on the basis of the rescuers. See Oliner and Oliner, *Personality*; Fogelman, "The Rescuers"; Fogelman, *Conscience & Courage*; Wolfson, "Zum Widerstand." However, there was no typical helper personality. Rescuers came from all walks of life and had diverse motivations. See Benz, "Juden im Untergrund," 43; Giesecke and Welzer, *Das Menschenmögliche*, 69.

56. On this, see also Giesecke and Welzer, *Das Menschenmögliche*, 56–57.

57. On *Judenfledderei* (Jew fleecing) and selfish motives, see Benz, "Juden," 23–24; Benz, "Gegenleistungen"; Neiss, "Herr Obersturmbannführer"; Schrafstetter, "Life in Illegality."

58. Grossmann, *Jews, Germans, and Allies*. On displaced persons, see Königseder and Wetzel, *Waiting for Hope*; Feinstein Myers, *Survivors*; Holian, *Between National Socialism*.

59. Riffel, *Unbesungene Helden*; Kabalek, "The Rescue of Jews," last accessed February 24, 2022, https://libraetd.lib.virginia.edu/public_view/x633f123t; Beer, *Banalität des Guten*.

60. Winstel, "Über die Bedeutung"; Winstel, *Verhandelte Gerechtigkeit*; Frei et al., *Praxis der Wiedergutmachung*.

61. On this, see, for example, Garbarini, *Numbered Days*, 4.

62. Strnad, *Zwischenstation "Judensiedlung,"* 178.

63. Rosenthal, *Zwei Leben*, 80.

1. UNDER NAZI RULE

1. These figures offer only approximate references. In comparison: according to Strnad, there were 10,737 Jews living in Munich in February 1933; according to Ophir and Wiesemann, on the other hand, there were only 9,005 in 1933. Strnad, *Zwischenstation "Judensiedlung,"* 178; and Ophir and Wiesemann, *Die jüdischen Gemeinden*, 33. According to Ophir and Wiesemann, there were 293 Jews in Lower Bavaria and 9,522 in Upper Bavaria; ibid., 24. The following cities had larger Jewish communities: Berlin (160,564), Frankfurt (26,158), Breslau (20,202), Hamburg (16,885), Cologne (14,816), and Leipzig (11,564). These figures were taken from Statistik des Deutschen Reiches, *Volkszählung*, 5, available through Freier, "Statistik und Deportation der jüdischen Bevölkerung aus dem Deutschen Reich," last accessed March 15, 2022, https://www.statistik-des-holocaust.de/VZ1933-5.jpg.

2. Angermair, "Eine selbstbewußte Minderheit (1892–1918)," 110.

3. Hanke, *Zur Geschichte der Juden in München*, 51–52; Specht, "Zerbrechlicher Erfolg," 139–40. For a detailed discussion, see Brenner, *Der lange Schatten*, 112–17, 159–80. On the antisemitic associations of Judaism, socialism, and Germany's defeat raised by national-conservative and *völkisch* groups, see Brenner, *Der lange Schatten*; Barth, *Dolchstoßlegenden und politische Desintegration*, 359–71.

4. Specht, "Zerbrechlicher Erfolg," 140. For a detailed discussion, see Brenner, *Der lange Schatten*. On this, see also Auerbach, "Hitlers politische Lehrjahre," 8–10; Heusler, *Das braune Haus*, 78–80.

5. There is a wide range of indications of this. See, for example, Selig, *Leben unterm Rassenwahn*, 316–18; Brenner, *Der lange Schatten*, 115; Specht, "Zerbrechlicher Erfolg," 145.

6. Ibid., 149. On the shift in mood, see also Hockerts, "Warum München," 389.

7. Specht, "Zerbrechlicher Erfolg," 152–53. For a detailed discussion, see Brenner, *Der lange Schatten.*

8. Brenner, *Der lange Schatten*, 292–93; Häntzschel, "Flucht vor Hitler," 187; Specht, "Zerbrechlicher Erfolg," 153; Ophir and Wiesemann, *Die jüdischen Gemeinden*, 34.

9. Ophir and Wiesemann, *Die jüdischen Gemeinden*, 36; Rösch, *Die Münchner NSDAP*, 410–20; Brenner, *Der lange Schatten*, 293–95.

10. Hanke, *Zur Geschichte der Juden in München*, 72.

11. Specht, "Zerbrechlicher Erfolg," 154.

12. Heusler, "Verfolgung und Vernichtung," 162. For a detailed presentation, see ibid., 163–84; Hanke, *Zur Geschichte der Juden in München*, 78–157.

13. Heusler, "Verfolgung und Vernichtung," 163.

14. Hanke, *Zur Geschichte der Juden in München*, 85.

15. Ibid. See also Heusler and Weger, *"Kristallnacht,"* 18–20.

16. Ophir and Wiesemann, *Die jüdischen Gemeinden*, 45.

17. Affidavit, March 1, 1950, BayHStA, LEA 33681 (BEG 3375). On the persecution of Jewish lawyers, see Weber, *Das Schicksal*, 95–146.

18. Wertheimer, "Magdalena Schwarz," 449; Ebert, *Zwischen Anerkennung und Ächtung*, 208. Pursuant to the Fourth Decree to the Reich Citizenship Law of July 25, 1938, Jewish physicians could no longer practice medicine in Germany. As "treaters of the sick," they were only allowed to treat Jewish patients. On the persecution of Jewish doctors in Munich and Bavaria, see Drecoll "Die Entjudung"; Damskis, *Zerrissene Biographien*, 30–44.

19. Hanke, *Zur Geschichte der Juden in München*, 153.

20. Schlösser and Rausch, "Schüler-Schicksale," 192–96, contains a summary of the legislation (1933–1939) and examples of experiences of students in Munich. For a discussion of the measures of social and cultural exclusion, see Kaplan, *Between Dignity and Despair*; Friedländer, *Nazi Germany and the Jews*, vol. 1.

21. Bergmann, "Vorgezeichnete Wege," 74. Bergmann's book on Jewish emigration from Munich is forthcoming as Bergmann, *Jüdische Emigration*. Slightly different figures appear in Ophir and Wiesemann, *Die jüdischen Gemeinden*, 50.

22. Kuller, *Finanzverwaltung und Judenverfolgung*, 18–23.

23. Ibid., 19.

24. Ibid., 21. See also Frank Bajohr, *"Aryanisation" in Hamburg*, 121–22. The Reich Flight Tax already existed in 1931 to stem the flight of capital, but after 1933, it was charged specifically to Jews wanting to emigrate.

25. Willstätter, as cited in Heusler and Weger, *"Kristallnacht,"* 177. Willstätter, *From My Life*, 425–26.

26. Kuller, *Bürokratie und Verbrechen*, 139.

27. Ibid., 140–44; Kuller, *Finanzverwaltung und Judenverfolgung*, 15.

28. BayHStA, LEA 202 (BEG 17 295). For a documentation of this situation, see in particular pp. 22–41.

29. *Der Stürmer*, June 24, 1933.

30. Bachmann to the Bavarian State Compensation Office (*Landesentschädigungsamt*), August 8, 1955, BayHStA, LEA 202 (BEG 17 295).

31. The fatal shooting of Ernst vom Rath, a German diplomat, by Herschel Grynszpan, a young Jew, in Paris on November 7 was used as a pretext to launch the wave of violence two

days later. See Steinweis, *Kristallnacht*; for Munich, see Heusler and Weger, *"Kristallnacht,"* 95–111.

32. On Hitler's responsibility for the pogrom and the role of the Stosstrupp Adolf Hitler, see Hermann, "Hitler und sein Stoßtrupp."

33. Ophir and Wiesemann, *Die jüdischen Gemeinden*, 52; Heusler and Weger, *"Kristallnacht,"* 65.

34. Heusler and Weger, *"Kristallnacht,"* 95–108. On the murder of Joachim Both, see ibid., 112–20.

35. Heusler, "Verfolgung und Vernichtung," 176. Two of the twenty-six men died shortly after returning from Dachau as a result of the incarceration, ibid.

36. Ibid.

37. Steinweis, *Kristallnacht*, 7.

38. Newspaper clipping from the *Abendzeitung* evening newspaper of November 7, 1963, on the twenty-fifth anniversary of the assassination of vom Rath and the Reich Pogrom Night in Munich: "9. November 1938: Die Nacht der Scherben und der Schergen," IfZ archive, ED 465/1.

39. Heusler and Weger, *"Kristallnacht,"* 51.

40. Behrend-Rosenfeld and Rosenfeld, *Leben in zwei Welten*, 93. In many communities in Upper Bavaria, the few Jews who lived there were ordered to leave their place of residence immediately; Kershaw, *Popular Opinion and Political Dissent*, 261.

41. Steinweis, *Kristallnacht*, 108; Heusler and Weger, *"Kristallnacht,"* 122.

42. Behrend-Rosenfeld and Rosenfeld, *Leben in zwei Welten*, 93.

43. Gerty Spies, "Erinnerungen an Dr. Julius Spanier," 3–4, IfZ archive, ZS 3142.

44. Ibid., 4.

45. Macek, "Judith Hirsch," 117.

46. Heusler and Weger, *"Kristallnacht,"* 150–51.

47. Hajak and Zarusky, "Verfolgung, Zerstörung, Neuanfang," 384–85.

48. Including Dr. Schweitzer, who found refuge in the deaconess house on Hess Strasse; Bühler, *Kirchenkampf*, 270. The family of Peter Sinclair had also been warned. His father escaped to Luxemburg, and his two uncles were hidden by non-Jewish friends; Heusler and Weger, *"Kristallnacht,"* 124. It is virtually impossible to determine the precise number of those who evaded arrest.

49. Behrend-Rosenfeld and Rosenfeld, *Leben in zwei Welten*, 96.

50. Barkow et al., *Novemberpogrom 1938*, 479–81. See also Heusler and Weger, *"Kristallnacht,"* 150–51.

51. Detjen, *Widerstand, Resistenz und Verweigerung*, 321. See also StAM, Stanw. 5573.

52. Cited in Heusler and Weger, *"Kristallnacht,"* 157.

53. Ibid.

54. Judgment, July 10, 1939, StAM, Stanw. 9327.

55. The phase of non–state-regulated Aryanization between 1933 and 1938, when private and business interests were the driving forces, was also referred to as "wild Aryanization"; see Kuller, *Bürokratie und Verbrechen*, 28, 248; and Drecoll, *Der Fiskus als Verfolger*, 10. From 1938 on, the state placed itself "at the pinnacle of the wealth grab." Kuller, *Bürokratie und Verbrechen*, 248.

56. On all these measures, see Kuller, "Finanzverwaltung und 'Arisierung,'" 179–81; Kuller, *Bürokratie und Verbrechen*, 263–65, 270–72.

57. On this, see Selig, *Leben unterm Rassenwahn*, 156–58; Strnad, *Privileg Mischehe?*, 109–13. For a detailed account on the efforts to target the businesses of mixed-marriages, see ibid., 98–129.

58. Selig, *Leben unterm Rassenwahn*, 180–81.

59. Ibid., 240.

60. Ibid., 244–45.

61. Kuller, *Finanzverwaltung und Judenverfolgung*, 94–95; Kuller, "Finanzverwaltung und 'Arisierung,'" 192; Kuller, *Das Hildebrandhaus*, 78–81.

62. Schelpmeier, "Siegfried und Flora Wilmersdörfer und ihre Familie," 261; Selig, *"Arisierung" in München*, 49–50.

63. Ibid., 49; Transcript of Dr. Benno Schülein's witness testimony, November 21, 1949, IfZ archive, Gm 07.94/8 vol. 1, Trial records: Investigation into the criminal charges against Wegner in connection with Aryanization.

64. Heusler and Weger, *"Kristallnacht,"* 134.

65. Hedwig Geng, "Bericht ueber Theresienstadt," 9–10, LBI, ME 183, last accessed March 15, 2022, http://digipres.cjh.org:1801/delivery/DeliveryManagerServlet?dps_pid=IE8404176.

66. Neuland to the Office for Compensation (*Wiedergutmachungsbehörde*), February 16, 1966, and appendix to the petition of February 19, 1950, StAM, WB I N 7700.

67. Haerendel, "Von der Mustersiedlung zur 'arisierten' Stadt," 244–45; Haerendel, "Der Schutzlosigkeit preisgegeben," 118–20. On Berlin, see Willems, *Der entsiedelte Jude*.

68. Haerendel, "Von der Mustersiedlung zur 'arisierten' Stadt," 244–45; Haerendel, "Der Schutzlosigkeit preisgegeben," 118–19. On "Jew houses" in Munich, see Strnad, "Das 'Judenhaus.'"

69. Judgment, June 13, 1960, IfZ archive, Gm 07.94/8, vol. 1, Trial records: Criminal case against Wegner Hans, Mugler Franz, Schrott Ludwig, and Gm 07.94/9, Criminal case on attempted extortion under threat of force, and StAM, Stanw. 9375.

70. Hans Bloch to the Special Court for the District of the Munich Regional Appeal Court, November 1, 1940, StAM, Stanw. 9375.

71. Kuller, *Das Hildebrandhaus*, 79; Modert, "Motor der Verfolgung," 165. See also Kuller, *Finanzverwaltung und Judenverfolgung*, 94–98.

72. Kuller, *Das Hildebrandhaus*, 79. On Hans Wegner, see Strnad, *Flachs für das Reich*, 35–36; Kasberger, "Hans Wegner." Wegner came from a Communist youth organization to the Stahlhelme (Steel Helmets) and joined the Nazi Party in 1929. One year later, he became a member of the SA. Modert, "Motor der Verfolgung," 166.

73. On this, see Hanke, *Zur Geschichte der Juden in München*, 237–39; Modert, "Motor der Verfolgung," 165–67; Kuller, *Finanzverwaltung und Judenverfolgung*, 96; Strnad, *Zwischenstation "Judensiedlung,"* 24–25.

74. Hanke, *Zur Geschichte der Juden in München*, 275.

75. Indictment, May 4, 1942, BayHStA, LEA 26715 (BEG 24 134).

76. On the judgment against Neuburger, see Detjen, *Widerstand, Resistenz und Verweigerung*, 258–59.

77. Hanke, *Zur Geschichte der Juden in München*, 174; the figures are cited from Bergmann, "Vorgezeichnete Wege," 74. A somewhat higher figure of roughly eight thousand emigrees from Munich in Heusler, "Verfolgung und Vernichtung," 177. On migration from rural areas of Bavaria to Munich, see also Bergmann, "Vorgezeichnete Wege," 50–51.

78. Witness questioning of Dietrich Lisberger, September 5, 1950, StAM, Stanw. 29499/1.

79. StAM, Stanw. 5592 and 9821.

80. Judgment, June 7, 1940, StAM, Stanw. 9821.

81. Strnad, *Flachs für das Reich,* 45.

82. Ibid.

83. Ibid., 49.

84. Gruner, *Der Geschlossene Arbeitseinsatz,* 113–14. See also Gruner, *Jewish Forced Labor Under the Nazis,* 8–9.

85. Strnad, *Zwischenstation "Judensiedlung,"* 94. The age limit in Berlin was evidently fifty-five for men (later raised to sixty), and in Breslau and Dresden, it was sixty years of age; see Gruner, *Der Geschlossene Arbeitseinsatz,* 133–34, 138, 162.

86. On this, see Strnad, *Flachs für das Reich.*

87. Ibid., 27–28.

88. StAM, Stanw. 46909–46914, 46968, 46969, 46978, 46981–46988, 46991, 46992, 46994, 46995, 47003, 47021, 47022.

89. Meyer, *"Jüdische Mischlinge,"* 30. Marriages were considered "non-privileged mixed marriages" if the children were raised Jewish, if the non-Jewish spouse had converted to Judaism prior to the wedding, or, regarding childless marriages, if the Jewish spouse was the man; ibid. See also Strnad, *Privileg Mischehe?,* 145–51.

90. Sworn statement by Benno Schülein, November 22, 1945, StAM, SpkA, K 833, Kammerer, Rudolf.

91. Sworn statement by Rudolf Zieglwallner, February 5, 1946, ibid.

92. Geismar to Heusler, March 25, 2010, StadtAM, Judaica, Mem. 34.

93. Penalty order, January 28, 1942, StAM, Stanw. 46981, case against Dietrich Lisberger. He was sentenced in January 1942 to three weeks in prison.

94. Grüner to Hitler's deputy, Reich Minister Rudolf Hess, February 14, 1939, LAN, Holdings: Church Aid Center for non-Aryan Christians in Munich, no. 1. On these petitions, see Meyer, *"Jüdische Mischlinge,"* 105–43.

95. Report on an acquaintance in a remark regarding the letters to her daughter Louise, March 14, 1940, LBI, AR 1587, Hedwig Geng Collection, box 1, folder 2.

96. On the categorization of *Mischlinge* and *Geltungsjuden* according to the Nuremberg Race Laws, see the introduction, 4.

97. Macek, "Werner Grube," 140.

98. On this, see Von der Heydt, "Wer fährt denn gerne mit dem Judenstern in der Straßenbahn," 70.

99. See, for example, the case of Ruth Butscheidt in Munich: StadtAM, Biographical Memorial Book of the Jews of Munich, 1933–1945, entry "Butscheidt, Ruth," last accessed March 15, 2022, https://gedenkbuch.muenchen.de/index.php?id=gedenkbuch_link&gid=1025.

100. Wertheimer, "Magdalena Schwarz," 449. On denunciations throughout the German Reich for "defiling the race," see Przyrembel, *"Rassenschande,"* 210–23.

101. Transcript, June 24, 1935, StAM, Pol. Dir. 12688. There were no further investigations.

102. Judgment, July 1, 1940, StAM, Stanw. 9839.

103. Selig, *Leben unterm Rassenwahn,* 118–19, 126–32.

104. Ibid., 334.

105. Transcript of the Munich Gestapo, September 11, 1939, StAM, Stanw. 5463.

106. Charge, August 30, 1939, StAM, Stanw. 5464.

107. Judgment of the Munich Special Court, July 27, 1940, StAM, Stanw. 9842.

108. The public plaintiff of the Nuremberg denazification tribunal to the Munich police headquarters, March 3, 1950, StAM, Pol. Dir. 15336.

109. Judgment, February 1, 1941, StAM, Stanw. 10342.

110. On the denunciations in Munich, see also Detjen, *Widerstand, Resistenz und Verweigerung*, 32–34.

111. Johnson, *Nazi Terror*, 23–25, also indicated this in his investigation for Cologne/Krefeld.

112. On this, see Gellately, *The Gestapo and German Society*, 14–15.

113. Sworn statement, April 2, 1964, BayHStA, LEA 3245 (EG 85157).

114. Gerty Spies's witness testimony, March 24, 1949, StAM, SpKA, K 1338, Poller, Ernst.

115. Johnson, *Nazi Terror*, 364.

116. Ibid.

117. Kasberger, "Karrierewege Münchner Gestapobeamter," 203–4.

118. Haerendel, "Der Schutzlosigkeit preisgegeben," 122–23; Strnad, *Zwischenstation "Judensiedlung,"* 27.

119. Strnad, *Zwischenstation "Judensiedlung,"* 84–85.

120. Heusler, "Verfolgung und Vernichtung," 181. On this in detail, see Strnad, *Zwischenstation "Judensiedlung,"* 63–66.

121. Strnad, *Zwischenstation "Judensiedlung,"* 51.

122. Ibid., 106; Gruner, "Von der Kollektivausweisung zur Deportation," 41–43. See also Gottwaldt and Schulle, *Die "Judendeportationen" aus dem Deutschen Reich*, 31–46.

123. Gruner, "Von der Kollektivausweisung zur Deportation," 43.

124. Strnad, *Zwischenstation "Judensiedlung,"* 178–79.

125. On Munich's pioneering role, see Heusler, "Verfolgung und Vernichtung," 161–62.

126. Drecoll, *Der Fiskus als Verfolger*, 54; Gruner, "Die NS-Judenverfolgung und die Kommunen," 123.

127. Gruner, *Öffentliche Wohlfahrt und Judenverfolgung*, 99–100, 161–62. On the municipal awarding of contracts, see Heusler, "Verfolgung und Vernichtung," 163.

128. Strnad, *Flachs für das Reich*, 36–37.

129. Meyer, *A Fatal Balancing Act*, 259. Similarly, see Strnad, *Flachs für das Reich*, 36–37.

130. Gruner, "Die NS-Judenverfolgung und die Kommunen," 118–19.

131. Gruner, *Öffentliche Wohlfahrt und Judenverfolgung*, 275–76; Gruner, "Die NS-Judenverfolgung und die Kommunen," 119. See also Strnad, *Zwischenstation "Judensiedlung,"* 166–67.

132. Gruner, *Öffentliche Wohlfahrt und Judenverfolgung*, 275.

133. Meyer compares the situation in Munich with that in Hamburg, where two "Jewish shops" sold overpriced goods, but were centrally located. Meyer, *A Fatal Balancing Act*, 259–60.

2. THE DEPORTATIONS

1. Hartmann to Weiss, January 12, 1950, StadtAM, Polizeidirektion 831. On this deportation and the subsequent murder of the deportees in Kaunas, see Heusler, "Fahrt in den Tod."

2. Kasberger, "Karrierewege Münchner Gestapobeamter," 213.

3. On the early deportations, see Gruner, "Von der Kollektivausweisung zur Deportation," 31–42; Gottwaldt and Schulle, *Die "Judendeportationen" aus dem Deutschen Reich*, 26–51; Löw, "Die frühen Deportationen."

4. Gruner, "Von der Kollektivausweisung zur Deportation," 51.

5. Gottwaldt and Schulle, *Die "Judendeportationen" aus dem Deutschen Reich*, 66–67.

6. Ibid., 444–46; and Gruner, "Von der Kollektivausweisung zur Deportation," 52–53. The transport from Munich was originally also supposed to go to Riga; see Heusler, "Fahrt in den Tod," 18.

7. Gruner, "Von der Kollektivausweisung zur Deportation," 55.

8. Stockdreher, "Heil- und Pflegeanstalt Eglfing-Haar," 347. The large number of Jewish patients can be explained by the fact that Eglfing-Haar served as an internment camp for Jewish patients from throughout Bavaria; see Hinz-Wessels, "Antisemitismus und Krankenmord," 78.

9. Hinz-Wessels, "Antisemitismus und Krankenmord," 82.

10. This is why references often state that the Jewish patients were in fact brought to the clinic in Cholm, Poland. On this, see Hinz-Wessels, "Antisemitismus und Krankenmord," 81–85.

11. Strnad, *Zwischenstation "Judensiedlung,"* 120. On the tens of thousands of German Jews who were deported to the General Government in the spring and summer of 1942, see Gottwaldt and Schule, *Die "Judendeportationen" aus dem Deutschen Reich*, 137–229; Gruner, "Von der Kollektivausweisung zur Deportation," 57.

12. Strnad, *Zwischenstation "Judensiedlung,"* 120–22.

13. Gruner, "Von der Kollektivausweisung zur Deportation," 56; Gottwaldt and Schulle, *Die "Judendeportationen" aus dem Deutschen Reich*, 266–78.

14. Strnad, *Zwischenstation "Judensiedlung,"* 182. There were forty-five people on the last transport.

15. Ibid., 126. On the deportation of July 13, 1942, referred to by the Munich Gestapo as a "penal transport," see Strnad, *Zwischenstation "Judensiedlung,"* 131–34.

16. Ibid., 135, 182.

17. Gruner, *Widerstand in der Rosenstraße*, 46.

18. Ibid., 59–70.

19. Gottwald and Schulle, *Die "Judendeportationen" aus dem Deutschen Reich*, 456–57.

20. Strnad, *Zwischenstation "Judensiedlung,"* 138, 140.

21. Ibid., 135.

22. The Nazis referred to buildings in which they forced a large number of Jews to live together in extremely cramped conditions as "Jew houses" (*Judenhäuser*). Hajak, "Letzte Adresse: Lindwurmstraße 125," 146.

23. Strnad, *Zwischenstation "Judensiedlung,"* 136. On Theodor Koronczyk, see ibid., 131–37; Meyer, *A Fatal Balancing Act*, 263–69, 290–94, and chapters 6 and 10 of this book.

24. Gruner, *Widerstand in der Rosenstraße*, 50–51. In Berlin, Jewish men who lived in mixed marriages were arrested—which led to the Rosenstrasse protest—but most of them were later released, according to Gruner, because their deportation had not yet been planned at that time; ibid., 157–66. Nathan Stolzfus has argued that they were released because of the protest by their wives and relatives. See Stolzfus, *Resistance of the Heart*. On the ensuing debate, see Gruner, "Ein Historikerstreit"; Stolzfus and Maier-Katkin, *Protest in Hitler's "National Community."*

25. Von der Heydt, "Wer fährt denn gerne mit dem Judenstern," 74.

26. Ibid. The same was the case in Munich; on this, see Schrafstetter, "'Geltungsjüdische' Jugendliche," 67.

27. Von der Heydt, "Wer fährt denn gerne mit dem Judenstern," 74.

28. On this, see Heusler and Weger, *"Kristallnacht,"* 191; and Strnad, *Zwischenstation "Judensiedlung,"* 126, 141; figures in ibid., 182.

29. Gruner, "Von der Kollektivausweisung zur Deportation," 59.

30. On differences between Hamburg and Berlin, see Meyer, "Fragwürdiger Schutz," 83.

31. Gottwaldt and Schulle, *Die "Judendeportationen" aus dem Deutschen Reich,* 466–67.

32. On this, see in particular Strnad, "Die Deportationen aus München," 87–96.

33. Strnad, *Zwischenstation "Judensiedlung,"* 182; and Strnad, "Die Deportationen aus München," 80–81. Of these 3,400 people, 2,576 lived in Munich and the rest came from the outskirts of Munich and from Swabia; ibid.

34. Strnad, *Zwischenstation "Judensiedlung,"* 178.

35. Ibid., 136. From 1943 on, roughly sixty Jewish forced laborers were deployed in street cleaning. Ten of them certified in July 1945 that their supervisor, Josef Hackner, treated them very decently, contrary to the instructions of the Aryanization Office. Hackner left his position in July 1944. Confirmation, July 1, 1945, StAM, SpkA, K 594, Hackner, Josef.

36. On the different Munich companies that employed Jewish forced laborers, see Strnad, *Flachs für das Reich,* 45–46.

37. Heusler, *Ausländereinsatz,* 121. Werner, *Kriegswirtschaft und Zwangsarbeit,* 187, lists the number of foreign forced laborers in Allach in 1941 as 2,215.

38. Strnad, *Zwischenstation "Judensiedlung,"* 108.

39. Ibid.

40. Kasberger, "Karrierewege Münchner Gestapobeamter," 194. On the Gestapo men, see ibid. On Isselhorst and Schäfer, see Mettig, "Der Münchner Gestapochef"; Eichmüller, *Keine Generalamnestie,* 17–23; Raim, *Justiz,* 1033–34.

41. Trial records: Criminal case against Wegner Hans, Mugler Franz, Schrott Ludwig, IfZ Archive, Gm 07.94/8 vol. 1. See also Kasberger, "Hans Wegner."

42. Strnad, *Zwischenstation "Judensiedlung,"* 111. Hanke, *Zur Geschichte der Juden in München,* 290.

43. It has not been fully clarified precisely who participated in compiling the lists; Meyer, *A Fatal Balancing Act,* 263.

44. Strnad, *Zwischenstation "Judensiedlung,"* 108–109; Heusler and Weger, *"Kristallnacht,"* 182.

45. Behrend-Rosenfeld and Rosenfeld, *Leben in zwei Welten,* 170.

46. On formal "self-administration," see, for example, Strnad, *Flachs für das Reich,* 85; on the dilemmas for the Jewish officials, see Meyer, *A Fatal Balancing Act,* 243–47. See ibid., 376–77, and chapters 6 and 10 of this book for postwar efforts to blame Jewish officials for the deportations.

47. Kuller, "Erster Grundsatz," 164–65; Gruner, "Von der Kollektivausweisung zur Deportation," 56.

48. Gertrud Spies to the investigation judge at the Regional Court (*Landgericht*) Munich I, May 16, 1951, IfZ archive, ED 102/3, estate of Gertrud Spies. On the "baggage checks," see also Strnad, *Zwischenstation "Judensiedlung,"* 113–14.

49. Kuller, "Finanzverwaltung und 'Arisierung,'" 187; and Kuller, *Finanzverwaltung und Judenverfolgung,* 24–32.

50. Kuller, *Finanzverwaltung und Judenverfolgung,* 159–60. The investigation by Christiane Kuller shows that the tax authorities did, in fact, consider the fate of those deported. A 1941 conversation transcript of the Nuremberg authorities includes the sentence, "No one is considering extermination." Kuller, *Bürokratie und Verbrechen,* 411. It is possible to read the

(self-)placating denial of the actual fate of those affected as a feeling they did not want to believe; see also ibid.

51. Jalowicz Simon, *Underground in Berlin*, 220.

52. Spies, *My Years in Theresienstadt*, 58.

53. Ibid., 59.

54. Bajohr and Pohl correctly indicate that what appears to be passive behavior cannot always be subsumed under the terms "indifference" or "tacit approval." Bajohr and Pohl, *Massenmord und schlechtes Gewissen*, 50.

55. Bajohr and Pohl, *Massenmord und schlechtes Gewissen*; Bajohr and Pohl, *Der Holocaust als offenes Geheimnis*; and Longerich, *"Davon haben wir nichts gewußt!"*

56. Reck, *Diary of a Man in Despair*, 160. Reck assumed the pen name Reck-Malleczewen.

57. Holzmann, *Woman Courageous*, 124–25, 224, StadtAM, Judaica, Mem. 22.

58. Ibid.

59. Strnad, *Flachs für das Reich*, 103–4.

60. Macek, "Walter Geismar," 163.

61. Behrend-Rosenfeld and Rosenfeld, *Leben in zwei Welten*, 18.

62. Hinz-Wessels, "Antisemitismus und Krankenmord," 81. On Rosa Hechinger, see also StadtAM, Biographical Memorial Book of the Jews of Munich, 1933–1945, entry "Hechinger, Rosa," last accessed March 21, 2022, https://gedenkbuch.muenchen.de/index.php?id=gedenkbuch_link&gid=5965.

63. On this, see Süß, *Der "Volkskörper" im Krieg*, 127–41.

64. Krauss, "Zur Einführung," 17–18.

65. Kosmala, "Zwischen Ahnen und Wissen," 149. For a detailed discussion of what the Berlin Jews knew, see ibid.

66. Bajohr and Pohl, *Massenmord und schlechtes Gewissen*, 60–61; and Bajohr and Pohl, *Der Holocaust als offenes Geheimnis*, 61.

67. For the second flyer of the White Rose see Weiße Rose Stiftung e.V., "Das zweite Flugblatt der Weißen Rose," last accessed February 24, 2022, https://www.weisse-rose-stiftung.de/widerstandsgruppe-weisse-rose/flugblaetter/ii-flugblatt-der-weissen-rose/ (German), https://www.weisse-rose-stiftung.de/white-rose-resistance-group/leaflets-of-the-white-rose/ii-leaflet-of-the-white-rose/ (English version). The literature on the White Rose is now so comprehensive that only a few central and recent publications shall be mentioned here: Scholl, *White Rose*; Zankel, *Mit Flugblättern*; Chaussy and Ueberschär, *"Es lebe die Freiheit!"*

68. The Holocaust as an open secret ("*offenes Geheimnis*"), as in the title of the work by Bajohr and Pohl. Longerich, *"Davon haben wir nichts gewußt!"* 201, also speaks of an "open secret." See also Dörner, *Die Deutschen und der Holocaust*; Fritzsche, *Babi Yar*.

69. Steckhan, "Was ihr getan habt," 201.

70. On this, see, for example, Longerich, *"Davon haben wir nichts gewußt!"* 305; Bajohr and Pohl, *Massenmord und schlechtes Gewissen*, 67–68; Fritzsche, *Babi Yar*, 95.

71. Behrend-Rosenfeld and Rosenfeld, *Leben in zwei Welten*, 150–51.

72. Ibid., 119–21.

73. Ibid., 118.

74. Ibid., 146–47.

75. Ibid., 159.

76. Ibid., 161; See also Goeschel, *Suicide in Nazi Germany*, 109.

77. Strnad, *Zwischenstation "Judensiedlung,"* 152. The actual number is presumably higher.
78. Goeschel, *Suicide in Nazi Germany*, 106–9.
79. Behrend-Rosenfeld and Rosenfeld, *Leben in zwei Welten*, 188.
80. Ibid., 200–201.

3. EARLY ESCAPES

1. Christopher Browning correlates the Nazi leadership's optimism for a victory in the fall of 1941 with the decision to murder European Jewry. See Browning, *The Origins of the Final Solution*, 309–30.

2. This group around the Swiss publisher Walter Classen will be dealt with in chapter 7 as part of the discussion of Christian assistance for people in hiding. The actual figures must in any case be presumed to be higher.

3. Sigmund W. to the State Office for Compensation (Landesamt für Wiedergutmachung, later LEA), March 17, 1950, BayHStA, LEA 39369 (BEG 11408).

4. Registration of claims: Damage to professional advancement, September 18, 1960, ibid.

5. Note, June 30, 1959, BLEA, EG 65335.

6. His future wife, Martha W., listed the date as September 1941, but she was evidently mistaken in her memory. Martha W. to the Bavarian State Compensation Office, October 20, 1960, BLEA, EG 65335.

7. Ibid.

8. Sigmund W. to the State Office for Compensation (Landesamt für Wiedergutmachung, later LEA), March 17, 1950, BayHStA, LEA 39369 (BEG 11408).

9. Ibid.; and Martha W. to the Bavarian State Compensation Office, May 25, 1957, BLEA, EG 65335.

10. Martha W. to the Bavarian State Compensation Office, May 25, 1957, BLEA, EG 65335.

11. Themal, "Meine Erlebnisse waehrend der Zeit der Judenverfolgungen in Deutschland, 1933–45," 5, AWL, Gale Primary Sources, Archives Unbound, Testaments to the Holocaust.

12. Martha W. to the Bavarian State Compensation Office, May 25, 1957, BLEA, EG 65335.

13. Judgment, January 3, 1950, StAM, SpkA, K 621, Hanisch, Stanislaus.

14. On the German Red Aid, see Brauns, *Schafft Rote Hilfe!*; Brauns, "Kraft wahrer Solidarität," 9–69; Hering and Schilde, *Die Rote Hilfe*.

15. Graf, *Gelächter von Außen*, 467.

16. Ibid.

17. Graf, *Gelächter von Außen*, 471. See also Brauns, "Wahre Solidarität," last accessed February 24, 2022, http://www.nikolaus-brauns.de/OMG_RHZ.htm; Brauns, "Kraft wahrer Solidarität," 55–56.

18. Brauns, "Kraft wahrer Solidarität," 61.

19. Meta L. to the Bavarian Relief Organization (Bayerische Hilfswerk), September 6, 1949, BLEA, BEG 3196/EG 1220.

20. Minutes of the public session of November 11, 1955, Testimony of Meta L., BLEA, BEG 3196/EG 1220.

21. Witness testimony of Meta L., January 3, 1950, StAM, SpkA, K 621, Hanisch, Stanislaus.

22. Minutes of the public session of November 11, 1955, Testimony of Meta L., BLEA, BEG 3196/EG 1220.

23. Witness testimony of Meta L., January 3, 1950, StAM, SpKA, K 621, Hanisch, Stanislaus.

24. Sworn statement by Meta L., October 21, 1946, StAM, SpkA, K 1441, Rodius, Alfred.

25. Witness testimony of Meta L., January 3, 1950, StAM, SpKA, K 621, Hanisch, Stanislaus.

26. Judgment, January 3 1950, StAM, SpkA, K 621, Hanisch, Stanislaus; sworn statement by Meta L., January 21, 1947, BLEA, BEG 3196/EG 1220.

27. Kosmala, "Mißglückte Hilfe und ihre Folgen," 207.

28. Statement by Stanislaus Hanisch, January 3, 1950, StAM, SpkA, K 621, Hanisch, Stanislaus.

29. Sworn statement by Meta L., January 21, 1947, BLEA, BEG 3196/EG 1220.

30. After the war, Maria H. referred to her fiancé as Epp's adjutant; file note, October 13, 1961, BayHStA, LEA 38189 (BEG 69840). It is unclear if this was true. It is certain, however, that he was a member of Epp's *Freikorps* (Free Corps).

31. Behrend-Rosenfeld and Rosenfeld, *Leben in zwei Welten*, 188.

32. Selig, *Leben unterm Rassenwahn*, 316.

33. Ibid.

34. Ibid.

35. Ibid.

36. Sworn statement, November 20, 1960, BayHStA, LEA 38189 (BEG 69840).

37. Cited in Selig, *Leben unterm Rassenwahn*, 318.

38. Ibid., 318–19.

39. Sworn statement by Maria V., November 20, 1960, BayHStA, LEA 38189 (BEG 69840).

40. File note October 13, 1961, ibid.

41. According to Katja-Maria Wächter in her generally noncritical biography. See Wächter, *Die Macht der Ohnmacht*, 175–80. What Epp referred to as "protective custody excesses" were what he felt were excessive, arbitrary arrests of political adversaries and their all too brutal mistreatment in various concentration camps. With that, however, he was not opposing the system of "protective custody," per se. On Epp's antisemitism, see ibid., 128–30.

42. Leugers, "Du hast alles vereint," 197–99.

43. Sworn statement, November 20, 1960, BayHStA, LEA 38189 (BEG 69840).

44. For example, Max Krakauer and his wife; see Krakauer, *Lights in Darkness*, 53–58.

45. German Resistance Memorial Center, Silent Heroes database, Dossier Rudolf V.

46. Undated confirmation, BayHStA, LEA 38189 (BEG 69840).

47. Comments from the letter of Rudolf V., n.d., LBI, AR 1587, Hedwig Geng Collection, box 1, folder 1.

48. Rudolf V. to Geng, November 18, 1943, ibid.

49. Ibid.

50. The correspondence and the deportation were not at all connected. Hedwig Geng was divorced from her non-Jewish husband in 1938, and, like many Jews who had lost the protection of being in a mixed marriage, she was deported in early 1944; Freier, "Statistik und Deportation der Juden aus dem Deutschen Reich," last accessed March 23, 2022, http://www.statistik-des-holocaust.de/II30-1.jpg.

51. Geng to Muehsam, February 4, 1963, LBI, AR 1587, Hedwig Geng collection, box 1, folder 3.

52. Letter of the Bavarian State Ministry of Justice, State Secretary Hartinger, July 4, 1959, BayHStA, LEA 38189 (EG 69840).

53. In Grabower's case, it was Hans Heinrich Lammers, chief of the Reich Chancellery, who prevented his deportation to Kaunas. Strnad, *Flachs für das Reich*, 90. Grabower was sent to Theresienstadt in June 1942.

54. Rolf Grabower, cited in Strnad, *Flachs für das Reich*, 93.

55. Ibid. On Grabower, ibid., 85–96; on Grabower in Theresienstadt, see Hájková, *The Last Ghetto*, 161, 241.

56. Supplementary details by Edith S., March 26, 1947, BLEA, BEG 6966.

57. Bavarian State Compensation Office (BLEA) (Dr. Klein) to the state health department in Erlangen, February 22, 1954, BLEA, BEG 6966.

58. StadtAM, database of the Biographical Memorial Book of the Jews of Munich, 1933–1945, entry "Max S." On the *Kindertransport*, see Craig-Norton, *The Kindertransport*.

59. Supplementary details by Edith S., March 26, 1947, BLEA, BEG 6966.

60. Bavarian State Compensation Office (BLEA) (Dr. Klein) to the state health department in Erlangen, February 22, 1954, ibid.

61. Dr. Hugo Rothschild's curriculum vitae in Weber, *Das Schicksal der jüdischen Rechtsanwälte*, 143.

62. Bavarian State Compensation Office (BLEA) (Dr. Klein) to the state health department in Erlangen, February 22, 1954, BLEA, BEG 6966.

63. Weber, *Das Schicksal der jüdischen Rechtsanwälte*, 143.

64. Behrend-Rosenfeld and Rosenfeld, *Leben in zwei Welten*, 188.

65. On the story of Dr. Sophie Mayer, see also Ebert, *Zwischen Anerkennung und Ächtung*, 181–84.

66. For biographical details of the members of the Mayer family see StadtAM, Biographical Memorial Book of the Jews of Munich, 1933–1945, entry "Mayer, Lieselotte," last accessed March 24, 2022, https://gedenkbuch.muenchen.de/index.php?id=gedenkbuch_link&gid=7460; entry "Mayer, Julius," last accessed March 24, 2022, https://gedenkbuch.muenchen.de/index.php?id=gedenkbuch_link&gid=7456; entry "Mayer, Paula," last accessed March 24, 2022, https://gedenkbuch.muenchen.de/index.php?id=gedenkbuch_link&gid=7467.

67. Sworn statement by Dr. Sophie Mayer, May 15, 1946, StAM, SpkA, K 3643, Mayer, Paul. We know very little about Maria Letnar other than that Sophie Mayer and Maria Letnar had met in the English Garden, where they both walked their dogs regularly; see Ebert, *Zwischen Anerkennung und Ächtung*, 182. See also Schrafstetter and Steinweis, *The Germans and the Holocaust*, 168–69.

68. Hedwig Geng, "Bericht ueber Theresienstadt," 19, LBI, ME 183, last accessed March 23, 2022, http://digipres.cjh.org:1801/delivery/DeliveryManagerServlet?dps_pid=IE8404176. On Paula and Lieselotte Mayer's helper and hiding place, see also German Resistance Memorial Center, Silent Heroes database, dossier: Paula and Lieselotte Mayer.

Hedwig Geng and Sophie Mayer knew each other through their forced labor for the Kammerer company. They met again in 1945, when Hedwig Geng, together with other survivors of Theresienstadt, was quartered in the Jewish nursing home on Kaulbachstrasse. Sophie Mayer worked there as a doctor (see chapter 9).

69. Ebert, *Zwischen Anerkennung und Ächtung*, 183.

70. Sophie Mayer to David Alcalay, December 31, 1967, Yad Vashem, M.31, file 0394b.

71. Wolffenstein, *Erinnerungen von Valerie Wolffenstein*, 60. Valerie Wolffenstein's helper Esther Seidel did not want to take in her friend until the thirteen-year-old son had returned to boarding school. On the role of Günter Mayer, see Statement by Dr. Sophie Mayer, *Data der Geretteten*, September 3, 1966, Yad Vashem, M.31, file 0394b.

72. Sophie Mayer described this detail in her letter to Kurt Grossmann, in Grossmann, *Die Unbesungenen Helden*, 134.

73. This information can be found in only one article on the honoring of Rosa Mayer and Maria Letnar by Yad Vashem; see *Abendzeitung*, April 1, 1971, Yad Vashem, M.31, file 0394b.

74. Sworn statement by Dr. Sophie Mayer, May 15, 1946, StAM, SpkA, K 3643, Mayer, Paul.

75. Ibid. The "clean bills of health" (so-called Persil certificates) often handed down in denazification proceedings must generally be taken with a grain of salt, but in this case, the activities of Mayer have been documented in detail by a wide range of people.

76. Questionnaire, February 19, 1946, StAM, SpkA, K 3643, Mayer, Paul.

77. Statement by Dr. Sophie Mayer, *Data der Geretteten*, September 3, 1966, Yad Vashem, M.31, file 0394b.

78. Ebert, *Zwischen Anerkennung und Ächtung*, 184.

79. Behrend-Rosenfeld and Rosenfeld, *Leben in zwei Welten*, 190.

80. Ibid., 195–96; and Krauss, "Zur Einführung," 17.

81. Behrend-Rosenfeld and Rosenfeld, *Leben in zwei Welten*, 197.

82. Ibid., 201–3.

83. Ibid., 205–7. Else Behrend-Rosenfeld changed the names of some people she mentioned to keep them anonymous. Hence, her sister Eva became her cousin Erna. The identities were clarified in the comments of Erich Kasberger and Marita Krauss; ibid., 191.

84. Ibid., 208–9, 215. On people who spontaneously became helpers and gradually expanded their assistance, see Giesecke and Welzer, *Das Menschenmögliche*, 61–64.

85. Behrend-Rosenfeld, *Leben in zwei Welten*, 215.

86. Ibid., 226. Peter Heilmann, born 1922, was the older son of Magdalena and Ernst Heilmann. Deemed a "half Jew," he fled in early 1945 from the Organization Todt labor camp and went into hiding himself; ibid., 235; Heilmann, "Ein neues Leben," 53–54.

87. Behrend-Rosenfeld and Rosenfeld, *Leben in zwei Welten*, 227–28.

88. Caplan, "Ausweis bitte!" 234. On the postal ID card, see ibid.

89. Behrend-Rosenfeld and Rosenfeld, *Leben in zwei Welten*, 235–39.

90. For a discussion on the difficulty in making such estimates, see Beer, *Die Banalität des Guten*, 121–23.

91. Ungar-Klein, *Schattenexistenz*, 107. In Austria, three quarters of all those in hiding evidently survived in a maximum of two hiding places. Moser, "Jewish 'U-Boote' in Austria," 59.

92. Kosmala, "Zwischenbilanz eines Forschungsprojektes," 22; Beer, *Die Banalität des Guten*, 122.

93. Lutjens, *Submerged on the Surface*, 2. On Anne Frank as a so-called model of life in hiding, see also Roseman, *A Past in Hiding*, 272; and Lutjens, "Vom Untertauchen," 50–51. The specific reasons for these differences between Berlin and Vienna still need to be examined. Also, a difference must be made between the situation in the occupied areas—such as France, the Netherlands, or Poland—and those in Germany (in its 1937 borders). In Poland, groups of people often built long-term underground hiding places; see Grabowski, *Hunt for the Jews*, 76; Aleksiun, "Neighbors in Borysław," 254–56.

94. Goeschel, *Suicide in Nazi Germany*, 102, 111.

95. Siegfried B. to the Bavarian State Compensation Office (BLEA), September 2, 1956, BayHStA, LEA 5514 (BEG 10675).

96. Roseman, *A Past in Hiding*, 292–93.

97. Hedwig Geng, "Bericht ueber Theresienstadt," 19, LBI, ME 183, last accessed March 23, 2022, http://digipres.cjh.org:1801/delivery/DeliveryManagerServlet?dps_pid=IE8404176.

98. Lutjens, "Jews in Hiding," 274.

99. See, for example, Jalowicz Simon, *Underground in Berlin*; Degen, *Nicht alle waren Mörder*; Lovenheim, *Survival in the Shadows*.

100. Krauss, "Zur Einführung," 17–18; Behrend-Rosenfeld and Rosenfeld, *Leben in zwei Welten*, 185.

101. On these issues, see also Beer, *Die Banalität des Guten*, 160–63.

102. Statement by Dr. Sophie Mayer, *Data der Geretteten*, September 3, 1966, Yad Vashem, M.31, file 0394b; Meta L. to the Bayerische Hilfswerk, August 26, 1949, BLEA, BEG 3196/EG 1220.

103. For a detailed analysis of the motivations and forms of help of this category of helpers, see Beer, *Die Banalität des Guten*, 246–51; Strnad, *Privileg Mischehe*, 317–22. On Jewish helpers, see Enzenbach, "Zur Problematik des Begriffs 'Retter,'" 246–48.

104. Beer, *Die Banalität des Guten*, 238–41.

105. Ibid., 241.

106. On Franz Kaufmann and Benno Heller, see Rudolph, *Hilfe beim Sprung ins Nichts*; Düring, *Verdeckte soziale Netzwerke*, 74–89; Jalocwicz-Simon, *Underground in Berlin*.

107. Riffel, Unbesungene Helden, 184–91; Beer, *Die Banalität des Guten*, 241.

108. Degen, *Nicht alle waren Mörder*, 77–82.

109. Lovenheim, *Survival in the Shadows*, 104–5; see also Frankenstein, "Ich habe eigentlich nie Angst gehabt," 103–04.

110. Orbach and Orbach-Smith, *Soaring Underground*, 119–30, 159.

111. Veit, "Non-Jews Helping Jews," 5, AWL, Gale Primary Sources, Archives Unbound, Testaments to the Holocaust.

112. Letter of January 28, 1946, LBI, AR 1587, Hedwig Geng collection, box 1, folder 1.

113. Themal, "Meine Erlebnisse waehrend der Zeit der Judenverfolgungen in Deutschland, 1933–45," 8, AWL, Gale Primary Sources, Archives Unbound, Testaments to the Holocaust.

114. Lovenheim, *Survival in the Shadows*, 86; Herman-Friede, *Für Freudensprünge keine Zeit*, 53.

115. Croes and Kosmala, "Facing Deportation," 119.

116. As Lutjens explains, in 1939, more than 57 percent of Berlin's Jews were women, and therefore it is not surprising that the percentage of surviving female U-boats was considerably higher than 50 percent. Lutjens, *Submerged on the Surface*, 216. On this, see also Lutjens, "Jews in Hiding," 283–84.

117. Lutjens, *Submerged on the Surface*, 218. As men ran a higher risk of being arrested, Lutjens assumes a lower survival rate for men, ibid., 216. A lower survival rate for men could not be determined by the research conducted for the present study.

118. Ungar-Klein, *Schattenexistenz*, 97.

119. This refers to an unknown number of people who were brought to Switzerland by a Christian support network (see chapter 7). There was probably also a small number of people who fled that can no longer be ascertained.

120. Kosmala, "Gedenkstätte Stille Helden," 172–73. The statistics are similar in Lutjens, "Jews in Hiding," 276.

121. Meyer, "A conto Zukunft," 214.

122. Bonavita, *Mit falschem Pass*, 175. For statistics for 1941, see Meyer, *A Fatal Balancing Act*, 256.

123. Meyer, *A Fatal Balancing Act*, 252; Bonavita, *Mit falschem Pass*, 8–9; Kingreen, "Die Aktion zur kalten Erledigung der Mischehen," 188.

124. Bonavita, *Mit falschem Pass*, 8.

125. Meyer, *A Fatal Balancing Act*, 253.

4. THE CONCLUSION OF THE MASS DEPORTATIONS IN 1943

1. For a detailed discussion, see Schoppman, "Die 'Fabrikaktion' in Berlin."

2. Ibid., 141–42.

3. Gruner, *Widerstand in der Rosenstraße*, 46.

4. Ibid. Gruner also notes that in the SS statistics of January 1943 on forced laborers still in Germany (in its 1937 borders), the cities of Frankfurt and Hamburg were no longer included in the lists, as the deportations there were already regarded as virtually completed.

5. Ibid., 46, 58–59. A total of only 5,306 Jewish forced laborers were still registered outside Berlin.

6. Schoppmann, "Die 'Fabrikaktion' in Berlin," 142.

7. Gruner, *Widerstand in der Rosenstraße*, 54, 59–60.

8. Andreas-Friedrich, *Berlin Underground, 1938–1945*, 90.

9. Gruner, "Die Berliner und die NS-Judenverfolgungen," 84–85.

10. Schoppmann, "Die 'Fabrikaktion' in Berlin," 139.

11. Lochner, ed. and trans., *The Goebbels Diaries 1942–1943*, 293–94 (March 11, 1943).

12. Dörner, *Die Deutschen und der Holocaust*, 452–56.

13. Longerich, *"Davon haben wir nichts gewusst!"* 255. Dörner views December 1942 as marking the transition from a phase in which "indications of the genocide of the Jews were consolidating" to a phase in which the genocide of the Jews was "increasingly becoming a certainty"; see Dörner, *Die Deutschen und der Holocaust*, 426, 452.

14. Kosmala, "Zwischen Ahnen und Wissen," 146–47.

15. See also Schoppmann, "Die 'Fabrikaktion' in Berlin," 143.

16. Strnad, *Zwischenstation "Judensiedlung,"* 140–41, 143–44.

17. Ibid., 136.

18. Ibid., 141. Walter Geismar also implied that several days passed between receipt of a deportation notice and the departure of the transport; see Geismar to Heusler, March 25, 2010, StadtAM, Judaica, Mem. 34.

19. For all of 1943 in Munich, only seven escapes have been documented; on top of that come another seven people who had fled to the Greater Munich area from elsewhere in 1943 and were hidden there.

20. On Dr. Benno Schülein in detail, see Weber, *Das Schicksal der jüdischen Rechtsanwälte*, 191–94.

21. Compensation proceedings of Siegfried B., Proposed settlement, October 25, 1961, and sworn statement by Leopold F., February 9, 1953, BayHStA, LEA 5514 (BEG 10675).

22. Witness testimony of Siegfried B., August 25, 1950, StAM, Stanw. 29499/1.

23. Investigation from the records of the Munich police headquarters, February 12, 1953, and dismissal of the case, July 28, 1942, BayHStA, LEA 5514 (EG 10 675).

24. Witness testimony of Siegfried B., October 7, 1949, StAM, SpkA, K 545, Grahammer, Hans.

25. Ibid.

26. Testimony of Hans Grahammer, October 7, 1949, ibid.

27. Witness testimony of Siegfried B., October 7, 1949; witness testimony of Julius B., May 26, 1952, ibid.

28. Mezger's wife was also told that her husband had been arrested for aiding an escape. Witness testimony of Almuth Mezger, September 5, 1950, StAM, Stanw. 29499/1.

29. StadtAM, Biographical Memorial Book of the Jews of Munich, 1933–1945, entry "Mezger, Curt," last accessed March 23, 2022, https://gedenkbuch.muenchen.de/index.php?id=gedenkbuch_link&gid=2605; Strnad, *Zwischenstation "Judensiedlung,"* 54–55.

30. Siegfried B. to the Bavarian State Compensation Office (BLEA), September 2, 1956, BayHStA, LEA 5514 (EG 10675).

31. Hartlapp, *Siebten-Tages Adventisten*, 585–89. The scientific studies on the Adventists that have been conducted up to now paint a picture of a Free Church whose stance on the persecution of the Jews was characterized by official silence and whose doctrine of salvation also contained antisemitic stereotypes; see ibid.; and Heinz, *Freikirchen und Juden*, 284–98.

32. Affidavit by Dr. Benno Schülein, February 28, 1946, StAM, SpkA, K 816, Jordan, Otto.

33. Ibid. On Schülein's time in hiding, see supplemental affidavit by Dr. Benno Schülein, February 29, 1948, StAM, SpkA, K 816, Jordan, Otto; see also Weber, *Das Schicksal der jüdischen Rechtsanwälte*, 191–92.

34. Affidavit by Dr. Benno Schülein, November 22, 1945, StAM, SpkA, K 833, Kammerer, Rudolf.

35. Weber, *Das Schicksal der jüdischen Rechtsanwälte*, 191.

36. Affidavit, March 1, 1950, BayHStA, LEA 33681 (BEG 3375).

37. Bayerischer Landtag, current and former members of the Bavarian state parliament since 1946, "August Melchner", last accessed February 23, 2022: https://www.bayern.landtag.de/abgeordnete/abgeordnete-von-a-z/profil/august-melchner/.

38. Stefan and Therese Steinbacher, Ilse Gerweck's helpers, were honored in 2014 as Righteous Among the Nations, Embassy of the State of Israel in Berlin, "Yad Vashem-Ehrung von vier 'Gerechten unter den Völkern' im Bayerischen Landtag," last accessed March 11, 2022, http://www.botschaftisrael.de/2014/06/26/yad-vashem-ehrung-von-vier-gerechte-unter-den-voelkern-im-bayerischen-landtag/.

39. Frau Baier to the Bavarian State Compensation Office (BLEA), October 27, 1954, BayHStA, LEA 33681 (BEG 3375); see also Weber, *Das Schicksal der jüdischen Rechtsanwälte*, 191.

40. Affidavit by Rudolf Kammerer, October 30, 1954; affidavit by Hans Fetzer, November 11, 1954, BayHStA, LEA 33681 (BEG 3375); affidavit by Benno Schülein, n.d., SpKA, K 833, Kammerer, Rudolf. See also Weber, *Das Schicksal der jüdischen Rechtsanwälte*, 192.

41. Witness testimony of Dr. Fritz Kuhn, December 8, 1947, StAM, SpkA, K 633, Kammerer, Rudolf.

42. Confirmation by Margarethe Günther, November 28, 1945, ibid.

43. Affidavit by Hans Günther, December 8, 1947, ibid.

44. Witness testimony of Eduard Meyer, December 8, 1947, ibid.

45. Grossmann, *Die unbesungenen Helden*, 124.

46. Widmann, "Die Kunst der Frechheit," 280; also in Grossmann, *Die unbesungenen Helden*, 122.

47. Widmann, "Die Kunst der Frechheit," 278. On Herda's strategy of referring to his knowing Göring, see ibid., 280.

48. Grossmann, *Die unbesungenen Helden*, 125–26; Widmann, "Kunst der Frechheit," 280–81.

49. Registration of claims: deprivation of liberty, September 30, 1949, BayHStA, LEA 16392 (BEG 6935).

50. Sworn statement by Albertine Gimpel, August 23, 1954, ibid.

51. Albertine Herda, questionnaire of the Bayerisches Hilfswerk, a Bavarian relief organization; remarks by Albertine Gimpel, April 26, 1946, ibid. Unfortunately, she does not elaborate on what exactly Franz Herda did to prevent her from being deported.

52. Sworn statement by Albertine Herda, August 23, 1954, BayHStA, LEA 16392 (BEG 6935).

53. Ibid.

54. Widmann, "Die Kunst der Frechheit," 282; interview with Richard Marx, February 14, 2014.

55. Interview with Richard Marx, February 14, 2014.

56. In his critical two-volume biography of Reck-Malleczewen, Alphons Kappeler treated first and foremost Reck's ostensibly wild imagination. He said that Reck evidently invented some episodes of his life. Friedrich Reck added the name of his parents' estate, Malleczewen, to his family name, and in the 1920s, he assumed Percyval as a middle name. Occasionally he referred to himself as Fritz von Reck-Malleczewen, adding the aristocratic "von"; see Kappeler, *Ein Fall von "Pseudologia phantastica,"* 15–82, and Geer, *Sophistication*, 77–87.

57. Reck-Malleczewen, *Bockelson*. See also von der Lippe and Reck-Malleczewen, *A History of the Münster Anabaptists*.

58. Kappeler, *Ein Fall von "Pseudologia phantastica,"* 432.

59. Sworn statement by Franz Herda, September 29, 1954, BayHStA, LEA 16392 (BEG 6935).

60. Kappeler, *Ein Fall von "Pseudologia phantastica,"* 8–9; Ebert and Hasselwander, "Schwadroneur," 30. Details in StAM, SpkA, K1487, Salat, Alfred.

61. Herda had driven to Dachau to obtain further information. He received contradictory information about the cause of death. It is likely that Fritz Reck-Malleczewen, who was healthy when he was admitted, was deliberately placed in the typhus barracks, where he was infected and died from the disease a short time later. Letter of Irmgard Reck-Malleczewen, April 29, 1946, and the letter of Mr. Sternberg, October 25, 1946, StAM, SpkA, K 1487, Salat, Alfred; Kappeler, *Ein Fall von "Pseudologia phantastica,"* 11.

62. Albertine Herda, sworn statement, n.d. [1954], BayHStA, LEA 16392 (BEG 6935).

63. Kappeler, *Ein Fall von "Pseudologia phantastica,"* 485.

64. Reck-Malleczewen, *Tagebuch eines Verzweifelten*. The English translation, *Diary of a Man in Despair*, was published in 1970; Reck-Malleczewen [Reck], *Diary of a Man in Despair*. A new English translation was released in 2013 and a new German edition in 2015. Reck never mentioned Albertine Gimpel in his diary with even a single word.

65. Reck, *Diary of a Man in Despair*, 170.

66. Evans, "Afterword," 228–29.

67. Judgment of the Munich denazification tribunal (*Spruchkammer*) X, May 19, 1948, StAM, SpkA, K 1487, Salat, Alfred. Salat was placed in Group I of "Major Offenders." The verdict in the appeal proceedings in 1949 is unfortunately not included in the dossier.

68. Frei, *Adenauer's Germany*, 406.

69. On the Naumann circle, see ibid., 277–302; Buchna, *Nationale Sammlung an Rhein und Ruhr*.

70. See chapter 8 ("Conclusion" section). On Herda's and Gimpel's postwar life, see Von Weitzel, "Franz Herda, (1887–1965)," last accessed February 24, 2022, http://www.christoph-von-weitzel.de/herda_2.html.

71. Bachmann to the Bavarian State Compensation Office (BLEA), November 6, 1954, BayHStA, LEA 202 (BEG 17295).

72. Bachmann, Max, statement, n.d., ibid.

73. Bachmann to the Bavarian State Compensation Office (BLEA), November 6, 1954, ibid.

74. Bachmann, Max, appendix to E: damage to economic advancement, n.d., ibid.

75. Düring, *Verdeckte soziale Netzwerke*, 190. Düring provides a detailed analysis of the largest networks in Berlin. On the situation in Berlin, see also Beer, *Die Banalität des Guten*; Lutjens, *Submerged on the Surface*.

76. Beer, *Die Banalität des Guten*, 169–74.

77. On the Dahlem group, see, for example, Rudolph, *Hilfe beim Sprung ins Nichts*; on the Uncle Emil group, see Düring, *Verdeckte soziale Netzwerke*, 103–17; Friedrich, "Er ist gemein zu unseren Freunden," 97–109; Andreas-Friedrich, *Berlin Underground, 1938–1945*.

78. The savings were gathered to provide for those in hiding; the "high stakes" referred to the high risk that members took on; see Schieb-Samizadeh (1991), "Die Gemeinschaft für Frieden und Aufbau," 192.

79. Schieb-Samizadeh (1993), "Die Gemeinschaft für Frieden und Aufbau," 37–81; and Schieb-Samizadeh (1991), "Die Gemeinschaft für Frieden und Aufbau," 189–222. Werner Scharff went into hiding in 1943; he was arrested and put in Theresienstadt in July 1943. From there, he managed to flee together with his girlfriend, Fancia Grün, and return to Berlin, where he came into contact with Hans Winkler. Werner Scharff was arrested in October 1944 and shot in the Sachsenhausen concentration camp in March 1945. Schieb-Samizadeh (1991), "Die Gemeinschaft für Frieden und Aufbau," 216–19.

80. Zahn, "Nicht mitgehen," 169. On Edith Wolff, see ibid., 165–73; Schwersenz and Wolff, "Jüdische Jugend im Untergrund."

81. On Franz Kaufmann, see Rudolph, *Hilfe beim Sprung ins Nichts*, 55–70; Schönhaus, *The Forger*, 92–162; Düring, *Verdeckte soziale Netzwerke*.

82. Schönhaus, *The Forger*, 135–62.

83. Andreas-Friedrich, *Berlin Underground, 1938–1945*, 83–84.

84. Jalowicz Simon, *Underground in Berlin*, 232.

85. Lovenheim, *Survival in the Shadows*, 103.

86. For some examples, see Beer, *Die Banaliät des Guten*, 153; and Lutjens, *Submerged on the Surface*, 135–46.

87. Behar, "*Versprich mir, dass Du am Leben bleibst*," 126–27. On the *Verwarier*, see also chapter 6.

88. Jalowicz Simon, *Underground in Berlin*, 3–8.

89. Ibid., 99.

90. Degen, *Nicht alle waren Mörder*, 47–48; Friedlander, *"Try to Make Your Life,"* 120, 144.

91. Orbach and Orbach-Smith, *Soaring Underground*, 80.

92. Ibid., 121; Behrend-Rosenfeld and Rosenfeld, *Leben in zwei Welten*, 232.

93. Schwersenz and Wolff, "Jüdische Jugend im Untergrund," 93–94.

94. Lotte Bamberg was subsequently deferred from the transport to Riga in January 1942; see Bamberg, *Erinnerung ans Dritte Reich*, 803.

95. Jan Grabowski attributes this statement to Marek Edelman, one of the surviving leaders of the Warsaw ghetto uprising: "In order to survive, Jews needed money, 'good' (Gentile) looks and reliable and trustworthy acquaintances on the 'Aryan side.'" Grabowski, *Rescue for Money*, 8. Even if the basic conditions for going underground in Poland were different, these factors also helped in Germany; on this, see Lutjens, *Submerged on the Surface*, 86–88; Kaplan, *Between Dignity and Despair*, 204–05.

96. Anonymous, "Complaint of a Jewish Survivor against Allied Occupation Authorities, 1946," 3, AWL, Gale Primary Sources, Archives Unbound, Testaments to the Holocaust. Similarly, Heskel, "Our Underground Life in Berlin During the War," 7, ibid.

97. Wolffenstein, *Erinnerungen*, 66; van Laak, *Die Nazis nannten sie Sara*, 181.

98. Schoppmann, "Die 'Fabrikaktion' in Berlin," 143.

99. Wolffenstein, *Erinnerungen*, 47.

100. Friedlander, *"Try to Make Your Life,"* 95.

101. Düring, *Verdeckte soziale Netzwerke*, 99.

102. Jalowicz Simon, *Underground in Berlin*, 196, 201.

103. Lutjens, *Submerged on the Surface*, 95, 215, 220.

104. Ibid., 215, 220.

105. Raggam-Blesch, "Mischlinge' und 'Geltungsjuden," 83.

106. Tausendfreund, *Erzwungener Verrat*, 211. On the "Vienna methods," see ibid., 211–39. On the "Vienna model," see Safrian, *Eichmann's Men*, 14–38.

107. Tausendfreund, *Erzwungener Verrat*, 237.

108. Löw, "Die frühen Deportationen," 60–61, 71. On the early deportations from Vienna, see Moser, *Nisko*; Safrian, *Eichmann's Men*, 46–58.

109. On statistics regarding mixed marriages and *Geltungsjuden*, see Bukey, *Jews and Intermarriage*, 148–49.

110. On the number of people deported from Vienna, see Gottwaldt and Schulle, *Die "Judendeportationen" aus dem Deutschen Reich*, 444–67.

111. Safrian, *Eichmann's Men*, 121.

112. Ungar-Klein, *Schattenexistenz*, 97, lists a figure of 1,634 U-boats in Vienna. Older estimates on the number of U-boats who survived in all of Austria range from at least 600 to 750 people. See Moser, "Jewish *U-Boote* in Austria," 54; Königseder, "Österreich," 229.

113. Moser, "Jewish *U-Boote* in Austria," 59.

114. Including Margarete Sterneck (see chapter 6) and Edith Hahn-Beer (see chapter 8).

115. Ungar-Klein, *Schattenexistenz*, 160–62.

116. Ibid., 104, 107.

117. Königseder, "Österreich," 229.

118. On the situation in Berlin and specifically on the dangers for the U-boats, see Lutjens, *Submerged on the Surface*, 89–90, 168–75; Lovenheim, *Survival in the Shadows*, 145–59.

119. Croes and Kosmala, "Facing Deportation," 142. There are no estimates of how many U-boats died as a result of the air war.

120. Ungar-Klein, *Schattenexistenz*, 326.

121. Richardi, *Bomber über München*, 258–74. On the air war, see Süß, *Tod aus der Luft*.
122. Strnad, *Zwischenstation "Judensiedlung,"* 141.
123. Geismar to Heusler, March 25, 2010, StadtAM, Judaica, Mem. 34.
124. On Geismar and Nussbaum, see Macek, "Walter Geismar," 160–63.
125. Affidavit, n.d., BLEA, EG 65146.
126. Themal, "Meine Erlebnisse waehrend der Zeit der Judenverfolgungen in Deutschland," 5, AWL, Gale Primary Sources, Archives Unbound, Testaments to the Holocaust; Jalowicz Simon, *Underground in Berlin*, 200–201.
127. Meyer, "A conto Zukunft," 218.
128. Ibid., 216.
129. Ibid., 219.
130. Lewyn and Saltzmann Lewyn, *On the Run*, 136.
131. Themal, "Meine Erlebnisse waehrend der Zeit der Judenverfolgungen in Deutschland," 6–7, AWL, Gale Primary Sources, Archives Unbound, Testaments to the Holocaust.
132. Kaplan, *Between Dignity and Despair*, 209.
133. Bonavita, *Mit falschem Pass*, 133–34.
134. Klemperer, *I Will Bear Witness*, vol. 2: 1942–45, 404, 415–16 (February 13 and 19, 1945). See also Brenner, *Das Lied ist aus*, 86–92.
135. Benz, "Gegenleistungen," 224.
136. Drach, "Deportations from Berlin," 7, AWL, Gale Primary Sources, Archives Unbound, Testaments to the Holocaust.
137. Strnad, *Privileg Mischehe*, 264–69.
138. Affidavit by Elfriede Seitz, August 29, 1952, BayHStA, LEA 34411 (BEG 28702).
139. Affidavit by Alois Rauch, August 20, 1952, ibid.; he joined the party on May 1, 1933, membership no. 3212322, BArchB, BDC 00029, Rauch, Alois.
140. Affidavit by Elfriede Seitz, August 29, 1952, BayHStA, LEA 34411 (BEG 28702).
141. Franz Gerlach to Hilde Dennis, November 5, 1945, StadtAM, Judaica, Varia 94. The letter has been published in Kastner, *Auf einmal da waren sie weg*, 29–33. See also Amtsgericht Ebersberg (Local Court), declaratory procedure, May 11, 1954, BayHStA, LEA 13085 (EG 39193).
142. Meyer, *"Jüdische Mischlinge,"* 238–41; Gruner, *Der Geschlossene Arbeitseinsatz*, 326–29; Gruner, *Jewish Forced Labor*, 93–101; Strnad, "The Fortune of Survival."
143. Strnad, ibid., 177; Meyer, *"Jüdische Mischlinge,"* 238–41.
144. Meyer, ibid., 239, mentions for Hamburg a figure of 1,088 conscripted for forced labor out of a total of 1,680 men who were called up. In Frankfurt, there were approximately six hundred to seven hundred people affected. Eichler, "Das 'Judenreferat' der Frankfurter Gestapo," 256.
145. Walter N., "Meine Gestapo Haft im Zwangsarbeitslager Tiefenort a. d. Werra, October 19, 1944–Easter 1945," StadtAM, Judaica Varia 46.
146. Ibid.
147. Schrey to the Munich denazification tribunal X, July 27, 1947, StAM, SpkA, K 939, Koronczyk, Theodor.
148. Gruner, *Der Geschlossene Arbeitseinsatz*, 305.
149. Interview with Richard Marx, February 14, 2014, and Widmann, "Die Kunst der Frechheit," 284–85.

150. Interview, ibid., and Widmann, ibid.

151. Interview with Richard Marx, February 14, 2014.

152. Ibid. and Widmann, "Die Kunst der Frechheit," 285.

153. Strnad, "The Fortune of Survival," 178.

154. Ibid.; and Lekebusch, *Not und Verfolgung*, 126–30, 380–81.

155. Strnad, "The Fortune of Survival," 178–79. It is unclear, however, whether the orders came from the Higher SS and Police Command (HSSPF) of Military District IV or the Reich Security Main Office (RSHA) in Berlin.

156. Lekebusch, *Not und Verfolgung*, 127, 129–30.

157. Middle Rhine regional group of Gegen Vergessen—Für Demokratie e. V. (Against Oblivion—For Democracy), "Projekt-Abschlussbericht," last accessed February 24, 2022, https://www.gegen-vergessen.de/fileadmin/user_upload/Gegen_Vergessen/Dokumente/Diverses/Abschlussbericht_Rettung_verfolgter_Juden_ManfredStruck.pdf.

158. Strnad, "Fortune of Survival," 180.

159. Ibid., 185; Gruner, *Der Geschlossene Arbeitseinsatz*, 328.

5. EVADING THE FINAL DEPORTATIONS IN FEBRUARY 1945

1. Meyer, *A Fatal Balancing Act*, 356; Strnad, *Privileg Mischehe*, 326–27. On the last deportations of February 1945, see ibid., 326–53.

2. Strnad, *Zwischenstation "Judensiedlung,"* 145, 182.

3. Klemperer, *I Will Bear Witness*, vol. 2: 1942–45, 404 (February 13, 1945).

4. Meyer, *A Fatal Balancing Act*, 356; Von der Heydt, "'Geltungsjuden' und jüdische Gemeinde in Berlin," 317.

5. Von der Heydt, "'Geltungsjuden' und jüdische Gemeinde in Berlin," 318.

6. Raggam-Blesch, "Alltag unter prekärem Schutz," 303.

7. Strnad, "The Fortune of Survival," 186.

8. Ibid.

9. Gottwald and Schulle, *Die "Judendeportationen" aus dem Deutschen Reich*, 466–67; Strnad, "The Fortune of Survival," 188–90.

10. Meyer, *A Fatal Balancing Act*, 350.

11. Strnad, "The Fortune of Survival," 190. On these last deportations from Munich see also Strnad, "Die Deportationen," 83-91.

12. Ibid., 88; Meyer, *A Fatal Balancing Act*, 357.

13 Statement by Clementine Grube and Minna Maier, October 25, 1950, StAM, Stanw. 29499/2.

14. Macek, "Werner Grube," 140–42. See also Freier, "Statistik und Deportation der jüdischen Bevölkerung aus dem Deutschen Reich, Deportationsliste München—Theresienstadt, February 22, 1945," last accessed March 31, 2022, https://www.statistik-des-holocaust.de/II35-SE. On Theresienstadt in 1945, see Hájková, *The Last Ghetto*, 235–37.

15. Strnad, *Zwischenstation "Judensiedlung,"* 178.

16. The Kammerer company managed to have nineteen of their forced laborers removed from deportation lists; sworn statement by August Kammerer, August 28, 1948, StAM, SpkA, K 558, Grimm, Gerhard.

17. The head of the district branch of the Reich Association of Jews, Theodor Koronczyk, asserted after the war that he managed to get roughly 450 Jews deferred from deportation; this number is very obviously exaggerated, as that would have meant he saved all of the remaining Jews in Munich. Minutes of the public session, statement by Theodor Koronczyk, October 29, 1947, StAM, SpkA, K 939, Koronczyk, Theodor.

18. Wertheimer, "Magdalena Schwarz," 449–50; Ebert, *Zwischen Anerkennung und Ächtung*, 208. On Magdalena Schwarz, see also Behrend-Rosenfeld and Rosenfeld, *Leben in zwei Welten*, 150–51, 190–202.

19. Wertheimer, "Magdalena Schwarz," 449–50; Ebert, *Zwischen Anerkennung und Ächtung*, 208.

20. Behrend-Rosenfeld and Rosenfeld, *Leben in zwei Welten*, 196–200.

21. Christians, *Amtsgewalt und Volksgesundheit*, 262.

22. Minutes of the public session of October 29–30, 1947, witness testimony of Magdalena Schwarz, StAM, SpkA, K 939, Koronczyk, Theodor.

23. Wertheimer, "Magdalena Schwarz," 450.

24. Ibid.

25. Wertheimer, "Kurt Schneider," 447.

26. Personnel file of Professor Kurt Schneider, StadtAM, Personalwesen 11030.

27. Wertheimer, "Kurt Schneider," 446–47.

28. Lamm, *Von Juden in München*, 347; Grossmann, *Die unbesungenen Helden*, 142–43.

29. Lamm, ibid.; Grossmann, ibid.

30. Witness testimony of Karl Rieger, June 1, 1955, BayHStA, LEA 22418 (BEG 12625).

31. Theodor Heller to the Munich local court, June 1, 1955, BayHStA, LEA 22418 (BEG 12625).

32. Rosa Vetter to the embassy of the State of Israel, June 22, 1970, Yad Vashem, M.31, file 0694.

33. Ibid.

34. Application for a concentration camp ID card, March 27, 1947, BLEA, BEG 14770, Vetter, Rosa. See also StadtAM, Biographical Memorial Book of the Jews of Munich, 1933–1945, entry "Weiss, Jeanette," last accessed March 31, 2022, https://gedenkbuch.muenchen.de/index.php?id=gedenkbuch_link&gid=1402.

35. Rosa Vetter to Yad Vashem, December 10, 1970, Yad Vashem, M. 31, file 0694.

36. Widmann, "Die Kunst der Frechheit," 282–83.

37. Ibid.; Macek, "Walter Geismar," 168.

38. Selig, *Leben unterm Rassenwahn*, 182.

39. Ibid., 183.

40. Interview with Richard Marx, February 14, 2014.

41. Widmann, "Die Kunst der Frechheit," 284.

42. Sworn statement by Justin Marx, February 16, 1953, BayHStA, LEA 25065 (EG 41968).

43. Ibid.; Widmann, "Die Kunst der Frechheit," 284.

44. Sworn statement by Justin Marx, February 16, 1953, BayHStA, LEA 25065 (EG 41968).

45. Selig, *Leben unterm Rassenwahn*, 183.

46. Wetzel, "Karriere nach der Rettung," 305–6.

47. Knobloch, *In Deutschland angekommen*, 31.

48. Weber, *Das Schicksal der jüdischen Rechtsanwälte*, 144; Knobloch, *In Deutschland angekommen*, 104, also mentions a work-related accident.

49. Geismar to Heusler, September 8, 2008, StadtAM, Judaica, Mem. 34.

50. Based on these recollections, see Wetzel, "Karriere nach der Rettung," 308.

51. Ibid.

52. Work log of Siegfried Neuland, BayHStA, LEA 2652 (EG 84999). The work log indicates that Siegfried Neuland worked for Kammerer until late April 1944. He confirmed this himself: Petition for recognition of damage to liberty, March 27, 1950, ibid. As he did not mention any other forced labor workplaces, it remains unclear where and how he spent the time from May 1944 to early 1945.

53. Neuland to the eye clinic at the University of Munich, August 4, 1955, BayHStA, LEA 2652 (EG 84999). He underwent another operation in late April. Siegfried Neuland was in the hospital when the war ended; see also Wetzel, "Karriere nach der Rettung," 308.

54. Kongregation der Schwestern der Heimsuchung Mariens, "Kloster der Heimsuchung Beuerberg: Gründung und Geschichte" (Convent of Salesian nuns Beuerberg: foundation and history), last accessed March 31, 2022, http://www.franz-sales-verlag.de/ovm/foederation/beuerberg.

55. For example, those who were given refuge by Karl Schörghofer, caretaker of the Jewish cemetery in Munich. This will be discussed in the next section.

56. See, for example, the report of February 17, 1961, BLEA, BEG 39359, or Kronheimer-Sinz, "Erinnerungen."

57. Witness testimony of Hedwig Schindler, October 20, 1954, BayHStA, LEA 24890 (BEG 11341); Amalie Surrer to the Central Filing Office for Compensation, November 24, 1948, StAM, WB Ia 4684.

58. Minutes of the meeting of January 24, 1955, testimony of Kurt R., BLEA, EG 75804.

59. Macek, "Judith Hirsch," 123.

60. Lisberger, "Die seelischen Schäden," 104–6.

61. Grossmann, *Die unbesungenen Helden*, 94–96; Weyerer, "Retter unter Einsatz des eigenen Lebens," 393–95; Fraenkel and Borut, *Lexikon der Gerechten*, 247–48.

62. Weyerer, "Retter unter Einsatz des eigenen Lebens," 393; Grossmann, *Die unbesungenen Helden*, 132–33.

63. Weyerer, ibid.; Grossmann, ibid.; *Neue Jüdische Zeitung*, March 9, 1956, Yad Vashem, M.31, file 0390.

64. Ibid.; Weyerer, "Retter unter Einsatz des eigenen Lebens," 393.

65. Vollmer to Schörghofer, May 2, 1945, Yad Vashem, M.31, file 0390.

66. Term of imprisonment, Vollmer, Karl, archive of the Dachau memorial site.

67. StadtAM, database of the Biographical Memorial Book of the Jews of Munich, 1933–45, entry "Vollmer, Karl."

68. According to Weyerer, "Retter unter Einsatz des eigenen Lebens," 394. However, there is no mention of this in the primary sources.

69. StAM, WB I JR 2122 and JR 2657, Vollmer, Karl.

70. Zeibig (General Building Inspector) to the city building office, September 6, 1940, and Johann Deininger (head of the Bavarian Peasants' League) to Fiehler, October 29, 1940, StadtAM, Jüdisches Vermögen 253.

71. Zeibig (General Building Inspector) to the city building office, September 6, 1940, StadtAM, Jüdisches Vermögen 253. On this, see also Haerendel, "Der Schutzlosigkeit preisgegeben," 115–16.

72. Dr. Schmid, lawyer, to the district president of Upper Bavaria, September 3, 1941, StadtAM, Jüdisches Vermögen 253.

73. Sales contract, January 23, 1942, StadtAM, Jüdisches Vermögen 253.

74. StadtAM, database of the Biographical Memorial Book of the Jews of Munich, 1933–45, entry "Schülein, Hermann."

75. Evidence 7b of Dr. Josef Cammerer, July 12, 1965, Yad Vashem, M.31, file 0390. For biographical information and details on the rescue effort, see also Florida Holocaust Museum, "Herta Pila and Salomon Pila oral history interview by Carolyn Ellis and Chris Patti, July 2, 2010," Holocaust & Genocide Studies Center Oral Histories, Paper 176, last accessed February 24, 2022, http://scholarcommons.usf.edu/hgstud_oh/176.

76. Florida Holocaust Museum, ibid.

77. Evidence 7b of Dr. Josef Cammerer, July 12, 1965, Yad Vashem, M.31 file 0390.

78. Sworn statement by Josef M., December 18, 1958, BLEA, BEG 44211.

79. Testimony of Kurt Kahn, August 21, 1950, StAM, Stanw. 29499/1. For biographical data on the Kahn and Schwalb families, see StadtAM, database of the Biographical Memorial Book of the Jews of Munich, 1933–1945.

80. Transcript of the preliminary investigation against Johann Pfeuffer: Questioning of the witness Kahn, Kurt, August 21, 1950, StAM, Stanw. 29499/1.

81. Klara Rambold to Yad Vashem, May 5, 1964, Yad Vashem, M.31, file 0390.

82. Transcript of the preliminary investigation against Johann Pfeuffer: Questioning of the witness Schwalb, Klara, September 4, 1950, StAM, Stanw. 29499/1.

83. Confirmation of the Jewish Community of Munich, August 23, 1949, BLEA, EG 37337.

84. Hearing, August 26, 1950, StAM, Stanw. 29499/1.

85. Minutes of the public session of January 14, 1949, Witness testimony, StAM, SpkA, K 558, Grimm, Gerhard.

86. Schwalb to the US military government, August 20, 1945, BayHStA, LEA 3245 (EG 85157).

87. Transcript of witness questioning Franz Xaver Schwalb, September 4, 1950, StAM, Stanw 29499/1.

88. Schwalb to the US military government, August 20, 1945, BayHStA, LEA 3245 (EG 85157).

89. *Neue Jüdische Zeitung*, March 9, 1956, Yad Vashem, M.31, file 0390. Grossmann, *Die unbesungenen Helden*, 133; Weyerer, "Retter unter Einsatz des eigenen Lebens," 394. In 1943, Schörghofer started paying rent for the nursery to the Munich tax office, which was responsible for the cemetery. The tax office generated considerable profit from the leasing of the arable land that belonged to the cemetery. This was also the reason why the cemetery on Ungererstrasse was not closed and sold, as was the case with many other Jewish cemeteries. See Kuller, *Finanzverwaltung und Judenverfolgung*, 178–80.

90. *Neue Jüdische Zeitung*, March 9, 1956, Yad Vashem, M.31, file 0390.

91. Vollmer to Schörghofer, May 2, 1945, Yad Vashem, M.31, file 0390.

92. Cahnman, "Die Juden in München," 446. On the two cemeteries, see Schubsky, "Jüdische Friedhöfe," 163–87.

93. List suggesting people to be honored by the city of Munich, n.d., StadtAM, Direktorium 3–18, no. 27, 50–7/13.

94. Lamm, *Von Juden in München*, 347; Rosa Vetter to Yad Vashem, December 10, 1970, Yad Vashem, M.31, file 0694.

95. Macek, "Judith Hirsch," 123. The two half-Jewish women were the daughters of the Jewish writer Alfred Reifenberg, who had found refuge in a small village close to the Alps. See undated investigation report, StAM, SpkA, K 558, Grimm, Gerhard.

96. Indictment, October 26, 1948, StAM, Stanw. 17413. StadtAM, Biographical Memorial Book of the Jews of Munich, 1933–1945, entry "Prölsdorfer, Heinrich," last accessed March 31, 2022, https://gedenkbuch.muenchen.de/index.php?id=gedenkbuch_link&gid=3310.

97. Paul, "Diese Erschießungen,"552– 55; Keller, *Volksgemeinschaft am Ende*, 262–68.

98. Paul, "Diese Erschießungen," 555; Strnad, "Fortune of Survival," 193.

99. Roseman, *A Past in Hiding*, 334.

100. Paul, "Diese Erschießungen," 558–59; and, in agreement, Keller, *Volksgemeinschaft am Ende*, 269.

101. Nerdinger, *Ort und Erinnerung*, 86.

102. On this, see Knoll, "Die Todesmärsche"; Mannheimer, *Spätes Tagebuch*, 114–15.

103. Statistics cited from Schwartz, "Death Marches," 136. The proportion of Jewish prisoners is known only for individual treks. See Schwartz, "Death Marches," 142.

104. Mannheimer, *Spätes Tagebuch*, 114–15; Knoll, "Die Todesmärsche," 208–9.

105. On this, see Weiße Rose Stiftung e.V., Projektarbeitskreis Franz-Marc-Gymnasium mit Schülern der Kollegstufe und des Arbeitskreises Politik und Zeitgeschichte unter der Leitung von Matthias Konrad und Heinrich Mayer, "Vergessener Widerstand." Resistenz, Verweigerung und Widerstand gegen den Nationalsozialismus in den Jahren 1933–1945 in Markt Schwaben und Umgebung; last accessed February 23, 2022, http://franz-marc-gymnasium.info/wp-content/uploads/2015/03/Vergessener-Widerstand_2.pdf, and Weiße Rose Stiftung e.V., Tätigkeitsbericht 2014, "Vergessener Widerstand," last accessed February 24, 2022, https://www.weisse-rose-stiftung.de/wp-content/uploads/pdf/Taetigkeitsbericht-2014.pdf.

106. Archive of the Dachau Memorial Site, DA Evakuierungsmärsche: Rettungsaktionen Bericht, A 3660, *Die Welt*, June 16, 2008, also online, last accessed March 29, 2022, https://www.welt.de/welt_print/article2108342/Chinas-Vater-der-Chirurgie-war-ein-Freund-Deutschlands.html. Qiu Fazu died in 2008 at the age of ninety-four in Wuhan.

107. Ergoldsbach Historical Study Group, "Das hätte doch jeder getan." English: Strasser, "Anyone Would Have Done That."

108. On other attempted escapes, see Zarusky, "Von Dachau nach nirgendwo," 55. As Zarusky shows, it is difficult to reconstruct the public reactions in towns the death marches passed through; ibid., 58–59.

6. DANGERS AND FAILED ESCAPES, 1941–1945

1. Beate Kosmala calculated the survival rate throughout Germany as roughly 26 percent on average; Croes and Kosmala, "Facing Deportation," 142.

2. Ibid., 124.

3. Tausendfreund, *Erzwungener Verrat*. On Frankfurt, see Meyer, *A Fatal Balancing Act*, 253.

4. Croes and Kosmala, "Facing Deportation," 141. Tausendfreund, *Erzwungener Verrat*, 288, assumes "at least several hundred" people.

5. The most notorious snatcher was Stella Goldschlag Kübler, who together with her later husband, Rolf Isaaksohn, denounced more than one hundred Jews. Stella Kübler had to account for her deeds in court after 1945; see Tausendfreund, *Erzwungener Verrat*, 142–52. In some cases, the snatchers helped Jews in hiding; see ibid., 114–24.

6. Ibid., 88–96.

7. Lutjens, "Vom Untertauchen," 60.
8. Ibid., Schoppman, "Rettung von Juden," 121.
9. Beer, *Die Banalität des Guten*, 167.
10. The actual number is probably higher. See, for example, the case of Sigmund Grauer, who lived in Munich until the fall of 1942. He died in Auschwitz in March 1943 but it is unclear where he was arrested. StadtAM, Biographical Memorial Book of the Jews of Munich, 1933–1945, entry "Grauer, Sigmund," last accessed March 31, 2022, https://gedenkbuch.muenchen.de/index.php?id=gedenkbuch_link&gid=3820.
11. Andreas-Friedrich, *Berlin Underground, 1938–1945*, 118–19.
12. On the Uncle Emil group, see Düring, *Verdeckte soziale Netzwerke*, 103–18.
13. It is not known how many German Jews in hiding died in their hiding places. According to Beate Kosmala, the Silent Heroes Memorial Center in Berlin knows of roughly ten such cases.
14. Künzel, "Erinnerungen," 340–41. Cammerer described how he met Fröhlich and the ensuing friendship in his letter to Yad Vashem, July 15, 1965, Yad Vashem, M.31, file 0396. For a more detailed account of this rescue story, see Yad Vashem, "Righteous Among the Nations: Josef Sebastian Cammerer," last accessed March 31, 2022, https://righteous.yadvashem.org/?search=Cammerer&searchType=righteous_only&language=en&itemId=4042997&ind=0.
15. Künzel, "Erinnerungen," 343. Josef Cammerer to Yad Vashem, July 15, 1965, Yad Vashem, M.31, file 0396.
16. Hans Fröhlich to Yad Vashem, April 30, 1970, ibid.
17. Confirmation of Josef Cammerer, July 12, 1965, ibid.
18. Josef Cammerer to Yad Vashem, July 15, 1965, Yad Vashem, M.31, file 0396.
19. Ibid.
20. Hans Fröhlich to Yad Vashem, April 30, 1970, Yad Vashem, M.31, file 0396.
21. Josef Cammerer to Yad Vashem, July 15, 1965, ibid.
22. Grossmann, *Die unbesungenen Helden*, 96, wrote that Gertrud Lustig committed suicide. Cammerer assured Gertrud Lustig's brother that his sister had died of natural causes due to her illness; Cammerer to Fröhlich, April 30, 1946, LBI, AR 25276, box 1, folder 25.
23. German Resistance Memorial Center, information from Beate Kosmala, September 26, 2013. For additional cases, see Kaplan, *Between Dignity and Despair*, 207–8; and Seligmann, "An Illegal Way of Life," 339.
24. Cited in Ungar-Klein, *Schattenexistenz*, 184–85. Square brackets in the original.
25. German Resistance Memorial Center, information from Beate Kosmala, September 26, 2013.
26. Cited in Roseman, *A Past in Hiding*, 291.
27. Concurring: Erna Rüppel (Solingen, Munich), Edith Hahn Beer (Vienna, Munich, Brandenburg), and Marianne Ellenbogen (Essen). See Roseman, *A Past in Hiding*, 292; Hahn-Beer, *The Nazi Officer's Wife*, 226; Sassin, "Überleben im Untergrund," 28 (https://www.gedenkbuch-wuppertal.de/sites/default/files/doc/ueberleben-im-untergrund-die-kinderaerztin-dr-erna-rueppel-1895-1970-von-horst-sassin.pdf). See also Kaplan, *Between Dignity and Despair*, 207.
28. Confirmation of Josef Cammerer, July 12, 1965, Yad Vashem, M.31, file 0396.
29. Letter of Hans Fröhlich to Yad Vashem, April 30, 1970, ibid.
30. Evidence 7b of Dr. Cammerer, July 12, 1965, ibid.
31. Letter of Hans Fröhlich to Yad Vashem, April 30, 1970, ibid.
32. Cammerer to Alcalay, August 6, 1965, ibid.

33. Cammerer to Alcalay, December 21, 1963, Yad Vashem, M.31, file 0396.

34. Möllmann, "Der Opernsänger Berthold Sterneck," 150.

35. Ibid., 155.

36. Ibid., 153.

37. Ibid., 150. Transport lists from the Munich Gestapo, 1.2.1.1./11194697, Arolsen Archives and USHMM, ITS Digital Archive.

38. Möllmann, "Der Opernsänger Berthold Sterneck," 154.

39. Röhm and Thierfelder, *Juden, Christen, Deutsche*, vol. 4.1, 205.

40. Ibid., 207.

41. Ibid.; Möllmann, "Der Opernsänger Berthold Sterneck," 154.

42. Dr. Margarete Hoffer to the Bavarian State Compensation Office, March 7, 1958, BayHStA, LEA 36498 (EG 76247); see also Röhm and Thierfelder, *Juden, Christen, Deutsche*, vol. 4.1, 208.

43. Röhm and Thierfelder, ibid., 207; and Dr. Margarete Hoffer to the Bavarian State Compensation Office, March 7, 1958, BayHStA, LEA 36498 (EG 76247).

44. Hahn Beer, *The Nazi Officer's Wife*, 226–27. Leonie Frankenstein, too, gave birth to a child while living under an assumed identity in Brandenburg; see Frankenstein, "Ich habe eigentlich nie Angst gehabt," 102. Sidonie Rottenberg gave birth to a son in Vienna; see Ungar-Klein, *Schattenexistenz*, 187.

45. Jalowicz Simon, *Underground in Berlin*, 104–6.

46. Aleksiun, "Gender and the Daily Lives of Jews in Hiding," 49–50.

47. Declaration to the Chief Financial Officer, June 21, 1944, StAM, OfD 8875.

48. Siegfried Neuland to the Central Filing Office Bad Nauheim, November 26, 1946, StAM, WB I a 2387.

49. Kingreen, "Die Aktion zur kalten Erledigung der Mischehen," 187–201.

50. Ibid., 190–91. The arrest of Jewish spouses in the Hesse-Nassau Gau was largely discontinued in June 1943 on pressure from Berlin; ibid., 201.

51. Ibid., 191.

52. Elsie Kühn-Leitz, cited in Ebertz and Ebertz, *Die jüdischen Familien in Wetzlar*, 218. See also Porezag, *Als aus Nachbarn Juden wurden*, 152. See also Smith, *Elsie's War*.

53. Porezag, *Ernst Leitz aus Wetzlar*, 76–77.

54. Penalty order, August 3, 1943, StAM, AG 47166, Bocks, Elisabeth.

55. Report by Elsie Kühn-Leitz, in Ebertz und Ebertz, *Die jüdischen Familien in Wetzlar*, 219.

56. Penalty order, August 3, 1943, StAM, AG 47166, Bocks, Elisabeth.

57. Ebertz and Ebertz, *Die jüdischen Familien in Wetzlar*, 220.

58. Porezag, *Als aus Nachbarn Juden wurden*, 155–56.

59. Ibid.

60. Ibid., 156.

61. Kosmala, "Mißglückte Hilfe," 207; Kosmala, "Resistance to the Persecution of Jews," 109; Benz, "Juden im Untergrund," 39.

62. Kosmala, "Mißglückte Hilfe," 207.

63. Ibid.

64. Ibid., 208; Benz, "Juden im Untergrund," 40.

65. Kosmala, "Mißglückte Hilfe," 212–14.

66. Moser, "Jewish *U-Boote* in Austria," 60–61; Ungar-Klein, *Schattenexistenz*, 224.

67. Kosmala, "Mißglückte Hilfe," 208.

68. Kosmala, "Resistance to the Persecution of Jews," 120.

69. Ibid., 122.

70. I would like to thank Beate Kosmala for this information.

71. According to Strnad, *Flachs für das Reich*, 51, the women performing forced labor there used this expression.

72. On the case of Elisabeth Kühl in detail, see Strnad, *Flachs für das Reich*, 75–76, and the Memorial Book of the Jews of Karlsruhe, entry "Elisabeth Kühl," last accessed March 31, 2022, http://my.informedia.de/gedenkbuch.php?PID=12%C2%A8name=335&name=2273&seite=4&suche=K. Biographical data cited from the Memorial Book of the Jews of Karlsruhe, information compiled by Jürgen Schuhladen-Krämer. I would like to thank Maximilian Strnad for the reference to Elisabeth Kühl.

73. This could not be confirmed because the Berlin Document Center has no records at all on Elisabeth Kühl, except for the file referenced below, which can now be found at the State Archives in Munich. There are indications that Kühl might have attempted to forge the membership card of her ex-husband; Nazi Party (NSDAP) district leadership in Rosenheim to the Munich Gestapo headquarters, November 11, 1941, StAM, Gestapo Leitstelle Schutzhaft (BDC Schutzhaft), Kühl, Elisabeth.

74. BArchB, BDC, NSDAP main membership file, Dr. Karl Busemann, membership number 6078718. Karl Busemann had applied for membership in December 1937. His membership was cancelled in 1940. No reasons were given. BArchB, BDC, NSDAP-Gaukartei, Herbert Kühl, membership no. 3463385.

75. BArchB, BDC, NSDAP-Gaukartei, Herbert Kühl.

76. Penalty order, January 17, 1942, StAM, AG 46987.

77. Bundesministerium der Finanzen, *Wenn im Amte*, 78.

78. Strnad, *Flachs für das Reich*, 76.

79. Memorial Book of the Jews of Karlsruhe, entry "Elisabeth Kühl," last accessed March 31, 2022, http://my.informedia.de/gedenkbuch.php?PID=12%-C2%A8name=335&name=2273&seite=4&suche=K; Strnad, *Flachs für das Reich*, 76.

80. Ibid.

81. Ibid.

82. StadtAM, Biographical Memorial Book of the Jews of Munich, 1933–1945, entry "Cosmann, Oskar," last accessed March 31, 2022, https://gedenkbuch.muenchen.de/index.php?id=gedenkbuch_link&gid=1524; and Cosmann to Landesamt für Wiedergutmachung, May 8, 1949, BLEA, EG 39426.

83. Testimony of Gertrud Hirschauer (Paulus), March 15, 1949, StAM, SpkA, K 545, Grahammer, Hans.

84. Witness testimony of Dr. Margarete Cosmann, October 7, 1949, ibid.

85. Ibid. On the Cosmann family, see also Behrend and Behrend-Rosenfeld, *Leben in zwei Welten*, 194.

86. Dr. Margarete Cosmann to the Bavarian Relief Organization for Those Affected by the Nuremberg Laws, December 10, 1948, StAM, SpkA, K 545, Grahammer, Hans.

87. Ibid.

88. Testimony of Gertrud Hirschauer (Paulus), March 15, 1949, ibid.

89. Dr. Margarete Cosmann to the Bavarian Relief Organization for Those Affected by the Nuremberg Laws, December 10, 1948, ibid.

90. StadtAM, Biographical Memorial Book of the Jews of Munich, 1933–1945, entry "Cosmann, Oskar," last accessed March 31, 2022, https://gedenkbuch.muenchen.de/index.php?id=gedenkbuch_link&gid=1524.

91. On the Swing Youth, see Kater, *Different Drummers*.

92. Detjen, *Zum Staatsfeind ernannt*, 201.

93. Ibid., 200–201.

94. Hearing transcription, Eugen Roth, March 4, 1943, StAM, Stanw. 6430. The files contain only a few totally apolitical caricatures.

95. Detjen, *Zum Staatsfeind ernannt*, 203.

96. Ibid., 202.

97. *Der Spiegel*, "Kennwort Georg," November 22, 1950, last accessed February 23, 2022, https://www.spiegel.de/spiegel/print/d-44451370.html.

98. Schilde, "Grenzüberschreitende Flucht und Fluchthilfe," 155–56.

99. Ibid.

100. Ibid., 157–60; Schoppmann, "Fluchtziel Schweiz," 206–8; Battel, *"Wo es hell ist,"* 197–210.

101. Behrend-Rosenfeld and Rosenfeld, *Leben in zwei Welten*, 191, 195. When Else Behrend-Rosenfeld's friends were scouting out various escape options in the summer of 1942, they rejected traveling from Munich to the Swiss border because they felt it was too risky.

102. Strnad, *Zwischenstation "Judensiedlung,"* 50–55; 131–33; Strnad, *Flachs für das Reich*, 117–19; Meyer, *A Fatal Balancing Act*, 258–66.

103. Strnad, *Flachs für das Reich*, 117.

104. Meyer, *A Fatal Balancing Act*, 259, 264–66.

105. Alfred Neumeyer, cited in Meyer, *A Fatal Balancing Act*, 258. Stahl referred to Hechinger as having been fostered by the Gestapo. Behrend-Rosenfeld and Rosenfeld, *Leben in zwei Welten*, 125.

106. Meyer, *A Fatal Balancing Act*, 258.

107. Ibid., 263–64.

108. Behrend-Rosenfeld and Rosenfeld, *Leben in zwei Welten*, 158–59.

109. Ibid., 171–74; Meyer, *A Fatal Balancing Act*, 264.

110. After the war, Wegner passed off the responsibility for Hechinger's deportation to Gau leader Wagner. Hearing transcription, Hans Wegner, February 20, 1954, StAM, Stanw. 29499/4. See also Meyer, *A Fatal Balancing Act*, 264.

111. Testimony of Theodor Koronczyk, January 30, 1951, StAM, Stanw. 29499/2.

112. Meyer, *A Fatal Balancing Act*, 152–53.

113. Strnad, *Zwischenstation "Judensiedlung,"* 132; Meyer, *A Fatal Balancing Act*, 265.

114. Hearing transcription, Hans Wegner, February 20, 1954, StAM, Stanw. 29499/4.

115. Witness testimony of Hans Wegner, December 28, 1950, StAM, Stanw. 29499/2.

116. Ibid.; hearing transcription, testimony of Hans Wegner, February 20, 1954, StAM, Stanw. 29499/4.

117. Strnad, *Flachs für das Reich*, 117–19, and Meyer, *A Fatal Balancing Act*, 265.

118. Meyer, *A Fatal Balancing Act*, 264–65.

119. Ibid., 269, 375–77; Strnad, *Zwischenstation "Judensiedlung,"* 50–53.

120. Meyer, *A Fatal Balancing Act*, 294.

121. Ibid., 267.

122. Ibid., 269.

123. Strnad, *Flachs für das Reich*, 118.

124. Vita (handwritten) of Marion V., BArchB, NS 9/15765.

125. Questionnaire on the implementation of the Editors' Law of October 4, 1933, submitted on February 15, 1934, StAM, Pol. Dir. 15286.

126. Account by Beate K., December 22, 1948, StAM, WB I a 4279.

127. Decision: party exclusion, August 24, 1938, BArchB, BDC, PK Johann V., and Lammer's letter to Wagner, May 25, 1941, ibid., R 9361I/40417.

128. Johann V. to the expert for race research at the Reich Ministry of the Interior, August 16, 1936, BArchB, BDC, R 9361 I/40417; decision: party exclusion; reasons, August 24, 1938, BArchB, BDC, PK Johann V., and Munich Gestapo to the director of the Foreign Organization (AO): Office for Return Migration (RWA), November 3, 1942, BArchB, NS 9/15765.

129. Account by Beate K., December 22, 1948, StAM, WB I a 4279.

130. Ancestry decision, June 25, 1942, BArchB, NS 9/15765.

131. Munich Gestapo to the director of the Foreign Organization (AO): Office for Return Migration (RWA), November 3, 1942, BArchB, NS 9/15765.

132. Witness testimony of Beate K., minutes of the public session of February 4, 1953, StAM, WB I a 4279.

133. Annemarie K. to the Denazification Tribunal (Spruchkammer) 3, October 12, 1948, StAM, SpkA, K 558, Grimm, Gerhard.

134. Account by Beate K., December 22, 1948, StAM, WB I a 4279.

135. Ibid.

136. Statement by August H., July 29, 1953, BLEA, EG 65147.

137. Benz, "Juden im Untergrund," 24. For more examples of these forms of exploitation, see Benz, "Gegenleistungen"; Neiss, "Herr Sturmbannführer." For a systematic analysis of the exploitation, see Schrafstetter, "Life in Illegality," 72–79.

138. Schrafstetter, ibid., 78.

139. Lutjens, "Ordinary Crime and the Persecution of Jewish Germans," 443.

140. Ibid., 433–34, 445–46.

141. See Schrafstetter, "Life in Illegality."

142. On *Verwarier*, or "custodaryans," a play on words combining *Verwahrer* (custodian) and *Arier* ("Aryan," non-Jew), see also chapter 4 in this book. On the terms *Judenfledderer* and *Aufbewarier*, see Barkai, "The Final Chapter," 384, and Schrafstetter, "Life in Illegality," 74–75. On *Judenfledderer*, see also Benz, "Juden im Untergrund," 24.

143. For a series of examples, see Schrafstetter, "Life in Illegality," 72–75.

144. For a typical example, see Barkai, "The Final Chapter," 385.

145. Else Krell, *Wir rannten um unser Leben*, 81.

146. Marcella Herrmann, *Aus Berliner Erinnerungen 1940/44*, 8, AWL, Gale Primary Sources, Archives Unbound, Testaments to the Holocaust.

147. Biographical data cited from BLEA, EG 120117.

148. Affidavit by Margot S., February 24, 1947, StAM, SpkA, K 384, Fahlbusch, Eduard.

149. Ibid.

150. Witness testimony of Margot S., August 27, 1947, StAM, SpkA, K 246, Cremer, Wally.

151. Ibid.; Witness testimony of Josef Bloch, Oberkommissar, August 27, 1947, ibid.

152. Cremer to the Munich Rural District Denazification Tribunal, July 31, 1947, ibid.

153. Affidavit by Eduard Fahlbusch, May 21, [year illegible], BLEA, EG 120117; affidavit by Margot S., February 24, 1947, StAM, SpkA, K 384, Fahlbusch, Eduard.

154. Witness testimony of Josef Bloch and Margot S., August 27, 1947, StAM, SpkA, K 246, Cremer, Wally.

155. Affidavit by Wilhelm Eder, July 2, 1947, StAM, SpkA, K 246, Cremer, Wally.

156. Schülein to Denazification Tribunal VIII, February 29, 1948, affidavit by Otto and Anny Jordan, April 14, 1947, StAM SpkA, K 816, Jordan, Otto.

157. Judgment, January 20, 1953, IfZ Archive, Gm 07.146/2. I would like to thank Marion Detjen for information about this case. On this, see also Detjen, *Zum Staatsfeind ernannt*, 322; and Schrafstetter, "Life in Illegality," 76.

158. Marszolek, "Denunziation im Dritten Reich," 103.

159. Lutjens, *Submerged on the Surface*, 98.

160. Kosmala, "Mißglückte Hilfe," 209–16.

161. Ibid. See, for example, Friedländer, *Nazi Germany and the Jews*, vol. 2: *The Years of Extermination, 1939–1945*, 518.

162. Archive of the Dachau Memorial Site, DA Deutsche Häftlinge, A 1493, List, Heinrich, files from the Hessian State Archive, Darmstadt, G 15, Q 83, police files Heinrich List.

163. Johnson, *Nazi Terror*, 366. Gellately shows on the basis of Lower Franconia that there, too, relatively many proceedings trace back to reports filed by the general population; Gellately, *Backing Hitler*, 134.

164. Johnson, *Nazi Terror*, 374.

165. Berschel, "Polizeiroutiniers und Judenverfolgung," 168–70, also indicated a high rate of Jews being denounced.

166. Jalowicz Simon, *Underground in Berlin*, 263, 277.

167. Declaratory proceedings, witness questioning, Emmy R., May 11, 1954, Bay HStA, LEA 13085 (EG39193).

168. Max Oeschey to the Bavarian State Compensation Office, February 2, 1957, BayHStA, LEA 22205 (EG 40389).

169. Witness testimony of Gerty Spies, March 24, 1949, StAM, SpKA, K 1338, Poller, Ernst.

170. Schubert, *Judasfrauen*.

171. Diewald-Kerkmann, *Politische Denunziation im NS-Regime*, 131–35; Dörner, "NS-Herrschaft und Denunziation," 58–61.

172. Johnson, *Nazi Terror*, 368.

173. Ibid., 370–71.

174. Diewald-Kerkmann, *Politische Denunziation im NS-Regime*, 127–30.

7. SPECIFIC GROUPS OF HELPERS AND THOSE THEY HELPED

1. Croes and Kosmala, "Facing Deportation," 118.

2. Hajak and Zarusky, "Verfolgung, Zerstörung, Neuanfang," 389.

3. Knobloch, *In Deutschland angekommen*, 31.

4. Ibid., 73–97. As Charlotte Knobloch recollects, she and her grandmother were both on the list for an upcoming transport to Theresienstadt. Her father succeeded in getting his daughter crossed off the list; ibid., 69. Wetzel, "Karriere nach der Rettung," 305, writes that Siegfried Neuland had evidently been warned by Theodor Koronczyk that Albertine and Charlotte Neuland were both on the deportation list for a scheduled *Alten- und Kindertransport* (transport of the elderly and children). He was told that he could cross one

off the list but not both, that either the grandmother Albertine Neuland or her granddaughter Charlotte would have to be deported. The grandmother evidently volunteered to go. Children who were younger than fourteen were generally deported with their parents or the Jewish parent. See, for example, Gottwaldt and Schulle, *Die "Judendeportationen" aus dem Deutschen Reich*, 269–70; von der Heydt, "Wer fährt denn gerne mit dem Judenstern," 74. Also, children with one parent who according to the Nazi race ideology was considered Aryan were usually not deported until later. It is possible that Siegfried Neuland was extorted for money or valuables in this way or that Koronczyk gave Neuland false information. There were also instances in which individuals who were actually not supposed to be deported at a certain time were mistakenly or arbitrarily placed on deportation lists.

5. The story of Charlotte Knobloch's survival has already been described numerous times. See, for example, Hajak and Zarusky, "Verfolgung, Zerstörung Neuanfang," 381–98; Knobloch, "Doch ich hatte die Tiere"; Wetzel, "Karriere nach der Rettung"; Knobloch, *In Deuschland angekommen*.

6. Croes and Kosmala, "Facing Deportation," 119.

7. Ibid., 118; Kosmala, "Rettung und Verrat," 70–72, 76–79. One of the best-known of these were actor Michael Degen and his mother; see Degen, *Nicht alle waren Mörder*.

8. Kosmala, "Rettung und Verrat," 65–72; Croes and Kosmala, "Facing Deportation," 118.

9. Kosmala, ibid., 65; Croes and Kosmala, ibid. It is uncertain how many children survived in monasteries and convents in Poland, for example. Nahum Bogner assumes that "the number is in the hundreds, not in the thousands." Bogner, *At the Mercy of Strangers*, 180; see also Bogner, "The Convent Children," 41–43, last accessed February 25,2022, https://www.yadvashem.org/yv/pdf-drupal/nachum_bogner.pdf. On hidden children across occupied Europe, see Dwork, *Children with a Star*, 31–110.

10. Croes and Kosmala, "Facing Deportation," 118.

11. Kosmala, "Rettung und Verrat," 62–63. On the *Kindertransports*, see, for example, Craig Norton, *The Kindertransport*; Benz and Aichinger, *Kindertransporte*; Curio, *Verfolgung, Flucht, Rettung*.

12. Knobloch, *In Deutschland angekommen*, 28–30.

13. The deportation of *Geltungsjuden* was not at all regulated up to May 1942. On this, see chapter 2; see also Schrafstetter, "'Geltungsjüdische' Jugendliche in München."

14. On the yellow star, see Kwiet, "Nach dem Pogrom," 614–31. As already shown in chapter 4, non-Jewish spouses in mixed marriages and male *Mischlinge* were conscripted starting in early 1944 to forced labor doing construction work for the Organization Todt. On this, see Meyer, *"Jüdische Mischlinge,"* 238–39. On privileged and non-privileged mixed marriages, see ibid., 30–31; Strnad, *Privileg Mischehe?*, 145–51; Kaplan, *Between Dignity and Despair*, 148–49.

15. Holzmann, "Woman Courageous," 19–36, StadtAM, Judaica, Mem. 22.

16. Holzmann, ibid., 121, StadtAM, Judaica, Mem. 22.

17. Ibid., 250.

18. Ibid., 357–58.

19. Ibid., 359.

20. Philipp, *Gerettet*, 12–13, 19.

21. Ibid., 20–22.

22. Ibid., 23.

23. Ibid., 26–28, 30.

24. Ibid., 24. Transcript of the hearing, April 2, 1948, StAM, SpkA, K 3558, Gailer, Leonhard.

25. Philipp, *Gerettet*, 33, 38.

26. Consulate of the Dominican Republic in Berlin to Gustav K., December 17, 1940, privately owned, Bernhard K.

27. Interview with Bernhard K., December 28, 2012.

28. Ibid.

29. Ibid.

30. Gudelius, "Die Jachenau," last accessed February 24, 2022, http://www.gudelius.de/jchronik.htm;see also StadtAM, Biographical Memorial Book of the Jews of Munich, 1933–1945, entry "Schwink, Elisabeth," last accessed April 4, 2022, https://gedenkbuch.muenchen.de/index.php?id=gedenkbuch_link&gid=8304.

31. Wetzel, "Karriere nach der Rettung," 308.

32. Ibid.

33. Knobloch, *In Deutschland angekommen*, 74–81.

34. Schreiber, *Versteckt*, 73–74.

35. Ibid., 74, 405; Marks, *Hidden Children*, 35.

36. Michalski, "Mein Vater konnte alles besorgen," 26; Michalski, *Als die Gestapo an der Haustür klingelte*, 59.

37. Interview with Bernhard K., December 28, 2012; Knobloch, *In Deutschland angekommen*, 77, 84.

38. Sworn statement submitted to Dr. Wilhelm Hoffmann, legation secretary of the German embassy in Montevideo, Uruguay, January 26, 954, BLEA, BEG 3766. On Denny F., see also Kitzmann, *Wagnis Widerstand*, 86–90, 128–33.

39. Mosbach, "Die Ohnmacht der Verzweiflung," 67.

40. Ibid.

41. Ibid.

42. Ibid., 67–69.

43. Ibid., 71–72. On Adam von Trott zu Solz, the Kreisau Circle, and the plot of July 20, 1944, to assassinate Hitler, see Hoffmann, *German Resistance to Hitler.*

44. Lamm, *Von Juden in München*, 344.

45. Ibid.

46. Sworn statement submitted to Dr. Wilhelm Hoffmann, legation secretary of the German embassy in Montevideo, Uruguay, January 26, 1954, BLEA, BEG 3766. See also Kitzmann, *Wagnis Widerstand*, 87–89.

47. Baier, *Liebestätigkeit unterm Hakenkreuz*, 97; Kitzmann, *Wagnis Widerstand*, 89.

48. Supplement to the petition for recognition of damages to body and health, March 3, 1958, BLEA, BEG 3766.

49. Schreiber, *Versteckt*, 405. On the reunification of families after the war, see also Cohen, "Starting Over," 64–67.

50. The literature generally deals with the psychological consequences for the children. Research is very rudimentary at best regarding how many children were hidden in Germany, as well as where they were and what their living conditions in hiding were like. On this, see Kosmala, "Rettung und Verrat."

51. Croes and Kosmala, "Facing Deportation," 119.

52. On the Netherlands, see ibid., 130.

53. Kosmala, "Rettung und Verrat," 72.

54. Bühler, *Der Kirchenkampf*; Schönlebe, "München im Netzwerk"; Baier, *Liebestätigkeit unterm Hakenkreuz*; Fix, *Glaubensgenossen in Not.* Whereas some of these were strikingly

critical of the stance taken by the two major churches, others displayed an effort to boast of having helped as many as possible. However, there were no clear-cut distinctions made between church aid and their representatives and institutions, on the one hand, and individual assistance by people who (might have) had religious motives for their actions, on the other. Bühler, *Der Kirchenkampf*, 258–73, contains a varied collection of stories and anecdotes, yet the motives of the helpers sometimes remain unclear. This definitely gives the impression that the main intention was to present as many stories as possible as having had religious motives. This pertains also to Leuner, *When Compassion Was a Crime*. In this case, countless helper stories are strung together, though often the author fails to offer any evidence or precise information.

55. Bühler, *Der Kirchenkampf*, 258.

56. Fix, *Glaubensgenossen in Not*.

57. Schönlebe and Bäumler, *Von ihren Kirchen verlassen*.

58. Büttner, "Von der Kirche verlassen," 47; Johannes Zwanzger, "Report to the State Church Council, Re: Support for Non-Aryan Jews, Munich, 25 Aug. 1945," published in Fix, *Glaubensgenossen in Not*, 188. When the German Christians (*Deutsche Christen*) movement developed, and Ludwig Müller was elected as the Reich Bishop, major parts of the Protestant church excluded converted Jews from their religious community. Röhm and Thierfelder, *Juden, Christen, Deutsche*, vol. 1, 190–98. On the debates on the exclusion of converted Jews within the Protestant church, see Röhm and Thierfelder, *Juden, Christen, Deutsche*, vol. 1 and vol. 2/I. On German Christians, see Heschel, *The Aryan Jesus*; Bergen, *Twisted Cross*.

59. On the Bureau Grüber, see Ludwig, *An der Seite der Entrechteten*, 15–86; Röhm and Thierfelder, *Juden, Christen, Deutsche*, vol. 3/I and 3/II.

60. Schönlebe, "München im Netzwerk," 62–63 (1,700); Röhm and Thierfelder, *Juden, Christen, Deutsche*, vol. 3/II, 294 (2,000).

61. Leichsenring, *Die Katholische Kirche*, 77, 191. On the *Hilfswerk*, see Leichsenring, *Die Katholische Kirche*; Röhm and Thierfelder, *Juden, Christen, Deutsche*, vol. 3/I and 4/I. On Margarete Sommer, see also Phayer, "The Catholic Resistance Circle in Berlin," 216–29.

62. There were connections, for example, to the Munich Caritas Association; Leichsenring, *Die Katholische Kirche*, 138–39.

63. Baier, *Liebestätigkeit unterm Hakenkreuz*, 149.

64. Schönlebe, "München im Netzwerk," 64–65; Fix, *Glaubensgenossen in Not*, 41, 189. State Bishop Meiser's attitudes toward Jews is controversial and increasingly viewed critically. This was apparent recently in the discussion on renaming Meiserstrasse in Munich. Landeshauptstadt München, *ThemenGeschichtsPfad*, 41. On Meiser's attitudes toward Jews, see Fix, "Landesbischof Meiser"; Röhm and Thierfelder, *Juden, Christen, Deutsche*, vol. 1, 75–83; vol. 2/I, 53–55; vol. 4/II, 285–96.

65. Schönlebe, "München im Netzwerk," 67–69.

66. Ibid., 69. On this, see Johannes Zwanzger, "Report to the State Church Council, Re: Support for Non-Aryan Jews, Munich, 25 Aug. 1945," published in Fix, *Glaubensgenossen in Not*, 188–92.

67. Baier, *Liebestätigkeit unterm Hakenkreuz*, 158; Schönlebe, "München im Netzwerk," 69.

68. Ibid., 120; Fix, *Glaubensgenossen in Not*, 58. For a list of visitors, see Zahn, *Hilfe für Juden*, 15.

69. Krauss "Zur Einführung," 16; Behrend-Rosenfeld and Rosenfeld, *Leben in zwei Welten*, 104. On Rudolf and Annemarie Cohen, see Schönlebe, "München im Netzwerk," 46–49; Zahn, *Hilfe für Juden*, 3–12.

70. Cited in Schönlebe, "München im Netzwerk," 89.

71. Cited in ibid., 28. The letter is reprinted in Volk, *Akten Kardinal Michael von Faulhabers*, vol. 2, Faulhaber to Bertram, October 23, 1936, 179.

72. Wirsching, "Mehr Nähe als Distanz," 213–14, quote by Faulhaber in ibid.

73. Schönlebe, "München im Netzwerk," 111–13.

74. Leichsenring, "Die Auswanderungsunterstützung," 112. According to Leichsenring, there were two lists: one with people who had been baptized before 1933 and a second one with people who were baptized between 1933 and 1937. The former was supposed to be preferred in the issuing of visas; ibid., 110. On the Brazil Operation, see also Leichsenring, *Die Katholische Kirche*, 154–60.

75. Schönlebe, "München im Netzwerk," 111; see also ibid., 29.

76. Büttner, "Die anderen Christen," 145–46. For Munich, see Schönlebe, "München im Netzwerk," 120–22.

77. Ibid. On this, see also Düring, *Verdeckte soziale Netzwerke*, 74–90. According to Düring, roughly four hundred people were involved in the largest network of the Confessing Church; ibid., 74.

78. Behrend-Rosenfeld and Rosenfeld, *Leben in zwei Welten*, 118.

79. Ibid., 213, 245.

80. Wollasch, *"Nachrichtenzentrale des Erzbischofs,"* 32. Luise Oestreicher, born April 12, 1910, was the daughter of the Jewish businessman Arthur Oestreicher, who had already died in 1929. Oestreicher and her two siblings lived with their non-Jewish mother. StadtAM, database of the Biographical Memorial Book of the Jews of Munich, 1933–1945, entry "Oestreicher, Luise."

81. See chapter 8; Wolffenstein, *Erinnerungen*, 58–59.

82. On Delp, see Saltin, "Alfred Delp"; Bleistein, *Alfred Delp*.

83. Luise Oestreicher to Ger van Roon, October 3, 1965, cited in Saltin, "Alfred Delp," 83. Unfortunately, no details such as names or family origin are mentioned.

84. Wollasch, *"Betrifft: Nachrichtenzentrale des Erzbischofs,"* 34–36.

85. Wollasch, ibid., 30–34; Schönlebe, "München im Netzwerk," 102–5; Borgstedt, "'Bruderring' und 'Lucknerkreis,'" 199–203.

86. Baier, *Liebestätigkeit unterm Hakenkreuz*, 97–98; Fix, *Glaubensgenossen in Not*, 191.

87. Röhm and Thierfelder, *Juden, Christen, Deutsche*, vol, 4/II, 283–85; Schönlebe, "München im Netzwerk," 86–87; Diem, "Wie wenig haben wir geholfen," 132–38.

88. Schönlebe, "München im Netzwerk," 87. On Lempp, see also Kitzmann, *Wagnis Widerstand*, 101–5.

89. Evangelische Kreuzkirche München, "Albert Lemp, 1884–1943, Verleger, Christ, Widerständler: Irmgard Meyenberg," last accessed February 24, 2022, http://www.albert-lempp.de/leben/isabellastrase-20/irmgard-meyenberg/. It is unclear precisely when Irmgard Meyenberg went underground, since Edith Holm and Irmgard Meyenberg moved in together at Isabellastrasse 20 in late 1942 and Irmgard Meyenberg officially registered as residing at c/o Holm, Isabellastrasse 20/III. That is, she did nothing (at that time) to conceal her place of residence. StadtAM, EWK 78, registration card. Irmgard Meyenberg was presumably half-Jewish and therefore initially protected from getting deported.

90. Evangelische Kreuzkirche München, "Albert Lemp, 1884–1943, Verleger, Christ, Widerständler: Irmgard Meyenberg," last accessed February 24, 2022, http://www.albert-lempp.de/leben/isabellastrasse-20/irmgard-meyenberg/.

91. Johannes Zwanzger, "Report to the State Church Council, re: Aid for non-Aryan Christians, Munich, 25 Aug. 1945," published in Fix, *Glaubensgenossen in Not*, 188–92.

92. Bühler, *Der Kirchenkampf*, 259.

93. Diem, "Wie wenig haben wir geholfen," 139.

94. Ibid., 139–40; see also Diem, *Ja oder Nein*, 132–34.

95. Armin Rudi Kitzmann compiled some documents and statements by Classen's family and secretary about the rescue efforts. See Kitzmann, *Wagnis Widerstand*, 90–94, 101–5. Classen's network also does not appear in the relevant literature on Switzerland: Unabhängige Expertenkommission, *Die Schweiz und die Flüchtlinge*; Stadelmann, *Umgang mit Fremden*; Picard, *Die Schweiz und die Juden*; Picard, "Die Schweiz."

96. Steckhan, "Was ihr getan habt," 180–205.

97. Ibid., 195–96.

98. Diem, "Wie wenig haben wir geholfen," 137–38.

99. Steckhan, "Was ihr getan habt," 198–99; and Schönlebe, "München im Netzwerk," 122.

100. Steckhan, "Was ihr getan habt," 199–202.

101. Ibid.

102. Schönlebe, "München im Netzwerk," 122.

103. Büttner, "Die anderen Christen," 145.

104. Ibid.; Schönlebe, "München im Netzwerk," 120–22.

105. On this, see Bonavita, *Mit falschem Pass*, 11–16.

106. Ibid., 15, 24–27.

107. Schaeffler, "Dr. Gertrud Schaeffler," 104.

108. Schönlebe, "München im Netzwerk," 115.

109. Ibid.; Schaeffler, "Dr. Gertrud Schaeffler," 104–5.

110. Ibid., 105.

111. Koppers-Weck, "Rettung einer katholischen Jüdin," 208.

112. Ibid.

113. Bühler, *Der Kirchenkampf*, 260, 265.

114. StadtAM, database of the Biographical Memorial Book of the Jews of Munich, 1933–45, entry "Borchardt, Karoline," last accessed February 24, 2022, https://gedenkbuch.muenchen.de/index.php?id=gedenkbuch_link&gid=939.

115. Schröder to Langenfass, November 2, 1941, in Bernard und Raulff, *Briefe aus dem 20. Jahrhundert*, 132–33; italics in the original. I would like to thank Pastor Armin Rudi Kitzmann for telling me about Karoline Borchardt.

116. Ibid.

117. Schröder to Langenfass, November 2, 1941, in Bernard und Raulff, *Briefe aus dem 20. Jahrhundert*, 134.

118. Ibid., 137.

119. StadtAM, Biographical Memorial Book of the Jews of Munich, 1933–1945, entry "Borchardt, Karoline," last accessed February 24, 2022, https://gedenkbuch.muenchen.de/index.php?id=gedenkbuch_link&gid=939. Karoline Borchardt had apparently been mistakenly placed on the deportation list to Kaunas since people her age (she was sixty-eight at the time) were not supposed to be deported at that time.

120. Report of church council member Leonhard Henninger for the one hundredth anniversary of the Inner Mission, 65, AIM, holdings: History of the Inner Mission.

121. Leichsenring, *Die Katholische Kirche*, 271.

8. TO AND FROM MUNICH

1. Wolffenstein, *Erinnerungen*, 26.
2. On their childhood, see ibid., 11–14.
3. Ibid., 14, 20–21.

4. Ibid., 28.

5. Ibid., 18, 35.

6. Ibid., 11, unfortunately not containing any details about her brother's fate.

7. On the circumstances of their flight, see ibid., 46–48.

8. Ibid., 55. The young graphic artist was Cioma Schönhaus. Rudolph, *Hilfe beim Sprung ins Nichts*, 124. On Franz Kaufmann and Helene Jacobs, see ibid., 55–70. See also Schönhaus, *The Forger*.

9. Wolffenstein, *Erinnerungen*, 55, 57.

10. Ibid., 57–58.

11. On Ellen Ammann, see Holtmann, *Ellen Ammann*. On her role during the putsch, see ibid., 229–32.

12. On the "Gralsburg," Rothenfels Castle, see Gerl, *Romano Guardini*, 164, 212–39. On Ammann's role and the confiscation of the castle in 1939, see ibid., 193–94, 244–46. On Quickborn, see also Binkowski, *Jugend als Wegbereiter*.

13. Sworn statement by Herr Heckl, June 13, 1948, StAM, SpkA, K 22, Ammann, Rolf (formerly Rudolf); see also Wolffenstein, *Erinnerungen*, 58, 66.

14. Wolffenstein, *Erinnerungen*, 58. On the mentioned stations of her flight, see ibid., 58–61.

15. Ibid., 62–65.

16. Ibid., 66.

17. Ammann to the Munich Denazification Tribunal X, June 2, 1948, StAM, SpkA, K 22, Ammann, Rolf (formerly Rudolf).

18. Schöler, "Totalitarismustheoretische Ansätze," 71.

19. Ibid.

20. Statement, political activities since 1933, n.d., StAM, SpkA, K 22, Ammann, Rolf (formerly Rudolf).

21. Statement by Eva Guttmann, n.d., BayHStA, LEA 14935 (EG 123883). On the story of Eva Guttmann, see also Grossmann, *Die unbesungenen Helden*, 114–19. On going underground and resurfacing, see also Lutjens, "Vom Untertauchen," 52.

22. Hahn Beer, *The Nazi Officer's Wife*, 156; Roseman, *A Past in Hiding*, 273, 275; Behrend-Rosenfeld and Rosenfeld, *Leben in zwei Welten*, 208; Krell, *Wir rannten um unser Leben*, 163–65.

23. Schönhaus, *The Forger*, 165–98.

24. Kosmala and Croes, "Facing Deportation," 124; Lutjens, "Jews in Hiding," 273–74.

25. Schwarzmüller, "Garmisch-Partenkirchen und seine jüdischen Bürger, 1933–1945," last accessed February 23, 2022, https://www.gapgeschichte.de/juden_in_gap_biographien/krohn_hans.htm.

26. Sworn statement by Anton Viehböck, December 16, 1948, BayHStA, LEA 5175 (EG 114032).

27. Bloch, "Gertrud und Margarete Zuelzer," 204–5. Gertrud Zuelzer survived Theresienstadt, but her friend Helene Marwitz was deported and murdered. I would like to thank Anna Hájková for the reference to Gertrud Zuelzer.

28. Sassin, "Überleben im Untergrund," 22–29, last accessed February 24, 2022, http://www.gedenkbuch-wuppertal.de/files/doc/ueberleben-im-untergrund--die-kinderaerztin-dr-erna-rueppel-1895-1970-von-horst-sassin.pdf. For biographical data and her story of survival, see ibid.

29. A couple in a mixed marriage from Odenthal reached Bavaria rather indirectly, whereby the wife took care of her husband, who was seriously ill. He died in 1943. In addition,

a Jewish woman from Bonn was hidden by her sister-in-law near Garmisch-Partenkirchen. Others who went from the Rhineland to Upper Bavaria were a half Jew and her husband. On this, see Middle Rhine regional group of Gegen Vergessen—Für Demokratie e.V. (Against Oblivion—For Democracy), "Projekt-Abschlussbericht," last accessed February 24, 2022, https://www.gegen-vergessen.de/fileadmin/user_upload/Gegen_Vergessen/Dokumente/Diverses/Abschlussbericht_Rettung_verfolgter_Juden_ManfredStruck.pdf.

30. Hahn Beer, "Johann Plattner," 44–45; Hahn Beer, *The Nazi Officer's Wife*, 151–52.

31. Hahn Beer, *The Nazi Officer's Wife*, 155.

32. Ibid., 215. Edith Hahn Beer used the "Aryan" certificates of the parents and grandparents of her friend Christl Denner.

33. Hahn Beer, *The Nazi Officer's Wife*, 286–88.

34. Croes and Kosmala, "Facing Deportation," 124.

35. On geographical Holocaust research, see Knowles, Cole, and Giordano, *Geographies of the Holocaust.*

36. On these issues, see also Schrafstetter, "The Geographies of Living Underground."

37. It can be said regarding France that there were far more attempted escapes from deportation trains in 1943 than in 1942. Meyer, *Täter im Verhör*, 251–63. On France, Belgium, and the Netherlands, see also Fransecky, *Escapees.*

38. Statistics cited from Heusler, "Verfolgung und Vernichtung," 180.

39. Kastner, *Auf einmal da waren sie weg*, 82.

40. Statistics cited from Voigt, *Zuflucht auf Widerruf*, vol. 1, 145. Precise numbers cannot be determined, as a substantial number of emigrants fled from there to a third country.

41. Schrafstetter, "Zwischen Skylla und Charybdis," 581.

42. StadtAM, Biographical Memorial Book of the Jews of Munich, 1933–1945, entry "Obarzanek, Samuel" last accessed February 24, 2022, https://gedenkbuch.muenchen.de/index.php?id=gedenkbuch_link&gid=8991; Schrafstetter, "Zwischen Skylla und Charybdis." On the fate of the Engelhard family, see Siegemund, "Zur Familiengeschichte," 316–20. The Rauch family of Munich first went to Genoa and from there to France. In September 1942, three members of the family were deported from the Drancy camp to Auschwitz; StadtAM, Biographical Memorial Book of the Jews of Munich, 1933–1945, entry "Rauch, Fanny," last accessed February 24, 2022, https://gedenkbuch.muenchen.de/index.php?id=gedenkbuch_link&gid=13295.

43. On the life of Irma Ortenau, see also Damskis, *Zerrissene Biographien*, 61–68; Ebert, *Zwischen Anerkennung und Ächtung*, 196–98; Koppers-Weck, "Die Ortenaus," 241–43.

44. Ebert, ibid., 196.

45. Ibid., 196–97; Damskis, *Zerrissene Biographien*, 65; Ortenau to Meier, May 4, 1954, BLEA, BEG 42220.

46. See Damskis, ibid., 65–66; Ebert, *Zwischen Anerkennung und Ächtung*, 197.

47. Ebert, ibid.

48. Ibid., 197–98.

49. Hametz, "Leben im Blut," 219–20.

50. Voigt, *Zuflucht auf Widerruf*, vol. 1, 280–84.

51. Koppers-Weck, "Die Ortenaus," 242.

52. Voigt, *Zuflucht auf Widerruf*, vol. 1, 312.

53. Letter from Irma Ortenau, petition for recognition of damage to liberty, October 10, 1956, BLEA, BEG 42220.

54. See Voigt, *Zuflucht auf Widerruf*, vol. 1, 292–312.

55. Letter from Irma Ortenau, petition for recognition of damage to liberty, October 10, 1956, BLEA, BEG 42220.

56. Ibid.

57. Sworn statement by Giovanni Savaldi, May 23, 1957, BLEA, BEG 42220.

58. Ibid. Unfortunately, nothing more is known about the lives of Hirschl and Savaldi.

59. Hametz, "Leben im Blut," 223.

60. Wedekind, *Nationalsozialistische Besatzungs- und Annexionspolitik*, 432.

61. Sworn statement by Giovanni Savaldi, May 23, 1957, BLEA, BEG 42220.

62. Voigt, *Zuflucht auf Widerruf*, vol. 2, 345–47. On the deportations from Italy, see Sarfatti, *The Jews*, 178–227. For a chronological and geographical analysis of the arrests, see Giordano and Holian, "Retracing the 'Hunt for the Jews.'"

63. Addendum to the petition for recognition of damage to health, November 1, 1956, BLEA, BEG 42220.

64. Voigt, *Zuflucht auf Widerruf*, vol. 2, 345. Only fifteen survivors returned; see Osti Guerrazzi, *Caino a Roma*, 75.

65. Osti Guerrazzi, ibid., 76–77.

66. Ibid., 78–105, 111.

67. Ibid., 115–21.

68. Addendum to the petition for compensation for damage to health, November 1, 1956, BLEA, BEG 42220.

69. Ebert, *Zwischen Anerkennung und Ächtung*, 198.

70. Grübler, *Journey through the Night*, 4–6. For biographical data on the Littner family, see ibid., xxi–xxii; and StadtAM, database of the Biographical Memorial Book of the Jews of Munich, 1933–1945, entries "Littner, Jakob and Katharina". In early October 1938, the Polish government passed a law, according to which Polish citizens who had been living outside the country for more than five years could have their citizenship revoked. The law, as well as stricter entry checks, intended to preempt the remigration or an increasingly feared mass expulsion of Polish Jews from Nazi Germany. The German authorities responded with the arrest and expulsion of thousands of Polish Jews. Many of them were long stranded on a strip of no-man's-land at the border between the two countries since the Polish authorities refused to grant them entry. On this, see Weiss, *Deutsche und polnische Juden*, 195–99.

71. Grübler, *Journey through the Night*, 7. The transport left Munich on October 28, 1938, and returned on October 30; see also Ophir and Wiesemann, *Die jüdischen Gemeinden*, 50; StadtAM, Biographical Memorial Book of the Jews of Munich, 1933–1945, entry "Hallerz, Moritz," last accessed February 24, 2022, https://gedenkbuch.muenchen.de/index.php?id=gedenkbuch_link&gid=5291.

72. Grübler, *Journey through the Night*, 10–11.

73. Ibid., 58–70.

74. Ibid., 82–85.

75. Ibid., 95–96, 106, 129. I would like to thank Anna Holian for the reference to Jakob Littner.

76. Statistics cited in Grabowski, *Hunt for the Jews*, 2–3, 248; and Friedländer, *Nazi Germany*, vol. 2, 632.

77. On the situation of Jews in hiding in German-occupied Poland, see Grabowski, *Hunt for the Jews*; Grabowski, "Rural Society"; Grabowski, *Rescue for Money*; Paulsson, *Secret City*, Aleksiun, "Neighbors in Borysław"; Engelking, *Such a Beautiful Day*; Mędykowski, "Modes of Survival."

78. Grabowski, *Hunt for the Jews*, 54. For an in-depth look at the conditions for going underground in occupied Poland, see ibid., 135–48.

79. Grübler, *Journey through the Night*, 88–89. Some of her letters were lost or stolen.

80. Specht, "Zerbrechlicher Erfolg," 147–48.

81. StadtAM, Biographical Memorial Book of the Jews of Munich, 1933–1945, entry "Kalter, Ernestine," last accessed February 24, 2022, https://gedenkbuch.muenchen.de/index.php?id=gedenkbuch_link&gid=6247.

82. Schrafstetter, "Zwischen Skylla und Charybdis," 586–87.

83. Kwiet and Eschwege, *Selbstbehauptung und Widerstand*, 145.

84. Behrend-Rosenfeld and Rosenfeld, *Leben in zwei Welten*, 257–58. The group around Luise Meier and Josef Höfler successfully brought a total of twenty-eight people across the border to safety. In May 1944, an escape failed, and Meier and Höfler were then arrested. Both of them survived the war in prison; see Schoppmann, "Fluchtziel Schweiz," 205–19.

85. Behrend-Rosenfeld and Rosenfeld, *Leben in zwei Welten*, 261–62.

86. Herbstrith, "Enge Freunde," 65–66.

87. Beckmann-Zöller, "Adolf und Anne Reinach," 81–82. On Edith Stein, see Berkman, *Contemplating Edith Stein*; Herbstrith, *Edith Stein, a Biography*.

88. Wendorff, "Meine Tante," 87.

89. Beckmann-Zöller, "Adolf und Anne Reinach," 83. On the oblation, see also Erzabtei St. Martin zu Beuron, "Oblatengemeinschaft Beuron," last accessed February 24, 2022, http://www.erzabtei-beuron.de/kloster/oblaten/index.html.

90. Beckmann-Zöller, "Adolf und Anne Reinach," 83; IfZ Archive, ZS 2424, Keller, Hermann, "Interview with Professor Harold Deutsch." On Keller, see Spicer, *Hitler's Priests*, 90–91, 262.

91. IfZ Archive, ZS 2424, Keller, Hermann, "Interview with Professor Harold Deutsch," 2–4. Keller evidently tried in 1939–40 to reveal the secret Vatican missions of Josef Müller ("Ochsensepp," "Joe Ox"), a member of the German military intelligence (Abwehr) who was involved in resistance efforts. Müller had probed for the conspiratorial group in the Abwehr whether, in the case of a coup against Hitler, the Vatican could help negotiate a peace with Britain. Admiral Wilhelm Canaris, also part of the conspiratorial Abwehr, was able to stop Keller at the last minute, and a short time later, the SD sent Keller to Paris; Deutsch, *The Conspiracy against Hitler*, 102–36; Müller, *Bis zur letzten Konsequenz*, 92–99.

92. Beckmann-Zöller, "Adolf und Anne Reinach," 83.

93. Ibid.; and Herbstrith, "Enge Freunde," 66.

94. IfZ Archive, ZS 2424, Keller, Hermann, "Interview with Professor Harold Deutsch," 20.

95. Beckmann-Zöller, "Adolf und Anne Reinach," 84.

96. Petition to the Bavarian State Compensation Office, March 31, 1951, BayHStA, LEA 29719 (EG 91493). Unfortunately, she made no remarks about the circumstances of her flight.

97. Fraenkel and Borut, *Lexikon der Gerechten*, 289–90; and Baum, *Widerstand in Auschwitz*, 66–68.

98. Fraenkel and Borut, *Lexikon der Gerechten*, 196–98. Meyer was the director of the Food and Agriculture Department in Zolochiv. The Wiener Holocaust Library, "Eyewitness account by Josef Meyer of his attempts to help Jews in Poland," last accessed February 24, 2022, https://wiener.soutron.net/Portal/Default/en-GB/recordview/index/105613; and JewishGen, "Yizkor Book Project, Altman, S., 'Haunting Memories,'" last accessed February 24, 2022, https://www.jewishgen.org/yizkor/Zolochiv1/zole029.html.

99. Isolated cases of help offered by members of the Wehrmacht are also known. See Wette and Haase, *Retter in Uniform*.

100. Fraenkel and Borut, *Lexikon der Gerechten*, 289–90.

101. Ibid.; see also Langbein, *People in Auschwitz*, 294–96.

102. Fraenkel and Borut, *Lexikon der Gerechten*, 289–90; Langbein, ibid., 639.

103. See, for example, Frankenstein, "Ich habe eigentlich nie Angst gehabt," 101; Orbach, *Soaring Underground*, 210–12; Lutjens, "Vom Untertauchen," 58; Kaplan, *Between Dignity and Despair*, 206.

104. Lutjens, ibid., 52.

105. Behrend-Rosenfeld and Rosenfeld, *Leben in zwei Welten*, 245. Else Behrend-Rosenfeld, for example, could not resist the temptation to go on an outing from Freiburg to Strasbourg.

106. Behrend-Rosenfeld and Rosenfeld, ibid., 250.

107. Especially the importance of remembering and passing on addresses of potential helpers and places to go is mentioned as a key element in numerous narrative accounts of former U-boats. Lewyn and Saltzman Lewyn, *On the Run*; Friedlander, *"Try to Make Your Life,"* 111–23.

108. Jalowicz Simon, *Underground in Berlin*, 238.

109. Vita, July 24, 1957, BLEA, BEG 56459.

110. Ibid.

111. Sworn statement, June 14, 1973, BLEA, BEG 56459.

112. Marriage certificate, November 25, 1942, ibid.

113. Vita, July 24, 1957, ibid.

114. *Mundfunk*, or word of mouth, literally "mouth radio," is a pun on *Rundfunk*, radio broadcasting.

115. Jalowicz Simon, *Underground in Berlin*, 86–88.

9. AFTER 1945

1. Grossmann, *Jews, Germans, and Allies*, 106.
2. Ibid.
3. Rosenthal, *Zwei Leben*, 80; and Schäbitz, "Banished from the Fatherland," 299.
4. Grossmann, *Jews, Germans, and Allies*, 243–45.
5. Königseder and Wetzel, *Waiting for Hope*.
6. Grossmann, *Jews, Germans, and Allies*, 97. See also Strnad, *Privileg Mischehe?*, 371–99.
7. On this important aspect, see Lutjens, *Submerged on the Surface*, 178–83.
8. Schieb, "How the Frankenstein Family Survived Underground," 290.
9. Lutjens, *Submerged on the Surface*, 179–80.
10. Ibid., 181–83.
11. Schäbitz, "Banished from the Fatherland," 307.
12. Ibid., 306–7.
13. Statistics cited in Strnad, *Zwischenstation 'Judensiedlung,'* 178.
14. Wolffenstein, *Erinnerungen*,66–67.
15. Schieb, "How the Frankenstein Family Survived Underground," 290.
16. Sophie Mayer, *Data der Geretteten*, September 3, 1966, Yad Vashem, M.31, file 0394b.
17. Berthold L., "Description of the process of persecution that compelled me to assume an illegal existence," November 7, 1953, BayHStA, LEA 2222 (EG 123263).

18. Ungar-Klein, "Überleben im Versteck," 38.
19. Holzmann, *Woman Courageous*, 413–14, StadtAM, Judaica, Mem. 22.
20. Wolffenstein, *Erinnerungen*, 67.
21. Hedwig Geng, "Bericht ueber Theresienstadt," 21, LBI, ME 183.
22. Holzmann, *Woman Courageous*, 428, StadtAM, Judaica, Mem. 22.
23. Ibid., 403–4.
24. Ibid., 416, 420–22, 433–34.
25. Transcript of a statement recorded in shorthand, submitted by Eduard Meyer on June 26, 1945, to the Munich Mayor's Office, StadtAM, Judaica, Varia 157/10.
26. Ibid.
27. Wetzel, *Jüdisches Leben*, 37–38.
28. Ibid., 38; Winstel, *Verhandelte Gerechtigkeit*, 28.
29. Winstel, ibid., 33; Wetzel, *Jüdisches Leben*, 39–40.
30. Auerbach assumed his position in September 1946. His predecessor was Hermann Aumer, who had a falling-out with the Allied Military Government and was therefore removed; Winstel, *Verhandelte Gerechtigkeit*, 29. On the Bavarian Aid Organization (Bayerisches Hilfswerk) and the State Commission (Staatskommissariat), see ibid., 28–30; Wetzel, *Jüdisches Leben*, 49–63.
31. Ludyga, *Philipp Auerbach*, 53.
32. Ibid., 51–54; Fürmetz, "Ein Fall für den Staatskommissar," 158–61.
33. Ludyga, ibid., 54.
34. Grossmann, *Jews, Germans, and Allies*, 97.
35. Aumer to Meiser, December 3, 1945, LAN, Bestand Landeskirchenrat, no. 2595, Pastoral care for non-Aryan Christians.
36. Meiser to Aumer, December 8, 1945, ibid.
37. Aumer to Meiser, February 16, 1946, ibid.
38. See Ludwig, *An der Seite der Entrechteten*, 140–41. Eugen Gerstenmaier, founder of the Aid Office of the Lutheran Church in Germany (Hilfswerk der Evangelischen Kirche in Deutschland), refused to incorporate the efforts of Grüber's aid office (Evangelische Hilfsstelle) to support former Jews into the Aid Office of the Lutheran Church. Consequently, the Central Committee of Christian Aid Societies for Racial Persecutees of Non-Jewish Faith in Germany was formed; ibid., 145–47. See also Hockenos, *A Church Divided*, 145–47.
39. Hermle, *Evangelische Kirche und Judentum*, 64–66.
40. Ibid., 159–60. On the activities of the Working Committee for the Lutheran Jewish Mission, see also Hockenos, *A Church Divided*, 158–59.
41. Hermle, *Evangelische Kirche und Judentum*, 160.
42. Faulhaber to the Military Government, June 14, 1945, *Akten Kardinal Michael von Faulhabers*, vol. 3, 12. I would like to thank Antonia Leugers for this information. In his letter, Faulhaber referred to Christians persecuted as Jews both as "baptized Israelites" and as "Jews."
43. Ibid.
44. Frau H. to Pollinger, May 31, 1946, DiCV, I/AR 121.
45. Frau E. to Jandl, July 10, 1946; Frau H. to Pollinger, July 2, 1946; Jandl to Frau E. and Frau H., July 13, 1946, ibid. The correspondence ended with the thank-you notes written by the two women.

46. On the founding of the new community, see Kauders, *Democratization and the Jews*, 41–42; Kauders and Levinsky, "Neuanfang mit Zweifeln," 185; Wetzel, *Jüdisches Leben*, 5–10.

47. Wetzel, ibid., 7–8.

48. Letter from Hedwig Geng, September 7, 1945, LBI, Hedwig Geng Collection, AR 1587, box 1, folder 1.

49. Wetzel, *Jüdisches Leben*, viii.

50. Kauders and Levinsky, "Neuanfang mit Zweifeln," 186.

51. Wetzel, *Jüdisches Leben*, 8. According to information from Charlotte Knobloch, many Eastern European Jews voted in 1952 for her father to be president of the Jewish Community of Munich since he had a Polish son-in-law; Hajak and Zarusky, "Verfolgung, Zerstörung, Neuanfang," 395.

52. Kauders and Levinsky, "Neuanfang mit Zweifeln," 188.

53. Ibid., 188–90, and Kauders, *Democratization and the Jews*, 45–46.

54. Kauders and Lewinsky, "Neuanfang mit Zweifeln," 196, 199.

55. Ibid., 199; see also Kauders, *Democratization and the Jews*, 46, 51–52.

56. Kauders and Levinsky, "Neuanfang mit Zweifeln," 197.

57. Ibid.

58. Ludyga, "Philipp Auerbach," 127.

59. On the trial against Auerbach, see Ludyga, ibid., 119–31; Kraushaar, "Die Affäre Auerbach."

60. Ohrenstein was initially convicted and sentenced to one year in prison, but he appealed the decision. The judgment was reversed in 1956, and in 1957, Ohrenstein received a suspended sentence with nine months' probation. See Balcar and Schlemmer, *An der Spitze der CSU*, 331.

61. Kauders, *Democratization and the Jews*, 49–51; and Kauders and Levinsky, "Neuanfang mit Zweifeln," 198.

62. Holzmann, *Woman Courageous*, 436, StadtAM, Judaica, Mem. 22.

63. Hajak and Zarusky, "Verfolgung, Zerstörung, Neuanfang," 393.

64. Margot S. to Keilhold, August 10, 1949, StAM, SpkA, K 246, Cremer, Wally.

65. Krauss, "Zur Einführung," 36, 38.

66. Weber, *Das Schicksal der jüdischen Rechtsanwälte*, 193.

67. Bavarian Aid Organization to Sigmund W., October 12, 1950, BayHStA, LEA 39369 (BEG 11408).

68. Welfare report, September 11, 1950, BayHStA, LEA 5514 (EG 10675).

69. On the conflicts regarding the Jewish community leadership, see BayHStA, MK 49560–49567 (formerly MK 9), and Kauders, *Democratization and the Jews*, 49–51.

70. Riffel, "Unbesungene Helden," 327.

71. Grube and Macek, "Erwin Weil," 151.

72. On this, see Wetzel, *Jüdisches Leben*, 84–85, 97–105.

73. Hajak and Zarusky, "Verfolgung, Zerstörung, Neuanfang," 392.

74. *Der Spiegel*, "Kennwort Georg," November 22, 1950, last accessed February 23, 2022, https://www.spiegel.de/spiegel/print/d-44451370.html.

75. Ibid.

76. Letter to the Bavarian State Compensation Office, March 18, 1955, BLEA, EG 69844.

77. Declaration by Felix B., July 20, 1954, BLEA, EG 65146.

78. Ibid.

79. Roseman, *A Past in Hiding*, 408.
80. Ibid.
81. Ibid., 407.
82. Ibid., 408.
83. See, for example, Bavarian Aid Organization (*Hilfswerk*) to the Bavarian State Compensation Office, August 14, 1950, BLEA, EG 1228.
84. Durst, "Eine Herausforderung für Therapeuten," 83–84; Brunner, "Gesetze, Gutachter, Geld," 58; Goltermann, "Psychisches Leid," 434.
85. On this, see, for example, Brunner, ibid., 50–57; Goltermann, ibid., 440–51; Goltermann, "Kausalitätsfragen," 276–80.
86. Von Baeyer et al., *Psychiatrie der Verfolgten*, III. On the importance of the book, see Brunner, "Gesetze, Gutachter, Geld," 55.
87. Von Baeyer et al., ibid., 19.
88. Sigmund W. to the Bavarian State Compensation Office, March 28, 1952, BayHStA, LEA 39369 (BEG 11408).
89. See, for example, Roseman, *A Past in Hiding*, 297–301, 409–10.
90. On this, see Ungar-Klein, "Überleben im Versteck," 39; Ungar-Klein, *Schattenexistenz*, 263–64.
91. Ungar-Klein, "Überleben im Versteck," 39; Ungar-Klein, *Schattenexistenz*, 263.
92. The following studies treat both camp survivors and some who survived in hiding: Von Baeyer et al., *Psychiatrie der Verfolgten*; Yehuda, "Individual Differences."
93. Muth, *Versteckte Kinder*; Keilson, *Sequential Traumatization in Children*; Delpard, *Überleben*; Marks, *The Hidden Children*; Schreiber, *Versteckt*; Frydman, *Le traumatisme de l'enfant caché*.
94. Schreiber, *Versteckt*, 66–67; Keilson, ibid., 53.
95. Keilson, ibid., 440; Schreiber, ibid.
96. Keilson, "Sequentielle Traumatisierung," 79.
97. Muth, *Versteckte Kinder*, 14–15. On the consequences for the children, see Schreiber, *Versteckt*, 30, 75.
98. Hefter to Auerbach, August 10, 1950, BLEA, EG 1228.
99. Petition for recognition of damage to professional advancement, September 13, 1966, BLEA, EG 4528.
100. Schreiber, *Versteckt*, 29–30; Cohen, *Child Survivors*, 132–36. In 1988, the "child survivors" started to form as a separate group of persecutees. In 1997, the World Federation of Jewish Child Survivors of the Holocaust and Descendants was founded. See World Federation of Jewish Child Survivors of the Holocaust and Descendants, "President's Message," last accessed February 24, 2022, https://www.holocaustchild.org/about/presidents-message/. On the story of its founding, see Cohen, *Child Survivors*, 141–48.
101. Meyer, *"Jüdische Mischlinge,"* 357.
102. Correspondence with J. S. Cammerer, LBI, AR 25276, box 1, folders 24 and 25. Cammerer and Fröhlich, who had met only once before the war, kept up their correspondence from 1946 until Cammerer's death in 1978.
103. Taube, "Errettung eines jüdischen Kindes," 344.
104. Wetzel, *Jüdisches Leben*, 338. Literature on Möhlstrasse has become quite extensive; see also, for example, Holian, "The Architecture of Jewish Trade"; Holian, "Die Möhlstrasse"; Crago-Schneider, "Antisemitism or Competing Interests"; Meier, "Der Schwarzmarkt in der Möhlstraße."

105. On Möhlstrasse as a "shopping center," see Wetzel, *Jüdisches Leben*, 338–42.

106. Ibid., 342–43; Crago-Schneider, "Antisemitism or Competing Interests," 169.

107. Wetzel, *Jüdisches Leben*, 343.

108. Crago-Schneider, "Antisemitism or Competing Interests," 183–87; Wetzel, ibid., 343–46.

109. Questioning of Karl Schörghofer Sr., January 10, 1948, StAM, Stanw. 19079. On the illegal butchering at the cemetery, see also *Neue Jüdische Zeitung* of March 9, 1956 (translation), Yad Vashem, M.31, file 0390.

110. Questioning of Karl Schörghofer Jr., January 9, 1948, StAM, Stanw. 19079.

111. Ibid.

112. Investigation report, January 12, 1948, ibid.

113. Ibid.

114. Ibid.

115. Ludyga, "Philipp Auerbach," 78–79.

116. Judgment, August 3, 1948, StAM, Stanw. 19079. Regional Court Judge Adalbert Gürthofer had been a member of the Nazi Party since May 1933, and from 1934 to 1938, he was a "supporting member" of the SS. Starting in 1940, he was a court martial counselor in France, the Netherlands, and elsewhere. StAM, SpkA, K 580, Gürthofer, Adalbert.

117. *Neue Jüdische Zeitung* of March 9, 1956, Yad Vashem, M.31, file 0390.

118. Ibid. Marian Gid, originally from Poland, went from Britain to Germany directly after the war to work as a journalist. A *Forverts* correspondent, he took over the *Neue Jüdische Zeitung* in 1950. Lewinsky, *Displaced Poets*, 45.

119. *Neue Jüdische Zeitung* of March 9, 1956 (translation), Yad Vashem, M.31, file 0390.

120. Kauders and Levinsky, "Neuanfang mit Zweifeln," 197–99. See also Kauders, *Unmögliche Heimat*, 166–69. These debates were also about the status of mixed marriages. Numerous representatives of the Jewish community feared that mixed marriages would be disadvantaged in the future. They argued that this was already apparent in the Jewish rest home, where the non-Jewish spouses in mixed marriages were turned away; ibid., 168; Kauders and Levinsky "Neuanfang mit Zweifeln," 198.

121. Ibid.; Kauders, *Democratization and the Jews*, 49–51; Details in BayHStA, MK 49567.

122. Pardoning of the cemetery gardener, Karl Schörghofer Jr., February 28, 1949, StAM, Stanw. 19079.

123. Weyerer, "Retter unter Einsatz des eigenen Lebens," 394; Fraenkel and Borut, *Lexikon der Gerechten*, 247–48.

10. POSTWAR ENCOUNTERS

1. Sworn statement by Sophie Mayer, May 15, 1946, StAM, SpkA, K 3643, Mayer, Paul. Parts of the document have been published in Schrafstetter and Steinweis, *The Germans and the Holocaust*, 168–69. Paul and Sophie Mayer were not related.

2. See StAM, SpkA, K 621, Hanisch, Stanislaus.

3. Transcription, Dr. Ing. Rolf M. Ammann, political activities since 1930, n.d., StAM, SpkA, K 22, Ammann, Rolf (formerly Rudolf).

4. Ammann to the Denazification Tribunal X, June 2, 1948, ibid.

5. Notification of atonement (*Sühnebescheid*) from the Denazification Tribunal (*Spruchkammer*) X, April 11, 1948, StAM, ibid.

6. Transcription, Dr. Ing. Rolf M. Ammann, political activities since 1930, n.d., ibid.

7. Ammann to the Denazification Tribunal (*Spruchkammer*) X, June 2, 1948, and sworn statement of Valerie Wolffenstein, June 16, 1948, ibid.

8. Statement, June 15, 1948, ibid.

9. Werner, *Kriegswirtschaft*, 99.

10. With almost twenty-nine thousand foreign workers at BMW in 1944, they made up more than 51 percent of the entire workforce. The turnover was 750 million reichsmarks; Werner, *Kriegswirtschaft*, 61. In the two Munich plants (Milbertshofen and Allach), there were a total of 11,632 foreign forced laborers in 1944. Both plants also deployed numerous prisoners from the Dachau concentration camp, 5,500 of them in the Allach plant in 1944. Statistics cited in Werner, *Kriegswirtschaft*, 187.

11. Ammann to the Denazification Tribunal X, June 2, 1948, StAM, SpkA, K 22, Ammann, Rolf.

12. Decision, July 16, 1948, ibid.

13. Ammann to the Denazification Tribunal X, June 2, 1948, ibid.

14. Benno Schülein to the Denazifiation Tribunal VIII, February 3, 1948, StAM SpkA, K 816, Jordan, Otto. On the information about Jordan's membership in Nazi institutions, see his denazification questionnaire of April 25, 1946, which is also in this file.

15. Affidavit by Dr. Benno Schülein, February 28, 1948, ibid.

16. Decision, March 13, 1948, ibid.

17. On the weaknesses of the denazification process, see Niethammer, *Die Mitläuferfabrik*.

18. Decision of the Munich Denazification Tribunal (*Spruchkammer*) VI, October 10, 1946, StAM, SpkA, K 633, Kammerer, Rudolf.

19. Complaint, September 12, 1946, ibid.

20. Transcription of a letter from Kurt J., September 14, 1946, ibid. Emphasis in the original.

21. Transcription of the testimony of Johanna G., August 27, 1946, and Hanna C., August 26, 1946, ibid.

22. Sworn statement by Hermann S., August 26, 1946, ibid.

23. Witness questioning, Hermann S., December 8, 1947, ibid.

24. Witness testimonies, December 8, 1947, ibid.

25. Sworn statement by Benno Schülein, November 22, 1945, ibid.

26. Sworn statement by Anton Geßler, February 1946 [no precise date], ibid.

27. Benno Schülein: "Meine Tätigkeit und meine Erfahrungen bei der Firma Kammerer," October 5, 1946, ibid.

28. Decision of the Appeals Chamber, December 8, 1947, ibid.

29. Ibid.

30. Decision of June 11, 1947, and of June 26, 1948, StAM, SpkA, K 833, Kammerer, August (replacement files).

31. Decision of the Munich Denazification Tribunal VI, June 11, 1947, ibid. Only the judgments (with reasons) are available, but not the individual witness testimonies.

32. Munich Appeals Chamber II. Senat, June 24, 1948, ibid.

33. Hedwig Geng, "Bericht ueber Theresienstadt," May 24, 1962, 17, LBI, ME 183.

34. Sworn statement by Robert B., July 23, 1954, BLEA, BEG 4735. The former operations manager Robert B. confirmed that a former forced laborer had to work under conditions that were hazardous to her health.

35. Judgments of July 7, 1947, and September 14, 1949, StAM, AG 58094.

36. Decision of July 7, 1947, ibid.

37. Decision and Reasons, August 27, 1947, StAM, SpkA, K 246, Cremer, Wally.

38. Judgment, December 17, 1948, ibid. In 1950, the fine was reduced to 4,000 marks, and the prison sentence was lifted. Written comment, July 24, 1950, ibid.

39. Mettig, "Der Münchner Gestapochef," 255.

40. Heusler, "Karl Fiehler," 133; Munich Documentation Center for the History of National Socialism, "Münchener Biographien, Karl Fiehler 1895–1969," last accessed February 24, 2022, https://www.ns-dokuzentrum-muenchen.de/en/events/details/?tx_ttnews%5Btt_news%5D=28&cHash=31d59dd675b914373995af91df3640b3.

41. Judgment of April 19, 1950, StAM, Stanw. 5464.

42. Decision of September 22, 1948, and of April 26, 1950, StAM, Stanw. 6430.

43. Niethammer, *Die Mitläuferfabrik*, 597.

44. Raim, *Justiz zwischen Diktatur und Demokratie*, 555.

45. Ibid., 556–57.

46. Ibid., 999–1000. Before general courts of law, according to Raim, the sentencing of the denouncer was "anything but successful"; ibid., 998. An assessment of the treatment of the denouncer by the denazification tribunals would require a systematic evaluation of the relevant files. Such an appraisal is still outstanding; ibid. For Munich, there are indications that denouncers received harsh punishments from denazification tribunals.

47. Raim, *Justiz zwischen Diktatur und Demokratie*, 951–52. On this, see also Eichmüller, *Keine Generalamnestie*, 265–84.

48. Grau, "Steigbügelhalter des NS-Staates," 30.

49. Minutes of the session, October 5, 1949, and letters from the lawyers Erhardt, September 21, 1950, and Stoeckle, April 8, 1949, StAM, SpkA, K 370, Ritter von Epp, Franz Xaver. On this, see also Grau, "Steigbügelhalter des NS-Staates," 30–32.

50. Wächter, *Die Macht der Ohnmacht*, 128–30.

51. Decision of February 7, 1949, Reasons of Presiding Judge von Dewitz, StAM, SpkA, K 370, Ritter von Epp, Franz Xaver. Emphasis and quotation marks in original.

52. Personal notes of General von Epp, n.d. [after May 1945], ibid.

53. Decision of February 7, 1949, Reasons of Presiding Judge von Dewitz, ibid.

54. Statement by Rudolf D., December 13, 1948, StAM, SpkA, K 1393, Reichhart, Johann. I would like to thank Martina Voigt of the German Resistance Memorial Center for telling me about this case.

55. *Die Zeit*, "Ich tät's nie wieder," October 30, 1964, last accessed February 23, 2022, https://www.zeit.de/1964/44/ich-taets-nie-wieder/komplettansicht; see also *Der Spiegel*, "Mit den Nerven herunter," April 23, 1949, last accessed February 23, 2022, https://www.spiegel.de/spiegel/print/d-44436112.html. On Reichhart, see also Ernst, *Der Vollstrecker*.

56. Witness testimony of Rudolf D., minutes of the public session of December 13, 1948, StAM, SpkA, K 1393, Reichhart, Johann. For additional biographical information about Rudolf D., see BLEA, EG 23333.

57. Decision of August 21, 1947, StAM, SpkA, K 1393, Reichhart, Johann.

58. Affidavit by Rudolf D., March 20, 1947, ibid.

59. Decision of August 21, 1947, ibid.

60. Witness testimony of Rudolf D., minutes of the public session of December 13, 1948, ibid.

61. Decision of the Munich Denazification Tribunal IV, December 17, 1948, ibid.

62. Judgment, November 30, 1949, ibid.

63. On this, see, for example, Ludyga, "Die Todesurteile"; Ledford, "Judging German Judges."

64. Hedwig Geng to "Meine Lieben," November 25, 1945, LBI, AR 1587, box 1, folder 1.

65. Grossmann, *Jews, Germans, and Allies*, 110–11.

66. Holzmann, "Woman Courageous," 428f., StadtAM, Judaica, Mem. 22.

67. Decision of the Munich Denazification Tribunal (*Spruchkammer*) X, October 16, 1946, StAM, SpkA, K 219, Buchner, Oskar.

68. Strnad, *Flachs für das Reich*, 91–92.

69. Witness testimony of Rolf Grabower, December 16, 1948, StAM, Stanw. 17856.

70. *Der Weg* 1:3 (March 15, 1946), cited in Grossmann, *Jews, Germans, and Allies*, 111.

71. Levi, *The Drowned and the Saved*, 45–46.

72. Ibid.

73. See, for example, StAM, Stanw. 29499/1-7 and Stanw. 17856.

74. See proceedings, StAM, Stanw. 17856. Ultimately, no main proceedings took place against the Gestapo staff.

75. Eichmüller, *Keine Generalamnestie*, 17–23.

76. Transcription, sworn statement by Gertrud Hirschauer, March 15, 1949, StAM, Stanw. 29499/1.

77. Witness testimonies of Margarete Cosmann, August 14, 1950; Kurt Kahn, August 21, 1950; and Siegfried B., August 25, 1950, ibid.

78. Witness testimony of Julius B., August 25, 1950, ibid.

79. Witness testimony of Kurt Kahn, August 21, 1950, ibid.

80. Affidavit by Margot S., February 24, 1947; statement by Eduard Fahlbusch, March 16, 1948; and decision of March 16, 1948, StAM, SpkA, K 384, Fahlbusch, Eduard.

81. Confirmation by Leonhard Henninger, January 4, 1947; and affidavit by Margot S., February 24, 1947, ibid.

82. Statement by Irmgard S., January 28, 1947, ibid.

83. Testimonies of Clementine Grube and Minna Maier, October 25, 1950, StAM, Stanw. 29499/2.

84. Petition concerning Hans Ebenbeck, Rosa Baumgartner, June 30, 1945, StAM, SpkA, K 322, Ebenbeck, Hans.

85. Sworn statement by Anna Westermayer-Rosenthal, January 6, 1947, ibid. Anna Westermayer was deported to Theresienstadt on January 14, 1944. Freier, "Statistik und Deportation der jüdischen Bevölkerung aus dem Deutschen Reich, Deportationsliste München—Theresienstadt, January 14, 1944," last accessed April 5, 2022, https://www.statistik-des-holocaust.de/II30-1.jpg.

86. Letter of Heinz Westermayer, January 5, 1947; and sworn statement, January 4, 1947, StAM, SpkA, K 322, Ebenbeck, Hans.

87. Letter of Erna Huber, May 5, 1947, ibid. On Ebenbeck, see also Kasberger, "Karrierewege Münchner Gestapobeamter," 218.

88. Judgment, October 25, 1949, StAM, SpkA, K 322, Ebenbeck, Hans.

89. Witness testimony of Rolf Grabower, December 16, 1948, StAM, Stanw. 17856.

90. Strnad, *Flachs für das Reich*, 94. On Grabower's ideas about discipline, see Grabower, *Wenn im Amte*, 83.

91. Witness testimony of Siegfried B., December 16, 1948, StAM, Stanw. 17856.

92. Transcript of the witness testimony of Siegfried Neuland, December 7, 1953, StAM, Stanw. 29499/4.

93. Decision, January 23, 1953; and minutes of the public session, May 31, 1950, StAM, SpkA, K 1316, Pfeuffer, Johann.

94. Decision of the Third Criminal Chamber of the Munich Regional Court I, October 8, 1953, StAM, Stanw. 29499/4; and the Decision of the Third Criminal Chamber of the Munich Regional Court I, April 29, 1954, StAM, Stanw. 29499/5.

95. Pfeuffer's first boss, Dr. Erich Isselhorst, was sentenced to death in France for war crimes and executed in 1948. Raim, *Justiz zwischen Diktatur und Demokratie,* 1133. His successor, Oswald Schäfer, was charged with accessory to manslaughter by the Munich Regional Court and acquitted. He received a short prison sentence for bodily injury; Eichmüller, *Keine Generalamnestie,* 22; Mettig, "Der Münchner Gestapochef," 254–56.

96. Minutes of the public session, October 29–30, 1947, witness questioning, Dr. Magdalena Schwarz, StAM, SpkA, K 939, Koronczyk, Theodor.

97. Questioning of Magdalena Schwarz-Bichlmeir, October 2, 1950, StAM Stanw. 29499/2.

98. Augsburg Regional Court, Judgment of June 8, 1953, file reference AK 207/51, IfZ, NSG database; according to the database, the files are missing, presumably destroyed. No main proceedings against Grahammer were introduced in Munich. In 1941, Grahammer transferred from the Augsburg Gestapo to Munich; see Kasberger, "Karrierewege Münchner Gestapobeamter," 201.

99. Kasberger, "Hans Wegner," 237.

100. Judgment, July 11, 1950, StAM Stanw. 17856.

101. Judgment, December 14, 1954, StAM Stanw. 29499/5.

102. Grossmann, *Jews, Germans, and Allies,* 108; Meyer, *A Fatal Balancing Act,* 370–71; Tausendfreund, *Erzwungener Verrat,* 261–78.

103. Orbach and Orbach-Smith, *Soaring Underground,* 335; see also Grossmann, *Jews, Germans, and Allies,* 109; and Lutjens, *Submerged on the Surface,* 103.

104. Grossmann, *Jews, Germans, and Allies,* 108; Tausendfreund, *Erzwungener Verrat,* 148.

105. Meyer, *A Fatal Balancing Act,* 371; Tausendfreund, ibid., 276–78.

106. Weiner to State Prosecutor Woerle, July 14, 1949, StAM, Stanw. 17856.

107. Strnad, *Flachs für das Reich,* 96.

108. Auerbach cited in Meyer, *A Fatal Balancing Act,* 375.

109. Ibid., 267–69, 375–77.

110. Meyer, *A Fatal Balancing Act,* 268.

111. Ibid., 375.

112. Written statement by Edith S., July 12, 1945; and transcript of the witness questioning, October 29, 1947, StAM, SpkA, K 939, Koronczyk, Theodor.

113. Minutes of the public session of October 29–30, 1947, witness testimonies of Kurt, Rolf, Julius, and Anna Kahn; Karl Schörghofer Sr. and Jr., ibid.

114. Minutes of the public session of October 29–30, 1947, statements of Theodor Koronczyk, witness testimonies of Katharina Baerlein, Kurt Kahn, Josef Schwed, Richard Riemer, Klara Schwalb and written statements of Julius Kahn, February 14, 1947, Hugo Jacob, April 14, 1947, Katharina Baerlein, May 8, 1947, ibid. See also Kasberger, "Hans Wegner," 241–42.

115. Minutes of the public session of October 29–30, 1947, witness testimonies of Otto Mösch, Leon Goldschmidt, and Hans Armin Schrey, ibid.

116. Minutes of the public session of October 29–30, 1947, witness testimonies of Richard Riemer and Oskar Maron, ibid.

117. On the problems connected with these sources, see Meyer, *A Fatal Balancing Act*, 376–77.

118. Decision of November 12, 1947, and decision of May 12, 1948, StAM, SpkA, K 939, Koronczyk, Theodor; Kasberger, "Hans Wegner," 236–37, 243–44.

119. Decision, with reasons, November 15, 1948; and transcript of the testimony of Magdalena Schwarz, November 15, 1948, StAM, SpkA, K 939, Koronczyk, Theodor.

120. Transcript of the testimony of Hans Wegner, December 28, 1950, StAM, Stanw. 29499/2. On the strategy of passing a share of the responsibility onto the Jews, see Meyer, *A Fatal Balancing Act*, 376–77; and Strnad, *Zwischenstation "Judensiedlung,"* 50–51. See also chapter 6.

121. See Levi, *The Drowned and the Saved*, 41–42.

11. COMPENSATION FOR SURVIVING U-BOATS, THEIR FAMILY MEMBERS, AND THEIR HELPERS

1. Notice of denial, June 17, 1953, BLEA, BEG 3196/EG 1220.

2. On this, see also Hockerts, "Wiedergutmachung," 183f. On compensation for victims of National Socialist persecution, see ibid.; Goschler, *Schuld und Schulden*; Goschler *Wiedergutmachung*; Winstel, *Verhandelte Gerechtigkeit*.

3. Grossmann, *Jews, Germans, and Allies*, 107.

4. Ibid., 112.

5. Kosmala and Croes, "Facing Deportation," 119.

6. Brenner, *After the Holocaust*, 42.

7. Winstel, *Verhandelte Gerechtigkeit*, 29–30.

8. Ibid., 30.

9. Ibid.

10. Ibid., 31.

11. Ibid., 30.

12. Goschler, *Wiedergutmachung*, 128. Law No. 35 on Creation of a Special Fund for the Purpose of Indemnification, August 1, 1946. Online at Bayerische Staatskanzlei, Bayern. Recht, Verkündungsplattform, "Law No. 35," *Bayerisches Gesetz- und Verordnungsblatt* 17 (1946): 258, last accessed February 23, 2022, https://www.verkuendung-bayern.de/files/gvbl/1946/17/gvbl-1946-17.pdf#page=1. On the development and the provisions of the law, see Goschler, *Wiedergutmachung*, 128–30; Winstel, *Verhandelte Gerechtigkeit*, 38–42.

13. Language used in the legal text, see "Law No. 35," *Bayerisches Gesetz- und Verordnungsblatt* 17 (1946): 258.

14. Goschler, *Wiedergutmachung*, 128.

15. Winstel, *Verhandelte Gerechtigkeit*, 39–40.

16. Goschler, *Wiedergutmachung*, 147–48; on its development, see ibid., 131–48; on its application, see ibid., 149–67.

17. Law for Compensation for National Socialist Injustice, Sec. 1(1), in Blessin and Wilden, *Bundes-Entschädigungsgesetze*, 1173. Online at Bayerische Staatskanzlei, Bayern. Recht, Verkündungsplattform, "Law for Compensation for National Socialist Injustice," *Bayerisches Gesetz- und Verordnungsblatt* 20 (1949): 196–204, last accessed February 23, 2022,

https://www.verkuendung-bayern.de/files/gvbl/1949/20/gvbl-1949-20.pdf. In the case of the deceased, the next of kin was entitled to compensation; see Sec. 13.

18. Non-Jewish DPs were entitled to apply, although it was never recognized that they were persecuted on grounds of religious beliefs or worldview; Goschler, *Wiedergutmachung*, 154.

19. Law for Compensation for National Socialist Injustice, Sec. 15, in Blessin and Wilden, *Bundes-Entschädigungsgesetze*, 1179. As of July 1952, due to a further implementation provision, forced labor in connection with wearing the yellow star was also recognized.

20. On this, see Pawlita, *Wiedergutmachung als Rechtsfrage*, 202–10; Goschler, *Wiedergutmachung*, 69–70.

21. Law for Compensation for National Socialist Injustice: Sec. 13 and Sec. 14, in Blessin and Wilden, *Bundes-Entschädigungsgesetze*, 1178–79.

22. Text of the law in Blessin and Wilden, *Bundes-Entschädigungsgesetze*, 1193–1237, online at Bundesanzeiger, "Federal Supplementary Law on Compensation for Victims of National Socialist Persecution," *Bundesgesetzblatt* 62, part 1 (1953), last accessed February 23, 2022, https://www.bgbl.de/xaver/bgbl/start.xav#__bgbl__%2F%2F*%5B%40attr_id%3D%27bgbl153s1387.pdf%27%5D__1592419095170. On its development, see Goschler, *Wiedergutmachung*, 286–98; Goschler, *Schuld und Schulden*, 189–93.

23. Text of the law in Blessin and Wilden, *Bundes-Entschädigungsgesetze*, 5–76, online at Bundesanzeiger, "Federal Compensation Law for Victims of National Socialist Persecution," *Bundesgesetzblatt* 31 part 1 (1956), last accessed March 22, 2022, https://www.bgbl.de/xaver/bgbl/start.xav?start=//*%5B@attr_id=%27bgbl156s0559.pdf%27%5D#__bgbl__%2F%2F*%5B%40attr_id%3D%27bgbl156s0559.pdf%27%5D__1647965442811. On its development and passage in parliament, see Goschler, *Schuld und Schulden*, 200–203; Hockerts "Wiedergutmachung," 182–85.

24. BErgG of September 18, 1953, Art. I, Sec. 1(2) in Blessin and Wilden, *Bundes-Entschädigungsgesetze*, 1193.

25. On this point, see also Riffel, *Unbesungene Helden*, 33; and Beer, *Die Banalität des Guten*, 305. Riffel and Beer have shown that a number of helpers who applied for compensation because they had been imprisoned as a direct result of their help for Jews were turned down; Riffel, ibid., 33–35; Beer, ibid., 307–10.

26. Blessin and Wilden, *Bundes-Entschädigungsgesetze*, 1201.

27. Ibid., 19–20.

28. Ibid., 15–16.

29. Notification of wrongful imprisonment compensation, August 16, 1954, BLEA, BEG 3196/EG 1220.

30. Notification of wrongful imprisonment compensation: Facts of the case and reasons for the decision, August 16, 1954, testimony by Meta L. and Stanislaus Hanisch, ibid.

31. Minutes of the session of the 2nd Compensation Chamber of the Munich Regional Court I on November 11, 1955, ibid.

32. Notification of compensation for damages to body and health, June 22, 1955, ibid.

33. See BLEA, EG 32176.

34. Edith S. to the State Compensation Office, June 5, 1949, BLEA, EG 32176.

35. Settlement, November 30, 1955, ibid.

36. Notification, March 5, 1956, BLEA, BEG 3766, including facts of the case and reasons for the decision, April 5, 1961, BayHStA, LEA 13085 (EG 39193).

37. Letter of Margot S., March 7, 1953, BLEA, EG 12117.

38. Note of Herr Troßmann, November 2, 1953, ibid.

39. Lawyer Hanns Dahn to the Bavarian State Compensation Office, September 4, 1954, ibid.
40. Decree of September 16, 1954, ibid.
41. Lawyer Georg Ott to the Bavarian State Compensation Office, October 14, 1965, ibid.
42. Letter of Margot S., December 1968, ibid.
43. Settlement, December 17, 1970, ibid.
44. Response to the complaint filed by Margot S., Memorandum of Herr Troßmann, November 2, 1953, ibid.
45. On the quality of the personnel, see Winstel, *Verhandelte Gerechtigkeit*, 122–24.
46. Certification of the Comite Uruguayo de Israelitas de Europa Central, Victimas del Nazismo, March 28, 1955, BLEA, BEG 11986.
47. Facts of the case and reasons for the decision, February 28, 1956, ibid.
48. Final judgment, December 1, 1959, ibid.
49. Notice of denial, June 26, 1961, BLEA, EG 65335.
50. Notification, April 13, 1953, BayHStA, LEA 39369 (BEG 11408).
51. Notice of denial, September 2, 1953, BayHStA, LEA 20771 (EG 4546).
52. Letter of January 12, 1973, BLEA, BEG 67271.
53. Notice of partial denial, June 17, 1953, BayHStA, LEA 202 (BEG 17295).
54. Assessment notice for compensation for wrongful imprisonment, October 1, 1952, BayHStA, LEA 16392 (BEG 6935).
55. Bachmann to the Bavarian State Compensation Office, November 6, 1954, BayHStA, LEA 202 (BEG 17295).
56. Bachmann to the State Compensation Office in Munich, June 4, 1956, ibid. On these issues, see also Winstel, *Verhandelte Gerechtigkeit*, 283–91.
57. Goschler, *Wiedergutmachung*, 151.
58. Winstel, *Verhandelte Gerechtigkeit*, 124.
59. Cited in ibid., 125.
60. Schrafstetter, "Von der Soforthilfe zur Wiedergutmachung," 322–26.
61. Ministerium des Inneren des Landes Nordrhein-Westfalen, Geltende Gesetze und Verordnungen, "Law on Granting Accident and Surviving Dependents' Pensions to the Victims of Nazi Oppression of March 5, 1947," last accessed February 24, 2022, https://recht.nrw.de/lmi/owa/br_bes_text?sg=0&menu=1&bes_id=4593&aufgehoben=N&anw_nr=2.
62. Ministerium des Inneren des Landes Nordrhein-Westfalen, "Law on Compensation for Deprivation of Liberty for Political, Racial, and Religious Reasons of February 11, 1949," *Gesetz- und Verordnungsblatt NRW* 3, no. 10 (1949), last accessed February 24, 2022, https://recht.nrw.de/lmi/owa/br_gv_show_jahr?anw_nr=6&parent_anw_nr=2&year=1949.
63. Klatt, *Unbequeme Vergangenheit*, 260–61. In the city of Hagen, thirty-one petitions were submitted by Jews for compensation on grounds of wrongful imprisonment; twenty-three of them were denied, ibid., 260.
64. Volmer-Naumann, *Bürokratische Bewältigung*, 131.
65. Klatt, *Unbequeme Vergangenheit*, 250–51, 260–62.
66. Marianne Ellenbogen to her lawyer, June 8, 1957, cited in Roseman, "It Went on for Years," 67.
67. Ibid., 67–68.
68. Feaux de la Croix and Rumpf, *Werdegang*, 21.
69. Hölscher, *NS-Verfolgte*, 58–59.
70. Ibid., 59.

71. Feaux de la Croix and Rumpf, *Werdegang*, 60.

72. Bukofzer and Radlauer, *Kommentar*, 13.

73. Ibid., 57.

74. Riffel, *Unbesungene Helden*, 44.

75. Ungar Klein, *Schattenexistenz*, 271. The text of the law is available online at Rechtsinformationssystem des Bundes, Dokumente, "12. Opferfürsorgegesetz-Novelle, March 22, 1961" (Austrian compensation law for victims of National Socialist persecution) *Bundesgesetzblatt für die Republik Österreich* 23 (1961), last accessed February 23, 2022, https://www.ris.bka.gv.at/Dokumente/BgblPdf/1961_101_0/1961_101_0.pdf.

76. Ungar Klein, *Schattenexistenz*, 272–73.

77. Ibid., 275. The text of the law is available online at Rechtsinformationssystem des Bundes, Dokumente, "21. Opferfürsorgegesetz-Novelle, November 11, 1970" (revised Austrian compensation law for victims of National Socialist persecution), *Bundesgesetzblatt für die Republik Österreich*, 89 (1970), last accessed March 23, 2022, https://www.ris.bka.gv.at/Dokumente/BgblPdf/1970_352_0/1970_352_0.pdf.

78. Winstel, *Verhandelte Gerechtigkeit*, 282–83.

12. U-BOATS AND THEIR HELPERS IN POSTWAR GERMAN SOCIETY

1. Riffel, *Unbesungene Helden*, 37–38; Grossmann, *Unbesungene Helden*, 11. Kurt Grossmann, Secretary General of the German League for Human Rights from 1926 until he fled in 1933 to Prague and then on to the United States in 1939. In New York, he worked as a freelance author for émigré newspapers. On Grossmann, see Mertens, *Unermüdlicher Kämpfer*.

2. See Grossmann, *Die Unbesungenen Helden*, 126. On Franz Herda's life, especially after 1945, see Von Weitzel, "Franz Herda (1887–1965)," last accessed April 10, 2022, http://www.christoph-von-weitzel.de/herda_2.html.

3. On the silence of the helpers, see Riffel, ibid., 29–32.

4. Wetzel, "Karriere nach der Rettung," 308.

5. Beer, *Die Banalität des Guten*, 304.

6. Riffel, *Unbesungene Helden*, 31–32.

7. Kingma, *Spuren der Menschlichkeit*, 37.

8. Roseman, *A Past in Hiding*, 409.

9. Jalowicz Simon, *Underground in Berlin*, 338.

10. See also Gudelius, "Die Jachenau," last accessed February 24, 2022, http://www.gudelius.de/jchronik.htm.

11. Ibid. Unfortunately, there is no mention of when or under what circumstances the plaque was installed.

12. Behrend, *Verfemt*; Behrend-Rosenfeld, *Ich stand nicht allein*. See also Krauss, "Zur Einführung," 39–40.

13. Krauss, ibid., 12, 40; Riffel, *Unbesungene Helden*, 31.

14. Kabalek, "The Rescue of Jews," 119, last accessed February 24, 2022, https://libraetd.lib.virginia.edu/public_view/x633f123t. See also Krakauer, *Lights in Darkness*, 8.

15. Andreas-Friedrich, *Berlin Underground, 1938–1945*; and *Der Schattenmann: Tagebuchaufzeichnungen, 1938–1945*.

16. Behrend-Rosenfeld, *Ich stand nicht allein*; see also Krauss, "Zur Einführung," 41. Andreas-Friedrich, *Der Schattenmann*; Krakauer, *Lichter im Dunkel*. Numerous printings and editions followed. See also Riffel, *Unbesungene Helden*, 30–31.

17. Riffel, ibid., 30–32. At the same time, however, many U-boats kept diaries or made notes while in hiding and wrote letters (even if they could not be mailed) to communicate, to record the events, or to stave off loneliness; Garbarini, *Numbered Days*, 104–6.

18. Grossmann, *Die unbesungenen Helden*. The book contains stories of helpers from throughout Europe. On this book, see Riffel, *Unbesungene Helden*, 39.

19. Grossmann, ibid., 119. The "Scarlet Pimpernel" is a character in the novel by Emma Orczy who saved people condemned to death at the time of Robespierre's Reign of Terror during the French Revolution. Orczy, *The Scarlet Pimpernel*.

20. Grossmann, ibid., 132–35, 142–43, 150–51. On the development of the book, see Mertens, *Unermüdlicher Kämpfer*, 269–71.

21. Sophie Mayer, too, was concerned about anonymity and therefore only described her hiding place but did not mention the town in which she was living; Grossmann, ibid., 151.

22. Beer, *Die Banalität des Guten*, 321.

23. Kabalek, "The Rescue of Jews," 224–36, last accessed February 24, 2022, https://libraetd.lib.virginia.edu/public_view/x633f123t.

24. On the impact of the miniseries on the remembrance discourse and the politics of memory in West Germany, see Bösch, "NS-Vergangenheit und Geschichtswissenschaft."

25. Kabalek, "The Rescue of Jews," 293–96, last accessed February 24, 2022, https://libraetd.lib.virginia.edu/public_view/x633f123t.

26. Riffel, "Der Umgang," 318. For a detailed history of the project's development, see Riffel, *Unbesungene Helden*, 43–60.

27. Riffel, "Der Umgang," 318.

28. Ibid. "Ehrung von Berliner Bürgern," *Amtsblatt für Berlin* 41 (1960), 958–59. For a detailed discussion, see Riffel, *Unbesungene Helden*, 65–102. On Joachim Lipschitz, ibid., 47–57.

29. Riffel, "Der Umgang," 318–19. For a detailed analysis of who was honored and who was not, see Riffel, *Unbesungene Helden*, 129–226.

30. Riffel, "Der Umgang," 319.

31. Riffel, *Unbesungene Helden*, 241–43.

32. Ibid., 246.

33. Letter from the German Federal Finance Ministry, cited in Riffel, *Unbesungene Helden*, 246.

34. Yad Vashem, "The Righteous Among the Nations: About the Program," last accessed February, 24, 2022, https://www.yadvashem.org/righteous/about-the-program.html; Fraenkel and Borut, *Lexikon der Gerechten*, 16–17. On the origins of the program, see Kabalek, "The Commemoration before the Commemoration."

35. Yad Vashem, "The Righteous Among the Nations: How to Apply," last accessed February 24, 2022, https://www.yadvashem.org/righteous/how-to-apply.html; Riffel, *Unbesungene Helden*, 169–83.

36. Yad Vashem, "Righteous Among the Nations Honored by Yad Vashem," last accessed April 7, 2022, https://www.yadvashem.org/yv/pdf-drupal/germany.pdf.

37. Fraenkel and Borut, *Lexikon der Gerechten*, 172–73; Lasker-Wallfisch, *Inherit the Truth*, 50–51. Anita Lasker-Wallfisch and Renate Lasker-Harpprecht survived Auschwitz and Bergen-Belsen; see Lasker-Wallfisch, *Inherit the Truth*.

38. Krumme to Kohl, November 25, 1965, StadtAM, DE-1992-DIR-ZR-1118.

39. Freudling to Vogel, January 24, 1966, StadtAM, DE-1992-DIR-ZR-1118. The last tributes in Berlin took place in 1966; Riffel, *Unbesungene Helden*, 240.

40. The resistance fighters connected to the July 20, 1944, plot to assassinate Hitler had received numerous honors; Riffel, ibid., 243. Georg Elser, a leftist whose assassination attempt almost succeeded in killing Hitler in November of 1939, was generally not honored as a resistance fighter until the 1980s; on this, see Steinbach and Tuchel, *Georg Elser*, 152–62.

41. Landeshauptstadt München, Muenchen.de. Das offizielle Stadtportal, "Gästebuch und Ehrungen: Die Medaille 'München leuchtet' (Munich shines)," last accessed February 24, 2022, https://stadt.muenchen.de/infos/muenchenleuchtet.html.

42. On Josef Meyer, see Fraenkel and Borut, *Lexikon der Gerechten*, 196–98.

43. List of names and merits, n.d., StadtAM, DE-1992-DIR-ZR-1120. For Frau Schulz, unfortunately neither her first name nor any other information is noted.

44. Cahnman, "Die Juden in München," 446; List of names and merits, n.d., StadtAM, DE-1992-DIR-ZR-1120.

45. Meyer to Brauchle, December 29, 1965, StadtAM, DE-1992-DIR-ZR-1120.

46. Riffel, *Unbesungene Helden*, 245. This prize has been awarded since 1957 to people who "stood up for the Jewish community in an outstanding manner" and who learned "lessons for the future" from Germany's history; Central Council of Jews in Germany, "Auszeichnungen: Der Leo Baeck Preis," last accessed February 23, 2022, https://www.zentralratderjuden.de/der-zentralrat/auszeichnungen/leo-baeck-preis/der-leo-baeck-preis/.

47. Mayor Hans-Jochen Vogel, cited in *Münchner Merkur*, March 1, 1966.

48. *Süddeutsche Zeitung*, March 1, 1966; *Süddeutsche Zeitung*, November 4, 1966; *Münchner Merkur*, March 1, 1966. Wörl maintained his political views after 1945 and was a cofounder of the Communist Party of Germany (KPD) in Munich; report on Ludwig Wörl's reputation, July 23, 1958, StAM, Pol. Dir. 15582. Wörl was considered "headstrong," however, and did not always follow the party line. Stengel, *Hermann Langbein*, 333. In the postwar period, he sometimes expressed clear criticism that in his opinion the KPD and the Association of the Victims of the Nazi Regime (VVN) did not do enough to build up a network of former Auschwitz prisoners and identify witnesses for the postwar trials; ibid., 333–35.

49. Bavarian State Office for Protection of the Constitution, February 12, 1960, StAM, Pol. Dir. 15582.

50. Riffel, *Unbesungene Helden*, 245.

51. Kabalek, "The Rescue of Jews," 262–64, last accessed February 24, 2022, https://libraetd.lib.virginia.edu/public_view/x633f123t; Beer, *Die Banalität des Guten*, 324–25; Riffel, ibid., 248.

52. Letter of Sophie Mayer, March 27, 1966, Yad Vashem, M.31, File 0394b.

53. In the newspaper articles about the honoring of Rosa Mayer and Maria Dora Letnar by Yad Vashem, her name was rendered anonymous. See, for example, *Abendzeitung*, April 1, 1971, Yad Vashem, M. 31, File 0394b.

54. Vetter to Vogel, July 3, 1970, and January 22, 1972, StadtAM, DE-1992-DIR-ZR-1121; Vetter to Yad Vashem, September 15, 1970 and December 10, 1970; Yad Vashem, M.31, File 0694.

55. Newspaper clippings from *Abendzeitung*, January 14, 1972; *Bild*, January 14, 1972; *Süddeutsche Zeitung*, January 15–16, 1972; and *Münchener Jüdische Nachrichten*, January 21, 1972; Yad Vashem, M.31, file 0694; newspaper clippings from the *tz*, January 14, 1972 [erroneously dated January 14, 1971, in the files]: StadtAM, DE-1992-DIR-ZR-1121.

56. Roseman, *A Past in Hiding*, 409–12. On the dynamic of the postwar relationships between survivors and their helpers, see Beer, *Banalität des Guten*, 310–14; Riffel, "Der Umgang," 325–26.

57. Multipartisan motion, January 19, 1960, StadtAM, DE-1992-DIR-ZR-1120.

58. Nikou, "Heimweh nach München," 84. On the antisemitic attacks, see Brochhagen, *Nach Nürnberg*, 299–313.

59. Thumser, *Heimweh nach München*, 16.

60. *Süddeutsche Zeitung*, July 24, 1965, StadtAM, DE-1992-DIR-ZR-1120. On the modalities, see also Nikou, "Heimweh nach München," 81–82. For a detailed, comparative analysis of the visitors' programs in Munich, Frankfurt, and Berlin, see Nikou, *Besuche in der alten Heimat*.

61. Nikou, *Zwischen Imagepflege*, 28–32; Nikou, "Heimweh nach München," 82. On the visitors' program in Munich, see also Heusler, *Das braune Haus*, 309–10.

62. The lists of names and addresses compiled by the Press and Information Office in connection with contacting former Munich residents included two former U-boats; address lists, n.d., StadtAM, DE-1992-DIR-ZR-1120.

63. Nikou, "Heimweh nach München," 86; *Süddeutsche Zeitung* of July 24, 1965; StadtAM, Direktorium, DE-1992-DIR-ZR-1120.

64. On this, see Thumser, *Journalistengift*, 64–65.

65. Nikou, "Heimweh nach München," 88–89.

66. Ibid., 89.

67. Thumser, *Heimweh nach München*, 2; Nikou, "Heimweh nach München," 89.

68. Thumser, ibid., 2; Nikou, ibid., 89.

69. Lamm, "Eine Generation wächst heran," 3.

70. Sinn, "*Und ich lebe wieder an der Isar.*"

71. Thumser, *Heimweh nach München*, 9. On the separation of the "years of shame" from the "longing of the emigrants," see also Nikou, "Heimweh nach München," 88–89.

72. Thumser, ibid., 9. Thumser cited these passages extensively in his 1999 book *Journalistengift* (*Journalist Poison*); in the chapter "Vom Hinsehen und Wegsehen" ("On Watching and Looking Away"), he treats the city's visitors' program in detail; Thumser, *Journalistengift*, 73–90, esp. 85. Thumser justifies his conclusion that "the love was stronger than the terror" with the results of his research; ibid., 85. Other examples are not cited, however. Even if the language is at times still very unsettling (esp. 90), this chapter—as well as the critical remarks about the failures at the time—clearly show Thumser's intense personal involvement in making contact with the Jewish emigrants.

73. Nikou, "Heimweh nach München," 90.

74. Ibid.; Nikou, *Zwischen Imagepflege*, 20–22. The completion of Hamburg's memorial book and its presentation to the Jewish Community of Hamburg in 1965 was used as an opportunity to place advertisements in various emigrant publications to inform former Hamburg residents about the memorial book and to request that they contact the city; ibid.

75. StadtAM, *Biographisches Gedenkbuch*.

76. It is not clear whether the article appeared in consultation with the mayor's office or the Press and Information Office of the city of Munich.

77. *Süddeutsche Zeitung* of July 24, 1965, StadtAM, DE-1992-DIR-ZR-1120.

78. Ibid.

79. Ibid.

80. Thumser, *Heimweh nach München*, 18.

81. On the role of the large group of victims of Nazi persecution in Munich's municipal administration, see, for example, StadtAM, Direktorium 3/18, no. 27, 50–7/M300. On Vogel's visit to Israel, see Nikou, *Besuche in der alten Heimat*, 79–81; Thumser, *Heimweh nach München*, 13–15.

82. Lamm, "Eine neue Generation wächst heran," 3.

83. Vogel, "Grußwort" (welcome address), 1. On the close connection between the Olympics application and politics of the past, see also Rosenfeld, *Munich and Memory*, 153–56.

84. Nikou, *Besuche in der alten Heimat*, 198.

85. *Münchener Jüdische Nachrichten* of April 1, 1966, StadtAM, DE-1992-DIR-ZR-1120.

86. Ibid. "Munich—cosmopolitan city with a heart" (*Weltstadt mit Herz*) was formally adopted as official slogan of the city in 1962; see Kurzhals, *"Millionendorf,"* 136–43.

87. Press and Information Office to the Directorate—Administrative Office, March 9, 1966; and Directorate—Administrative Office to the Press and Information Office, March 14, 1966, StadtAM, DE-1992-DIR-ZR-1120.

88. Lamm to Vogel, April 4, 1966, ibid.

89. Kauders, *Unmögliche Heimat*, 129–31, 150.

90. Ibid., 126, 129–31.

91. Sinn, *"Und ich lebe wieder an der Isar,"* 121.

92. Lamm, *Von Juden in München*. See also Sinn, *"Und ich lebe wieder an der Isar,"* 122–23.

93. Lamm, "Einführung," 13.

94. Ibid.

95. *Münchener Jüdische Nachrichten* of April 1, 1966, StadtAM, DE-1992-DIR-ZR-1120.

96. See in particular the article by Else Behrend-Rosenfeld, "Leben und Sterben der Münchner Gemeinde 1938–1942," as well as the letter from Rabbi Bruno Finkelscherer to Alfred Neumeyer dated November 30, 1942.

97. Kurt Grossmann wrote about Karl Schörghofer, Karl Rieger about Cäcilie Langenwalter, and Otto von Taube about saving Denny F.; Lamm, *Von Juden in München*, 344–47.

98. Ophir and Wiesemann, "Geschichte und Zerstörung." The 1982 edition had a different title, see Lamm, *Vergangene Tage*.

99. Rosenfeld, *Munich and Memory*, 211; Heusler, *Das Braune Haus*, 307–8. There has been a memorial in the new Jewish cemetery since 1946, but it remains largely hidden from public view; Rosenfeld, ibid., 139–40.

100. Rosenfeld, ibid., 211–13.

101. Mayor Vogel, cited in Rosenfeld, ibid., 226. On the memorial stone, see ibid., 225–26.

102. Rosenfeld, ibid., 294–95. The impetus for the monument at Berg am Laim came from a local high school class and its history teacher, Erich Kasberger. The class started a research project on the Berg am Laim camp. On this, see Krauss, "Zur Einführung," 41; and Rosenfeld, *Munich and Memory*, 295. Both the erection of the monument at Berg am Laim and the installation of a plaque at the site of the former Jewish hospital led to public protests, calling for greater visibility and more information. On the controversies, see Rosenfeld, ibid., 295–97; and Krauss, "Zur Einführung," 41–43. On this, see also Nerdinger, "Der Umgang," 555–56.

103. Yad Vashem, "Righteous Among the Nations Honored by Yad Vashem," last accessed April 7, 2022, https://www.yadvashem.org/yv/pdf-drupal/germany.pdf. It is not known who initiated the honoring of these helpers.

104. There is a small commemorative plaque in the Munich city hall that memorializes the deportation of Jews from Munich to Kaunas. An underground "path of remembrance" connects the new synagogue with the Jewish community center. On the walls are the names of the Munich Jews who were murdered during the Nazi period. On this, for example, see Landeshauptstadt München, *ThemenGeschichtsPfad*, 58–59, 70–71, last accessed April 10,

2022, https://stadt.muenchen.de/service/info/orte-des-erinnerns-und-gedenkens/10314423/#k-sf3.

105. Gedenkstätte Stille Helden, "The Silent Heroes Memorial Center," https://www.gedenkstaette-stille-helden.de/en/memorial-center/.

106. See, for example, Behar, *"Versprich mir"*; Lewyn, *On the Run*; Friedlander, *"Try to Make Your Life"*; Lévy, *Nichts wie raus*.

107. Friedlander, ibid., 277.

108. Inge Deutschkron spoke in the German Bundestag in 2013, and Hanni Lévy was a guest speaker at the Green Party convention in 2018; *Süddeutsche Zeitung*, "Worauf es in diesen Zeiten ankommt: nichts vergessen," January 27, 2018, last accessed February 24, 2022, https://www.sueddeutsche.de/politik/hanni-levy-bei-den-gruenen-worauf-es-in-diesen-zeiten-ankommt-nichts-vergessen-1.3843482. Inge Deutschkron's speech can be read online at Deutscher Bundestag, "Webarchiv, Texte von 2013," last accessed February 23, 2022, https://www.bundestag.de/dokumente/textarchiv/2013/rede_deutschkron-252298.

109. The film *Aimee & Jaguar* opened in movie theaters in 1999; it tells of the love story between Lilly Wust and the U-boat Felice Schragenheim, a Berlin Jew. The television film *Ein blinder Held—die Liebe des Otto Weidt* (*A Blind Hero: The Love of Otto Weidt*) was aired in 2014. Otto Weidt was one of the best-known helpers in Berlin. On Weidt, see Kain, *Otto Weidt. Die Unsichtbaren/The Invisibles* opened in movie theaters in 2017, and two years later it was aired on German television. On the movie, see Kosmala, "Hanni Lévy in Berlin," 172–77.

CONCLUSION

1. Croes and Kosmala, "Facing Deportation," 119.

2. In Berlin, 58 percent of the surviving U-boats were women, and the surviving U-boats were mainly in their thirties and forties. Lutjens, *Submerged on the Surface*, 216, 218.

3. Ungar-Klein, *Schattenexistenz*, 97.

4. See also Moore, *Survivors*, 4–5; Roseman, *A Past in Hiding*, 272; Lutjens, "Vom Untertauchen," 50–51.

5. Hilberg, *Perpetrators, Victims, Bystanders*, xi. If and how this diffuse group should be divided into subcategories is a subject of lively discussion among Holocaust researchers. See, for example, Cesarani, *"Bystanders" to the Holocaust*; Morina and Thijs, *Probing the Limits of Categorization*; Bajohr and Löw, "Beyond the 'Bystander.'"

6. Bajohr and Löw, ibid., 4.

7. Tausendfreund, "'Jüdische Fahnder,'" 239.

8. Lutjens, "Vom Untertauchen," 49.

9. Welzer, "Collateral Damage of History Education," 297–304.

10. Welzer, Moller, and Tschuggnall, *"Opa war kein Nazi,"* 67–69, 101–3, 149–50, 208.

11. Ibid. This was also revealed in school discussions about family memories of Nazism; see Hamann, "'Uropa war ein Guter,'" 381–86.

12. Kabalek, "The Rescue of Jews," 326, last accessed February 24, 2022, https://libraetd.lib.virginia.edu/public_view/x633f123t. *"Der gute Deutsche"* ("The Good German") was the cover story in the German news magazine *Der Spiegel*, with a picture of actor Liam Neeson, who played Oskar Schindler, on the cover; *Der Spiegel*, February 21, 1994. On the Spiegel cover and article, see Kabalek, "The Rescue of Jews," 322–24.

13. Terminology borrowed from Jureit and Schneider, *Gefühlte Opfer*.

BIBLIOGRAPHY

ARCHIVAL COLLECTIONS

Archiv der Inneren Mission München (Archive of the Inner Mission, Munich, AIM)
Bestand: Geschichte der Inneren Mission
Bericht von Kirchenrat Leonhard Henninger zum 100-jährigen Bestehen der Inneren Mission
Bestand: Pfarrer Hofmann
Entnazifizierung
"Nichtarische Christen"
Archiv des Caritasverbands der Erzdiözese München und Freising e.V. (Archive of the Caritas Association of the Archdiocese of Munich and Freising, DiCV)
I/AR 121, 206, 544, 545, 776
Arolsen Archives, Bad Arolsen, Germany
Transportlisten aus dem Gestapo-Bereich München, 1.2.1.1./11194608–11194735, ITS Digital Archive.
Bayerisches Hauptstaatsarchiv München (Bavarian Main State Archive, Munich, BayHStA)
Finanzministerium: Landesentschädigungsamt (LEA)
Kultusministerium: MK 49560–49567
Staatskommissariat für rassisch, religiös und politisch Verfolgte
Bayerisches Landesentschädigungsamt München (Bavarian State Compensation Office, Munich, BLEA)
Entschädigungsakten
Bundesarchiv, Berlin (Federal Archive, Berlin, BArchB)
Auslandsorganisation der NSDAP (NS 9)

Berlin Document Center (BDC): Mitgliederkartei der NSDAP (Zentralkartei), NSDAP-Gaukartei, Personenbezogene Unterlagen der NSDAP, Parteikorrespondenz

Gale Primary Sources, Archives Unbound, digital collection from the Archives of the Wiener Library (AWL): *Testaments to the Holocaust. Documents and Rare Printed Materials from the Wiener Library London.*

Anonymous. "Complaint of a Jewish Survivor Against Allied Occupation Forces." Manuscript Number: 063-EA-1606. Letters. P.IV.a. No. 704.

Drach, Anna. "Deportations from Berlin." Manuscript Number: 050-EA-0679. P.III.C. No. 597.

Herrmann, Marcella. "Aus Berliner Erinnerungen 1940/1944." Manuscript Number: 049-EA-0634. P.III.A. No. 54.

Heskel, Lotte. "Our Underground Life In Berlin During The War." Manuscript Number: 050-EA-0732. P.III.D. No. 706.

Themal, Ilselotte. "Meine Erlebnisse Waehrend der Zeit der Judenverfolgungen in Deutschland 1933–1945." Manuscript Number:050-EA-0719. P.III.D. No.460.

Veit, Susanne. "Non-Jews Helping Jews." Manuscript Number: 051-EA-0825. P.III.F. No. 535.

Gedenkstätte Dachau, Archiv (Archive of the Dachau Concentration Camp Memorial Site)

DA Deutsche Häftlinge

DA Evakuierungsmärsche

List, Heinrich, A 1493

Reck-Malleczewen, Friedrich, A 1575

Rettungsaktionen Bericht, A 3660

Gedenkstätte Deutscher Widerstand, Berlin (The German Resistance Memorial Center, Berlin)

Datenbank Stille Helden (database silent heroes)

Institut für Zeitgeschichte, München, Archiv (Institute for Contemporary History, Munich, IfZ Archiv)

ED 465 Winkler, Eduard

ED 102 Spies, Gerty

FA 208, 209

Gm 07.94/8 Prozessakten: Strafsache gegen Wegner Hans, Mugler Franz, Schrott, Ludwig

Gm 07.146/1-2

NSG-Datenbank

ZS 2213 Hirsch, Rudolf Frhr. v.

ZS 2424 Keller, Hermann

ZS 3142 Spies, Gerty

Landeskirchliches Archiv der Evangelisch-Lutherischen Kirche in Bayern, Nürnberg (Archive of the Lutheran State Church of Bavaria, Nuremberg, LAN)
Dekanat München I: 18 (Nichtarische Christen 1935–46)
Diakonisches Werk der Evang.-Luth. Kirche in Bayern: 1552, 1553
Kirchliche Hilfsstelle für nichtarische Christen in München: 1–10
Landeskirchenrat: 2595
Leo Baeck Institute New York (LBI)
Gerty Spies Collection, AR 6903
Gerty Spies: Ein Stück Weges, ME 294
Hans Froehlich Collection, AR 25276
Hedwig Geng: "Bericht ueber Theresienstadt," ME 183
Hedwig Geng Collection, AR 1587
Julius Spanier Collection, AR 5705
Munich Jewish Community Collection, AR 143
Suse Veit: Erinnerungen, ME 655
Some of these are available online, see cjh.org.
Staatsarchiv München (State Archive, Munich, StAM)
Amtsgericht München (AG)
Oberfinanzdirektion (OFD)
Polizeidirektion (Pol. Dir.)
Rückerstattungsakten (WB)
Spruchkammern (SpkA)
Staatsanwaltschaften (Stanw.)
Stadtarchiv München (Munich City Archive, StadtAM)
Datenbank zum biographischen Gedenkbuch der Münchner Juden, 1933–1945
Direktorium
Einwohnerkartei
Judaica
Jüdisches Vermögen
Nachlässe (NL)
Personalwesen
Polizeidirektion (Pol. Dir.)
United States Holocaust Memorial Museum, Washington (USHMM)
Transportlisten aus dem Gestapo-Bereich München, 1.2.1.1./11194608–11194735, ITS Digital Archive.
Yad Vashem, World Holocaust Remembrance Center, Jerusalem
Record Group M.31: Files of the Department for the Righteous among the Nations
File 0390 Karl Schörghofer, Katharina Schörghofer, Karl Schörghofer (jun.), Martha Schörghofer-Schleipfer
File 0394b Paul Mayer, Rosa Mayer, Maria Lethnar

File 0396 Josef Sebastian Cammerer
File 0694 Gisela Scherer, Josy Hofmann-Scherer

INTERVIEWS AND CORRESPONDENCE

Hugo Holzmann
Bernhard K.
Richard Marx
Herta Pila

NEWSPAPERS, MAGAZINES, AND ONLINE RESOURCES

Abendzeitung (abendzeitung-muenchen.de)

Bayerischer Landtag, Landtagsamt, Munich, "August Melchner," Abgeordnete A-Z, (current and former members of the Bavarian State parliament since 1946), last accessed February 23, 2022, https://www.bayern.landtag.de/abgeordnete/abgeordnete-von-a-z/profil/august-melchner/.

Bayerischer Rundfunk, "Ellen Ammann: Die Grenzgängerin," BR Mediatek, BR Fernsehen, June 27, 2020, last accessed February 23, 2022, https://www.br.de/mediathek/video/ellen-ammann-die-grenzgaengerin-av:5ef63ee499c6de001b743f34.

Bayerische Staatskanzlei, Bayern.Recht, Verkündungsplattform, "Gesetz Nr. 35 vom 1. August 1946 über Bildung eines Sonderfonds zum Zwecke der Wiedergutmachung," (Law No. 35 for a Special Indemnification Fund), *Bayerisches Gesetz- und Verordnungsblatt, Amtliches Nachrichtenblatt der bayerischen Landesregierung*, 17, (1946): 258, last accessed February 23, 2022, https://www.verkuendung-bayern.de/files/gvbl/1946/17/gvbl-1946-17.pdf#page=1.

———, "Gesetz zur Wiedergutmachung nationalsozialistischen Unrechts (Entschädigungsgesetz) vom 12. August 1949," (Law for Compensation for National Socialist Injustice), *Bayerisches Gesetz- und Verordnungsblatt*, 20, (1949): 196–204, last accessed February 23, 2022, https://www.verkuendung-bayern.de/files/gvbl/1949/20/gvbl-1949-20.pdf.

Botschaft des Staates Israel in Berlin (Embassy of the State of Israel in Berlin), "Yad Vashem-Ehrung von vier 'Gerechten unter den Völkern' im Bayerischen Landtag, 26. Juni 2014," last accessed March 11, 2022, http://www.botschaftisrael.de/2014/06/26/yad-vashem-ehrung-von-vier-gerechte-unter-den-voelkern-im-bayerischen-landtag/.

Brauns, Nikolaus, "Wahre Solidarität: Der bayerische Heimatschriftsteller Oskar Maria Graf und die Rote Hilfe," last accessed February 24, 2022, http://www.nikolaus-brauns.de/OMG_RHZ.htm.

Bundesanzeiger Verlag, Cologne, Bundesgesetzblatt online:
"Bundesergänzungsgesetz zur Entschädigung für Opfer der nationalsozialistischen Verfolgung, September 18, 1953," (Federal Supplementary Law on Compensation for Victims of National Socialist Persecution), *Bundesgesetzblatt* Teil 1, 1953, Nr. 62, last accessed February 23, 2022, https://www.bgbl.de/xaver/bgbl/start.xav#__bgbl__%2F%2F*%5B%40attr_id%3D%27bgbl153s1387.pdf%27%5D__1592419095170.

———, "Bundesgesetz zur Entschädigung für Opfer der nationalsozialistischen Verfolgung, (BEG)," June 29, 1956, (Federal Compensation Law for Victims of National Socialist Persecution), *Bundesgesetzblatt* Teil 1, 1956, Nr. 31, last accessed March 22, 2022, https://www.bgbl.de/xaver/bgbl/start.xav?start=//*%5B@attr_id=%27bgbl156s0559.pdf%27%5D#__bgbl__%2F%2F*%5B%40attr_id%3D%27bgbl156s0559.pdf%27%5D__1647965442811.

Bundesarchiv der Bundesrepublik Deutschland, "Gedenkbuch: Opfer der Verfolgung der Juden unter der nationalsozialistischen Gewaltherrschaft in Deutschland 1933–1945," (Memorial Book Victims of the Persecution of Jews under the National Socialist Tyranny in Germany 1933–1945), last accessed February 24, 2022, https://www.bundesarchiv.de/gedenkbuch/.

Der Spiegel (spiegel.de):

———, "Kennwort Georg", November 21, 1950, last accessed February 23, 2022, https://www.spiegel.de/spiegel/print/d-44451370.html.

———, "Mit den Nerven herunter," April 22, 1949, last accessed February 23, 2022, https://www.spiegel.de/spiegel/print/d-44436112.html.

———, "Täter, Opfer, Zuschauer," February 14, 1993, last accessed February 24, 2022, https://www.spiegel.de/politik/taeter-opfer-zuschauer-a-dd3ed3cd-0002-0001-0000-000013681126.

Deutscher Bundestag, "Rede von Inge Deutschkron," Webarchiv, Texte von 2013, last accessed February 23, 2022, https://www.bundestag.de/dokumente/textarchiv/2013/rede_deutschkron-252298.

Die Welt (welt.de), *Die Welt*, "Chinas Vater der Chirurgie war ein Freund Deutschlands," June 16, 2008, last accessed March 29, 2022, https://www.welt.de/welt_print/article2108342/Chinas-Vater-der-Chirurgie-war-ein-Freund-Deutschlands.html.

Die Zeit (zeit.de), *Die Zeit*, "Ich täts nie wieder," October 30, 1964, accessed February 23, 2022, https://www.zeit.de/1964/44/ich-taets-nie-wieder/komplettansicht.

Dokumentationsarchiv des österreichischen Widerstandes (Documentation Center of Austrian Resistance), Vienna, "Personendatenbank Shoah-Opfer," last accessed February 24, 2022, http://www.doew.at/personensuche.

Erzabtei St. Martin zu Beuron, "Oblatengemeinschaft Beuron," last accessed February 24, 2022: http://www.erzabtei-beuron.de/kloster/oblaten/index.html.

Evangelische Kreuzkirche München, "Albert Lemp, 1884-1943, Verleger, Christ, Widerständler," last accessed February 24, 2022, http://www.albert-lempp.de/.

Florida Holocaust Museum in conjunction with University of South Florida Tampa Library and Holocaust & Genocide Studies Center, "Herta Pila and Salomon Pila oral history interview by Carolyn Ellis and Chris Patti, July 2, 2010," Holocaust & Genocide Studies Center Oral Histories, Paper 176, last accessed February 24, 2022, http://scholarcommons.usf.edu/hgstud_oh/176.

Freier, Thomas, "Statistik und Deportation der jüdischen Bevölkerung aus dem Deutschen Reich," last accessed February 24, 2024, http://www.statistik-des-holocaust.de/.

———, "Jüdische Bevölkerung in Deutschland am 16.6.1933:" Statistik des Deutschen Reiches. Volkszählung. Die Bevölkerung des Deutschen Reiches nach den Ergebnissen der Volkszählung 1933, Band 451, 5. Berlin: Verlag für Sozialpolitik Wirtschaft und Statistik, 1936, https://www.statistik-des-holocaust.de/stat_ger_pop33.html.

———, Deportationsliste München—Theresienstadt, January 14, 1944, last accessed March 30, 1945, http://www.statistik-des-holocaust.de/II30-1.jpg.

———, Deportationliste München—Theresienstadt, February 22, 1945, last accessed March 30, https://www.statistik-des-holocaust.de/II35-SE.

Gedenkstätte Stille Helden (Silent Heroes Memorial Center), Widerstand gegen die Judenverfolgung in Europa 1933 bis 1945, "Die Gedenkstätte Stille Helden," last accessed February 24, 2022, https://www.gedenkstaette-stille-helden.de/en/memorial-center/.

Gegen Vergessen—Für Demokratie e.V./Regionalgruppe Mittelrhein, Projektgruppe Rettung verfolgter Juden und Jüdinnen 1933–1945, Projektleitung: Manfred Struck, Bonn, "Projekt-Abschlussbericht zu erkundeten Rettungen von Juden und als Juden Verfolgten, und als Juden Verfolgten mit Bezug zur Projektregion Mittelrhein 1933–1945," Bonn 2014, last accessed February 24, 2022, https://www.gegenvergessen.de/fileadmin/user_upload/Gegen_Vergessen/Dokumente/Diverses/Abschlussbericht_Rettung_verfolgter_Juden_ManfredStruck.pdf.

Geyer, Hermann, "Irmgard Meyenberg," last accessed February 24, 2022, http://www.albert-lempp.de/leben/isabellastrase-20/irmgard-meyenberg/.

Gudelius, Jost, "Die Jachenau, unter Einbeziehung der Chronik von Johannes Nar von 1933 einschließlich des Beitrags von Josef Demleitner von 1933 und des Geologischen Beitrags von Kurt Kment von 2004," herausgegeben von der Gemeinde Jachenau, Jachenau, 2013, last accessed February 24, 2022, http://www.gudelius.de/jchronik.htm.

JewishGen, Yizkor Book Project, Altman, S., "Haunting Memories," last accessed February 24, 2022, https://www.jewishgen.org/yizkor/Zolochiv1/zole029.html.

Jüdische Allgemeine: juedische-allgemeine.de.

Kabalek, Kobi, "The Rescue of Jews and the Memory of Nazism in Germany from the Third Reich to the Present," PhD thesis, Department of History, University of Virginia, Charlottesville, VA, 2013, last accessed February 24, 2022, https://libraetd.lib.virginia.edu/public_view/x633f123t.

Kongregation der Schwestern der Heimsuchung Mariens, Deutschsprachige Föderation, "Kloster der Heimsuchung Beuerberg: Gründung und Geschichte," last accessed February 24, 2022, http://www.franz-sales-verlag.de/ovm/foederation/beuerberg/index.html.

Landeshauptstadt München, Muenchen.de. Das offizielle Stadtportal. München im Porträt: "Gästebuch und Ehrungen: Die Medaille München leuchtet (Munich shines)," last accessed February 24, 2022, https://stadt.muenchen.de/infos/muenchenleuchtet.html.

Landeshaupstadt München, "ThemenGeschichtsPfad: Orte des Erinnerns und Gedenkens," last accessed April 10, 2022, https://stadt.muenchen.de/service/info/orte-des-erinnerns-und-gedenkens/10314423/#k-sf3.

Leo Baeck Institute New York Berlin, *Aufbau* (Reconstruction), New York (1934–2004) *Aufbau*, "Juden in München, Rückwanderer, Dritte Liste," August 24, 1945, last accessed March 19, 2022, https://archive.org/details/aufbau.

Ministerium des Inneren des Landes Nordrhein-Westfalen, Geltende Gesetze und Verordnungen (SGV. NRW.) mit Stand vom 17.2.2022: "Gesetz über die Gewährung von Unfall- und Hinterbliebenenrenten an die Opfer der Naziunterdrückung vom 5. März 1947," (Law on Granting Accident and Surviving Dependents' Pensions to the Victims of Nazi Oppression of March 5, 1947)," last accessed February 24, 2022, https://recht.nrw.de/lmi/owa/br_bes_text?sg=0&menu=1&bes_id=4593&aufgehoben=N&anw_nr=2.

Ministerium des Inneren des Landes Nordrhein-Westfalen, Gesetz- und Verordnungsblatt NRW 1949, 3. Jahrgang, Nr. 10, Düsseldorf, April 30, 1949: "Gesetz über die Entschädigung von Freiheitsentziehung aus politischen, rassischen und religiösen Gründen," February 11, 1949," ("Law on Compensation for Deprivation of Liberty for Political, Racial, and Religious Reasons,") last accessed February 24, 2022, https://recht.nrw.de/lmi/owa/br_gv_show_jahr?anw_nr=6&parent_anw_nr=2&year=1949.

Memorial and Museum Auschwitz-Birkenau, "Auschwitz Prisoners," last accessed February 23, 2022, http://auschwitz.org/en/museum/auschwitz-prisoners/.

Münchener Jüdische Nachrichten

Münchener Merkur (merkur.de)

Neue Jüdische Zeitung

NS-Dokumentationszentrum München (Munich Documentation Center for the History of National Socialism), "Münchener Biographien, Karl Fiehler 1895–1969," last accessed February 24, 2022, https://www.ns-dokuzentrum-muenchen.de/dauerausstellung/muenchner-biographien/detail/?tx_ttnews%5Btt_news%5D=28&cHash=31d59dd675b914373995af91df3640b3.

Rechtsinformationssystem des Bundes, Dokumente: "12. Opferfürsorgegesetz-Novelle," March 22, 1961, (Austrian compensation law for victims of National

Socialist persecution) *Bundesgesetzblatt für die Republik Österreich*, 23. Stück, Jahrgang 1961, last accessed February 23, 2022, https://www.ris.bka.gv.at/Dokumente/BgblPdf/1961_101_0/1961_101_0.pdf.

———, "21. Opferfürsorgegesetz-Novelle," November 11, 1970, (revised Austrian compensation law for victims of National Socialist persecution), *Bundesgesetzblatt für die Republik Österreich*, 89. Stück, Jahrgang 1970, last accessed March 23, 2022, https://www.ris.bka.gv.at/Dokumente/BgblPdf/1970_352_0/1970_352_0.pdf.

Sassin, Horst, "Überleben im Untergrund. Die Kinderärztin Dr. Erna Rüppel (1895–1970)," Gedenkbuch für die NS-Opfer aus Wuppertal (Memorial Book dedicated to the Victims of National Socialism in Wuppertal), last accessed February 24, 2022, https://www.gedenkbuch-wuppertal.de/de/doc/%C3%BCberleben-im-untergrund-die-kinder%C3%A4rztin-dr-erna-r%C3%BCppel-1895%E2%80%931970-von-horst-sassin.

Schwarzmüller, Alois, "Beiträge zur Geschichte des Marktes Garmisch-Partenkirchen im 20. Jahrhundert: Garmisch-Partenkirchen und seine jüdischen Bürger, 1933–1945," Garmisch-Partenkirchen, 2006, entry for Krohn, Hans, last accessed February 23, 2022, https://www.gapgeschichte.de/juden_in_gap_biographien/krohn_hans.htm.

Stadtarchiv München, Biographisches Gedenkbuch der Münchner Juden (Munich City Archive, Biographical Memorial Book of the Jews of Munich), all the following URLs last accessed February 24, 2022, https://gedenkbuch.muenchen.de/,

Borchardt, Karoline, https://gedenkbuch.muenchen.de/index.php?id=gedenkbuch_link&gid=939.

Butscheidt, Ruth, https://gedenkbuch.muenchen.de/index.php?id=gedenkbuch_link&gid=1025.

Cosmann, Oskar, https://gedenkbuch.muenchen.de/index.php?id=gedenkbuch_link&gid=1524.

Grauer, Sigmund, https://gedenkbuch.muenchen.de/index.php?id=gedenkbuch_link&gid=3820.

Hallerz, Moritz, https://gedenkbuch.muenchen.de/index.php?id=gedenkbuch_link&gid=5291.

Hechinger, Julius, https://gedenkbuch.muenchen.de/index.php?id=gedenkbuch_link&gid=80.

Hechinger, Rosa, https://gedenkbuch.muenchen.de/index.php?id=gedenkbuch_link&gid=5965.

Kalter, Ernestine, https://gedenkbuch.muenchen.de/index.php?id=gedenkbuch_link&gid=6247.

Mayer Julius, https://gedenkbuch.muenchen.de/index.php?id=gedenkbuch_link&gid=7456.

Mayer, Lieselotte, https://gedenkbuch.muenchen.de/index.php?id=gedenkbuch_link&gid=7460.
Mayer, Paula, https://gedenkbuch.muenchen.de/index.php?id=gedenkbuch_link&gid=7467.
Mezger, Kurt, https://gedenkbuch.muenchen.de/index.php?id=gedenkbuch_link&gid=2605.
Obarzanek, Samuel, https://gedenkbuch.muenchen.de/index.php?id=gedenkbuch_link&gid=8991.
Prölsdorfer, Heinrich, https://gedenkbuch.muenchen.de/index.php?id=gedenkbuch_link&gid=3310.
Rauch, Fanny, https://gedenkbuch.muenchen.de/index.php?id=gedenkbuch_link&gid=13295.
Schwink, Elisabeth, https://gedenkbuch.muenchen.de/index.php?id=gedenkbuch_link&gid=8304.
Weiss, Jeanette, https://gedenkbuch.muenchen.de/index.php?id=gedenkbuch_link&gid=1402.

Stadt Karlsruhe, Gedenkbuch für die Karlsruher Juden (Memorial Book for the Karlsruhe Jews), "Eintrag für Elisabeth Kühl" von Jürgen Schuhladen-Krämer, Karlsruhe, 2014, last accessed February 24, 2022, https://gedenkbuch.karlsruhe.de/namen/2273.

Süddeutsche Zeitung (www.sueddeutsche.de) *Süddeutsche Zeitung*, "Worauf es in diesen Zeiten ankommt: nichts vergessen," January 27, 2018, last accessed February 24, 2022, https://www.sueddeutsche.de/politik/hanni-levy-bei-den-gruenen-worauf-es-in-diesen-zeiten-ankommt-nichts-vergessen-1.3843482.

TZ (tz.de)

Weiße Rose Stiftung e.V., "Das zweite Flugblatt der Weißen Rose (The second flyer of the White Rose)," last accessed February 24, 2022, https://www.weisse-rose-stiftung.de/widerstandsgruppe-weisse-rose/flugblaetter/ii-flugblatt-der-weissen-rose/ (German version); https://www.weisse-rose-stiftung.de/white-rose-resistance-group/leaflets-of-the-white-rose/ii-leaflet-of-the-white-rose/ (English version); Weiße Rose Stiftung e.V., Tätigkeitsbericht 2014, "Vergessener Widerstand," last accessed February 24, 2022, https://www.weisse-rose-stiftung.de/wp-content/uploads/pdf/Taetigkeitsbericht-2014.pdf.

Weiße Rose Stiftung e.V., Projektarbeitskreis Franz-Marc-Gymnasium mit Schülern der Kollegstufe und des Arbeitskreises Politik und Zeitgeschichte unter der Leitung von Matthias Konrad und Heinrich Mayer, "Vergessener Widerstand." Resistenz, Verweigerung und Widerstand gegen den Nationalsozialismus in den Jahren 1933–1945 in Markt Schwaben und Umgebung. (Ausstellungsprojekt der Weiße Rose Stiftung e.V. und des Franz-Marc-Gymnasiums Markt Schwaben in Zusammenarbeit mit der Bayerischen Landeszentrale für Politische Bildungsarbeit.) Munich, 2015, last accessed

February 23, 2022, http://franz-marc-gymnasium.info/wp-content/uploads/2015/03/Vergessener-Widerstand_2.pdf.

Weitzel, Christoph von, "Franz Herda, 1887–1965," last accessed February 24, 2022, http://www.christoph-von-weitzel.de/herda_2.html.

Wiener Holocaust Library, "Eyewitness account by Josef Meyer of his attempts to help Jews in Poland," last accessed February 24, 2022, https://wiener.soutron.net/Portal/Default/en-GB/recordview/index/105613.

World Federation of Jewish Child Survivors of the Holocaust and Descendants, "President's Message," last accessed February 24, 2022 https://www.holocaustchild.org/about/presidents-message/.

Yad Vashem, Shoah Resource Center: Nahum Bogner, "The Convent Children. The Rescue of Jewish Children in Polish Convents during the Holocaust," https://www.yadvashem.org/yv/pdf-drupal/nachum_bogner.pdf.

Yad Vashem—The World Holocaust Remembrance Center, Jerusalem, "The Righteous Among the Nations," all the following URLs last accessed February 25, 2022, https://www.yadvashem.org/righteous.html.

"The Righteous Among the Nations: About the Program," https://www.yadvashem.org/righteous/about-the-program.html.

"The Righteous Among the Nations: How to Apply," https://www.yadvashem.org/righteous/how-to-apply.html.

"Righteous Among the Nations: Honored by Yad Vashem by 1 January 2021: Germany," https://www.yadvashem.org/yv/pdf-drupal/germany.pdf.

"The Righteous Among the Nations: Numbers of Righteous by Country," https://www.yadvashem.org/righteous/statistics.html.

"The Righteous Among the Nations: Sebastian Cammerer," https://righteous.yadvashem.org/?search=Cammerer&searchType=righteous_only&language.

Zentralrat der Juden in Deutschland (Central Council of Jews in Germany), "Auszeichnungen: Der Leo Baeck Preis," last accessed February 23, 2022, https://www.zentralratderjuden.de/der-zentralrat/auszeichnungen/leo-baeck-preis/der-leo-baeck-preis/.

MEMOIRS, DIARIES, DISSERTATIONS, AND DOCUMENT COLLECTIONS

Akten Kardinal Michael von Faulhabers, Band II 1935–1945 bearbeitet von Ludwig Volk (Veröffentlichungen der Kommission für Zeitgeschichte, herausgegeben von Rudolf Morsey, Reihe A: Quellen, Band 26). Mainz: Matthias-Grünewald-Verlag, 1978; Band III 1945–1952, bearbeitet von Heinz Hürten (Veröffentlichungen der Kommission für Zeitgeschichte, Reihe A: Quellen, Band 48). Paderborn: Ferdinand Schöningh, 2002.

Andreas-Friedrich, Ruth. *Berlin Underground, 1938–1945*. Translated by Barrows Mussey. New York: Holt, 1947.

———. *Der Schattenmann. Tagebuchaufzeichnungen 1938–1945*. Berlin: Suhrkamp, 1947. Second edition: *Der Schattenmann*. Reinbek: Rowohlt, 1964.

Balcar, Jaromir, and Thomas Schlemmer, eds. *An der Spitze der CSU. Die Führungsgremien der Christlich-Sozialen Union 1946–1955*. Munich: Oldenbourg, 2007.

Bamberg, Lotte. "Erinnerung ans Dritte Reich. An der Oberfläche untergetaucht." *Frankfurter Hefte* 10 (1955): 803–8.

Barkow, Ben, et al., eds. *Novemberpogrom 1938. Die Augenzeugenberichte der Wiener Library*. Frankfurt am Main: Suhrkamp, 2008.

Baum, Bruno. *Widerstand in Auschwitz*. Berlin: Kongress-Verlag, 1957.

Beck, Gad. *An Underground Life. Memoirs of a Gay Jew in Nazi Berlin*. Translated by Allison Brown. Madison: The University of Wisconsin Press, 1999.

Behar, Isaak. *"Versprich mir, dass Du am Leben bleibst": Ein jüdisches Schicksal*. Berlin: Ullstein, 2002.

Behrend, Rahel. *Verfemt und Verfolgt. Erlebnisse einer Jüdin in Nazi-Deutschland 1933–1944*. Zürich: Buchergilde Gutenberg, 1945.

Behrend-Rosenfeld, Else. *Ich stand nicht allein. Erlebnisse einer Jüdin in Deutschland 1933–1944*. Hamburg: Europäische Verlagsanstalt, 1949.

Behrend-Rosenfeld, Else, and Siegfried Rosenfeld. *Leben in zwei Welten. Tagebücher eines jüdischen Paares in Deutschland und im Exil*. Edited and annotated by Erich Kasberger and Marita Krauss. Munich: Volk-Verlag, 2011.

Behrend-Rosenfeld, Else, and Siegfried Rosenfeld. *Living in Two Worlds: Diaries of a Jewish Couple in Germany and in Exile*, edited by Marita Krauss and Erich Kasberger, translated by Deborah Langton. Foreword by Richard Evans. Cambridge: Cambridge University Press, 2022.

Beimler, Hans. *Im Mörderlager Dachau. Vier Wochen in den Händen der braunen Banditen*. Edited by Friedbert Mühldorfer. Köln: PapyRossa, 2012.

Bergmann, Katharina. "Vorgezeichnete Wege? Einflussfaktoren auf die jüdische Emigration aus dem nationalsozialistischen Reich am Beispiel der Münchner Gemeinde." Inaugural-Dissertation zur Erlangung des Doktorgrades der Philosophie an der Ludwig-Maximilians-Universität München. Munich, 2020.

Blau, Bruno. "Vierzehn Jahre Not und Schrecken." In *Jüdisches Leben in Deutschland. Selbstzeugnisse zur Sozialgeschichte 1918–1945, Vol. 3*, edited by Monika Richarz, 459–75. Stuttgart: Deutsche Verlags Anstalt, 1982.

Brenner, Henny. *"Das Lied ist aus:" Ein jüdisches Schicksal in Dresden*. Zürich: Pendo, 2001.

Bundesministerium der Finanzen. *Wenn im Amte, arbeite, wenn entlassen, verbirg Dich. Prof. Dr. jur. Dr. phil. Rolf Grabower in Zeugnissen aus der Finanzgeschichtlichen Sammlung der Bundesfinanzakademie*. Bonn: BMF, 2010.

Degen, Michael. *Nicht Alle waren Mörder: Eine Kindheit in Berlin*. Munich: Econ, 1999.

Deutschkron, Inge. *Outcast: A Jewish Girl in Wartime Berlin*. Translated by Jean Steinberg. New York: Fromm, 1989.

———. *We Survived. Berlin Jews Underground*. Translated by Kathy Derbyshire. Berlin: Eppler & Buntdruck, 2008.

Diem, Hermann. *Ja oder Nein. 50 Jahre Theologe in Kirche und Staat*. Stuttgart: Kreuz-Verlag, 1974.

———. "Wie wenig haben wir geholfen." In *Stärker als die Angst*, edited by Heinrich Fink, 132–40. Berlin: Union Verlag, 1968.

Fink, Heinrich, ed. *Stärker als die Angst*. Berlin: Union-Verlag, 1968.

Fogelman, Eva. "The Rescuers: A Socio-Psychological Study of Altruistic Behavior during the Nazi Era." PhD thesis, City University of New York, 1987.

Frankenstein, Walter. "Ich habe eigentlich nie Angst gehabt." In *Uns kriegt Ihr nicht*, edited by Tina Hüttl and Alexander Meschnig, 83–107. Munich: Piper, 2013.

Friedlander, Margot, and Malin Schwerdtfeger. *"Try to Make Your Life." A Jewish Girl Hiding in Nazi Berlin*. Translated by William Gilcher. Potomac, MD: BEA Press, 2014.

Fröhlich, Elke, ed. *Die Tagebücher von Joseph Goebbels. Im Auftrag des Instituts für Zeitgeschichte und mit Unterstützung des Staatlichen Archivdienstes Russlands. Teil II Diktate 1941–1945, Band 7, Januar–März 1943*. Munich: Saur, 1993.

Graf, Oskar Maria. *Gelächter von Außen. Aus meinem Leben 1918–1933*. Munich: Desch, 1966.

Grübler, Kurt Nathan, ed. and trans. *Journey through the Night. Jakob Littner's Holocaust Memoir*. New York: Continuum, 2000.

Hahn Beer, Edith, with Susan Dworkin. "Johann Plattner, Sippenforscher." In *Mit falschem Pass und fremden Namen. Junge Menschen im Holocaust*, edited by Harald Roth, 42–45. Gerlingen: Bleicher, 2002.

———. *The Nazi Officer's Wife: How One Jewish Woman Survived the Holocaust*. New York: William Morrow, 1999.

Heilmann Peter. "Ein neues Leben." In *So begann meine Nachkriegszeit*, edited by Peter Heilmann, 52–58. Berlin: Wichern-Verlag, 1985.

———, ed. *So begann meine Nachkriegszeit. Männer und Frauen erzählen vom Mai 45*. Berlin: Wichern-Verlag, 1985.

Herman-Friede, Eugen. *Für Freudensprünge keine Zeit. Erinnerungen an Illegalität und Aufbegehren 1942–1948*. Berlin: Metropol, 1991.

Hüttl, Tina, and Alexander Meschnig. *Uns kriegt Ihr nicht. Als Kinder versteckt—jüdische Überlebende erzählen*. Munich: Piper, 2013.

Jalowicz Simon, Marie. *Underground in Berlin: A Young Woman's Extraordinary Tale of Survival in the Heart of Nazi Germany*. Translated by Anthea Bell. New York: Back Bay Books, 2016.

Kabalek, Kobi. "The Rescue of Jews and the Memory of Nazism in Germany from the Third Reich to the Present." PhD thesis, Department of History, University of Virginia, Charlottesville, VA, 2013.

Klemperer, Victor. *The Diaries of Victor Klemperer, vol. 2: To the Bitter End, 1942–45.* Translated by Martin Chalmers. London: Phoenix, Orion Books, 2000.

———. *I Will Bear Witness: A Diary of the Nazi Years, 2 vols.* London: Random House, 1998.

Knobloch, Charlotte. "Doch ich hatte die Tiere. Kühe, Gänse, Hühner und Katzen als Verbündete." In *... und bleiben wollte keiner. Jüdische Lebensgeschichten im Nachkriegsbayern,* edited by Roman Haller, 12–25. Munich: Dölling & Galitz, 2004.

Knobloch, Charlotte, and Raphael Seligmann. *In Deutschland angekommen. Erinnerungen.* Munich: Deutsche Verlags-Anstalt, 2012.

Krakauer, Max. *Lichter im Dunkel.* Stuttgart: Calwer, 1947.

———. *Lights in Darkness.* Translated by Hans Martin Wuerth. Stuttgart: Calwer, 2007.

Krell, Else. *Wir rannten um unser Leben. Illegalität und Flucht aus Berlin 1943,* edited by Claudia Schoppmann. Berlin: Metropol, 2015.

Kronheimer-Sinz, Lola. "Erinnerungen einer Pianistin." In *Frauenleben in München. Lesebuch zur Geschichte des Münchner Alltags,* edited by the Landeshauptstadt München, 121–24. Munich: Buchendorfer, 1995.

Langbein, Hermann. *Die Stärkeren. Ein Bericht.* Vienna: Stern-Verlag, 1949.

———. *People in Auschwitz.* Translated by Harry Zohn. Auschwitz: Auschwitz-Birkenau State Museum, 2017.

Lasker-Wallfisch, Anita. *Inherit the Truth. A Memoir of Survivial and the Holocaust.* London: Giles de la Mare, 1996.

Lévy, Hanni, *Nichts wir raus und durch! Lebens- und Überlebensgeschichte einer jüdischen Berlinerin,* edited by Beate Kosmala. Berlin: Metropol, 2019.

Lewyn, Bert, and Bev Saltzmann Lewyn. *On the Run in Nazi Berlin. A Memoir.* Chicago: Chicago Review Press, 2001.

Lisberger, Helmut. "'Die seelischen Schäden sieht keiner . . .'" In *"Jüdisch Versippt." Schicksale von "Mischlingen" und "nichtarischen" Christen in Schwaben,* edited by Gernot Römer, 99–106. Augsburg: Wißner, 1996.

Lochner, Louis P., ed. and trans. *The Goebbels Diaries 1942–1943.* New York: Eagle Books, 1948.

Mannheimer, Max. *Spätes Tagebuch: Theresienstadt, Auschwitz, Warschau, Dachau.* Munich: Pendo, 2000.

Michalski, Franz. *Als die Gestapo an der Haustür klingelte. Eine Familie in "Mischehe" und ihre Helfer,* edited by Barbara Schieb. Berlin: Metropol, 2013.

———. "'Mein Vater konnte alles besorgen, auch überlebenswichtige Kontakte.'" In *Uns kriegt ihr nicht,* edited by Tina Hüttl and Alexander Meschnig, 25–45. Munich: Piper, 2013.

Müller, Josef. *Bis zur letzten Konsequenz. Ein Leben für Frieden und Freiheit.* Munich: Süddeutscher Verlag, 1975.

Neumeyer, Alfred, Alexander Karl Neumever, and Imanuel Noy-Meir. *"Wir wollen den Fluch in Segen verwandeln." Drei Generationen der jüdischen Familie Neumeyer: eine autobiografische Trilogie.* Berlin: Metropol, 2007.

Orbach, Larry, and Vivien Orbach-Smith. *Soaring Underground: A Young Fugitive's Life in Nazi Berlin.* Washington: Compass Press, 1996.

Reck-Malleczewen, Friedrich. *Tagebuch eines Verzweifelten.* Stuttgart: Burger Verlag, 1947. English translation: Reck, Friedrich. *Diary of a Man in Despair.* Translated by Paul Rubens. Afterword by Richard Evans. New York: NRB Classics, 2013.

Rosenthal, Hans. *Zwei Leben in Deutschland.* Bergisch-Gladbach: Lübbe, 1980.

Roth, Harald, ed. *Mit falschem Pass und fremden Namen. Junge Menschen im Holocaust.* Gerlingen: Bleicher, 2002.

Ruch, Martin, ed. *"Inzwischen sind wir nun besternt worden." Das Tagebuch der Esther Cohn (1926–1944) und die Kinder vom Münchner Antonienheim.* Norderstedt: Books on Demand, 2006.

Salewsky, Anja, ed. *Der olle Hitler soll sterben. Erinnerungen an den jüdischen Kindertransport nach England.* Munich: Claassen, 2001.

Scholl, Inge. *The White Rose: Munich 1942–1943.* Trans. Arthur R. Schultz. Middletown, Conn.: Wesleyan University Press, 1983.

Schönhaus, Cioma. *The Forger: An Extraordinary Story of Survival in Wartime Berlin.* Translated by Alan Bance. London: Granta, 2007.

Spies, Gerty. *My Years in Theresienstadt: How One Woman Survived the Holocaust.* Translated by Jutta R. Tragnitz. Amherst, NY: Prometheus, 1997.

———. "Wie ich es überlebte. Ein Dokument." *Hochland* 50 (1958): 350–60.

Steckhan, Beate. "Was ihr getan habt einem unter diesen meinen geringsten Brüdern, das habt ihr mir getan." In *Stärker als die Angst,* edited by Heinrich Fink, 180–205. Berlin: Union-Verlag, 1968.

Van Laak, Gert. *Die Nazis nannten sie Sara.* Munich and Zurich: Pendo, 2000.

Willstätter, Richard. *From My Life.* Edited by Arthur Stoll. Translated by Lilli S. Hornig. New York and Amsterdam: W. A. Benjamin, 1965.

Wolffenstein, Valerie. *Erinnerungen von Valerie Wolffenstein unte Berücksichtigung der Aufzeichnungen von Andrea Wolffenstein.* Edited and introduced by Robert A. Kann. Vienna: Kriesche, 1981.

Zwanzger, Johannes. "Jahre der Unmenschlichkeit. Eine Rückbesinnung von Kirchenrat Johannes Zwanzger." *Concordia* 73 (1988): 1–15.

SECONDARY LITERATURE

Albert, Reinhard, Roland Hartung, and Günter Saltin, eds. *Alfred-Delp-Jahrbuch,* 4 (2010). Berlin: LIT Verlag, 2010.

Aleksiun, Natalia. "Gender and the Daily Lives of Jews in Hiding in Eastern Galicia." *Nashim: A Journal of Jewish Women's Studies & Gender Issues* 27 (2014): 38–61.

———. "Neighbors in Borysław: Jewish Perceptions of Collaboration and Rescue in Eastern Galicia." *The Holocaust and European Societies. Social Processes and Social Dynamics*, edited by Andrea Löw and Frank Bajohr, 243–66. London: Palgrave, 2016.

Angermair, Elisabeth. "Eine selbstbewußte Minderheit (1892–1918)." In *Jüdisches München. Vom Mittelalter bis zur Gegenwart*, edited by Richard Bauer and Michael Brenner, 110–36. Munich: C. H. Beck, 2006.

Arbeitskreis Geschichte Ergoldsbach. *"Das hätte doch jeder getan!" Die Rettung der 13 Juden von Ergoldsbach*. Regensburg: Marquardt, 2006.

Auerbach, Hellmut. "Hitlers politische Lehrjahre und die Münchener Gesellschaft 1919–1923." *Vierteljahrshefte für Zeitgeschichte* 25, no. 1 (1977): 1–45.

Baeyer, Walter von, Heinz Kisker, and Karl Peter. *Psychiatrie der Verfolgten. Psychopathologische und gutachtliche Erfahrungen an Opfern der nationalsozialistischen Verfolgung und vergleichbarer Extrembelastungen*. Berlin: Springer, 1964.

Baier, Helmut. *Kirche in Not. Die bayerische Landeskirche im Zweiten Weltkrieg*. Neustadt an der Aisch: Degener, 1979.

———. *Liebestätigkeit unter dem Hakenkreuz. Die Innere Mission München in der Zeit des Nationalsozialismus*. Nuremberg: Verein für bayerische Kirchengeschichte, 2008.

Bajohr, Frank. *"Aryanisation" in Hamburg: The Economic Exclusion of Jews and the Confiscation of their Property in Nazi Germany*. Translated by George Wilkes. New York: Berghahn, 2002.

———. *Parvenüs und Profiteure. Korruption in der NS-Zeit*. Frankfurt am Main: Fischer, 2001.

Bajohr, Frank, and Andrea Löw. "Beyond the Bystander. Social Processes and Social Dynamics in European Societies as Context for the Holocaust." In *The Holocaust and European Societies*, edited by Frank Bajohr and Andrea Löw, 3–14. London: Palgrave Macmillan, 2016.

———, eds. *The Holocaust and European Societies. Social Processes and Social Dynamics*. London: Palgrave Macmillan, 2016.

Bajohr, Frank, and Dieter Pohl. *Der Holocaust als offenes Geheimnis. Die Deutschen, die NS-Führung und die Alliierten*. Munich: Beck, 2006.

———. *Massenmord und schlechtes Gewissen. Die deutsche Bevölkerung, die NS-Führung und der Holocaust*. Frankfurt am Main: Fischer, 2008.

Barkai, Avraham, and Paul Mendes-Flohr. *Reneval and Destruction 1918–1945*. Vol. 4, German-Jewish History in Modern Times, edited by Michael A. Meyer. New York: Columbia University Press, 1998.

Barth, Boris. *Dolchstoßlegenden und politische Desintegration: Das Trauma der deutschen Niederlage im Ersten Weltkrieg*. Düsseldorf: Droste, 2003.

Battel, Franco. *"Wo es hell ist, dort ist die Schweiz." Flüchtlinge und Fluchthilfe an der Schaffhauser Grenze zur Zeit des Nationalsozialismus*. Zürich: Chronos-Verlag, 2000.

Bauer, Richard, and Michael Brenner, eds. *Jüdisches München. Vom Mittelalter bis zur Gegenwart.* Munich: C. H. Beck, 2006.

Bauer, Richard, and Brigitte Schütz, eds. *München—"Hauptstadt der Bewegung." Bayerns Metropole und der Nationalsozialismus.* Munich: Minerva, 2002.

Baumann, Angelika, and Andreas Heusler, eds. *München arisiert. Entrechtung und Enteignung der Juden in der NS-Zeit.* Munich: C. H. Beck, 2004.

Beckmann-Zöller, Beate. "Adolf und Anne Reinach—Edith Steins Mentoren im Studium und auf dem Glaubensweg." *Edith Stein Jahrbuch* 13 (2007): 77–101.

Beer, Susanne. *Die Banalität des Guten. Hilfeleistungen für jüdische Verfolgte 1941–1945.* Berlin: Metropol, 2018.

Benz, Wolfgang. "Gegenleistungen. Stationen eines Kirchenasyls zwischen Weserbergland und Lausitz." In *Überleben im Dritten Reich: Juden im Untergrund und ihre Helfer,* edited by Wolfgang Benz, 220–28. Munich: C. H. Beck, 2003.

———. "Juden im Untergrund und ihre Helfer." In *Überleben im Dritten Reich: Juden im Untergrund und ihre Helfer,* edited by Wolfgang Benz, 11–50. Munich: C. H. Beck, 2003.

———, ed. *Die Juden in Deutschland 1933–1945. Leben unter nationalsozialistischer Herrschaft.* Munich: C. H. Beck, 1988.

———. "Solidarität und Hilfe für Juden während der NS-Zeit. Eine Einführung." In *Überleben im Untergrund. Hilfe für Juden in Deutschland, 1941–1945,* edited by Beate Kosmala and Claudia Schoppmann, 9–16. Berlin: Metropol, 2002.

———, ed. *Spuren des Nationalsozialismus. Gedenkstättenarbeit in Bayern.* Munich: Bayerische Landeszentrale für politische Bildungsarbeit, 2000.

———, ed. *Überleben im Dritten Reich: Juden im Untergrund und ihre Helfer.* Munich: C. H. Beck, 2003.

Benz, Wolfgang, and Ilse Aichinger, eds. *Die Kindertransporte 1938/39. Rettung und Integration.* Frankfurt am Main: Fischer, 2003.

Benz, Wolfgang, and Juliane Wetzel, eds. *Regionalstudien 1: Polen, Rumänien, Griechenland, Luxemburg, Norwegen, Schweiz* (Solidarität und Hilfe für Juden während der NS-Zeit, Vol. 1). Berlin: Metropol, 1996.

———, eds. *Regionalstudien 2: Frankreich, Österreich, Ukraine, Lettland, Litauen, Estland, Tschechoslowakei* (Solidarität und Hilfe für Juden während der NS-Zeit, Vol. 2). Berlin: Metropol, 1998.

———, eds. *Regionalstudien 4: Slowakei, Bulgarien, Serbien, Kroatien mit Bosnien und Herzegowina, Belgien, Italien* (Solidarität und Hilfe für Juden während der NS-Zeit, Vol. 4). Berlin: Metropol, 2004.

Bergen, Doris. *Twisted Cross: The German Christian Movement in the Third Reich.* Chapel Hill: University of North Carolina Press, 1996.

Berger, Franz, and Christiane Holler. *Überleben im Versteck. Schicksale in der NS-Zeit.* Vienna: Ueberreuter, 2002.

Bergmann, Katharina. *Jüdische Emigration aus München. Entscheidungsfindung und Auswanderungswege 1933–1941*. Munich: Oldenbourg/De Gruyter, 2021.

Bernard, Andreas, and Ulrich Raulff, eds. *Briefe aus dem 20. Jahrhundert*. Frankfurt am Main: Suhrkamp, 2005.

Berschel, Holger. "Polizeiroutiniers und Judenverfolgung. Die Bearbeitung von 'Judenangelegenheiten' bei der Stapo-Leitstelle Düsseldorf." In *Gestapo*, edited by Gerhard Paul and Klaus-Michael Mallmann, 155–78. Darmstadt: Wissenschaftliche Buchgesellschaft, 2000.

Binkowski, Johannes. *Jugend als Wegbegleiter. Der Quickborn von 1909 bis 1945*. Stuttgart: Konrad Theiss Verlag, 1981.

Bleistein, Roman. *Alfred Delp. Geschichte eines Zeugen*. Frankfurt am Main: Knecht, 1989.

Blessin, Georg, and Hans Wilden. *Bundes-Entschädigungsgesetze. Kommentar*. Munich: Oldenbourg, 1957.

Bloch, Max. "Gertrud und Margarethe Zuelzer. Zwei Schwestern im Holocaust." *Aschkenas* 24 (2014): 195–213.

Boehm, Eric. *We Survived. The Stories of 14 of the Hidden and the Hunted of Nazi Germany*. New Haven: Yale University Press, 1949. Republished as *We Survived. Fourteen Histories of the Hidden and the Hunted of Nazi Germany*. Boulder: Basic Books, 2003.

Bogner, Nahum. *At the Mercy of Strangers. The Rescue of Jewish Children with Assumed Identities in Poland*. Jerusalem: Yad Vashem, 2009.

Bokovoy, Douglas, and Stefan Meining, eds. *Versagte Heimat. Jüdisches Leben in Münchens Isarvorstadt 1914–1945*. Munich: Glas, 1994.

Bon, Silva. *Gli Ebrei a Trieste 1930–1945*. Gorizia: Libreria editrice goriziana, 2000.

Bonavita, Petra. *Mit falschem Pass und Zyankali. Retter und Gerettete aus Frankfurt am Main in der NS-Zeit*. Stuttgart: Schmetterling, 2009.

Borgstedt, Angela. "'Bruderring' und 'Lucknerkreis': Rettung im deutschen Südwesten." In *Überleben im Untergrund*, edited by Beate KosmalaandClaudia Schoppmann, 191–204. Berlin: Metropol, 2002.

———. "Hilfen für Verfolgte: Judenretter und Judenhelfer." In *Widerstand gegen die nationalsozialistische Diktatur*, edited by Peter Steinbach and Johannes Tuchel, 307–21. Bonn: Bundeszentrale für politische Bildung, 1994.

Bösch, Frank Film. "NS-Vergangenheit und Geschichtswissenschaft von 'Holocaust' zu 'Der Untergang.'" *Vierteljahrshefte für Zeitgeschichte* 55 (2007): 1–32.

Brauns, Nikolaus. "'Kraft wahrer Solidarität'—Oskar Maria Graf und die Rote Hilfe in München (mit einem bisher unveröffentlichten Brief Grafs an ein Mitglied der Roten Hilfe)." In *Oskar Maria Graf 2008/09, Jahrbuch der Oskar Maria Graf-Gesellschaft*, 9–69. Munich: Allitera, 2009.

———. *Schafft Rote Hilfe! Geschichte und Aktivitäten der proletarischen Hilfsorganisation für poltische Gefangene in Deutschland (1919–1938)*. Bonn: Pahl-Rugenstein, 2003.

Brenner, Michael. *After the Holocaust: Rebuilding Jewish Lives in Postwar Germany*. Princeton: Princeton University Press, 1997.

———. *Der lange Schatten der Revolution. Juden und Antisemiten in München 1918–1923*. Berlin: Suhrkamp, 2019.

———, ed. *Geschichte der Juden in Deutschland von 1945 bis zur Gegenwart. Politik, Kultur und Gesellschaft*. München: C. H. Beck, 2012.

Bronowski, Alexander. *Es waren so Wenige. Retter im Holocaust*. Stuttgart: Quell-Verlag, 1991.

Browning, Christopher, with contributions by Jürgen Matthäus. *The Origins of the Final Solution: The Evolution of Nazi Jewish Policy, September 1939–March 1942*. Lincoln: University of Nebraska Press, 2004.

Brunner, José. "Gesetze, Gutachter, Geld—Das Trauma als Paradigma des Holocaust." In *Holocaust und Trauma*, edited by José Brunner and Nathalie Zajde, 40–71. Göttingen: Wallstein, 2011.

Brunner, José, and Nathalie Zajde, eds. *Holocaust und Trauma. Kritische Perspektiven zur Entstehung und Wirkung eines Paradigmas*. Göttingen: Wallstein, 2011.

Buchna, Kristian. *Nationale Sammlung an Rhein und Ruhr. Friedrich Middelhauve und die nordrhein-westfälische FDP 1945–1953*. Munich: Oldenbourg, 2010.

Bühler, Anne Lore. *Der Kirchenkampf im evangelischen München. Die Auseinandersetzung mit dem Nationalsozialismus und seinen Folgeerscheinungen im Bereich des Evang.-Luth. Dekanates München 1923–1950*. Nürnberg: Selbstverlag des Vereins für bayerische Kirchengeschichte, 1974.

Bukey, Evan Burr. *Jews and Intermarriage in Nazi Austria*. Cambridge: Cambridge University Press, 2011.

Bukofzer, Ernst, and Curt Radlauer. *Kommentar zum Gesetz über die Entschädigung der Opfer des Nationalsozialismus vom 10. Januar 1951*. Koblenz: Humanitas-Verlag, 1951.

Büttner, Ursula. "Die anderen Christen. Ihr Einsatz für verfolgte Juden und 'Nichtarier' im nationalsozialistischen Deutschland." In *Überleben im Untergrund*, edited by Beate Kosmala and Claudia Schoppmann, 127–50. Berlin: Metropol, 2002.

———. "Von der Kirche verlassen: Die deutschen Protestanten und die Verfolgung der Juden und Christen jüdischer Herkunft im 'Dritten Reich.'" In *Die verlassenen Kinder der Kirche. Der Umgang mit Christen jüdischer Herkunft im 'Dritten Reich,'* edited by Ursula Büttner and Martin Greschat, 15–69. Göttingen: Vandenhoeck & Ruprecht, 1998.

Cahnman, Werner. "Die Juden in München 1918–43." *Zeitschrift für bayerische Landesgeschichte* 42 (1979): 403–61.

Caplan, Jane. "Ausweis bitte! Identity and Identification in Nazi Germany." In *Identification and Registration Practices in Transnational Perspective*, edited by Ilsen About, James Brown, and Gayle Lonergan, 224–42. London: Palgrave Macmillan, 2013.

Cesarani, David, ed. *"Bystanders" to the Holocaust: A Re-evaluation*. London: Cass, 2002.

Chaussy, Ulrich, and Gerd Ueberschär. *"Es lebe die Freiheit!" Die Geschichte der Weißen Rose und ihrer Mitglieder in Dokumenten und Berichten*. Frankfurt am Main: Fischer, 2013.

Christians, Annemone. *Amtsgewalt und Volksgesundheit. Das öffentliche Gesundheitswesen im nationalsozialistischen München*. Göttingen: Wallstein, 2013.

Cohen, Beth. *Child Survivors of the Holocaust. The Youngest Remnant and the American Experience*. New Brunswick: Rutgers University Press, 2018.

———. "Starting Over. Reconstituted Families after the Holocaust." In *Children in the Holocaust and its Aftermath*, edited by Sharon Kangisser Cohen, Eva Fogelman and Dalia Ofer, 62–80. New York: Berghahn, 2017.

Cole, Tim. *Holocaust Landscapes*. London: Bloomsbury, 2016.

Crago-Schneider, Kierra. "Antisemitism or Competing Interests? An Examination of German and American Perceptions of Jewish Diplaced Persons Active on the Black Market in Munich's Möhlstrasse." *Yad Vashem Studies* 38 (2010): 167–94.

Craig Norton, Jennifer. *The Kindertransport. Contesting Memory*. Bloomington: Indiana University Press, 2019.

Cranach, Michael von, and Hans-Ludwig Siemen. *Psychiatrie im Nationalsozialismus. Die bayerischen Heil- und Pflegeanstalten zwischen 1933 und 1945*. Munich: Oldenbourg, 1999.

Croes, Marnix, and Beate Kosmala. "Facing Deportation in Germany and the Netherlands. Survival in Hiding." In *Facing the Catastrophe: Jews and Non-Jews in Europe during World War II*, edited by Beate Kosmala and Georgi Verbeek, 97–158. Oxford: Berg, 2011.

Curio, Claudia. *Verfolgung, Flucht, Rettung. Die Kindertransporte 1938/39 nach Großbritannien*. Berlin: Metropol, 2006.

Dams, Carsten, and Michael Stolle. *Die Gestapo. Herrschaft und Terror im Dritten Reich*. Munich: C. H. Beck, 2008.

Damskis, Linda Lucia. *Zerrissene Biografien. Jüdische Ärzte zwischen nationalsozialistischer Verfolgung, Emigration und Wiedergutmachung*. Munich: Allitera, 2009.

Delpard, Raphael. *Überleben im Versteck. Jüdische Kinder 1940–1944*. Bonn: Dietz, 1994.

Detjen, Marion. *"Zum Staatsfeind ernannt . . ." Widerstand, Resistenz und Verweigerung gegen das NS-Regime in München*. Munich: Buchendorfer, 1998.

Deutsch, Harold. *The Conspiracy against Hitler in the Twilight War*. Minneapolis: University of Minnesota Press, 1968.

Diewald-Kerkmann, Gisela. *Politische Denunziation im NS-Regime oder die kleine Macht der "Volksgenossen."* Bonn: Dietz, 1995.

Dörner, Bernward. *Die Deutschen und der Holocaust. Was keiner wissen wollte, aber jeder wissen konnte*. Berlin: Propyläen, 2007.

———. "NS-Herrschaft und Denunziation. Anmerkungen zu Defiziten in der Denunziationsforschung." *Historical Social Research* 26 (2001): 55–69.

Drecoll, Axel. *Der Fiskus als Verfolger. Die steuerliche Diskriminierung der Juden in Bayern 1933–1941/42*. Munich: Oldenbourg, 2009.

———. "Die Entjudung der Münchner Ärzteschaft 1933–1941." In *München arisiert. Entrechtung und Enteignung der Juden in der NS-Zeit*, edited by Angelika Baummann and Andreas Heusler, 70–86. Munich: Beck, 2004.

Düring, Marten. *Verdeckte soziale Netzwerke im Nationalsozialismus. Die Entstehung und Arbeitsweise von Berliner Hilfsnetzwerken für verfolgte Juden*. Berlin: De Gruyter Oldenbourg, 2015.

Durst, Nathan. "Eine Herausforderung für Therapeuten. Psychotherapie mit Überlebenden der Shoah." In *Das Trauma des Holocaust zwischen Psychologie und Geschichte*, edited by Revital Ludewig-Kedmi et al., 79–96. Zurich: Chronos, 2001.

Dwork, Deborah. *Children with a Star. Jewish Youth in Nazi Europe*. New Haven: Yale University Press, 1991.

Ebert, Helmut, and Thomas Hasselwander. "Schwadroneur, Excentriker, Polemiker und Opfer: Reck-Malleczewen." *Pasinger Archiv* 11 (1992): 20–32.

Ebert, Monika. *Zwischen Anerkennung und Ächtung. Medizinerinnen der Ludwig-Maximilians-Universität in der ersten Hälfte des 20. Jahrhunderts*. Neustadt an der Aisch: Schmidt, 2003.

Ebertz, Doris, and Walter Ebertz. *Die jüdischen Familien in Wetzlar. Ein Gedenkbuch*. Wetzlar: Wetzlarer Geschichtsverein, 2010.

Eichler, Volker. "Das 'Judenreferat' der Frankfurter Gestapo." In *Kristallnacht*, edited by Monica Kingreen, 237–58. Frankfurt am Main: Campus, 1999.

Eichmüller, Andreas. *Keine Generalamnestie. Die strafrechtliche Verfolgung von NS-Verbrechen in der frühen Bundesrepublik*. Munich: Oldenbourg, 2012.

Engelking, Barbara. *Such a Beautiful Sunny Day. Jews Seeking Refuge in the Polish Countryside, 1942–1945*. Translated by Jerzy Michalowicz. Jerusalem: Yad Vashem, 2016.

Enzenbach, Isabel. "Zur Problematik des Begriffes 'Retter.'" In *Überleben im Untergrund. Hilfe für Juden in Deutschland, 1941–45 (Solidarität und Hilfe für*

Juden während der NS-Zeit, Vol. 5), edited by Beate Kosmala and Claudia Schoppmann, 241–56. Berlin: Metropol, 2002.

Erler, Hans, Arnold Paucker, and Ernst Ludwig Ehrlich, eds. *"Gegen alle Vergeblichkeit." Jüdischer Widerstand gegen den Nationalsozialismus*. Frankfurt am Main: Campus, 2003.

Ernst, Roland. *Der Vollstrecker. Johann Reichhart: Bayerns letzter Henker*. Munich: Allitera Verlag, 2019.

Evans, Richard. "Afterword." In *Diary of a Man in Despair*, by Friedrich Reck, 215–35. New York: NRB Classics, 2013.

Feaux de la Croix, Ernst, and Helmut Rumpf. *Der Werdegang des Entschädigungsrechts unter national- und völkerrechtlichem und politologischem Aspekt, München 1985 (Die Wiedergutmachung nationalsozialistischen Unrechts durch die Bundesrepublik Deutschland)*. Edited by the Bundesminster der Finanzen in Zusammenarbeit mit Walter Schwarz, Band III. Munich: C. H. Beck, 1985.

Feinstein Myers, Margarete. *Holocaust Survivors in Postwar Germany*. New York: Cambridge University Press, 2010.

Fix, Karl-Heinz. *Glaubensgenossen in Not. Die Evangelisch-Lutherische Kirche in Bayern und die Hilfe für aus rassischen Gründen verfolgte Protestanten. Eine Dokumentation*. Gütersloh: Gütersloher Verlags-Haus, 2011.

———. "Landesbischof Meiser und die Hilfe für 'Glaubensgenossen in Not.'" In *Die Kirchen und die Verbrechen im nationalsozialistischen Staat*, edited by Thomas Brechenmacher and Harry Oelke, 219–41. Göttingen: Wallstein, 2011.

Fogelman, Eva. *Conscience & Courage: Rescuers of Jews During the Holocaust*. New York: Doubleday, 1994.

———. "The Psychology behind Being a Hidden Child." In *The Hidden Children*, edited by Jane Marks, 292–307. New York: Ballantine, 1993.

Fraenkel, Daniel, and Jakob Borut, eds. *Lexikon der Gerechten unter den Völkern. Deutsche und Österreicher*. Göttingen: Wallstein, 2005.

Fransecky, Tanja von. *Escapees: The History of Jews Who Fled Nazi Deportation Trains in France, Belgium and the Netherlands*. Translated by Benjamin Liebelt. New York: Berghahn Books, 2019.

Frei, Norbert. *Adenauer's Germany and the Nazi Past. The Politics of Amnesty and Integration*. Translated by Joel Golb. New York: Columbia University Press, 2002.

Frei, Norbert, José Brunner, and Constantin Goschler, eds. *Die Praxis der Wiedergutmachung. Geschichte, Erfahrung und Wirkung in Deutschland und Israel*. Göttingen: Wallstein, 2009.

Friedländer, Saul. *Nazi Germany and the Jews. Vol. 1, The Years of Persecution, 1933–1939*. New York: HarperCollins, 1997.

———. *The Years of Extermination. Nazi Germany and the Jews, 1939–1945*. New York: HarperCollins, 2007.

Friedrich, Karin. "'Er ist gemein zu unseren Freunden . . .' Das Retternetz der Gruppe 'Onkel Emil.'" In *Überleben im Dritten Reich*, edited by Wolfgang Benz, 97–112. Munich: C. H. Beck, 2003.

Fritzsche, Peter. "Babi Yar, but not Auschwitz. What did the Germans Know About the Final Solution?" In *The Germans and the Holocaust. Popular Responses to the Persecution and Murder of the Jews*, edited by Susanna Schrafstetter and Alan Steinweis, 85–106. New York: Berghahn, 2016.

Frydman, Marcel. *Le traumatisme de l'enfant caché. Répercussions psychologiques à court et à long termes*. Paris: L'Harmattan, 2002.

Fürmetz, Gerhard. "Ein Fall für den Staatskommissar. Philipp Auerbach und die frühe Praxis der Wiedergutmachung in Bayern." In *Wiedergutmachung als Auftrag. Begleitband zur gleichnamigen Ausstellung, Geschichtsort Villa ten Hompel*, edited by Alfons Kenkmann, 157–70. Essen: Klartext, 2007.

Garbarini, Alexandra. *Numbered Days. Diaries and the Holocaust*. New Haven: Yale University Press, 2006.

Geer, Nadja. *Sophistication. Zwischen Denkstil und Pose*. Göttingen: V & R unipress, 2012.

Gellately, Robert. *Backing Hitler: Consent and Coercion in Nazi Germany*. Oxford: Oxford University Press, 2001.

———. *The Gestapo and German Society, Enforcing Racial Policy 1933–1945*. Oxford: Clarendon, 1990.

Gerl, Hanna-Barbara. *Romano Guardini, 1885–1968. Leben und Werk*. Mainz: Matthias Grünewald, 1985.

Giesecke, Dana, and Harald Welzer. *Das Menschenmögliche. Zur Renovierung der deutschen Erinnerungskultur*. Hamburg: Edition Körber-Stiftung, 2012.

Ginzel, Günther, ed. *Mut zur Menschlichkeit. Hilfe für Verfolgte während der NS-Zeit*. Cologne: Rheinland-Verlag, 1993.

Giordano, Alberto, and Anna Holian. "Retracing the 'Hunt for Jews.' A Spatio-Temporal Analysis of Arrests during the Holocaust in Italy." In *Geographies of the Holocaust*, edited by Kelly Ann Knowles, Tim Cole, and Alberto Giordano, 52–87. Bloomington: Indiana University Press, 2014.

Goeschel, Christian. *Suicide in Nazi Germany*. Oxford: Oxford University Press, 2009.

Goltermann, Svenja. "Kausalitätsfragen. Psychisches Leid und psychiatrisches Wissen in der Entschädigung." In *Die Praxis der Wiedergutmachung. Geschichte, Erfahrung und Wirkung in Deutschland und Israel*, edited by Norbert Frei, José Brunner, and Constantin Goschler, 427–51. Göttingen: Wallstein, 2009.

———. "Psychisches Leid und herrschende Lehre. Der Wissenschaftswandel in deutschen Psychiatrie der Nachkriegszeit." In *Akademische Vergangenheitspolitik.*

Beiträge zur Wissenschaftskultur der Nachkriegszeit, edited by Bernd Weisbrod, 263–80. Göttingen: Wallstein, 2002.

Goschler, Constantin. *Schuld und Schulden. Die Politik der Wiedergutmachung für NS-Verfolgte seit 1945*. Göttingen: Wallstein, 2005.

———. *Wiedergutmachung. Westdeutschland und die Verfolgten des Nationalsozialismus (1945–1954)*. Munich: Oldenbourg, 1992.

Gottwaldt, Alfred, and Diana Schulle. *Die "Judendeportationen" aus dem Deutschen Reich 1941–1945. Eine kommentierte Chronologie*. Wiesbaden: Marix Verlag, 2005.

Grabowski, Jan. *Hunt for the Jews: Betrayal and Murder in German-Occupied Poland*. Bloomington: Indiana University Press, 2013.

———. *Rescue for Money. Paid Helpers in Poland 1939–1945*. Jerusalem: Yad Vashem, 2008.

———. "Rural Society and the Jews in Hiding: Elders, Night Watches, Firefighters, Hostages and Manhunts." *Yad Vashem Studies* 40 (2012): 49–74.

Grau, Bernhard. "Steigbügelhalter des NS-Staates—Franz Xaver Ritter von Epp und die Zeit des 'Dritten Reiches.'" In *Rechte Karrieren*, edited by Marita Krauss, 29–51. Munich: Volk Verlag, 2010.

Gribl, Dorle. *Solln in den Jahren 1933–1945*. Munich: Volk Verlag, 2006.

Groothuis, Rainer-Maria. "Pater Aurelius Arkenau OP: Einsatz für Verfolgte." In *Geistliche und Gestapo. Klerus zwischen Staatsallmacht und kirchlicher Hierarchie*, edited by Joachim Kurpoka, 255–73. Münster: LIT Verlag, 2004.

Gross, Leonard. *The Last Jews in Berlin*. New York: Simon & Schuster, 1982.

Grossmann, Atina. *Jews, Germans, and Allies: Close Encounters in Occupied Germany*. Princeton: Princeton University Press, 2007.

Grossmann, Kurt. *Die Unbesungenen Helden. Menschen in Deutschlands dunklen Tagen*. Berlin: Arani, 1957.

Grube, Werner, and Ilse Macek. "Erwin Weil (Kusel, Pfalz): '. . . überfällt mich eine unbeschreibliche Traurigkeit.'" In *Ausgegrenzt – Entrechtet – Deportiert*, edited by Ilse Macek, 145–54. Munich: Volk Verlag, 2008.

Gruner, Wolf. *Der Geschlossene Arbeitseinsatz deutscher Juden. Zur Zwangsarbeit als Element der Verfolgung 1938–1943*. Berlin: Metropol, 1997.

———. "Die Berliner und die NS-Judenverfolgung. Eine mikrohistorische Studie individueller Handlungen und sozialer Beziehungen." In *Berlin im Nationalsozialismus*, edited by Rüdiger Hachtmann, Thomas Schaarschmidt, and Winfried Süß, 57–87. Göttingen: Wallstein, 2011.

———. "Die NS-Judenverfolgung und die Kommunen. Zur wechselseitigen Dynamisierung von zentraler und lokaler Politik 1933–1941." *Vierteljahrshefte für Zeitgeschichte* 48 (2000): 75–126.

———. "Ein Historikerstreit? Die Internierung der Juden aus Mischehen in der Rosenstraße 1943. Das Ereignis, seine Diskussion und seine Geschichte." *Zeitschrift für Geschichtswissenschaft* 52 (2004): 5–22.

———. "'The Germans Should Expel the Foreigner Hitler . . .' Open Protest and Other Forms of Defiance in Nazi Germany." *Yad Vashem Studies* 39 (2011): 13–53.

———. *Jewish Forced Labor under the Nazis: Economic Needs and Racial Aims 1933–1944*. Translated by Kathleen M. Dell'Orto. Cambridge/New York: Cambridge University Press, 2006.

———. *Öffentliche Wohlfahrt und Judenverfolgung. Wechselwirkung lokaler und zentraler Politik im NS-Staat (1933–1942)*. Munich: Oldenbourg, 2002.

———. "Von der Kollektivausweisung zur Deportation der Juden *aus Deutschland* (1938–1945). Neue Perspektiven und Dokumente." In *Die Deportation der Juden aus Deutschland*, edited by Beate Meyer and Birthe Kundrus, 21–62. Göttingen: Wallstein, 2011.

———. *Widerstand in der Rosenstraße. Die Fabrikaktion und die Verfolgung der 'Mischehen' 1943*. Frankfurt am Main: Fischer, 2005.

Hachtmann, Rüdiger, Thomas Schaarschmidt, and Winfried Süß, eds. *Berlin im Nationalsozialismus. Politik und Gesellschaft 1933–1945*. Göttingen: Wallstein, 2011.

Haerendel, Ulrike. "Der Schutzlosigkeit preisgegeben: Die Zwangsveräußerung jüdischen Immobilienbesitzes und die Vertreibung der Juden aus ihren Wohnungen." In *München arisiert*, edited by Angelika Baumann and Andreas Heusler, 105–25. Munich: C. H. Beck, 2004.

———. "Von der Mustersiedlung zur 'arisierten' Stadt: Wohnungsmarkt, Wohnungspolitik und Wohnungsraub in München." In *München und der Nationalsozialismus*, edited by Stefanie Hajak and Jürgen Zarusky, 227–48. Berlin: Metropol, 2008.

Hajak, Stefanie. "Letzte Adresse: Lindwurmstraße 125. Die Zerstörung der Israelitischen Kultusgemeinde Münchens." In *München und der Nationalsozialismus*, edited by Stefanie Hajak and Jürgen Zarusky, 133–50. Berlin: Metropol, 2008.

Hajak, Stefanie, and Jürgen Zarusky. "Verfolgung Zerstörung Neuanfang, Ein Gespräch mit Charlotte Knobloch." In *München und der Nationalsozialismus*, edited by Stefanie Hajak and Jürgen Zarusky, 381–98. Berlin: Metropol, 2008.

Hajak, Stefanie, and Jürgen Zarusky, eds. *München und der Nationalsozialismus. Menschen, Orte, Strukturen*. Berlin: Metropol, 2008.

Hájková, Anna. *The Last Ghetto: An Everyday History of Theresienstadt*. New York: Oxford University Press, 2020.

Haller, Roman. *. . . und bleiben wollte keiner. Jüdische Lebensgeschichten im Nachkriegsbayern*. Munich: Dölling und Galitz, 2004.

Hamann, Christoph. "'Uropa war ein Guter.' Retten und Überleben im Nationalsozialismus als Thema des Geschichtsunterrichts." In *Überleben im Untergrund*, edited by Beate Kosmala and Claudia Schoppman, 381–94. Berlin: Metropol, 2002.

Hametz, Maura. "'Leben im Blut' in der schönen Stadt: Juden und Nationalsozialisten in Triest 1943–1945." In *Alltag im Holocaust*, edited by Andrea Löw, Doris Bergen, and Anna Hájková, 217–36. Munich: Oldenbourg, 2013.

Hanke, Peter. *Zur Geschichte der Juden in München zwischen 1933 und 1945*. Munich: Stadtarchiv, 1967.

Häntzschel, Hiltrud. "'Flucht vor Hitler.' Zur Emigration aus München." In *München und der Nationalsozialismus*, edited by Stefanie Hajakand Jürgen Zarusky, 185–204. Berlin: Metropol, 2008.

Hardtmann, Gertrud, and Dan Bar-On, eds. *Spuren der Verfolgung. Seelische Auswirkungen des Holocaust auf die Opfer und ihre Kinder*. Gerlingen: Bleicher, 1992.

Hartlapp, Johannes. *Siebenten-Tags-Adventisten im Nationalsozialismus*. Göttingen: V&R unipress, 2008.

Heim, Susanne, Beate Meyer, and Francis R. Nicosia, eds. *"Wer bleibt, opfert seine Jahre, vielleicht sein Leben." Deutsche Juden 1938–1941*. Göttingen: Wallstein, 2010.

Heinz, Daniel, ed. *Freikirchen und Juden im "Dritten Reich." Instrumentalisierte Heilsgeschichte, antisemitische Vorurteile und verdrängte Schuld*. Göttingen: V&R unipress, 2011.

Herbstrith, Waltraud. *Edith Stein, a Biography*. Translated by Bernard Bonowitz. San Francisco: Harper and Row, 1985.

———, ed. *Edith Steins Unterstützer: Bekannte und unbekannte Helfer während der NS-Diktatur*. Münster: LIT Verlag, 2010.

———. "Enge Freunde Edith Steins—Anne Reinach-Stettenheimer und Hans Lipps." In *Edith Steins Unterstützer*, edited by Waltraud Herbstrith, 65–72. Münster: LIT Verlag, 2010.

Hering, Sabine, and Kurt Schilde, eds. *Die Rote Hilfe. Die Geschichte der internationalen kommunistischen "Wohlfahrtsorganisation" und ihrer sozialen Aktivitäten in Deutschland (1921–1941)*. Opladen: Leske und Budrich, 2003.

Hermann, Angela. "Hitler und sein Stoßtrupp in der 'Reichskristallnacht.'" *Vierteljahrshefte für Zeitgeschichte* 56 (2008): 603–20.

Hermle, Siegfried. "Die antijüdische NS-Politik als Herausforderung des Protestantismus." In *Die Kirchen und die Verbrechen im nationalsozialistischen Staat*, edited by Thomas Brechenmacher and Harry Oelke, 175–98. Göttingen: Wallstein, 2011.

———. *Evangelische Kirche und Judentum—Stationen nach 1945*. Göttingen: Vandenhoeck & Ruprecht, 1990.

Heschel, Susannah. *The Aryan Jesus. Christian Theologians and the Bible in Nazi Germany*. Princeton: Princeton University Press, 2008.

Heusler, Andreas. *Ausländereinsatz. Zwangsarbeit für die Münchner Kriegswirtschaft 1939–1945*. Munich: Hugendubel, 1996.

———. *Das Braune Haus. Wie München zur "Hauptstadt der Bewegung" wurde.* Munich: Deutsche Verlags-Anstalt, 2008.

———. "Fahrt in den Tod. Der Mord an den Münchner Juden in Kaunas (Litauen) am 25. November 1941." In *" . . . verzogen, unbekannt wohin." Die erste Deportation von Münchner Juden im November 1941*, edited by Stadtarchiv München, 13–24. Zürich: Pendo, 2000.

———. "Karl Fiehler (1933–1945)." In *Die Münchner Oberbürgermeister. 200 Jahre gelebte Stadtgeschichte*, 117–34. Munich: Volk Verlag, 2008.

———. "Verfolgung und Vernichtung (1933–1945)." In *Jüdisches München*, edited by Richard Bauer and Michael Brenner, 161–84. Munich: C. H. Beck, 2006.

Heusler, Andreas, and Tobias Weger. *"Kristallnacht." Gewalt gegen die Münchner Juden im November 1938*. Munich: Buchendorfer, 1998.

Heydt, Maria von der. "'Geltungsjuden' und jüdische Gemeinde in Berlin 1939–1945." *Zeitgeschichte* 43, no. 5 (2016): 308–23.

———. "'Wer fährt denn gerne mit dem Judenstern in der Straßenbahn?' Zur Ambivalenz des 'geltungsjüdischen' Alltags 1941–1945." In *Alltag*, edited by Andrea Löw, Doris Bergen, and Anna Hájková, 65–80. Munich: Oldenbourg, 2013.

Hilberg, Raul. *The Destruction of the European Jews, 3 Vols.* New Haven and London: Yale University Press, 2003.

———. *Perpetrators, Victims, Bystanders. The Jewish Catastrophe 1933–1945*. New York: HarperCollins, 1992.

Hinz-Wessels, Annette. "Antisemitismus und Krankenmord. Zum Umgang mit jüdischen Anstaltspatienten im Nationalsozialismus." *Vierteljahrshefte für Zeitgeschichte* 61 (2013): 65–92.

Hockerts, Hans Günter. "Warum München? Wie Bayerns Metropole die 'Hauptstadt der Bewegung' wurde." In *München und der Nationalsozialismus*, edited by Winfried Nerdinger, 387–97. Munich: C. H. Beck, 2015.

———. "Wiedergutmachung in Deutschland. Eine historische Bilanz 1945–2000." *Vierteljahrshefte für Zeitgeschichte* 49 (2001): 167–214.

Hockerts, Hans Günter, and Christane Kuller, eds. *Nach der Verfolgung. Wiedergutmachung nationalsozialistischen Unrechts?* Göttingen: Wallstein, 2003.

Hoffmann, Peter. *German Resistance to Hitler.* Harvard: Harvard University Press, 1988.

Holian, Anna. *Between National Socialism and Soviet Communism: Displaced Persons in Postwar Germany.* Ann Arbor: University of Michigan Press, 2011.

———. "Die Möhlstraße und der Wiederaufbau jüdischen Wirtschaftslebens in Nachkriegsdeutschland." *Münchner Beiträge zur jüdischen Geschichte und Kultur* 12 (2018): 23–34.

———. "The Architecture of Jewish Trade in Postwar Germany: Jewish Shops and Shopkeepers between Provisionality and Permanence." *Jewish Social Studies* 23 (2017): 101–33

Hölscher, Christoph. *NS-Verfolgte im "antifaschistischen Staat." Vereinnahmung und Ausgrenzung in der ostdeutschen Wiedergutmachung (1945–1989)*. Berlin: Metropol, 2002.

Holtmann, Gunda. *Ellen Ammann—eine intellektuelle Biographie*. Würzburg: Ergon, 2017.

Horbach, Michael. *Wenige. Zeugnisse der Menschlichkeit 1933–1945*. Munich: Kindler, 1964.

Johnson, Eric. *Nazi Terror: The Gestapo, Jews, and Ordinary Germans*. New York: Basic Books, 1999.

Johnson, Eric, and Karl Heinz Reuband, eds. *What We Knew: Terror, Mass Murder, and Everyday Life in Nazi Germany. An Oral History*. London: John Murray, 2005.

Jureit, Ulrike, and Christian Schneider. *Gefühlte Opfer. Illusionen der Vergangenheitsbewältigung*. Stuttgart: Klett-Cotta, 2010.

Kabalek, Kobi. "The Commemoration before the Commemoration: Yad Vashem and the Righteous Among the Nations, 1945–1963." *Yad Vashem Studies* 39, no. 1 (2011): 169–211.

Kain, Robert. *Otto Weidt. Anarchist und "Gerechter unter den Völkern."* Berlin: Lukas Verlag für Kunst- und Geistesgeschichte, 2017.

Kangisser Cohen, Sharon, Eva Fogelman and Dalia Ofer, eds. *Children in the Holocaust and its Aftermath*. New York: Berghahn, 2017.

Kaplan, Marion. *Between Dignity and Despair: Jewish Life in Nazi Germany*. New York, Oxford: Oxford University Press, 1998.

Kappeler, Alphons. *Ein Fall von "Pseudologia phantastica" in der deutschen Literatur: Fritz Reck-Malleczewen*. Göppingen: A. Kümmerle, 1975.

Kasberger, Erich. "Hans Wegner und Theodor Koronczyk—zwei Pole des Täterspektrums." In *Rechte Karrieren*, edited by Marita Krauss, 230–44. Munich: Volk Verlag, 2008.

———. "Karrierewege Münchner Gestapobeamter aus dem 'Judenreferat'; eine Kollektivbiografie." In *Rechte Karrieren*, edited by Marita Krauss, 189–229. Munich: Volk Verlag, 2008.

Kastner, Wolfram, ed. *Auf einmal da waren sie weg . . . Zur Erinnerung an Münchner Juden; ein Beispiel, das zur Nachahmung anregen könnte*. Munich: Allitera, 2004.

Kater, Michael H. *Different Drummers: Jazz in the Culture of Nazi Germany*. New York and Oxford: Oxford University Press, 1992.

Kauders, Anthony. "Catholics, the Jews and Democratization in Post-war Germany: Munich, 1945–1965." *German History* 18 (2000): 461–84.

———. *Democratization and the Jews: Munich, 1945–1965*. Lincoln: University of Nebraska Press, 2004.

———. *Unmögliche Heimat. Eine deutsch-jüdische Geschichte der Bundesrepublik.* Munich: Deutsche Verlags-Anstalt, 2007.

Kauders, Anthony, and Tamar Levinsky. "Neuanfang mit Zweifeln (1945–1970)." In *Jüdisches München*, edited by Richard Bauer and Michael Brenner, 185–208. Munich: C. H. Beck, 2006.

Keilson, Hans. "Die Entwicklung des Traumakonzepts in der Psychiatrie. Psychiatrie und Man-made-disaster." *Mittelweg* 36, no. 6 (1997/98): 73–82.

———. "Sequentielle Traumatisierung bei Kindern." In *Spuren der Verfolgung. Seelische Auswirkungen des Holocaust auf die Opfer und ihre Kinder*, edited by Gertrud Hardtmann, 69–79. Gerlingen: Bleicher, 1992.

Keilson, Hans, and H. R. Sarphatie. *Sequential Traumatization in Children (A Clinical and Statistical Follow-up Study on the Fate of the Jewish War Orphans in the Netherlands)*. Translated by Yvonne Bearne, Hilary Coleman, and Deirdre Winter. Jerusalem: Magnus Press, 1992.

Keim, Anton. *Die Judenretter aus Deutschland*. Mainz: Grünewald, 1983.

Keller, Sven. *Volksgemeinschaft am Ende. Gesellschaft und Gewalt 1944/45*. Munich: Oldenbourg, 2013.

Keneally, Thomas. *Schindler's Ark*. London: Hodder and Stoughton, 1982.

Kershaw, Ian. *Popular Opinion and Political Dissent in the Third Reich: Bavaria, 1933–1945*. Oxford: Clarendon, 2002.

Kestenberg, Judith, and Charlotte Kahn, eds. *Children Surviving Persecution: An International Study of Trauma and Healing*. Westport: Praeger, 1998.

Kingma, Renate. *Spuren der Menschlichkeit: Hilfe für jüdische Frankfurter*. Hanau: CoCon, 2006.

Kingreen, Monica. "'Die Aktion zur kalten Erledigung der Mischehen'—die reichsweit singuläre systematische Verschleppung und Ermordung jüdischer Mischehepartner im NSDAP-Gau Hessen-Nassau 1942/43." In *NS-Gewaltherrschaft. Beiträge zur historischen Forschung und juristischen Aufarbeitung*, edited by Alfred Gottwaldt et al., 187–201. Berlin: Hentrich, 2005.

———. "Gewaltsam verschleppt aus Frankfurt. Die Deportationen der Juden in den Jahren 1941–1945." In *"Nach der Kristallnacht,"* edited by Monica Kingreen, 357–402. Frankfurt am Main: Campus, 1999.

———, ed. *"Nach der Kristallnacht." Jüdisches Leben und antijüdische Politik in Frankfurt am Main 1938–1945*. Frankfurt am Main: Campus, 1999.

Kitzmann, Armin Rudi. *Mit Kreuz und Hakenkreuz. Die Geschichte der Protestanten in München 1918–1945*. Munich: Claudius, 1999.

———. *Wagnis Widerstand. Evangelische Christen in München gegen den Nationalsozialismus*. Munich: Allitera Verlag, 2016.

Klatt, Marlene. *Unbequeme Vergangenheit. Antisemitismus, Judenverfolgung und Wiedergutmachung in Westfalen 1925–1965*. Paderborn: Verlag Ferdinand Schöningh, 2009.

Knoll, Albert. "Die Todesmärsche des KZ Dachau im Spiegel der Berichte Überlebender." In *Freilegungen. Auf den Spuren der Todesmärsche,* edited by Jean-Luc Blondel et al., 198–213. Göttingen: Wallstein, 2012.

Knowles, Anne Kelly, Tim Cole, and Alberto Giordano, eds. *Geographies of the Holocaust.* Bloomington: Indiana University Press, 2014.

Königseder, Angelika. "Österreich—ein Land der Täter?" In *Solidarität und Hilfe für Juden während der NS-Zeit, Band 2 Regionalstudien: Frankreich, Österreich, Ukraine, Lettland, Litauen, Estland, Tschechoslowakei,* edited by Wolfgang Benz and Juliane Wetzel, 173–229. Berlin: Metropol, 1998.

———. "Polizeihaftlager." In *Der Ort des Terrors. Vol. 9: Arbeitserziehungslager, Ghettos, Jugendschutzlager, Polizeihaftlager, Sonderlager, Zigeunerlager, Zwangsarbeiterlager,* edited by Wolfgang Benz and Barbara Distel, 19–52. Munich: C. H. Beck, 2009.

Königseder, Angelika, and Juliane Wetzel. *Waiting for Hope: Jewish Displaced Persons in Post-World War II Germany.* Translated by John Broadwin. Evanston: Northwestern University Press, 2001.

Koppers-Weck, Gudrun. "Die Ortenaus in Pasing." In *Ins Licht gerückt,* edited by Bernhard Schoßig, 241–45. Munich: Herbert Utz Verlag, 2008.

———. "Rettung einer katholischen Jüdin—Klara Mayr." In *Ins Licht gerückt,* edited by Bernhard Schoßig, 205–10. Munich: Herbert Utz, 2008.

———. "Ruth Jordan. Überleben auf dem Bauernhof." In *Ins Licht gerückt,* edited by Bernhard Schoßig, 211–13. Munich: Herbert Utz, 2008.

Kosmala, Beate. "Gedenkstätte Stille Helden. Ein Erinnerungsort in Berlin." In *Helfer im Verborgenen. Retter jüdischer Menschen in Südwestdeutschland* (Laupheimer Gespräche 2009), edited by Irene Pill, 167–89. Heidelberg: Winter, 2012.

———. "Hanni Lévy in Berlin und Paris." In *Nichts wie raus und durch! Lebens- und Überlebensgeschichte einer jüdischen Berlinerin* edited by Beate Kosmala, 161–77. Berlin: Metropol, 2019.

———. "Mißglückte Hilfe und ihre Folgen: Die Ahndung der 'Judenbegünstigung' durch NS-Verfolgungsbehörden." In *Überleben im Untergrund. Hilfe für Juden in Deutschland 1941–1945,* edited by Beate Kosmala and Claudia Schoppmann, 205–22. Berlin: Metropol, 2002.

———. "Resistance to the Persecution of the Jews: Non-Jewish and Jewish Germans Caught in the Wheels of Justice and the Gestapo, 1942–1945." In *Hiding, Sheltering, and Borrowing Identities,* edited by Dan Michman, 107–22. Jerusalem: Yad Vashem, 2017.

———. "Rettung und Verrat: Jüdische Kinder in Deutschland 1941–1945." In *'So spricht der Ewige: . . . Und die Straßen der Stadt Jerusalem werden voll sein mit Knaben und Mädchen, die in ihren Straßen spielen.' Das jüdische Kind zwischen hoffnungsloser Vergangenheit und hoffnungsvoller Zukunft,* edited by Miriam

Gillis-Carlebach and Barbara Vogel, 62–84. Munich and Hamburg: Dönitz and Galitz Verlag, 2008.

———. "Ungleiche Opfer in extremer Situation. Die Schwierigkeiten der Solidarität im okkupierten Polen." In *Regionalstudien 1*, edited by Wolfgang Benz and Juliane Wetzel, 19–97. Berlin: Metropol, 2002.

———. "Zwischen Ahnen und Wissen. Flucht vor der Deportation, (1941–1943)." In *Die Deportation der Juden aus Deutschland. Pläne, Praxis, Reaktionen 1938–1945*, edited by Beate Meyer and Birthe Kundrus, 235–59. Göttingen: Wallstein, 2004.

Kosmala, Beate, and Claudia Schoppmann, eds. *Überleben im Untergrund. Hilfe für Juden in Deutschland 1941–1945 (Solidarität und Hilfe für Juden während der NS-Zeit, Vol.5)*. Berlin: Metropol, 2002.

———. "Überleben im Untergrund. Zwischenbilanz eines Forschungsprojektes." In *Überleben im Untergrund. Hilfe für Juden in Deutschland 1941–1945*, edited by Beate Kosmala and Claudia Schoppmann, 17–31. Berlin: Metropol, 2002.

Kosmala, Beate, and Felix Tych, eds. *Facing the Nazi Genocide: Non-Jews and Jews in Europe*. Berlin: Metropol, 2004.

Kosmala, Beate, and Georgi Verbeek, eds. *Facing the Catastrophe: Jews and Non-Jews in Europe during World War II*. Oxford: Berg, 2011.

Krafft, Sybille, and Christina Böck, eds. *Zwischen den Fronten. Münchner Frauen in Krieg und Frieden 1900–1950*. Munich: Buchendorfer, 1995.

Krakowski, Shmuel. *The War of the Doomed: Jewish Armed Resistance in Poland 1942–1944*. New York: Holmes & Meier, 1984.

Kraushaar, Wolfgang. "Die Affäre Auerbach. Zur Virulenz des Antisemitismus in den Gründerjahren der Bundesrepublik." In *Menora: Jahrbuch für deutsch-jüdische Geschichte 1995*, edited by Julius H. Schoeps, 319–43. Munich and Zurich: R. Piper GmbH & Co. KG.

Krauss, Marita, ed. *Rechte Karrieren in München: Von der Weimarer Republik in die Nachkriegsjahre*. Munich: Volk, 2010.

———. "Zur Einführung." In *Leben in zwei Welten* by Else Behrend-Rosenfeld and Siegfried Rosenfeld, 9–44. Munich: Volk-Verlag, 2011.

Kuller, Christiane. *Bürokratie und Verbrechen. Antisemitische Finanzpolitik und Verwaltungspraxis im nationalsozialistischen Deutschland*. Munich: Oldenbourg, 2013.

———. "'Erster Grundsatz: Horten für die Finanzverwaltung.' Die Verwertung des Eigentums der deportierten Nürnberger Juden." In *Die Deportation der Juden aus Deutschland*, edited by Beate Meyer and Birthe Kundrus, 160–79. Göttingen: Wallstein, 2004.

———. "Finanzverwaltung und 'Arisierung' in München." In *München arisiert*, edited by Angelika Baumann and Andreas Heusler, 176–97. Munich: C. H. Beck, 2004.

———. *Finanzverwaltung und Judenverfolgung. Die Entziehung jüdischen Vermögens in Bayern während der NS-Zeit*. Munich: C. H. Beck, 2008.

Kuller, Christiane, and Maximilian Schreiber. *Das Hildebrandhaus. Eine Münchner Künstlervilla und ihre Bewohner in der Zeit des Nationalsozialismus*. Munich: Allitera, 2006.

Künzel, Helmut. "Erinnerungen an Dr. Ing.-Habil. Josef Sebastian Cammerer." *Bauphysik* 30 (2008): 340–45.

Kurzhals, Anna. *"Millionendorf" und "Weltstadt mit Herz." Selbstdarstellung der Stadt München 1945–1978*. Munich: Herbert Utz Verlag, 2018.

Kwiet, Konrad. "Nach dem Pogrom: Stufen der Ausgrenzung." In *Die Juden in Deutschland,* edited by Wolfgang Benz, 545–659. Munich: C. H. Beck, 1988.

Kwiet, Konrad, and Helmut Eschwege. *Selbstbehauptung und Widerstand. Deutsche Juden im Kampf um Existenz und Menschenwürde 1933–1945*. Hamburg: Christians, 1984.

Lamm, Hans. "Einführung." In *Von Juden in München,* edited by Hans Lamm, 13–15. Munich: Ter-Namid-Verlag, 1958.

———, ed. *Von Juden in München. Ein Gedenkbuch*. Munich: Ter-Namid Verlag, 1982. Revised edition: *Vergangene Tage. Jüdische Kultur in München*. Munich: Ter-Namid Verlag, 1982.

Landeshauptstadt München, Kulturreferat. *ThemenGeschichtsPfad. Orte des Erinnerns und Gedenkens. Nationalsozialismus in München*. Munich: Kulturreferat, 2010.

Ledford, Kenneth. "Judging German Judges in the Third Reich: Excusing and Confronting the Past." In *The Law in Nazi Germany,* edited by Alan Steinweis and Robert Rachlin, 161–90. New York: Berghahn, 2013.

Leichsenring, Jana. "Die Auswanderungsunterstützung für katholische 'Nichtarier' und die Grenzen der Hilfe. Der St. Raphaelsverein in den Jahren 1938–1941." In *"Wer bleibt, opfert seine Jahre, vielleicht sein Leben." Deutsche Juden 1938–1941,* edited by Susanne Heim, Beate Meyer, and Francis Nicosia, 96–114. Berlin: Metropol, 2010.

———. *Die Katholische Kirche und "ihre" Juden. Das "Hilfswerk beim Bischöflichen Oridinariat Berlin" 1938–1945*. Berlin: Metropol, 2007.

Lekebusch, Sigrid. *Not und Verfolgung der Christen jüdischer Herkunft im Rheinland 1933–1945*. Cologne: Rheinland-Verlag, 1995.

Leugers, Antonia. "'Du hast alles vereint: Seele und Geist und Körper.' Kardinal Faulhaber und seine Freundin." *Rottenburger Jahrbuch für Kirchengeschichte* 35 (2016): 173–211.

———. "The 1943 Rosenstrasse Protest and the Churches." In *Protest in Hitler's "National Community,"* edited by Nathan Stoltzfus and Birgit Maier-Katkin, 143–76. New York: Berghahn, 2016.

Leuner, Heinz David. *When Compassion Was a Crime: Germany's Silent Heroes, 1933–1945*. London: Oswald Wolff, 1978.

Levi, Primo. *The Drowned and the Saved*. New York: Random House, 1989.

Lewinsky, Tamar. *Displaced Poets. Jüdische Schriftsteller im Nachkriegsdeutschland 1945–1951*. Göttingen: Vandenhoeck & Ruprecht, 2008.

Lippe, George von der, and Viktoria Reck-Malleczewen, eds. and trans. *A History of the Münster Anabaptists: Inner Emigration and the Third Reich: A Critical Edition of Friedrich Reck-Malleczewen's Bockelson: A Tale of Mass Insanity*. New York: Palgrave, 2008.

Litzka, Traude. *Kirchliche Hilfe für verfolgte Juden und Jüdinnen im nationalsozialistischen Wien*. Münster: LIT Verlag, 2011.

Löhken, Wilfried, and Werner Vathke, eds. *Juden im Widerstand. Drei Gruppen zwischen Überlebenskampf und politischer Aktion, Berlin 1939–1945*. Berlin: Hentrich, 1993.

Longerich, Peter. *"Davon haben wir nichts gewusst!" Die Deutschen und die Judenverfolgung 1933–1945*. Munich: Siedler, 2006.

Lovenheim, Barbara. *Survival in the Shadows: Seven Jews Hidden in Hitler's Berlin*. Rochester: Center for Holocaust Awareness and Information, 2002.

Löw, Andrea. "Die frühen Deportationen aus dem Reichsgebiet von Herbst 1939 bis Frühjahr 1941." In *"Wer bleibt, opfert seine Jahre, vielleicht sein Leben." Deutsche Juden 1938–1941*, edited by Susanne Heim, Beate Meyer, and Francis Nicosia, 59–76. Göttingen: Wallstein, 2010.

Löw, Andrea, Doris Bergen, and Anna Hájková, eds. *Alltag im Holocaust. Jüdisches Leben im Großdeutschen Reich 1941–1945*. Munich: Oldenbourg, 2013.

Löw, Konrad. *Die Münchner und ihre jüdischen Mitbürger 1900–1950 im Urteil der NS-Opfer und Gegner*. Munich: Olzog, 2008.

Löwenthal, Richard and Patrik von zur Mühlen. *Widerstand und Verweigerung in Deutschland 1933 bis 1945*. Bonn: Dietz, 1997.

Ludewig-Kedmi, Revital et al., eds. *Das Trauma des Holocaust zwischen Psychologie und Geschichte*. Zurich: Chronos, 2002.

Ludwig, Hartmut. *An der Seite der Entrechteten und Schwachen. Zur Geschichte des "Büro Pfarrer Grüber" (1938 bis 1940) und der Ev. Hilfsstelle für ehemals Rasseverfolgte nach 1945*. Berlin: Logos-Verlag, 2009.

Ludyga, Hannes. "Die Todesurteile des Oberlandesgerichts München im 2. Weltkrieg." *Journal der juristischen Zeitgeschichte* 9 (2015): 58–63.

———. "Eine antisemitische Affäre im Nachkriegsdeutschland. Der 'Staatskommissar für politisch, religiös und rassisch Verfolgte' Philipp Auerbach (1906–1952)." *Kritische Justiz* 40 (2007): 410–28.

———. *Philipp Auerbach (1906–1952). "Staatskommissar für rassisch, religiös und politisch Verfolgte."* Berlin: BWV, 2005.

Lustiger, Arno, ed. *Rettungswiderstand. Über die Judenretter in Europa während der NS-Zeit*. Göttingen: Wallstein, 2011.

———. *Zum Kampf auf Leben und Tod! Das Buch vom Widerstand der Juden 1933–1945*. Cologne: Kiepenheuer & Witsch, 1994.

Lutjens, Richard. "Jews in Hiding in Nazi Berlin, 1941–1945: A Demographic Survey." *Holocaust and Genocide Studies* 31, no. 2 (2017): 268–97.

———. "Ordinary Crime and the Persecution of Jewish Germans in Deportation-Era Berlin." *Holocaust and Genocide Studies* 31, no. 3 (2017): 433–56.

———. *Submerged on the Surface. The Not-So-Hidden Jews of Nazi Berlin, 1941–1945*. New York: Berghahn, 2019.

———. "Vom Untertauchen: 'U-Boote' und Berliner Alltag 1941–1945." In *Alltag im Holocaust*, edited by Andrea Löw, Doris Bergen, and Anna Hájková, 49–63. Munich: Oldenbourg, 2013.

Macek, Ilse, ed. *Ausgegrenzt—Entrechtet—Deportiert. Schwabing und Schwabinger Schicksale 1933 bis 1945*. Munich: Volk Verlag, 2008.

———. "Judith Hirsch, heute Judy Rosenberg (Montreal, Kanada)." In *Ausgegrenzt—Entrechtet—Deportiert*, edited by Ilse Macek, 115–27. Munich: Volk Verlag, 2008.

———. "Walter Geismar (South Caulfield, Australien)—'Man konnte nicht glauben, dass Deutsche das tun." In *Ausgegrenzt—Entrechtet—Deportiert*, edited by Ilse Macek, 155–69. Munich: Volk Verlag, 2008.

———. "Werner Grube (München)—'Mitzunehmen sind sämtliche Kinder zwecks Wohnsitzverlegung an Einsatzort.'" In *Ausgegrenzt—Entrechtet—Deportiert*, edited by Ilse Macek, 128–44. Munich: Volk Verlag, 2008.

Madievskij, Samson. *Die anderen Deutschen. Rettungswiderstand im Dritten Reich*. Aachen: Shaker Media, 2008.

Mahl, Tobias. "Die 'Arisierung' der Hofmöbelfabrik Ballin in München." In *München arisiert*, edited by Angelika Baumann and Andreas Heusler, 54–69. Munich: C. H. Beck, 2004.

Mann, Reinhard. *Protest und Kontrolle im Dritten Reich. Nationalsozialistische Herrschaft im Alltag einer rheinischen Großstadt*. Frankfurt am Main: Campus, 1987.

Marks, Jane, ed. *The Hidden Children: The Secret Survivors of the Holocaust*. New York: Fawcett Columbine, 1993.

Marszolek, Inge. "Denunziation im Dritten Reich. Kommunikationsformen und Verhaltensweisen." In *Überleben im Untergrund*, edited by Beate Kosmala and Claudia Schoppmann, 89–107. Berlin: Metropol, 2002.

Mędykowski, Witold. "Modes of Survival. Techniques of Hiding, and Relations with the Local Population: the Polish Case." In *Hiding, Sheltering, and Borrowing Identities: Avenues of Rescue during the Holocaust* edited by Dan Michman, 45–56. Jerusalem: Yad Vashem, 2017.

Mertens, Lothar. *Unermüdlicher Kämpfer für Frieden und Menschenrechte. Leben und Wirken von Kurt R. Grossmann*. Berlin: Dunker & Humblot, 1997.

Mettig, Marcel. "Der Münchner Gestapochef Oswald Schäfer." In *Rechte Karrieren*, edited by Marita Krauss, 245–61. Munich: Volk Verlag, 2010.

Meyer, Ahlrich. *Täter im Verhör. Die Endlösung der Judenfrage in Frankreich*. Darmstadt: Wissenschaftliche Buchgesellschaft, 2005.

Meyer, Beate. "A conto Zukunft. Hilfe und Rettung für untergetauchte Hamburger Juden." *Zeitschrift des Vereins für hamburgische Geschichte* 88 (2002): 205–33.

———. "Alltagsgeschichtliche Aspekte der Verfolgung. Funktionäre, Mitarbeiter und Mitglieder der Reichsvereinigung der Juden in Deutschland zur Zeit der Deportationen (1941–1943)." In *Alltag im Holocaust*, edited by Andrea Löw, Doris Bergen, and Anna Hájková, 13–28. Munich: Oldenbourg, 2013.

———. *A Fatal Balancing Act. The Dilemma of the Reich Association of Jews in Germany, 1939–1945*. Translated by William Templer. New York: Berghahn, 2013.

———. "Fragwürdiger Schutz—Mischehen in Hamburg (1933–1945)." In *Die Verfolgung und Ermordung der Hamburger Juden*, edited by Beate Meyer, 79–88. Göttingen: Wallstein, 2006.

———. *"Jüdische Mischlinge." Rassenpolitik und Verfolgungserfahrung 1933–1945*. Hamburg: Dölling und Galitz, 1999.

———. *Tödliche Gratwanderung. Die Reichsvereinigung der Juden in Deutschland zwischen Hoffnung, Zwang, Selbstbehauptung und Verstrickung (1939–1945)*. Göttingen: Wallstein, 2011.

———, ed. *Die Verfolgung und Ermordung der Hamburger Juden 1933–1945. Geschichte. Zeugnis. Erinnerung, Hamburg: Landeszentrale für politische Bildung*. Göttingen: Wallstein, 2006.

Meyer, Beate, and Birthe Kundrus, eds. *Die Deportation der Juden aus Deutschland. Pläne, Praxis, Reaktionen 1938–1945*. Göttingen: Wallstein, 2004.

Meyer, Beate, Hermann Simon and Chana Schütz, eds. *Jews in Nazi Berlin: From Kristallnacht to Liberation*, translated by Caroline Gay and Miranda Robbins. Chicago: University of Chicago Press, 2009.

Michman, Dan, ed. *Hiding, Sheltering, and Borrowing Identities. Avenues of Rescue during the Holocaust*. Jerusalem: Yad Vashem, 2017.

Modert, Gerd. "Motor der Verfolgung—Zur Rolle der NSDAP bei der Entrechtung und Ausplünderung der Münchner Juden." In *München arisiert*, edited by Angelika Baumann and Andreas Heusler, 145–77. Munich: C. H. Beck, 2004.

Möllmann, Bernhard. "Der Opernsänger Berthold Sterneck und seine Familie." In *Ins Licht gerückt*, edited by Bernhard Schoßig, 145–57. Munich: Herbert Utz Verlag, 2008.

Moore, Bob. *Survivors: Jewish Self-Help and Rescue in Nazi-Occupied Western Europe*. Oxford: Oxford University Press, 2010.

Morina, Christina, and Krijn Thijs, eds. *Probing the Limits of Categorization: The Bystander in Holocaust History*. New York: Berghahn, 2019.

Mosbach, Regina. "Die Ohnmacht der Verzweiflung. 'Innere Emigration' am Beispiel Otto von Taubes." In *Die Totalitäre Erfahrung: Deutsche Literatur und Drittes Reich*, edited by Frank-Lothar Kroll, 55–75. Berlin: Dunker & Humblot, 2003.

Moser, C. Gwyn. "Jewish *U-Boote* in Austria, 1938–1945." *Simon Wiesenthal Center Annual* 2 (1985): 53–62.

Moser, Jonny. *Nisko. Die ersten Judendeportationen*. Vienna: Ed. Steinbauer, 2012.

Müller, Klaus-Jürgen. *Der deutsche Widerstand 1933–1945*. Paderborn: Schöningh, 1986.

Muth, Kerstin. *Versteckte Kinder. Trauma und Überleben der "Hidden Children" im Nationalsozialismus*. Gießen: Halandt und Wirth, 2004.

Neander, Joachim. "Auschwitz, the Fabrik-Aktion, Rosenstrasse: A Plea for a Change of Perspective." In *Protest in Hitler's "National Community": Popular Unrest and the Nazi Response*, edited by Nathan Stoltzfus and Birgit Maier-Katkin, 125–42. New York: Berghahn, 2016.

Neiss, Marion. "'Herr Obersturmbannführer lässt daran erinnern, dass die Rate noch nicht da ist.' Eine Rettung auf Abzahlung." In *Überleben im Dritten Reich*, edited by Wolfgang Benz, 198–204. Munich: C. H. Beck, 2003.

Nerdinger, Winfried. "Der Umgang mit der 'zerlumpten Vergangenheit' Münchens." In *München und der Nationalsozialismus*, edited by Winfried Nerdinger, 548–56. Munich: C. H. Beck, 2015.

———, ed. *München und der Nationalsozialismus. Katalog des NS-Dokumentationszentrums München*. Munich: C. H. Beck, 2015.

———, ed. *Ort und Erinnerung. Nationalsozialismus in München*. Munich and Salzburg: Pustet, 2006.

Niethammer, Lutz. *Die Mitläuferfabrik. Die Entnazifizierung am Beispiel Bayerns*. Berlin: Dietz, 1982.

Nikou, Lina. *Besuche in der alten Heimat. Einladungsprogramme für ehemals Verfolgte des Nationalsozialismus in München, Frankfurt am Mainund Berlin*. Berlin: Neofelis, 2020.

———. "'Heimweh nach München.' Städtische Einladung für Verfolgte des Nationalsozialismus als Geschichts- und Imagepolitik in den sechziger Jahren." *Zeitgeschichte in Hamburg* 2012 (2013): 81–94.

———. *Zwischen Imagepflege, moralischer Verpflichtung und Erinnerungen. Das Besuchsprogramm für jüdische ehemalige Hamburger Bürgerinnen und Bürger*. Hamburg: Dölling und Galitz, 2011.

Oliner, Samuel, and Kathleen Lee. *Who Shall Live: The Wilhelm Bachner Story*. Chicago: Academy Chicago Publishers, 1996.

Oliner, Samuel P., and Pearl M. Oliner. *The Altruistic Personality: Rescuers of Jews in Nazi Europe*. New York: Free Press, 1992.

Ophir, Baruch, and Falk Wiesemann. *Die jüdischen Gemeinden in Bayern 1918–1945. Geschichte und Zerstörung*. Munich: Oldenbourg, 1979.

———. "Geschichte und Zerstörung der jüdischen Gemeinde in München, 1918–1945." In *Vergangene Tage. Jüdische Kultur in München*, edited by Hans Lamm, 462–89. Munich: Ter-Namid-Verlag, 1982.

Orczy, Emmuska. *The Scarlet Pimpernel*. New York: G. P. Putnam's Sons, 1920.

Osti Guerrazzi, Amedeo. *Caino a Roma. I complici romani della Shoah*. Rome: Cooper, 2006.

Paucker, Arnold. *Die Juden im nationalsozialistischen Deutschland, 1933–1943*. Tübingen: Mohr, 1986.

Paul, Gerhard. "'Diese Erschießungen haben mich innerlich gar nicht mehr berührt.' Die Kriegsendphasenverbrechen der Gestapo 1944/45." In *Die Gestapo im Zweiten Weltkrieg*, by Gerhard Paul and Klaus-Michael Mallmann, 543–68. Darmstadt: Wissenschaftliche Buchgesellschaft, 2000.

Paul, Gerhard, and Klaus-Michael Mallmann. *Die Gestapo im Zweiten Weltkrieg*. Darmstadt: Wissenschaftliche Buchgesellschaft, 2000.

Paulsson, Gunnar. *Secret City. The Hidden Jews of Warsaw, 1940–1945*. New Haven: Yale University Press, 2002.

Pawlita, Cornelius. *Wiedergutmachung als Rechtsfrage? Die politische und juristische Auseinandersetzung um Entschädigung für die Opfer nationalsozialistischer Verfolgung (1945 bis 1990)*. Frankfurt am Main: Lang, 1993.

Peukert, Detlev. *Volksgenossen und Gemeinschaftsfremde. Anpassung, Ausmerze und Aufbegehren unter dem Nationalsozialismus*. Cologne: Bund-Verlag, 1982.

Phayer, Michael. "The Catholic Resistance Circle in Berlin and German Catholic Bishops during the Holocaust." *Holocaust and Genocide Studies* 7, no. 2 (1993): 216–29.

Philipp, Eleonore. *Gerettet. Erinnerungen an zwei Familien im Nationalsozialismus*. Niederroth: Selbstverlag, 1998.

Picard, Jacques. "Die Schweiz. Hilfe, Selbsthilfe und Solidarität entlang der Grenze." In *Regionalstudien 1*, edited by Wolfgang Benz and Juliane Wetzel, 233–70. Berlin: Metropol, 1996.

———. *Die Schweiz und die Juden 1933–1945*. Zürich: Chronos, 1994.

Porezag, Karsten. *Als aus Nachbarn Juden wurden. Die Deportation und Ermordung der letzten Wetzlarer Juden 1938–1943/45*. Wetzlar: Porezag, 2006.

———. *Ernst Leitz aus Wetzlar und die Juden—Mythos und Fakten*. Berlin: Metropol, 2009.

Przyrembel, Alexandra. *"Rassenschande." Reinheitsmythos und Vernichtungslegitimation im Nationalsozialismus*. Göttingen: Vandenhoeck & Ruprecht, 2003.

Rabinovici, Doron. *Instanzen der Ohnmacht: Wien 1938–1945. Der Weg zum Judenrat*. Frankfurt am Main: Jüdischer Verlag, 2000.

Raggam-Blesch, Michaela. "Alltag unter prekärem Schutz. *Mischlinge* und *Geltungsjuden* im NS-Regime in Wien." *Zeitgeschichte* 43, no. 5 (2016): 292–307.

———. "'Mischlinge' und 'Geltungsjuden.' Alltag und Verfolgungserfahrungen von Frauen und Männern halbüdischer Herkunft in Wien 1938–1945." In *Alltag im Holocaust*, edited by Andrea Löw, Doris Bergen, and Anna Hájková, 81–98. Munich: Oldenbourg, 2013.

Raim, Edith. *Justiz zwischen Diktatur und Demokratie, Wiederaufbau und Ahndung von NS-Verbrechen in Westdeutschland 1945–1949*. Munich: Oldenbourg, 2013.

Rayski, Adam. *The Choice of the Jews under Vichy*. Notre Dame: University of Notre Dame Press, 2005.

Reck-Malleczewen, Friedrich. *Bockelson. Geschichte eines Massenwahns*. Berlin: Schützen-Verlag, 1937.

Richardi, Hans Günter. *Bomber über München. Der Luftkrieg von 1939 bis 1945, dargestellt am Beispiel der "Hauptstadt der Bewegung."* Munich: Ludwig, 1992.

Richarz, Monika, ed. *Jüdisches Leben in Deutschland. Selbstzeugnisse zur Sozialgeschichte 1918–1945*. Stuttgart: Deutsche Verlags-Anstalt, 1982.

Riffel, Dennis. "'Unbesungene Helden': Der Umgang mit 'Rettung' im Nachkriegsdeutschland." In *Überleben im Untergrund*, edited by Beate Kosmala and Claudia Schoppmann, 317–34. Berlin: Metropol, 2002.

———. *Unbesungene Helden. Die Ehrungsinitiative des Berliner Senats 1958 bis 1966*. Berlin: Metropol, 2007.

Ritter von Baeyer, Walter et al. *Psychiatrie der Verfolgten. Psychopathologische und gutachtliche Erfahrungen an Opfern der nationalsozialistischen Verfolgung und vergleichbarer Extrembelastungen*. Berlin: Springer, 1964.

Röhm, Eberhard, and Jörg Thierfelder. *Juden, Christen, Deutsche. Vol. 1: 1933–1935: Ausgegrenzt*. Stuttgart: Calwer, 1990.

———. *Juden, Christen Deutsche, Vols. 2/I and 2/II: 1935–1938: Entrechtet*. Stuttgart: Calwer, 1992.

———. *Juden Christen Deutsche, Vols. 3/I and 3/II: 1938–1941: Ausgestoßen*. Stuttgart: Calwer, 1995.

———. *Juden Christen, Deutsche, Vols. 4/I and 4/II: 1941–1945: Vernichtet*. Stuttgart: Calwer, 2007.

Römer, Gernot, ed. *"Jüdisch Versippt." Schicksale von "Mischlingen" und nichtarischen Christen in Schwaben*. Augsburg: Wißner, 1996.

———. *"Wir haben uns gewehrt." Wie Juden aus Schwaben gegen Hitler kämpften und wie Christen Juden halfen*. Augsburg: Wißner, 1995.

Roon, Ger van. *Widerstand im Dritten Reich*. Munich: C. H. Beck, 1997.

Rösch, Mathias. *Die Münchner NSDAP 1925–1933; eine Untersuchung zur inneren Struktur der NSDAP in der Weimarer Republik*. Munich: Oldenbourg, 2002.

Roseman, Mark. *A Past in Hiding. Memory and Survival in Nazi Germany*. New York: Metropolitan Books, 2001.

———. "'It Went On for Years and Years.' Der Wiedergutmachungsantrag der Marianne Ellenbogen." In *Praxis der Widergutmachung*, edited by Norbert Frei, José Brunner, and Constantin Goschler, 51–78. Göttingen: Wallstein, 2009.

———. *Lives Reclaimed: A Story of Rescue and Resistance in Nazi Germany*. New York: Metropolitan Books, 2019.

Rosenfeld, Gavriel. *Munich and Memory: Architecture, Monuments, and the Legacy of the Third Reich*. Berkeley: University of California Press, 2000.

Rudolph, Katrin. *Hilfe beim Sprung ins Nichts. Franz Kaufmann und die Rettung von Juden und nichtarischen Christen*. Berlin: Metropol, 2005.

Rüter, Christiaan, and Dirk Welmoed de Mildt. *Die Westdeutschen Strafverfahren wegen Nationalsozialistischer Tötungsverbrechen 1945–1997. Eine systematische Verfahrensbeschreibung*. Amsterdam: APA-Holland University Press, 1998.

Safrian, Hans. *Eichmann's Men*. Cambridge: Cambridge University Press, 2009.

Saltin, Günther. "Alfred Delp: Einsatz für verfolgte Juden." In *Alfred-Delp-Jahrbuch*, edited by Reinhard Albert et al., 78–93. Münster: LIT Verlag, 2010.

Sarfatti, Michele. *The Jews in Mussolini's Italy: From Equality to Persecution*. Translated by John and Anne Tedeschi. Madison: The University of Wisconsin Press, 2006.

Schäbitz, Michael. "Banished from the Fatherland." In *Jews in Nazi Berlin: From Kristallnacht to Liberation*, edited by Beate Meyer, Hermann Simon, and Chana Schütz, translated by Caroline Gay and Miranda Robbins, 298–308. Chicago: University of Chicago Press, 2009.

Schaeffler, Richard. "Dr. Gertrud Schaeffler, Chemikerin." In *Solln in den Jahren 1933–1945*, edited by Dorle Gribl, 102–5. Munich: Volk Verlag, 2006.

Schelpmeier, Holger. "Siegfried und Flora Wilmersdörfer und ihre Familie." In *Ausgegrenzt-Entrechtet-Deportiert*, edited by Ilse Macek, 251–87. Munich: Volk, 2008.

Schieb, Barbara. "How the Frankenstein Family Survived Underground 1943–45." In *Jews in Nazi Berlin: From Kristallnacht to Liberation*, edited by Beate Meyer, Hermann Simon, and Chana Schütz, translated by Caroline Gay and Miranda Robbins, 276–97. Chicago: University of Chicago Press, 2009.

———. "Nachwort." In *Überleben im Verborgenen*, edited by Barbara Lovenheim, 210–21. Munich: Siedler, 2002.

Schieb-Samizadeh, Barbara. "Die Gemeinschaft für Frieden und Aufbau." In *Für Freudensprünge keine Zeit*, by Eugen Hermann-Friede, 189–222. Berlin: Metropol, 1991.

———. "Die Gemeinschaft für Frieden und Aufbau." In *Juden im Widerstand*, edited by Wilfried Löhken and Werner Vathke, 37–81. Berlin: Hentrich, 1993.

Schilde, Kurt. "Grenzüberschreitende Flucht und Fluchthilfe (1941–1945): Ereignisse, Interessen und Motive." In *Überleben im Untergrund*, edited by Beate Kosmala and Claudia Schoppmann, 151–65. Berlin: Metropol, 2002.

Schlemmer, Thomas. *Aufbruch, Krise und Erneuerung. Die Christlich-Soziale Union 1945–1955*. Munich: Oldenbourg, 1998.

Schlösser, Stella, and Christina Rausch. "Schüler-Schicksale am Schwabinger Alten Realgymnasium—Der Schüler Günter Koppel." In *Ausgegrenzt-Entrechtet-Deportiert*, edited by Ilse Macek, 192–202. Munich: Volk Verlag, 2008.

Schöler, Uli. "Totalitarismustheoretische Ansätze bei Alexander Schifrin, ein Grenzgänger zwischen russischer und deutscher Sozialdemokratie." *Totalitarismuskritik von links* (2007): 69–82.

Schönlebe, Dirk. "München im Netzwerk der Hilfe für 'nicht-arische' Christen 1938–1941." In *Von ihren Kirchen verlassen und vergessen?*, edited by Dirk Schönlebe and Klaus Bäumler, 1–145. Munich: Franz Schiermeier Verlag, 2006.

Schönlebe, Dirk, and Klaus Bäumler. *Von ihren Kirchen verlassen und vergessen? Zum Schicksal Christen jüdischer Herkunft im München der NS-Zeit*. Munich: Franz Schiermeier Verlag, 2006.

Schoppmann, Claudia. "Die 'Fabrikaktion' in Berlin. Hilfe für untergetauchte Juden als Form humanitären Widerstandes." *Zeitschrift für Geschichtswissenschaft* 53 (2005): 138–48.

———. "Fluchtziel Schweiz. Das Hilfsnetz um Luise Meier und Josef Höfler." In *Überleben im Dritten Reich*, edited by Wolfgang Benz, 205–19. Munich: C. H. Beck, 2003.

———. "Rettung von Juden: ein kaum beachteter Widerstand von Frauen." In *Überleben im Untergrund*, edited by Beate Kosmala and Claudia Schoppmann, 109–26. Berlin: Metropol, 2002.

Schoßig, Bernhard, ed. *Ins Licht gerückt. Jüdische Lebenswege im Münchner Westen. Eine Spurensuche in Pasing, Obermenzing und Aubing*. Munich: Herbert Utz Verlag, 2008.

Schrafstetter, Susanna. "'Geltungsjüdische' Jugendliche in München 1938–1945." In *Münchner Beiträge zur Jüdischen Geschichte und Kultur* 8 (2014), edited by Alan E. Steinweis, 57–75. Munich: Ludwig-Maximilians-Universität, 2014.

———. "The Geographies of Living Underground: Escape Routes and Hiding Spaces of Fugitive Jews in Germany, 1939–1945." In *Lessons and Legacies XIV: The Holocaust in the Twenty-First Century; Relevance and Challenges in the Digital Age*, edited by Tim Cole and Simone Gigliotti, 109–38. Evanston: Northwestern University Press, 2020.

———. "'Life in Illegality Cost an Extortionate Amount of Money.' Ordinary Germans and German Jews Hiding from Deportation." In *The Holocaust and European Societies: Social Processes and Social Dynamics*, edited by Frank Bajohr and Andrea Löw, 69–85. London: Palgrave, 2016.

———. "Von der Soforthilfe zur Wiedergutmachung: Die Umsetzung der Zonal Policy Instruction No. 20 in der britischen Besatzungszone." In *Arisierung und Wiedergutmachung in deutschen Städten*, edited by Christiane Fritsche and Johannes Paulmann, 309–34. Cologne and Vienna: Böhlau, 2014.

———. "Zwischen Skylla und Charybdis? Münchner Juden in Italien 1933 bis 1945." *Vierteljahrshefte für Zeitgeschichte* 66, no. 4 (2018): 577–616.

Schrafstetter, Susanna, and Alan E. Steinweis, eds. *The Germans and the Holocaust: Popular Responses to the Persecution and Murder of the Jews* (Vermont Studies on Nazi Germany and the Holocaust). New York: Berghahn, 2016.

Schreiber, Birgit. *Versteckt: Jüdische Kinder im nationalsozialistischen Deutschland und ihr Leben danach*. Frankfurt am Main: Campus, 2005.

Schubert, Helga. *Judasfrauen. Zehn Fallgeschichten weiblicher Denunziation im "Dritten Reich."* Frankfurt am Main: Luchterhand, 1990.

Schubsky, Karl. "Jüdische Friedhöfe." In *Synagogen und jüdische Friedhöfe in München*, edited by Wolfram Selig, 149–88. Munich: Aries Verlag, 1988.

Schwartz, Eliezer. "The Death Marches from the Dachau Camps to the Alps during the Final Days of World War II in Europe." *Dapim. Studies on the Shoah* 25 (2011): 129–60.

Schwersenz, Jizchak, and Edith Wolff. "Jüdische Jugend im Untergrund. Eine zionistische Gruppe in Deutschland während des Zweiten Weltkrieges." *Bulletin des Leo Baeck Instituts* 12 (1969): 1–100.

Selig, Wolfram. *"Arisierung" in München: die Vernichtung jüdischer Existenz 1937–1939*. Berlin: Metropol, 2004.

———. *Leben unterm Rassenwahn: vom Antisemitismus in der "Hauptstadt der Bewegung."* Berlin: Metropol, 2001.

Seligmann, Avraham. "An Illegal Way of Life in Nazi Germany." *Leo Baeck Institute Yearbook* 37 (1992): 327–61.

Semelin, Jacques. *Persécutions et entraides dans la France occupée. Comment 75% des Juifs en France ont échappé à la mort*. Paris: Seuil, 2013.

Serup-Bilfeldt, Kirsten. *Zwischen Dom und Davidstern. Jüdisches Leben in Köln von den Anfängen bis heute*. Cologne: Kiwi, 2001.

Shephard, Ben. "Die frühen Befunde der Psychiatrie zum Holocaust (1945–1950)." In *Holocaust und Trauma. Kritische Perspektiven zur Entstehung und Wirkung eines Paradigmas*, edited by José Brunner and Nathalie Zajde, 72–85. Göttingen: Wallstein, 2011.

Siegemund, Anja. "Zur Familiengeschichte der Engelhards." In *Versagte Heimat. Jüdisches Leben in Münchens Isarvorstadt 1914–1945*, edited by Douglas Bokovoy and Stefan Meining, 311–20. Munich: Glas, 1994.

Silver, Eric. *The Book of the Just: The Silent Heroes Who Saved Jews from Hitler*. London: Weidenfeld and Nicolson, 1992.

Sinn, Andrea. *"Und ich lebe wieder an der Isar." Exil und Rückkehr des Münchner Juden Hans Lamm*. Munich: Oldenbourg, 2008.

Smith, Frank Dabba. *Elsie's War: A Story of Courage in Nazi Germany*. London: Frances Lincoln Limited, 2003.

Specht, Heike. "Zerbrechlicher Erfolg (1918–1933)." In *Jüdisches München*, edited by Richard Bauer and Michael Brenner, 137–60. Munich: C. H. Beck, 2006.

Spicer, Kevin. *Hitler's Priests. Catholic Clergy and National Socialism*. DeKalb: Northern Illinois University Press, 2008.

Stadelmann, Jürg. *Umgang mit Fremden in bedrängter Zeit. Schweizerische Flüchtlingspolitik 1940–1945 und ihre Beurteilung bis heute*. Zürich: Orell Füssli, 1998.

Stadtarchiv München, ed. *Biographisches Gedenkbuch der Münchner Juden*, Band I: A-L, Band II: M-Z. Munich: Stadtarchiv, 2003 and 2007.

Steinbach, Peter, and Johannes Tuchel. *Georg Elser. Der Hitler-Attentäter*. Berlin: be.bra verlag, 2010.

———, eds. *Widerstand gegen die nationalsozialistische Diktatur 1933–45*. Bonn: Bundeszentrale für politische Bildung, 2004.

———, eds. *Widerstand gegen den Nationalsozialismus*. Bonn: Bundeszentrale für politische Bildung, 1994.

Steinweis, Alan E. *Kristallnacht 1938*. Cambridge: Harvard University Press, 2009.

———, ed. *Judenverfolgung in München. Münchner Beiträge zur Jüdischen Geschichte und Kultur* 8 (2014). Munich: Ludwig-Maximilians-Universität, 2014.

Steinweis, Alan E., and Robert D. Rachlin, eds. *The Law in Nazi Germany. Ideology, Opportunism, and the Perversion of Justice*. New York: Berghahn, 2013.

Stengel, Katharina. *Hermann Langbein. Ein Auschwitz-Überlebender in den erinnerungspolitischen Konflikten der Nachkriegszeit*. Frankfurt am Main: Campus, 2012.

Stockdreher, Petra. "Heil- und Pflegeanstalt Eglfing-Haar." In *Psychiatrie im Nationalsozialismus*, edited by Michael von Cranach and Hans-Ludwig Siemen, 327–62. Munich: Oldenbourg, 1999.

Stoltzfus, Nathan, and Birgit Maier-Katkin, eds. *Protest in Hitler's "National Community." Popular Unrest and the Nazi Response*. New York: Berghahn, 2016.

Strasser, Gerhard F. "Anyone Would Have Done That." In *Leaflets of Our Resistance*, vol. 1, edited by Ruth Hanna Sachs, translated by Lidia Zimmermann, 25–33. Los Angeles: Exclamation! Publishers, 2009.

Strnad, Maximilian. "Das 'Judenhaus' in der Frundsbergstraße 8." *Neuhauser Werkstatt-Nachrichten* 16 (2006): 16–21.

———. "Die Deportationen aus München." In *Münchner Beiträge zur Jüdischen Geschichte und Kultur* 8 (2014), edited by Alan E. Steinweis, 76–96. Munich: Ludwig-Maximilians-Universität, 2014.

———. *Flachs für das Reich. Das jüdische Zwangsarbeitslager "Flachsröste Lohhof" bei München*. Munich: Volk Verlag, 2013.

———. “The Fortune of Survival—Intermarried German Jews in the Dying Breath of the ‘Thousand-Year-Reich.’” *Dapim: Studies on the Holocaust* 29, no. 3 (2015): 173–96.

———. *Privileg Mischehe? Handlungsräume “jüdisch versippter” Familien, 1933–1945*. Göttingen: Wallstein, 2021.

———. *Zwischenstation “Judensiedlung.” Verfolgung und Deportation der jüdischen Münchner 1941–1945*. Munich: Oldenbourg, 2011.

Süß, Dietmar. *Tod aus der Luft. Kriegsgesellschaft in Deutschland und England*. Munich: Siedler, 2011.

Süß, Winfried. *Der “Volkskörper” im Krieg. Gesundheitspolitik, Gesundheitsverhältnisse und Krankenmord im nationalsozialistischen Deutschland 1939–1945*. Munich: Oldenbourg, 2003.

Taube, Otto Freiherr von. *Das Opferfest*. Leipzig: Insel-Verlag, 1926.

———. “Errettung eines jüdischen Kindes in München 1943.” In *Von Juden in München*, edited by Hans Lamm, 343–44. Munich: Ter-Namid-Verlag, 1982.

Tausendfreund, Doris. *Erzwungener Verrat. Jüdische “Greifer” im Dienst der Gestapo 1943–1945*. Berlin: Metropol, 2006.

———. “‘Jüdische Fahnder.’ Verfolgte, Verfolger und Retter in einer Person.” In *Überleben im Dritten Reich*, edited by Wolfgang Benz, 239–58. Munich: C. H. Beck, 2003.

Thumser, Gerd. *Heimweh nach München. Das Schicksal der emigrierten jüdischen Bürger Münchens*. Munich: Alfred Wurm Verlag, 1967.

———. *Journalistengift. Events und Begegnungen*. Husum: Verlag der Nation, 1999.

Unabhängige Expertenkommission Schweiz—Zweiter Weltkrieg. *Die Schweiz und die Flüchtlinge zur Zeit des Nationalsozialismus*. Zurich: Chronos, 2001.

Ungar-Klein, Brigitte. “‘Don’t Go—You Will Stay with Me!:’ Hidden Jews in Vienna and Their Supporters.” In *Hiding, Sheltering, and Borrowing Identities*, edited by Dan Michman, 195–205. Jerusalem: Yad Vashem, 2017.

———. *Schattenexistenz. Jüdische U-Boote in Wien, 1938–1945*. Vienna: Picus, 2019.

———. “Überleben im Versteck—Rückkehr in die Normalität?” In *Überleben der Shoah—und danach: Spätfolgen der Verfolgung aus wissenschaftlicher Sicht*, edited by Alexander Friedmann et al., 31–41. Vienna: Picus, 1999.

Voigt, Klaus. *Zuflucht auf Widerruf. Exil in Italien 1933–1945*, 2 vols. Stuttgart: Klett-Cotta, 1993.

Volmer-Naumann, Julia. *Bürokratische Bewältigung. Entschädigung für nationalsozialistisch Verfolgte im Regierungsbezirk Münster*. Essen: Klartext, 2012.

Wachsmann, Nikolaus. *Hitler’s Prisons. Legal Terror in Nazi Germany*. New Haven and London: Yale University Press, 2004.

Wächter, Katja-Maria. *Die Macht der Ohnmacht. Leben und Politik des Franz Xaver von Epp*. Frankfurt am Main: Peter Lang, 1999.

Weber, Reinhard. *Das Schicksal der jüdischen Rechtsanwälte in Bayern nach 1933*. Munich: Oldenbourg, 2006.

Wedekind, Michael. *Nationalsozialistische Besatzungs- und Annexionspolitik in Norditalien. Die Operationszonen "Alpenvorland" und "Adriatisches Küstenland."* Munich: Oldenbourg, 2003.

Weiss, Yfaat. *Deutsche und polnische Juden vor dem Holocaust. Jüdische Identität zwischen Staatsbürgerschaft und Ethnizität 1933–1940*. Munich: Oldenbourg, 2000.

Welzer, Harald. "Collateral Damage of History Education: National Socialism and the Holocaust in German Family Memory." *Social Research* 75 (2008): 287–314.

Welzer, Harald, Sabine Moller, and Karoline Tschuggnall. *"Opa war kein Nazi." Nationalsozialismus und Holocaust im Familiengedächtnis*. Frankfurt am Main: Fischer, 2002.

Wendorff, Ruth. "Meine Tante Anne Reinach-Stettenheimer." In *Edith Steins Unterstützer*, edited by Waltraud Herbstrith, 87–89. Freiburg and Basel: Herder, 1983.

Werner, Constanze. *Kriegswirtschaft und Zwangsarbeit bei BMW*. Munich: Oldenbourg, 2006.

Wertheimer, Waltraut. "Kurt Schneider." In *Ausgegrenzt-Entrechtet-Deportiert*, edited by Ilse Macek, 443–48. Munich: Volk, 2008.

———. "Magdalena Schwarz." In *Ausgegrenzt-Entrechtet-Deportiert*, edited by Ilse Macek, 449–51. Munich: Volk, 2008.

Wette, Wolfram. "Rettungswiderstand aus der Wehrmacht." In *Widerstand gegen die nationalsozialistische Diktatur*, edited by Peter Steinbach and Johannes Tuchel, 322–37. Bonn: Bundeszentrale für politische Bildung, 2004.

———, ed. *Stille Helden. Judenretter im Dreiländereck während des Zweiten Weltkriegs*. Freiburg: Herder, 2005.

———. "Vorwort." In *Rettungswiderstand*, edited by Arno Lustiger, 12–16. Göttingen: Wallstein, 2011.

Wette, Wolfram, and Detlef Bald, eds. *Zivilcourage. Empörte, Helfer und Retter aus Wehrmacht, Polizei und SS*. Frankfurt am Main: Fischer, 2004.

Wette, Wolfram, and Norbert Haase, eds. *Retter in Uniform. Handlungsspielräume im Vernichtungskrieg der Wehrmacht*. Frankfurt am Main: Fischer, 2002.

Wetzel, Juliane. *Jüdisches Leben in München 1945–1951. Durchgangsstation oder Wiederaufbau?* Munich: Uni-Druck, 1987.

———. "Karriere nach der Rettung. Charlotte Knoblochs Weg zur Vizepräsidentin der Juden in Deutschland." In *Überleben im Dritten Reich*, edited by Wolfgang Benz, 301–11. Munich: C. H. Beck, 2003.

———. "Retter in der Not? Das faschistische Italien und die Hilfe für jüdische Verfolgte." In *Regionalstudien 4*, edited by Wolfgang Benz and Juliane Wetzel, 281–366. Berlin: Metropol, 2004.

Weyerer, Benedikt. *München 1933–1949. Stadtrundgänge zur politischen Geschichte.* Munich: Buchendorfer, 2006.

———. "Retter unter Einsatz des eigenen Lebens—die Familie Schörghofer." In *Ausgegrenzt-Entrechtet-Deportiert,* edited by Ilse Macek, 393–95. Munich: Volk Verlag, 2008.

Widmann, Peter. "Die Kunst der Frechheit. Ein Maler und das Überleben in München." In *Überleben im Dritten Reich,* edited by Wolfgang Benz, 278–86. Munich: C. H. Beck, 2003.

Willems, Susanne. *Der entsiedelte Jude. Albert Speers Wohnungsmarktpolitik für den Berliner Hauptstadtbau.* Berlin: Hentrich, 2002.

Wimmer, Florian. *Die völkische Ordnung von Armut. Kommunale Sozialpolitik im nationalsozialistischen München.* Göttingen: Wallstein, 2014.

Winstel, Tobias. "Über die Bedeutung der Wiedergutmachung im Leben der jüdischen NS-Verfolgten. Erfahrungsgeschichtliche Annäherungen." In *Nach der Verfolgung,* edited by Hans Günter Hockerts and Christiane Kuller, 199–228. Göttingen: Wallstein, 2003.

———. *Verhandelte Gerechtigkeit. Rückerstattung und Entschädigung für jüdische NS-Opfer in Bayern und Westdeutschland.* Munich: Oldenbourg, 2006.

Wirsching, Andreas. "Mehr Nähe als Distanz? Kardinal Michael von Faulhaber und der Nationalsozialismus." In *Distanz und Nähe zugleich? Die christlichen Kirchen im "Dritten Reich,"* edited by Friedrich Wilhelm Graf and Hans Günter Hockerts, 199–223. Munich: Munich Documentation Center for the History of National Socialism, 2017.

Wolfson, Manfred. "Zum Widerstand gegen Hitler: Umriß eines Gruppenporträts deutscher Retter von Juden." In *Tradition und Neubeginn. Internationale Forschungen zur deutschen Geschichte im 20. Jahrhundert,* edited by Joachim Hütter, Reinhard Meyers and Dietrich Papenfuss, 391–407. Cologne: Carl Hezmanns Verlag, 1975.

Wollasch, Hans-Josef. *"Betrifft: Nachrichtenzentrale des Erzbischofs Gröber in Freiburg." Die Ermittlungsakten der Geheimen Staatspolizei gegen Gertrud Luckner 1942–1944.* Konstanz: UVK, 1999.

Yehuda, Rachel et al. "Individual Differences in Posttraumatic Stress Disorder Symptom Profiles in Holocaust Survivors in Concentration Camps or in Hiding." *Journal of Traumatic Stress* 10 (1997): 453–63.

Zahn, Christine. "'Nicht mitgehen, sondern weggehen!' Chug Chaluzi—eine jüdische Jugendgruppe im Untergrund." In *Juden im Widerstand,* edited by Wilfried Löhken and Werner Vathke, 159–205. Berlin: Hentrich, 1993.

Zahn, Peter, ed. *Hilfe für Juden in München. Annemarie und Rudolf Cohen und die Quäker 1938–1941.* Munich: Oldenbourg, 2013.

Zajde, Nathalie. "Die Schoah als Paradigma des psychischen Traumas." In *Holocaust und Trauma,* edited by José Brunner and Nathalie Zajde, 17–39. Göttingen: Wallstein, 2011.

Zámečnik, Stanislav. *Das war Dachau*. Frankfurt am Main: Fischer, 2007.
Zankel, Sönke. *Mit Flugblättern gegen Hitler. Der Widerstandskreis um Hans Scholl und Alexander Schmorell*. Cologne: Böhlau, 2008.
Zarusky, Jürgen. "Von Dachau nach nirgendwo. Der Todesmarsch der KZ-Häftlinge im April 1945." In *Spuren des Nationalsozialismus. Gedenkstättenarbeit in Bayern*, edited by Wolfgang Benz, 42–63. Munich: Landeszentrale für politische Bildungsarbeit, 2000.

INDEX

SUSANNA SCHRAFSTETTER is professor of history at the University of Vermont. Her work focuses on Jews who went into hiding in Germany during the Holocaust, on German-Jewish refugees in Fascist Italy, and on the legacy of Nazism in postwar Germany. She has also published extensively on the diplomacy of nuclear nonproliferation. Her most recent publications include *After Nazism: Relaunching Careers in Germany and Austria*, coedited with Jürgen Zarusky and Thomas Schlemmer.

ALLISON BROWN has been a freelance translator from German into English of scholarly books and essays and exhibition texts and catalogues since 1988. Her main fields of expertise include history, art, religion, and the social and political sciences, especially women's and cultural studies. She has studied linguistics (Free University, Berlin) and German studies (BA, Stanford University), and she has an MA in translation science (Humboldt University, Berlin). She lives in Berlin.